OUR YOUNG FOLKS' PLUTARCH

OUR YOUNG FOLKS' PLUTARCH

BY

ROSALIE KAUFMAN

with illustrations

YESTERDAY'S CLASSICS

CHAPEL HILL, NORTH CAROLINA

Cover and arrangement © 2007 Yesterday's Classics.

This edition, first published in 2007 by Yesterday's Classics, is an unabridged republication of the work originally published by J. B. Lippincott & Co. in 1883. For a complete listing of the books published by Yesterday's Classics, please visit www.yesterdaysclassics.com. Yesterday's Classics is the publishing arm of the Baldwin Online Children's Project which presents the complete text of hundreds of classic books for children at www.mainlesson.com.

ISBN-10: 1-59915-208-8

ISBN-13: 978-1-59915-208-0

Yesterday's Classics
PO Box 3418
Chapel Hill, NC 27515

PREFACE

The lives which we here present in a condensed, simple form are prepared from those of Plutarch, of whom it will perhaps be interesting to young readers to have a short account. Plutarch was born in Chæronea, a town of Bœotia, about the middle of the first century. He belonged to a good family, and was brought up with every encouragement to study, literary pursuits, and virtuous actions. When very young he visited Rome, as did all the intelligent Greeks of his day, and it is supposed that while there he gave public lectures in philosophy and eloquence. He was a great admirer of Plato, and, like that philosopher, believed in the immortality of the soul. This doctrine he preached to his hearers, and taught them many valuable truths about justice and morality, of which they had previously been ignorant.

After his return to his native land, Plutarch held several important public offices, and devoted his time to forming plans for the benefit of his countrymen. Living to an advanced age, he wrote many important books; but the one which gave him most celebrity is the "Lives" from which we have derived this work. He consulted all the historians of his day, but did not follow them blindly; for after carefully comparing and weighing their statements, he selected those which seemed most probable. There can be no doubt that he shared the belief of the age in which he lived, for his works give evidence of devotion to the pagan gods. The legends of the Heroic age must not be accepted as historical facts, nor must any importance be attached to the prophecies of priests, omens, oracles, and the divinations of soothsayers, except in so far as they afford a picture of ancient superstitions, and show how even the most powerful minds had their weaknesses. They may be traced to natural causes, and it seems probable that the Roman and Greek armies were victorious or the reverse, because they went into battle impressed by the favorable or unfavorable prophecies, as the case might be, of their soothsayers. Plutarch says, "It must be borne in mind that my design is not to write histories, but lives." This is why anecdotes, short sayings or a word or two of repartee are frequently recorded. For they furnish a better insight into the thoughts and character of a man than his most glorious exploit, famous siege, or blood battle. So it is lives, and not a history, that we offer; this must be borne in mind when some of the most important events the world has ever known receive insufficient mention.

R.K.

Theseus & Romulus
Solon & Poplicola/Publicola
Themistocles & Camillus
Aristides & Cato the Elder
Cimon & Lucullus
Pericles & Fabius Maximus
Nicias & Crassus
Alcibiades & Coriolanus
Lysander & Sulla/Sylla

Lycurgus & Numa Pompilius
Phocion & Cato the Younger
Dion & Brutus
Agesilaus & Pompey
Alexander & Caesar
Demosthenes & Cicero
Demetrius & Mark Antony

CONTENTS

Theseus	1
Lycurgus	16
Romulus	34
Numa Pompilius	48
Solon	62
Publicola	78
Caius Marcius Coriolanus	94
Themistocles	110
Aristides	127
Cimon	138
Pericles	148
Nicias	158
Alcibiades	167
Lysander	179
Camillus	187
Artaxerxes	203
Agesilaus	210
Dion	222

PHOCION 236

PELOPIDAS 248

TIMOLEON 261

DEMOSTHENES 274

ALEXANDER 284

EUMENES 310

DEMETRIUS 318

PYRRHUS 329

ARATUS 342

AGIS 355

CLEOMENES 364

FABIUS 373

MARCELLUS 388

PHILOPOEMEN 402

FLAMININUS 411

MARCUS CATO 420

AEMILIUS PAULUS 433

TIBERIUS GRACCHUS 449

CAIUS GRACCHUS 458

CAIUS MARIUS 467

SYLLA 487

Crassus 498
Lucullus 512
Pompey 525
Cicero 543
Caesar 553
Cato the Younger 569
Marcus Brutus 584
Antony 597
Sertorius 606
Galba 616
Otho 623

THESEUS

Theseus was one of the most celebrated heroes of ancient times, but he lived so many centuries ago that no one knows the date of his birth. He was a Greek of noble descent, Æthra, his mother, being the granddaughter of one of the most powerful of all the Peloponnesian kings. Ægeus, his father, was not of royal blood, but he was descended from the oldest inhabitants of Attica, and became a sovereign before Theseus was born. A short time after he was chosen to rule over Athens he had occasion to travel, and one of the cities he visited was Trœzene, where he was invited to court. There he met the Princess Æthra, with whom he fell in love. She returned his affection, and the two were married; but Ægeus did not mention this important event when he returned to Athens, because of the displeasure that he knew it would cause his relations, and still less did he dare to do so when the birth of his son was announced to him.

This was on account of his nephews, the Pallantidæ, a band of fifty brothers who expected to mount the throne in turn, and would not have hesitated to destroy anybody who might stand in their way. So Ægeus carefully preserved his secret, although it was his intention to recognize his son as soon as he felt that it would be safe to do it.

Before his departure from Trœzene, Ægeus had hidden a sword and a pair of sandals beneath a huge stone, and had told Æthra that when their boy should reach manhood and should become sufficiently strong to raise the stone without aid, he was to carry the articles concealed under it to Athens. In that way, after the lapse of many years, Ægeus hoped to recognize his son. He had no fear that Æthra would betray the secret, for he had taken great pains to make her understand the danger to himself and Theseus if the existence of the latter should become known to the Pallantidæ.

Pittheus, Æthra's father, took charge of his grandson, and engaged a tutor named Connidas to educate him. In later years the Athenians sacrificed a ram to this tutor on the day before the celebration of the Thesean feasts, simply because he had been honored with the care of the person whom they loved, and for whom they entertained the most profound reverence.

Æthra was true to her trust, and told nobody who was the father of her son; but Pittheus declared that it was Neptune, the god of the sea. This pleased the Trœzenians, because they considered Neptune their special deity, offered sacrifices to him, and stamped their money with a three-pronged sceptre called a trident, which was the symbol of his power.

In course of time Theseus became a robust, healthy youth, and his mother was so pleased on account of his strength of mind and body, as well as the excellent judgment he displayed on various occasions, that when he was only sixteen years of age she resolved to inform him of the secret of his birth; so taking him by the hand one day, she led him to the stone under which his father had placed the sword and sandals, bade him remove it, and with what he would find concealed beneath hasten to Athens and present himself before Ægeus.

The youth obeyed in so far as lifting the stone was concerned, for, as we have said, he was strong, and the task was by no means a difficult one; but he astonished his mother by refusing to sail to Athens at her request. To Athens, he replied, he would certainly go, but not by sea. This announcement troubled the fond Æthra, for traveling by land was at that time made extremely dangerous by the bandits and cut-throats who overran Greece, and whose cruelty, strength, and desperate deeds were world-renowned. But Theseus was inspired with the spirit of the Heroic age in which he lived, and before following him in his travels we will say a few words about this period.

What is known as the Heroic age in history is supposed to have extended over about two hundred years. The Greeks believed that during that time their country was governed by a noble race of beings who, though not divine, possessed more than human strength, and were in many ways superior to ordinary men. These are the heroes, mentioned in Grecian mythology, whose exploits and noble deeds furnished themes for the early writers. The Heroic age closed with the Trojan war, 1184 B.C. Homer has given the best picture of the government, customs, and society of that age, and his poems furnish the earliest knowledge we have of the Greeks. This renders them valuable, even though they may not always be based on facts.

Among the most prominent heroes of Grecian mythology are Hercules, Theseus, and Minos.

Now Hercules and Theseus were of the same family, and the latter had heard so much about the wonderful feats of strength and the glorious valor of his ancestor that he burned to imitate him and have his name enrolled among the heroes. He had longed for the day when he might set forth to perform great deeds, and when at last it dawned he eagerly began his plans, and before long he started on his journey, determined to destroy all those who should offer violence to himself or who had been cruel to other travellers. Thus he hoped to benefit his country and all mankind.

The first creature who tried to stop him was Periphetes, the Club-bearer. Theseus killed him and took the enormous club with which he had put an end to his victims for so many years. As Hercules carried a huge lion's skin to show what a ferocious beast he had slain, so now did Theseus appear with the club of Periphetes, which, in his hands, became a most formidable weapon.

Theseus next slew Sinnis, the Pine-bender, whose very name had long been a terror to the world. His way of destroying people was to fasten their limbs to branches of pine-trees which were bent together for that purpose; then suddenly the trees would be unfastened, when they would return to their upright position and tear the victim to pieces. Sinnis suffered the very fate he had imposed on others.

At Commyon there was an immense sow, so fierce and wild as to keep the whole neighborhood in a state of constant dread. Theseus went out of his way to meet the horrible creature, because he did not wish it to appear that he would avoid peril of any sort; besides, he thought that a truly brave man ought to rid the world of dangerous beasts as well as of wicked human beings. So he put an end to the sow, and then travelled on to Megara.

At Megara there lived a notorious robber named Sciron, who made any person that came his way wash his feet. That would not have been a fatal operation performed in the ordinary way, but Sciron would seat himself at the edge of a lofty precipice for the washing, and while it was going on he would give his victim a violent kick and send him headlong down the rock into the sea. Theseus did not go through the ceremony of foot-washing with Sciron, but seized him and dashed him over the precipice. In putting these creatures out of the world in the same way they disposed of others, Theseus imitated Hercules, as students of mythology will perceive. Thus, in boxing-matches he killed Cycnus and Cercyon, celebrated wrestlers; he broke to pieces the skull of Termerus, who had killed people by butting his head against theirs; and Procrustes, a famous robber of Attica, he punished in the following way: Procrustes had a bed on which he made all his victims lie to see how nearly they would fit, but it was of a size that was sure to be too short for some people and too long for others. So the tall ones were lopped off and the short ones stretched out. The powerful giant's whole head had to come off before he could lie on the bed, and so Theseus punished him, much to the delight of the neighbors.

On his arrival at Athens, Theseus found public affairs all in confusion, for the inhabitants were divided into parties that were constantly disputing with one another. He did not at once present himself before his father, but Medea, to whom Ægeus was then married, found out who he was, and made up her mind that he should not stay to inherit the throne if she could help it, particularly as she had a son of her own for whom she desired it. So she told Ægeus that the appearance of the young stranger at court just then, when the government was so disturbed, meant mischief, and he must be put out of the way. She advised him to give a banquet and invite Theseus, for whom she would prepare a cup of poison. Ægeus, who was always in dread of plots against his throne, readily consented. When all the guests were assembled he took the cup of poison in his hand and was on the point of offering it, when Theseus drew out his sword and prepared to cut the meat with it. The father recognized the token and dashed the cup to the ground. A few questions convinced him that the stranger was his son, and he forthwith tenderly embraced him and publicly proclaimed him his heir. The Athenians, who had heard of the daring deeds of Theseus, shouted with joy, for they were delighted at the prospect of one day having so brave a king.

Not so the Pallantidæ; seeing their hopes thus destroyed, they became desperate, and, dividing themselves into two companies, they broke out into open warfare. Their plan was for one party to attack the city while the other lay in ambush ready to set upon the enemy from the opposite side. They might have met with success had it not been for a herald named Leos. He pretended to work with them, but treacherously repeated all he heard to Theseus. That young hero speedily destroyed one party, whereupon the other thought best to disperse.

Having no special business to attend to after that, Theseus amused himself by going to Marathon to destroy a furious bull that was doing great damage to the fields and frightening the people. This bull Hercules had brought from Crete, and when Theseus led it in chains through Athens, the people were filled with wonder at his having captured so ferocious a creature alive.

THESEUS

Theseus was now ranked next to Hercules among the heroes; but the adventure which won for him the greatest glory was this:

The island of Crete was governed by Minos, a wise, good king, much beloved by his subjects on account of his justice and honesty. It so happened that his son, Androgeus, when on a visit to Attica, had been treacherously murdered, and in order to avenge the dreadful deed the disconsolate father made perpetual war against the Athenians. The gods sided with Minos, and not only sent famine and pestilence to punish his enemy, but dried up all their rivers.

At last their sufferings became so intense that the Athenians could no longer bear them, so they sent to the oracle for advice. The oracle told them that if they could devise some means of satisfying Minos the anger of the gods would be appeased, and their distress would come to an end. Messengers were forthwith despatched to Crete to see what could be done. The king proposed a treaty, which required that every nine years seven young Athenian men and as many girls, of noble families, should be sent to Crete as victims to the Minotaur.

The Minotaur was a huge monster that had the body and limbs of a man and the head of a bull. His abode was at the central point of several winding paths, that crossed and recrossed one another in such a puzzling manner that nobody who got into the labyrinth, as it was called, could ever find his way out again.

Well, Ægeus had agreed to King Minos's treaty, and two sets of Athenian maids and youths had been devoured by the Minotaur. The period for sending the third lot came around just after Theseus had captured the Marathon bull.

The sorrow in Athens was so great that Theseus was much affected by it. Parents lamented loudly, and in the bitterness of their grief accused the king of signing the cruel treaty only because he had no child to sacrifice. No sooner did Theseus hear this than he unhesitatingly offered himself. Ægeus was shocked, and tried to dissuade his son from taking such a rash step, but Theseus remained firm, and the other thirteen victims were chosen as usual, by lot.

The treaty provided that the Athenians should furnish their own ships, and that no weapons of war should be carried to Crete. But it set forth distinctly that if, by any fair means, the Minotaur should be destroyed, the tribute should cease forever. On the two previous occasions the ships had carried black sails only, but Theseus had so encouraged his father by declaring that he felt certain of being able to kill the monster, that Ægeus gave the pilot a white sail, commanding him to hoist it on his return if he brought Theseus safely back, but should such not be the case, the black one was to appear as a sign of misfortune.

On his arrival in Crete, Theseus took part in the public games that Minos yearly celebrated in memory of his lost son, and showed such superiority as a wrestler that Ariadne, the daughter of Minos, fell in love with him. This proved a blessing, for she secretly informed Theseus how to reach the centre of the labyrinth, and gave him a thread which he was to unwind as he passed along, and thus be able to find his way back.

With such a clue the killing of the Minotaur became an easy task to so powerful a man as Theseus, and having accomplished it, he set out with his companions in triumph for Athens. But when the ship neared the coast, so great was the excitement on board that neither Theseus nor the pilot remembered the signal of success they had been ordered to hoist. So when Ægeus beheld the vessel with its black sail, he naturally concluded that his son was dead. In despair he threw himself headlong from a rock and perished in the sea.

The first thing Theseus did on stepping ashore was to offer sacrifices to the gods, but while thus engaged he sent a messenger to Athens to announce his victory and safe return. The city was filled with mourning on account of the king's death, but the lamentations were changed to rejoicing when the good news was made known. The messenger was crowned with garlands, which he hung upon his staff, and hastened back to the sea-shore.

Theseus was still sacrificing when the death of his father was reported to him. He was much grieved, and so were his companions, all of whom took part in the funeral ceremonies, and helped Theseus to do honor to the memory of the late king. They then marched through the city in triumph, the people flocking out to welcome them, and to gaze at the hero who had relieved them from the cruel tribute imposed on them by King Minos.

Theseus was now king of Attica, and he set about improving the condition of his subjects at once. Instead of living near together, they were scattered over such a large space that they could not be easily governed, so disputes, and even battles, were constantly taking place. Theseus thought of a remedy, and, after consulting the Oracle of Delphi and getting a favorable answer, proceeded to apply it.

He went from town to town, from tribe to tribe, and explained his plan for establishing a commonwealth, which

DEATH OF ÆGEUS

he promised to protect. It required a vast deal of persuasion before he could convince people that he was working for their good, and not for the purpose of increasing his own power; but at last he was rewarded for his trouble by seeing the various little state houses closed and one grand council hall established for the use of the whole kingdom. A public feast was given to celebrate this union of the people, and the state was henceforth called Athens.

Strangers from other countries were now invited to settle in Athens, and they flocked there in crowds. Much confusion might have resulted; but Theseus was wise enough to provide against this at the outset. He divided the people into three classes,—the noblemen, the husbandmen, and the mechanics,—each class having its duties and position clearly defined. The nobles had charge of religious affairs, appointed the magistrates, and saw that the laws were not violated. The husbandmen tilled the ground and raised cattle, and the mechanics attended to buildings and improvements in machinery, etc.

The new money was stamped with the image of an ox; probably in memory of the brute Theseus had slain at Marathon; so the Athenians valued an article at so many oxen, instead of dollars, as we do.

Theseus took possession of the country about Megara and added it to Athens, but wisely set up a pillar to mark the boundary-line, so as to avoid dispute on that point. Indeed, he seemed to be ever on the alert for anything that might disturb the peace and order he had established at home; but he was not so considerate of other nations, as his expedition against the Amazons proves. The Amazons were a race of warlike women represented in the ancient pictures and writings as fighting the Greek heroes. Theseus seized Antiope, their queen, fled with her to his ship, and set sail forthwith.

The rash act led to a disastrous war, which lasted four months; for the Amazons followed their queen to Athens and fought desperately. Antiope was slain, and so were many of her race, before peace was declared.

Theseus performed several exploits which we need not relate, because they were not of great importance, but when he reached the age of fifty he was guilty of a deed that by no means adds to his glory. That was the carrying off of Helen, who was supposed to be the daughter of the god Jupiter. She was considered the greatest beauty in the world, although she was then only nine years old.

Helen was dancing in the temple of Diana when Theseus went there, accompanied by his friend Pirithoüs, and stole her away. Armed men pursued the robbers, but could not overtake them, for they hastened on through Peloponnesus, and were soon beyond danger of arrest. Then they drew lots to see which of them should marry Helen when she should grow up, agreeing beforehand that the successful one should assist the other in getting a wife. Theseus proved the lucky man, and he bore the beauty to the house of a friend of his named Aphidnus, bidding him take the very best care of her and keep her hiding-place a profound secret. Æthra was conducted to the same house by Theseus, who begged her to assist in the care of the precious charge.

Now Pirithoüs had to be provided with a wife, and Cora, daughter of Pluto, god of the lower regions, was fixed upon. Accordingly, the two friends set out to secure Cora; but this was by no means so easy a task as they had supposed, for Pluto kept a fierce dog, named Cerberus, and all the suitors

THESEUS

for Cora's hand had to fight the brute before they could be received. Cerberus must have been wonderfully intelligent, for he knew that Pirithoüs had come to steal the young lady, not to sue for her, so he rushed at him and tore him to pieces. Theseus escaped a similar fate; but he was captured by Pluto and locked up.

Theseus was still in prison when Helen's brothers, Castor and Pollux, went to Athens to seek their sister. The inhabitants assured them that she was not with them, and that they did not know where she was to be found. But an Athenian, named Academus, had discovered her hiding-place, and informed Castor and Pollux of it. They gathered together an army, marched to the town where Aphidnus lived, assaulted and got possession of it. Helen was rescued and sent to Troy, where it is supposed Æthra went to live with her.

Castor and Pollux returned to Athens and became citizens; for the people felt so grateful to them for not punishing them on account of Theseus's crime that they received them with every mark of friendship.

In course of time Hercules, while travelling, went to visit Pluto, who related to him how Theseus and Pirithoüs had tried to steal his daughter, and the punishment each had received. Hercules was grieved at what he heard of Theseus, whom he had long admired, so he entreated Pluto to release his prisoner, telling him that so great a hero deserved a better fate.

So Pluto opened the prison door, and Theseus returned home, where, as a mark of gratitude, he dedicated all the sacred places to Hercules.

Now Theseus expected to resume his place on the throne and govern the Athenians as before, but he soon found he was mistaken. All the good he had done was overshadowed by the silly actions that had made the people despise and distrust him. At first he thought of fighting for his rights; but deciding that no benefit could result from that, he gave up hope and set sail for Scyros, where he owned land that had belonged to his father.

He thought that Lycomedes, King of Scyros, was his friend, and that he should have no trouble in laying claim to his own possessions; but such was not the case. Lycomedes received him courteously, and invited him to walk with him to a cliff, under pretence of pointing out the estate he owned. When they reached the highest point Lycomedes threw his visitor headlong into the sea, killing him instantly.

In course of time the Athenians began to worship Theseus as a demi-god; and when they were at war with the Medes and Persians part of their army declared that he appeared at their head, completely armed, and led them against the enemy. After that sacrifices were offered to him, and the Oracle of Apollo ordered that his bones should be placed in a sacred spot at Athens. But for a long time it was impossible to find them, for the people of Scyros were not friendly, and would not tell where Theseus was buried.

At last Cimon, who had conquered the island, saw an eagle one day pecking at a certain mound and trying to scrape up the earth. It suddenly struck him that the gods were thus pointing out to him the burial-place of Theseus; so he dug until he came to a coffin, which he opened. It contained the bones of a very large man, by whose side lay a sword and a brass spear-head. Cimon was now convinced, and lost no time in carrying the coffin to Athens. Had Theseus returned alive his countrymen could scarcely have rejoiced more than they did when his remains were brought to them. They made a grand public funeral, and erected a tomb in his memory just in the heart of the city.

Ever after, sacrifices in honor of the benefactor of Athens were offered on the anniversary of his return from Crete.

LYCURGUS

THERE is so much uncertainty about the life of Lycurgus, the law-giver of Sparta, that circumstances related by one historian are often contradicted or differently represented by all the others. No two agree as to the date of his birth, his voyages, or the manner of his death. One reason for this disagreement is that there were two men in Sparta at different periods named Lycurgus. The earlier one, of whom we write, lived not long after Homer, and some of the exploits of the later Lycurgus are often confused with his. However, we shall be careful to present only such facts as are given by the most reliable authors. It must be borne in mind that the capital of Laconia was sometimes called Sparta and sometimes Lacedæmon. The names are used indiscriminately, both meaning the same city.

The most renowned of all the ancestors of Lycurgus was Soüs, who, while king of the Lacedæmonians, gained a tract of land called Helos. He reduced the inhabitants to slavery, and from that time all the slaves that the Lacedæmonians captured in their wars were called by the general name of Helots.

A remarkable story is told of Soüs, which is worth repeating, because it gives an example of wonderful self-control. He was once besieged by the Clitorians in a barren spot where it was impossible to get fresh water. This occasioned the soldiers so much suffering that Soüs was forced to appeal to the besiegers, and he agreed to restore to them all he had conquered providing that he and his men should drink of a neighboring spring. The Clitorians, thinking that they had nothing to lose and much to gain, readily acceded to the terms. Then Soüs assembled his forces and offered his entire kingdom to any man among them who would forbear to drink; but they were so thirsty that they scarcely paid any heed to the offer, and eagerly partook of the cool, refreshing water. When all were satisfied, Soüs approached the spring, and, in the presence of his own soldiers and those of the enemy, merely sprinkled his face; then, without allowing a drop of water to enter his mouth, looked around with an air of triumph, and loudly declared that, since all his army had not drunk, the articles of the agreement were unfulfilled. Thus the country remained in his possession.

When the father of Lycurgus died, his eldest son, Polydectes, succeeded to the throne of Sparta, but he lived only a few months, and at his death it was unanimously agreed that Lycurgus should be king. But it so happened that a short time after her husband died the widow of Polydectes gave birth to a son, when Lycurgus, being too just to deprive the child of his right, presented him to the magistrates, and said, "Spartans, behold your new-born king!" He then placed the infant in the chair of state and named him Charilaus.

Lycurgus acted as guardian of the little king, and was for many months the real ruler of Sparta; but in course of time the friends and relations of the queen-mother became jealous of his power, and complained because they thought they did not receive proper consideration. They went further, and accused Lycurgus of desiring the death of Charilaus in order that he might ascend the throne. This, and various other accusations which they brought against him, so aroused the suspicions of the people that Lycurgus determined to go away, and not return until his nephew had reached manhood. So, in indignation that any one should believe him capable of such baseness, he set sail with the intention of visiting different countries and studying their various forms of government.

The first place he landed at was Crete, where he became acquainted with one Thales, a poet and musician, renowned for his learning and for his political abilities. Thales wrote poems which he set to music, exhorting people to obedience and virtue, and so effective were they that private quarrels were often ended, and peace and order restored by their influence, and Thales had in consequence become a most important and useful person. He and Lycurgus were soon warm friends, and the latter persuaded him to go to Sparta, where, by means of his melodies, he did much towards civilizing the inhabitants.

Lycurgus travelled on, only stopping long enough in each country to find out what was better or worse in its institutions than in those of his native land. While on this journey he first saw some of Homer's poetry, which he admired so much that he introduced it wherever it was not known.

Although Lycurgus remained away from Sparta several years, he was very much missed, and his countrymen frequently sent ambassadors to entreat him to return. They compared their condition with what it had been under his rule, and were convinced that he had a genius for governing, whereas Charilaus was only a king in name. In course of time

LYCURGUS

public affairs went from bad to worse, and then the king himself expressed a wish to have Lycurgus back. When this was made known to the traveller he no longer hesitated.

Lycurgus saw at once, on his arrival in Sparta, that no sort of patching up would restore the government to its proper state, and the only way to remedy the evil condition of public affairs was to begin at the very foundation and frame an entirely new set of laws. The first step he took was to visit the oracle at Delphi, where he offered a sacrifice and asked advice. The priestess called him the "beloved of the gods," and, in answer to his request that he might be inspired to enact good laws, assured him that Apollo had heard him, and promised that the constitution he should establish would be the wisest and best in the whole world. This was so encouraging that Lycurgus went to his friends and to all the prominent men of Sparta and begged them to assist him in his undertaking. They consented, and when his plans were completed Lycurgus requested thirty of the best-known Spartans to meet him at break of day in the market-place, well armed and prepared to attack any one who should oppose him. Such a tumult arose when the new form of government was announced that King Charilaus became alarmed, and thought there was a conspiracy against his person. So he rushed to the Temple of Minerva of the Brazen Horse for safety. There Lycurgus and his party followed, and explained their intentions so satisfactorily that the king was easily won over to their side.

The most important feature of the new government was the establishment of a senate, whose duty it should be to prevent the king on one hand, and the people on the other, from assuming too much control. After this was accomplished a difficult task presented itself in the new division of the land, which was all owned by a few wealthy men of Sparta. Lycurgus considered this a bad state of affairs, but it required a great deal of discussion and persuasion before he could convince these land-owners to part with their estates. He succeeded, however, and nine thousand lots were distributed among as many citizens of Sparta. Then the country of Laconia was divided into thirty thousand equal shares for her citizens. After that, all being rich and poor alike, the only distinction a man could hope for was in acts of virtue. Once when Lycurgus was travelling through the country at harvest-time he smiled to see how equal were the stacks of grain on each division of land, and said, "Laconia looks like a large family estate distributed among a number of brothers."

To divide movables was such an impossible matter that the law-giver had to resort to stratagem to accomplish this. He made gold and silver coin worthless, and substituted iron instead; but it was so heavy and bulky that a whole roomful was not very valuable, and a yoke of oxen was required to remove a small sum. This put an end to robbery, for it was difficult to steal enough of such money to make the crime an object, and impossible to conceal a large sum. Another peculiarity of the iron coin was that it prevented the Spartans from making purchases of their neighbors, who laughed at it, and would not receive it in exchange for their wares. Hence the Spartans were forced to manufacture whatever they needed, so they turned their attention to the production of such useful articles as tables, chairs, and beds, and were willing to dispense with luxuries. Finding that very little money was required for necessities, the Spartans were easily satisfied, and had no reason to covet wealth. This was a state of affairs that Lycurgus particularly desired. Wandering fortune-tellers and venders of trashy trinkets ceased their visits to a country that had undesirable money, and as such people do more harm than good, their absence was an advantage.

Public tables were introduced, and did more than any other institutions of the law-giver in placing the citizens on a more equal footing, by forcing every man to partake of the same description and quality of food as his neighbor. In no circumstance would it do for any one to take a private meal beforehand, even though he made his appearance afterwards at the public table, for a person with a poor appetite was suspected and accused of being dainty and effeminate, and that no Spartan could stand. But the men who had been wealthy objected to eating what Lycurgus prescribed, and one day they collected in the market-place and attacked him with abusive language, which they followed up by throwing stones. Finding that he was in danger, Lycurgus ran for a sanctuary, but he was pursued by a young man named Alcander, who overtook him and struck him such a violent blow in the face with a stout stick as to put out one of his eyes. Lycurgus did not attempt to resent his injury, but turned towards the rest of his tormentors, who, at the sight of his horrible condition, with his face streaming with blood, were so repentant and ashamed that they placed Alcander in his hands for punishment, and conducted Lycurgus to his home with great care and tenderness.

The law-giver thanked them for assisting him, and then dismissed all excepting Alcander, whom he took into his house. No word of reproach or ill treatment of any sort awaited the offender. The usual servants and attendants were sent away, and Alcander was ordered to wait upon Lycurgus instead. This he did without a murmur, because he was sorry for the dreadful injury he had done, and knew that he deserved punishment. Day by day his admiration of Lycurgus increased, and he constantly spoke to his friends of the goodness, the temperance, the industry, and the gentleness of the man he had once deemed proud and severe. Alcander knew that he could not do better than to imitate his master, and by so doing he became a wise, prudent citizen. In memory of his accident Lycurgus built a temple to Minerva, and to prevent the recurrence of such violence, the Lacedæmonians made it a rule never to carry sticks to their public assemblies.

Now we must give a description of the public dining-tables. Fifteen persons sat at a table, each being obliged to furnish monthly a bushel of meal, eight gallons of wine, five pounds of cheese, two pounds and a half of figs, and a little money to buy meat and fish. Any man who offered a sacrifice of first fruits, or killed a deer, had the privilege of eating at home for one day, providing he sent part of the venison to the public table. Besides repressing luxury, these assemblages for dining had another object: they were a kind of school for the young, where they were instructed in state affairs by learned statesmen, who discoursed while eating. Conversation was encouraged among the diners, who chatted freely and made jests, though they were always exceedingly careful not to hurt one another's feelings, that being considered ill bred.

The first time a youth entered the eating-place, the oldest citizen present would say, pointing to the door, "Not a word spoken in this company goes out there." This gave freedom to the conversation, and taught the young not to repeat what they heard. The manner of admitting a candidate to a particular table was as follows: each man who occupied a seat at it took a bit of soft bread and rolled it into a little ball, which he silently dropped into a vessel carried around for that purpose by a waiter. This vessel was called Caddos. If the candidate was desired, the shape of the ball was preserved by the person who made it, but if, for any reason, he preferred somebody else, the ball was flattened before being deposited in the Caddos. One flattened ball was sufficient to exclude an applicant, and such being the case, the fifteen men who occupied each table were always acceptable to one another. A rejected person was said to have ill luck with the Caddos.

The Lacedæmonians drank wine in moderation, and only at the public table; at the conclusion of the meal they went home in the dark. Their reason for not carrying lanterns was that they might accustom themselves to march boldly without light, and thus be prepared for midnight forays against an enemy.

It is remarkable that none of the laws made by Lycurgus were put into writing; indeed, he particularly enjoined that they should not be. He preferred rather to educate people to proper habits than to enforce them by writing. He said that matters of importance would have more weight if they were woven into the actions of everyday life, and imprinted on the hearts of the young by wise discipline and good example. Even for business contracts no writing was deemed necessary; the idea being so to educate men that their judgment would become sufficiently correct to enable them to adhere to an agreement or alter it as time and circumstances might require.

One of the laws of Lycurgus required the ceilings of the houses be wrought with no tool but an axe, and the doors and gates be only so smooth as a saw could make them. This was to prevent extravagance and luxury, for in a house so roughly constructed a man would not be likely to place bedsteads with silver feet, showy drapery, or gold and silver cups and salvers. Such costly articles would seem out of place;

plain, substantial ones were selected in preference. So accustomed did the Spartans become to simplicity that when Leotychidas, one of their kings, was entertained in a room at Corinth where the ceilings and door-posts were richly carved, he asked whether the trees of that country grew like that. It is not probable that the question arose from ignorance, but the king had learned to sneer at such sumptuous and expensive buildings as he saw at Corinth.

Lycurgus thought the good education of the Spartan youth the noblest part of his work, and required girls as well as boys to take plenty of exercise in the open air, such as running, wrestling, and throwing quoits, that they might become strong and healthy. Every child was regarded as the property of the state, so it was carried, soon after birth, to a place called Lesche to be examined by certain elders, who decided its fate. If it were found to be well-formed and healthy, an order was given for its rearing, and a portion of land set apart for its maintenance. But a puny or deformed baby was thrown into a chasm, for the Spartans would have no weaklings. Their object was to build up a martial race, and they did not see, as we do, that people whose bodies are not strong often become the most valuable members of the human family.

Those children that were permitted to live were nursed with the greatest care, not tenderly, but with a view to making them robust. Their clothing was loose, their food coarse and plain; they were not afraid to be left alone or in the dark, nor were they permitted to indulge ill humor or to cry at trifles. The Lacedæmonian nurses were so famous that people of other countries often purchased them for their children.

LYCURGUS

No tutors or nurses were obtained in that way for Spartan children, nor were their parents at liberty to educate them as they pleased. For at the age of seven they were enrolled in companies, and all subjected to the same discipline, performing their tasks and enjoying their recreations in common. The boy who showed most courage was made captain of the company, and the rest had to obey his orders implicitly and submit without a murmur to the punishments he inflicted. Old men were always present at the games, and often suggested some reason for a quarrel, in order that they might study the characters of the different boys and see which were brave and which cowardly. A slight knowledge of reading and writing was all that was required; but a Spartan youth was taught to endure pain, and to conquer in battle; as he advanced in years the severity of his discipline was increased, his head was shaved, he wore no shoes or stockings, and no clothing whatever when at play.

After reaching the age of twelve the boys discarded underclothing, which up to that time they were permitted to wear, and one coat a year was allotted to each. Bathing was not considered a necessity, and in order to render the skin hard and tough it was indulged in only on specified days at rare intervals. The Spartan boys slept together, forming themselves into bands and assisting each other in breaking and gathering the rushes of which their beds were composed. They were allowed to use no tools, their bare hands being considered sufficient for the work. In winter they added thistle-down to their rushes for warmth. They were constantly and carefully watched by the older men of the nation, and promptly punished for neglect of duty.

The bands were selected by the ablest and best citizen, who was appointed for that purpose. He governed them all, selected a captain for each, and exercised a general supervision over them. The captains were chosen from among the Irens, as those who had reached the age of twenty were called, bravery, good temper, and self-control being the necessary qualifications. The position, therefore, was considered one of high honor. It was the captain's duty to command in battle; but in time of peace he was waited on by the members of his band, who obeyed his orders implicitly. The older ones did the hard work, such as fetching logs of wood, while to the younger and weaker ones fell the duty of gathering salads, herbs, meats, or any other food, as best they could, even though it became necessary to steal it. For this purpose they would creep into the gardens or sneak into the eating-houses which chanced to be left unguarded, and help themselves. If caught in the act, these youths were whipped unmercifully for their awkwardness. Their supper was purposely made such a scant meal that they were encouraged to steal from actual hunger. This was done as an exercise of courage and address, for if a youth could not steal or beg food he had to suffer the pangs of hunger. Fortunately for the morals of the Spartan boys, they had no need of riches or luxury, consequently their thefts were limited to the requirements of their stomachs. This was bad enough, but the object was to render children who were destined for war expert in escaping the watchfulness of an enemy, and to accustom them to expose themselves to the severest punishment in case of detection. Another reason for feeding them so sparingly was to make them tall and pliant, rather than short and fat.

The Spartan boys performed their stealing so earnestly that one of them having hidden a young fox under his cloak suffered the animal to tear out his very bowels, choosing rather to die on the spot than be detected and accused of awkwardness. This story might appear incredible in any other nation, but Plutarch assures us that he himself saw several Lacedæmonian youths whipped to death at the foot of the altar of Diana, on which their blood was sprinkled as a sacrifice. All the institutions of Lycurgus tended towards excessive self-control, by which he desired to render Spartans superior to other human beings.

It was the custom of the Iren to spend some time with the boys every evening after supper, when he would test their wits and find out which were the bright and which the stupid ones. For example: one boy was ordered to sing a song, and was expected to comply instantly whether he chose or not. Another was asked who was the best man in the city, or what he thought of the various actions of such and such men. The object of these questions was not only to encourage the boys in forming opinions, but also to oblige them to inform themselves as to the defects and abilities of their countrymen. If a boy was not prepared with an answer he was considered dull and indifferent, and supposed to be wanting in a proper sense of virtue and honor. A good reason had to be given, in as few words as possible, for every statement made, and if it were not clear and sensible the boy had his thumb bitten by his captain. This was done in the presence of the old men and magistrates, who expressed no opinions in the presence of the boys, but as soon as they were gone reproved the Iren if he had been too severe or too indulgent.

The art of talking was so cultivated that the boys became sharp and quick at repartee. Indeed, it was the aim of every Lacedæmonian to condense a deal of sense into as few words as possible. Lycurgus set the example, as the anecdotes related about him prove.

On being questioned as to why he allowed such mean and trivial sacrifices to the gods, he replied, "That we may always have something to offer them." When asked what sort of martial exercises he preferred, he said, "All, excepting those in which you stretch out your hands." That attitude meant a demand for quarter in battle. Lycurgus was once consulted by letter as to how his countrymen might best oppose an invasion of their enemies. His answer was, "By continuing poor, and not coveting each man to be greater than his fellow." When asked whether the city ought not to be enclosed by a wall, he wrote, "The city is well fortified which hath a wall of men instead of brick."

King Charilaus was once asked why Lycurgus had made so few laws: he replied, "Men of few words require few laws." It was said by a learned Spartan in defence of another, who had been admitted to one of the public repasts and had observed profound silence throughout, "He who knows how to speak knows also when to speak." A troublesome, impertinent fellow asked one of the wise men four or five times, "Who was the best man in Sparta?" and got for his answer, "He that is least like you." An orator of Athens declared that the Lacedæmonians had no learning. "True," answered one who was present, "for we are the only people of Greece that have learnt no ill of you." These are enough examples to show how chary the Spartans were of their words.

Music and poetry were cultivated to a great extent, and the songs were such as to excite enthusiasm and inspire men to fight. They were always simple in their expression, serious and moral in their tone; often they were praises of such men as had died in defence of their country, declaring them to be happy and glorified, or they were written to ridicule cowards, who chose rather to drag out a life which was regarded with contempt than seek glory on the field of battle.

At no time was the discipline of the Spartans less severe than when they were engaged in a war. Then they were permitted to have fine clothes and costly armor, and to curl their hair, of which they had a great quantity. They were particular about the arrangement of this ornament, because the law-giver had said that a large head of hair added beauty to a good face and terror to an ugly one. During their campaigns they were better fed and forced to exercise less severely than in time of peace, and their whole treatment was so much more indulgent that they were never better satisfied than when under military rule. They went to battle dancing and keeping step to the music without disturbing their ranks. They were gay, cheerful, and so eager that they resembled race-horses full of fire and neighing for the start. When the king advanced against the enemy, he was always surrounded by those who had been crowned at the public games. Spartans considered it such a favor to be so placed in battle, that one of them, who had gained a difficult victory in an Olympic game, upon being asked what reward he expected, since he would not accept money as other combatants did, replied, "I shall have the honor to fight foremost in the ranks before my prince."

When they had routed an enemy they continued in pursuit until they were assured of the victory, but no longer, for they deemed it unworthy of a Grecian to destroy those who did not resist. This manner of dealing with their enemies was not only magnanimous, but was wise, for their opponents often gave up the fight and fled, knowing that their lives would be spared as soon as they did so. Lycurgus made great improvements in the art of war, and proved himself a brave, competent commander.

He made Lacedæmon resemble one great camp, where each person had his share of provisions and his occupation marked out. Even a man advanced in years could not live according to his own fancy, for he had always to consider the interest of his country before his own. If nothing else was required of him, he watched the boys in the performance of their exercises, and taught them something useful. Lycurgus forbade his people to engage in any mechanical trade, consequently they had plenty of leisure. They required no money, and thought that time devoted to the accumulation of wealth was sinfully wasted. The Helots tilled the ground and did all the menial work which a Lacedæmonian freeman considered beneath his dignity.

Lawsuits ceased, because there was no silver or gold to dispute about, and everybody's wants were supplied without any anxiety on his part. When not engaged in war, the Spartans spent their time in dancing, feasting, hunting, exercises, and conversation, and they were taught to believe that there was nothing more unworthy than to live by themselves or for themselves. They gathered about their commander, and devoted themselves entirely to the welfare of their country, esteeming no honor so great as that of being selected as a member of the senate. This is not remarkable when we remember that it was only the wisest and best of the citizens who were chosen, and only those who could count sixty years of honorable life.

With regard to burials Lycurgus made some wise rules. He tried to lessen superstition by ordering the dead to be buried within the city, and even near the temples, so that the young might become accustomed to seeing dead bodies without fearing them, and that they might touch them or tread upon a grave without fancying themselves defiled thereby. Nothing was allowed to be put into the ground with a corpse except a few olive-leaves and the scarlet cloth in which it was wrapped. Only the names of such men as fell in war, and of such women as died in sacred offices, were inscribed on the graves. Eleven days were devoted to mourning, which terminated on the twelfth day by a sacrifice to Ceres, the goddess of agriculture.

Travelling abroad was forbidden, because Lycurgus did not wish his people to adopt the bad habits and manners of the ill-educated, and, for the same reason, all strangers who could not give a good account of themselves, and a sensible reason for coming to Sparta, were banished.

It seems strange that a man who thought so much of honesty and valor as Lycurgus did should have allowed the Helots to be used with injustice, but such was the fact. The Lacedæmonians treated these poor slaves, who performed for them all the menial offices that they were too proud to stoop to themselves, with positive cruelty. Everything about the downtrodden Helots indicated that they were in bondage. Their dress, their manners, their gestures, all their surroundings, differed from those of their masters. They wore dog-skin bonnets and sheep-skin vests; they were forbidden to study art or to perform any act that was not menial; once a day they received a certain number of stripes, whether they deserved punishment or not, merely to remind them that they were slaves. If they dared, even in the most trivial matter, to imitate their masters, they were made to suffer for the offence, and sometimes they were actually murdered in cold blood by the Lacedæmonian young men. Other shameful cruelties were practised upon them, which it is not necessary to recount.

After Lycurgus had got his ordinances into working order, and was satisfied that the government was firmly established on the principles he had introduced, he felt so pleased that he wanted to do something to make it last forever. Having thought out a plan, he called an assembly of the people, and when they had gathered in large numbers he told them that, although the happiness and well-being of the state seemed assured, there was one very important matter that needed attention, but he did not wish to mention it until he had consulted the oracle. He then begged them to continue to observe the laws strictly, without the slightest alteration, until his return, promising that he would act precisely as the gods should direct. Everybody consented, and urged him to set out at once on his journey. This did not satisfy Lycurgus, however; he needed more binding assurance; and for that purpose the senate, as well as all those in authority, were required to take a solemn oath that they would abide by the laws and maintain them until his return. That done, he departed for Delphi.

On his arrival he offered a sacrifice to the god, and asked whether the laws he had established were acceptable. The reply was that they were excellent, and that so long as they were observed Sparta would be the most glorious city of the world. Having sent this flattering announcement of the Delphic Apollo to Sparta in writing, the law-giver resolved to put an end to his existence, hoping thereby to compel his countrymen to be faithful to their oath for an indefinite period. He therefore starved himself to death, for he considered it a statesman's duty to set an example of heroism, even in his exit from the world.

LYCURGUS

The oath that Lycurgus had exacted before his departure for Delphi was religiously observed, and Sparta retained her position as the chief city of Greece for five hundred years in consequence. During that period fourteen kings succeeded one another to the throne, but no change was made in the laws until the reign of Agis, who restored gold and silver money, which encouraged avarice and its attending evils. This is not the Agis whose life forms part of this volume, but one of his early ancestors.

The body of Lycurgus was burned at Crete, and the ashes were scattered into the sea. He had requested this, because he feared that if any part of himself went back to Sparta the people would consider themselves released from their oath. A temple was erected in honor of the law-giver, and sacrifices were yearly offered to him by his grateful and loving countrymen.

ROMULUS

NO author has stated with certainty how the city of Rome received its name, which signifies strength, but it is supposed to have been called after Romulus, who built it.

Romulus and his twin brother, Remus, were the sons of a priestess named Rhea Sylvia and of Mars, the god of war. Rhea Sylvia was the daughter of Numitor, who was the rightful king of Alba, but the throne had been taken away from him by his wicked brother Amulius. Amulius, being afraid that the children of Numitor might try to take his crown as he had taken their father's, had killed Numitor's sons and obliged his daughter, Rhea Sylvia, to become a vestal virgin. Vestal virgins were the priestesses of Vesta, one of the heathen goddesses, and their chief duty was to look after the sacred fire that burned in her temples, and to see that it never went out. There was a severe law against their marrying and having children. So, when Amulius made Rhea Sylvia a vestal virgin, it thought there would be no fear of any one after her doing him any harm. He was therefore very angry when Rhea Sylvia became the mother of Romulus and Remus, and declared that Mars was her husband. He had her buried alive, and the two little infants were put in a basket and thrown in the river Tiber to be drowned. It happened, however, that the river had overflowed its banks and covered part of the land near, and the basket was carried by the tide till it reached a place where the water was very shallow. Here it rested on the ground, and so the children were saved. But they would have perished of hunger and cold had it not been for a she-wolf, who fondled and fed them as if they were her own offspring until a shepherd named Faustulus found the two boys and carried them home to his wife.

Romulus and Remus were unusually robust and beautiful infants, and as they grew into boyhood they were noted for their bravery. In public games both showed remarkable skill, and their manners were so kind and affable that everybody loved them. In course of time they became famous because of their readiness to defend the oppressed, and their courage in punishing robbers and other wicked people.

Thus they were led to take part in a quarrel between the herdsmen of Amulius and those of Numitor, because the latter had stolen some of the king's cattle. Romulus and Remus attacked the offenders and got back nearly all the cattle, but Numitor vowed vengeance against them.

One day when Remus was taking a walk, some of Numitor's herdsmen seized him and carried him before their master. He was determined that the young man should be punished, and so led him to the king for sentence. Now, this placed Amulius in an embarrassing position, for it was in defending his rights that Remus had got into trouble. While he was still hesitating, the officers of Alba, who surrounded his throne, cried out that as Numitor was the person who had been insulted, Remus ought to be placed into his hands to be used as he saw fit.

This was accordingly done, and Numitor departed for home with his prisoner. But he was struck with admiration for the young man's fine face and robust form, and for the courage and coolness he displayed in so trying a position. He therefore resolved to be kind to Remus, and he encouraged him to talk, and asked him who he was and whence he had come.

"I will hide nothing from you," answered the prisoner, "for you seem to be of a more princely nature than Amulius, since you are willing to hear and examine before you punish. He has delivered me over into your hands without even inquiring into the nature of my offence." Remus then told all he knew about his birth, and how he and his twin brother Romulus had been nourished and tended in their infancy by a wolf. Numitor became more and more interested as Remus continued his story, and after hearing all that the young man could tell of his parentage, he at last discovered that Romulus and Remus were his own grandchildren.

Meanwhile, Romulus had not been idle. No sooner did he hear of the fate that had befallen his brother than he gathered together a large force, which he divided into companies of a hundred men each, and marched on Alba. So many of the citizens either feared or hated Amulius, that as Romulus advanced with his army they hastened to join his ranks, while Remus, on his part, excited those in the city to revolt.

So violent was the attack, both within and without the walls of Alba, that Amulius was incapable of defending himself or his subjects, and he was easily seized and put to death. Order was soon restored, but Romulus and Remus did not wish to stay at Alba, because so long as their grandfather lived they would not assume the reins of government. So, after placing Numitor on the throne, they resolved to return to the spot where their infancy had been passed, and there try to build up a city.

ROMULUS

They were accompanied by their soldiers, many of whom had selected wives from among the women of Alba, and as soon as the foundation of the city was laid, a sanctuary, called the temple of the god Asylæus, was opened to serve as a place of refuge for all fugitives. There a servant could find protection from his master, a debtor from his creditor, or a murderer from the magistrates; for it was proclaimed that the oracle had declared the temple a privileged place. So many availed themselves of this asylum that the city soon became very populous.

Romulus and Remus occupied themselves at once with the laying out of their city, but a dispute arose as to its site, for the former selected a square which he called Rome, while the latter chose a piece of ground on the Aventine Mount which he called Remonium. Neither was willing to yield, for each thought that the spot he had chosen possessed more natural advantages than the other. At last, no amount of argument proving of any avail in bringing the brothers to an agreement, it was decided to settle the question by means of an augury. Placing themselves at a considerable distance apart in the open air, Romulus and Remus waited to see what would happen.

After a while the latter announced that he had seen six vultures, whereupon the former declared that he had seen twelve, and the contest was therefore decided in favor of Romulus. These birds were so scarce, and their young were so seldom seen, that they were regarded by the ancients with superstitious awe. It is said that if Hercules, when setting out upon an important expedition, chanced to behold a vulture, he was filled with joy, because he considered it a good omen. The ancient soothsayers believed that vultures came from another world, and that they were divine messengers. Such being the case, their appearance just when Romulus and Remus were on the lookout for an augury was quite opportune.

But Romulus told an untruth, for he did not really see more vultures than his brother did. When Remus discovered the cheat, he was so angry that he ridiculed the ditch that Romulus had dug for his foundation wall, and jumped over it, contemptuously exclaiming, "Just so will the enemy leap over." "And in this manner will our citizens repulse the enemy," cried a bystander, as he dealt Remus a deadly blow.

Romulus buried his brother, and then proceeded with the building of his city. He sent to Tuscany for workmen, because they understood all the ceremonies to be observed, and were just as particular concerning them as if they had been religious rites. First they built a circular ditch around the spot where the Comitium, or Hall of Justice, afterwards stood. In this ditch the first-fruits of all things good and useful were solemnly deposited; then every man threw in a handful of earth brought from his own country. Romulus marked out the bounds of the city with a brazen ploughshare, to which he yoked a bull and a cow, and as he drove along making a deep furrow, those who followed were careful to see that all the earth turned up was thrown inwards towards the city, so as not to lose a single clod. The line thus made described the wall, which was called the Pomœrium. Wherever it was intended to make a gate, the plough was carried over and the earth left unbroken.

It is supposed that on the 21st of April the building of Rome began, and the Romans always regard that day as their country's birthday.

ROMULUS

As soon as the city was built, Romulus formed militia companies numbering three thousand foot and three hundred horse soldiers, and called them legions. A hundred counsellors from among the most influential citizens were selected, under the title of Patricians; their assembly was called the Senate, or Council of Elders.

The Patricians shared in the government and took care of those beneath them in station, and the people were taught to respect them and look to them for advice. Each man could select his own patron, whom he was bound to serve, and to whom he applied for protection and help, and the ties of affection and loyalty between patron and client were as strong as those between father and child.

Now, Romulus had proved himself a benefactor, by offering an asylum to those who had neither house nor home; but there were many lawless, depraved men among those who flocked to Rome, who did not make good citizens. Romulus thought to improve their morals by providing them with wives, and this is how he managed it.

First he gave out that he had discovered an altar of a certain god hidden under ground; and in order to celebrate the discovery he appointed a day for a splendid sacrifice, public games, and shows of all sorts. Neighbors were invited to witness the grand display, and flocked to the pleasure-grounds in great numbers. Among these were the Sabines, a tribe of people settled near Rome, who were accompanied by their wives and daughters.

By a previous understanding it was arranged that Romulus, who sat on a platform, clad in a purple robe, should at a certain stage of the performance rise and gather his garment about him, whereupon his men were to draw their swords, rush forward, and each secure for himself a wife. The signal was duly given, and the Sabine girls were carried off. Their fathers and brothers were naturally enough exceedingly angry, and they declared war against Rome.

After several severe struggles, peace was made, one of the conditions being that the stolen wives should be compelled to do no meaner work for their Roman husbands than spinning.

Meanwhile, several powerful armies were sent against Romulus by neighboring kings who feared his increasing power; but he defeated each in turn, and forced them to surrender their cities and territories and become citizens of Rome. All the lands thus acquired Romulus distributed among the inhabitants, with the exception of those that belonged to the parents of the stolen virgins. It so enraged the rest of the Sabines that such partiality should be shown, even to their own people, that, choosing Tatius for their captain, they straightway marched against Rome; but the city was so well fortified that had it not been for the treachery of Tarpeia, the daughter of Tarpeius, captain of the Roman guard, the Sabines would have been totally defeated. Tarpeia coveted the gold bracelets she observed on the left arms of the Sabines, and promised Tatius that she would assist him if he would give her what his soldiers wore on their left arms. He promised to do so, and at night she opened the gate of the citadel, and admitted the enemy. But the traitress did not enjoy the reward of her base deed, for Tatius was so filled with contempt and hatred of her that he tore off his bracelet and dashed it at her feet, then threw his buckler against her with all his strength, and commanded his soldiers to follow his example, and she was soon killed. In this way he fulfilled

ROMULUS

his promise, for the soldiers wore their bucklers also on their left arms.

Romulus was so enraged when he found the Sabines in possession of the Capitol hill that he offered them battle, though the field on which the conflict was to take place was so surrounded by lofty hills that there seemed little chance for either army to escape. However, Tatius was under the impression that his was the better position. He and his forces were on the point of marching across a plain that had been under water a few days before through the overflow of the river, when Curtius, a brave, gallant soldier, dashed on in advance. His horse sank so deep into the mire that it became impossible to extricate him, and the rider was forced to abandon him and save himself as best he could. An army so placed would have been thrown into confusion and probably destroyed. The Sabines felt much elated on account of their escape from this danger, and, looking upon it as a good omen, they fought all the more desperately. Many were slain on both sides, and for a long time there was doubt as to the result of the battle. At last Romulus was struck on the head by a stone that almost felled him to the ground. Then his soldiers, being driven out of the level plain, fled towards the Palatium; but Romulus soon recovered from his shock, and encouraged them to return to the fight. They dared not do so, however, until Romulus stretched his hands towards heaven and prayed aloud to Jupiter to assist the Roman cause. Then the fugitives felt ashamed of their cowardice, and determined to stand by their commander. Another fight ensued, and the Sabines were repulsed. Both armies were preparing to attack again, when the stolen Sabine wives came running towards them in a body, crying and lamenting like creatures possessed, and with their babies in their arms made their way among the dead bodies strewn upon the ground, entreating both sides to desist. The soldiers fell back in amazement, whereupon the women placed themselves between the armies. So eloquent were they in their appeals that a truce was made, and the chief officers decided to hold a council of war. Meanwhile, the women presented their husbands and children to their fathers and brothers, gave meat and drink to those that were hungry, and carried the wounded home to be cured. They took special pains to prove to their countrymen that they governed in their own houses, and that their husbands were the kindest and the most indulgent in the world. Finally it was agreed that those women who chose to stay should do so, providing that they continued to do no work but spinning; that the Romans and Sabines should inhabit the city together; that the city should be called Rome, and that both Romans and Sabines should govern and command in common. The place where this treaty was made was called the Comitium.

Thus was the population of the city increased. A hundred Sabines were added to the senators. The legions were increased to six thousand foot and six hundred horsemen, and the people were divided into three tribes, called the Ramnenses, from Romulus; the Tatienses, from Tatius; and the Luceres, from the grove where the asylum for refugees stood.

At first each of the princes took council with his own hundred representatives in the senate, but afterwards all assembled together. The house of Tatius was where the temple of Moneta afterwards stood, while that of Romulus was close by the steps that led from the Palatine Hill to the Circus Maximus. It is said that near the house of Romulus grew the holy Cornel tree, which had been planted in this wise. Once, to try his strength, Romulus threw a dart which

ROMULUS

stuck so fast into the ground that nobody could withdraw it. The soil being fertile, the wood took root, and in course of time grew into a good-sized tree. Posterity worshipped it as a sacred object, and placed a wall around it for protection, and if any one chanced to observe that it was not flourishing, or that it looked somewhat wilted, he would raise the alarm, when all those within hearing would run to fetch buckets of water, as though they had been warned of a house on fire. The tree withered when Collis Cæsar ordered the garden-steps to be repaired, because some of the workmen dug too close to the roots and destroyed them.

The Sabines adopted the Roman months, and Romulus, on the other hand, introduced into his army the armor and long shields that the Sabines used, instead of the Greek buckler, which he and his soldiers had worn before. The feasts and sacrifices of both nations were continued and partaken of in common, and some new ones were added to the list. One of these was the Matronalia, instituted in honor of the women who put an end to the war. During this feast the married Roman women served their slaves at table and received presents from their husbands. Another was the Carmentalia, a very solemn feast kept on the 11th of January. Carmenta was supposed to preside over the birth of babies, therefore all mothers worshipped her. The Lupercalia, or feast of wolves, was celebrated in February, and one of the rites consisted in the killing of a dog. The meaning of this is that dogs are enemies to wolves, and the Romans honored the latter because it was a wolf that nourished Romulus.

We have seen that the mother of Romulus was a vestal virgin. It was probably in memory of his mother that Romulus introduced the sacred and perpetual fire into his city, and appointed the Vestals to tend it. He was a religious man, and so skilled in divination that he carried the crooked rod used by soothsayers when observing the flight of birds. The one that belonged to Romulus was kept in the Capitol, but it disappeared when Rome was taken by the Gauls. Long afterwards it was found buried beneath a pile of ashes, uninjured by the fire that had destroyed everything about it.

For five years there was peace and harmony under the two rulers at Rome, and it did not seem probable that any disturbance would arise. But one day some of the friends and kinsmen of Tatius chanced to meet certain ambassadors from a neighboring town called Laurentium, who had gone to Rome to complain of incursions made upon their territories, and attempted to rob them. The ambassadors made a bold resistance, but, being unarmed, were put to death. Romulus was indignant at this cowardly crime, and demanded that the offenders should be punished forthwith. Tatius objected because they were his friends. He could not with justice declare that they did not deserve punishment, but he hesitated to give the order, whereupon the relatives of the murdered ambassadors became so indignant that one day when Tatius was engaged in offering sacrifices, they set upon him and put him to death.

The Sabines took no steps towards avenging the fate of their ruler, but peaceably submitted to Romulus.

Not long after this event a dreadful plague broke out, and caused the death of a great number of people as well as cattle; even the grain was blighted, and it was universally believed that the gods used this means to express displeasure. When Laurentium was similarly visited, the belief was strengthened, and no further proof was needed to convince the Romans that the murderers of the ambassadors, as well as those of Tatius, ought to have been punished. They were accordingly put to death, and it is said that the pestilence soon ceased. But, while it lasted, several nations, taking advantage of the distress it occasioned, made attacks on the Romans, under the belief that they were not in condition to resist. They found they were mistaken, however, for Romulus conquered so many of them that they were forced to accept whatever terms he chose to dictate.

Of course, so much prosperity had its effect on Romulus, as it would have on almost any man whom fortune favors to such an extent, and he became exceedingly haughty and arrogant. The people who had adored him now began to hate him, particularly as he assumed grand airs and made a display of his power. For he dressed himself in scarlet, and wore a regal, flowing, purple robe; then he would lie on a couch of state, and so give audience to those who sought him, while young men, called Celeres, from their swiftness in running errands, stood by ready to do his bidding. When he went out, these Celeres preceded him with long staves to make way for him, and they had leather thongs tied around their waists with which to bind anybody Romulus saw fit to punish. His conduct was entirely different from what it had been at the beginning of his reign, and he had become so despotic that the Patricians no longer had a share in the government. They retained their honorable title, and met at the senate-house, but this was a mere matter of form, for they heard their king give orders without daring to offer an opinion or to interfere in any way. At last this behavior became intolerable, and when Romulus went a step further and divided the conquered lands among his soldiers, and restored hostages without the consent of the senate, that body openly expressed profound indignation.

Shortly after, Romulus suddenly and mysteriously disappeared. Suspicion of foul play fell upon the senators, and many were under the impression that when they had assembled at the temple of Vulcan on a certain day they had killed the king and cut up his body, each senator carrying away a portion and concealing it.

The excitement caused by this event was increased by a total eclipse of the sun, accompanied by a wind-storm, vivid flashes of lightning, and loud peals of thunder. The nobility gathered together in the senate-house, but the common people were so terrified that they fled to their homes and hid themselves. They did not understand the laws which governed an eclipse, and always looked upon one with superstitious awe.

When the sun shone forth again, inquiries about the fate of Romulus were renewed, and the people insisted upon knowing what had happened to him. But they got little satisfaction, for the Patricians gave them no answer, except that they were to honor and worship Romulus because he had been a good and wise king, who had gone to heaven, where he would henceforth prove a propitious deity to the Romans.

Some went away, expecting now to have special favors and protection, but others accused the Patricians of imposing an absurd tale upon them for the sake of concealing a crime; for they felt certain that Romulus had been murdered. The excitement became so great that considerable uneasiness was felt as to the result.

At last Julius Proculus, a distinguished senator, who had come from Alba with Romulus and had been his faithful friend, went into the Forum and declared upon oath, before all the people assembled, that as he was travelling along the

ROMULUS

road he met Romulus, looking more noble and august than ever, and clad in bright, glittering armor. He further declared that in his astonishment at the sight, he said, "For what misbehavior of ours, O king, or by what accident have you left us to labor under the heaviest calumnies, and the whole city to sink under inexpressible sorrow?" To this Romulus answered, "It pleased the gods, my good Proculus, that we should dwell with men, for a time, and after having founded a city, which will be the most powerful and glorious in the world, return to heaven whence we came. Farewell, then, and go tell the Romans that by the exercise of temperance and fortitude they shall attain the highest pitch of human greatness, and I, the god Quirinus, will ever be propitious to them."

Proculus was so highly esteemed by the Romans that they did not doubt a word of his recital. All suspicion concerning the murder of Romulus vanished forever, and from that time the devotions of the Romans were addressed to the god Quirinus, who they believed had power to extend towards them special benefits.

NUMA POMPILIUS

No sooner had the disturbance caused by the death of Romulus ceased than a new cause for trouble arose, for a new king had to be chosen, and the Patricians were so jealous of one another that it was hard to decide which of their number was worthy of the honor.

The Sabines, as we know, after being made citizens, composed half of the senate; but the original Romans, who had helped Romulus to lay out and build the city, were not willing to submit to any person who had been raised to citizenship afterwards. On the other hand, the Sabines argued that as they had peaceably suffered Romulus to rule after their king Tatius had been killed, they ought to have the privilege of naming the new sovereign, particularly as they had united with the Romans as equals and were in no way their inferiors.

This seems fair; but the older men of Rome would not listen to such a proposition, and it was a long time before the matter could be settled. While it was pending, it was agreed that each of the two hundred senators, in turn, should wear the robes of state for one day and transact all public business.

Of course no one could feel jealous of a ruler whose reign was to last only a few hours; but it was impossible that such a system of government could last. The necessity for a permanent king soon made itself felt, and the senators arranged that a member of one party should be chosen by the other party. Thus, if a Roman were named he would without doubt favor his own countrymen on the one hand, and he would feel kindly towards the Sabines for favoring him on the other.

But no Roman would have been satisfied to be elevated to the throne by the Sabines; so their senators announced their decision to name a Sabine for the honor, and this arrangement gave perfect satisfaction. It seemed that at last there was to be an end to party spirit, and that peace was to be established in Rome.

The choice fell on Numa Pompilius, a man of high standing, to whom no objection could be raised by either Roman or Sabine. Representatives from both nations were appointed to wait upon him with the news of his elevation to the throne, for he was then living at Cures, a city of the Sabines, from which they and the Romans afterwards called themselves by the common name of Quirites.

Numa was born on the 21st of April, the birthday of Rome. Tatius, whose subject he was, had considered him such a wise, good man that he had chosen him for the husband of his only daughter. Numa, though grateful for such an honor, could never be induced to go to Rome to live, even when Tatius was ruling there. He preferred to stay at Cures and take care of his aged father, who was too infirm to be moved. His duty as a son would not permit him to neglect his parent for the sake of the honors that awaited him at court.

Fortunately, Tatia, his wife, shared his fancy for a retired life, and so the two lived happily together for thirteen years. Then Tatia died, and Numa was so grieved that he left the city and passed his time wandering about alone in the sacred groves and other solitary places.

The ambassadors who were sent to offer the kingdom to Numa willingly undertook a task that seemed an easy one, for they had no idea that any man would hesitate to accept the government of so famous a city as Rome. They therefore stated their errand in a few words; but, much to their surprise, Numa was not so elated at their proposition as they had anticipated. He listened quietly, and then replied, "Every change in life has its dangers, and it would be madness in a man who is satisfied with all he has, and who needs nothing, to abandon a course that has at least the advantage of certainty for one wholly strange. I know some of the difficulties of your government, for was not Romulus accused of plotting against the life of Tatius? and was not the senate suspected of having treacherously murdered Romulus? Yet Romulus was thought to be of divine origin and miraculously preserved in his infancy for a great future. I am only mortal, and men whom you all know have been my instructors. I am not fit to be a king, for I love retirement; I am fond of study, and have no knowledge of business; I prefer the society of those whose lives are spent upon their farms and their pastures, and I have studiously avoided warlike occupations. Your people have made many conquests, and desire to increase them; they have more need of a general than of a king; I should become a laughing-stock, therefore, were I to go among them to promote the worship of the gods and preach lessons of religion and justice to men who love violence and war."

The Romans were greatly perplexed at Numa's thus refusing the crown, and assured him that it would certainly plunge them into a civil war, because there was no other man whom both parties would unanimously elect. They begged him, therefore, to reconsider his decision. Then his father and his friend Marcius, who were present, drew him aside and privately argued the matter with him. "Though you are content with what you have," they said, "and desire neither riches, fame, nor authority, because you prize the virtues you have above these, yet you must not forget that as a king you will be always acting in the service of the gods, who call you from your retirement to exercise your qualities of justice and wisdom. Therefore do not turn your back upon an office in which you may perform great and honorable deeds. Tatius was beloved by the Romans, though he was a foreigner, and Romulus has received divine honors; perhaps the people have now had enough of war, and are ready to rejoice at the prospect of peace, and anxious to have a just prince who will preserve order and quiet for them."

These and other arguments, added to the persuasions of his fellow-citizens, had their weight, and Numa yielded. The ambassadors were delighted, and immediately accompanied him to Rome, where he was received with loud shouts and joyful acclamations by the senate and people, who came out on the road to meet him. Sacrifices were offered in all the temples, and great rejoicings marked the arrival of the new king. He was forthwith conducted to the Forum, where Spurius Vettius, who happened to be the senator in power that day, put it to the vote whether Numa Pompilius should be king. With one voice the citizens exclaimed in his favor. The regalia and royal robes were then brought, but Numa refused to receive any distinctions of office until he had first consulted the gods; so, accompanied by the priests and augurs, he went up to the Capitol, which at that time the Romans called the Tarpeian Hill. Then the chief of the augurs covered Numa's head and turned his face towards the south.

Standing behind Numa, the augur placed his right hand upon his head and prayed, while he looked around for some signal from the gods. Meanwhile perfect silence was maintained by the multitude assembled in the Forum. Presently their suspense was relieved by the appearance of a flock of birds that flew towards the right. This was regarded as a favorable omen, and Numa immediately put on the royal robes, in which he descended the hill. As he approached the Forum he was greeted with shouts of welcome from the people, who proclaimed him a holy king, beloved of all the gods.

Numa's first act after assuming office was to discharge the Celeres, or body-guard of three hundred, which Romulus had always kept near him. He explained that he neither chose to distrust those who put confidence in him nor to reign over people that could distrust him. The next thing he did was to add to the two priests of Jupiter and Mars a third in honor of Romulus, whom he called Flamen Quirinalis.

Numa saw that these acts pleased his subjects, so he resolved to go a step further and try to make them less bold and warlike, and more like gentle, reasonable human beings. For this purpose he called in the aid of religion, offered frequent sacrifices, formed processions, and instituted religious dances, in which he generally took part himself. His idea was to calm the people by associating their social pleasures with their religious ceremonies, which would render their festivities of a more refined nature. Sometimes he found it necessary to excite their imaginations by telling them of the dreadful apparitions he had seen and the strange, threatening voices he had heard. Their terror was thus aroused, and superstition made them humble and lowly.

NUMA POMPILIUS

Numa pretended that a certain goddess or mountain nymph was in love with him, and that it was through her and the Muses that he received all his revelations. He desired the Romans to show special veneration to one Muse in particular, and that was Tacita, the Silent, no doubt with the belief that if his subjects talked seldom they would not give utterance to much nonsense.

He made reforms in religious observances, the most important of which were these: All images representing the Deity in any form whatever, whether of man or beast, he ordered to be removed from the temples and chapels, and declared it impious to represent the Divine Being by anything capable of being created or destroyed by man; he put a stop to the shedding of blood upon the altars, and ordered the sacrifices to consist, instead, of flour, wine, and other inexpensive offerings.

Next he instituted an order of priests called Pontifices, or bridge-makers, because not only did they perform their religious ceremonies on bridges, which were considered sacred spots, but it was their duty to keep the structures in perfect order. It was accounted a sacrilege for anybody to deface a bridge, because they were supposed, in obedience to an oracle, to have been built of timber and fastened with wooden pins, not a single bit of metal having been employed in any part.

Numa himself was Pontifex Maximus, or chief of the priests, and it was his duty to explain the divine law, preside over sacred rites, and make rules for both public and private worship, so that no one might alter the prescribed form of any of the ceremonies. He increased the number of vestal virgins who kept the sacred fire alive. This fire might not be kindled in the usual way, so if by accident it became extinguished, it was only by concentrating the rays of the sun that it could be relighted. At first there were only two vestal virgins, but their number was doubled by the new Pontifex Maximus.

The rules laid down for the vestals were these: They had to promise not to marry for thirty years; the first ten were devoted to learning their duties, the second ten to performing them, and the third to instructing others. At the end of the term the vestals were permitted to marry or choose any condition of life they pleased; but very few ever cared to make a change, preferring to remain single until death. It was observed that those who did marry were never happy, but always seemed sad and dissatisfied, which is perhaps one reason why so many preferred to remain vestals even after their thirty years of service had expired.

They had privileges, however, that were not accorded to other women. For example, they could make a will while their fathers lived, and were permitted to manage their own affairs without a guardian or tutor. When they went abroad, the *fasces* was carried before them. The fasces consisted of an axe tied up with a bundle of rods, and they were used by the Roman magistrates as a badge of authority. If a vestal chanced to meet a criminal on his way to execution, his life was spared, but she had to swear that the meeting was purely accidental. If a person pushed against the chair in which one of these holy women was carried, he was put to death. Great honors were paid to the vestal virgins, but their punishments were very severe. For trifling faults the high-priest had power to scourge them, which he did in a dark place, with a curtain drawn between him and the offender. If one of them broke her vow and married she was buried alive, in this way: being

NUMA POMPILIUS

securely fastened to a litter by ropes, she was first carried to the Forum, the priests following in solemn procession, and everybody either making way for them or accompanying them with downcast and sorrowful mien. When the procession arrived at the place of execution, not far from the Forum, the officers cut the ropes which bound the prisoner, and the high-priest raised his hands to heaven, pronouncing certain prayers. Then the prisoner, covered from head to foot with a loose white robe, was made to descend a flight of steps that led under ground to a cell in which were a bed, a lighted lamp, and a small supply of food; the stairs were then drawn up and the entrance to the cell was securely closed with earth, care being taken that no mark should distinguish the spot.

Numa founded several orders of priests besides the Pontifices, but we shall mention only the Faciales and the Salii. The Faciales were the peace-makers, whose duty it was to settle all quarrels, and not allow two parties to go to war until it became impossible to reason with them. If any nation offered the Romans an insult, the Faciales were sent to demand satisfaction. In case it was refused, they called on the gods to curse them and their country if they were acting unjustly, and then declared war. Neither king nor soldiers dared take up arms until the Faciales gave their consent.

The origin of the Salii was as follows. In the eighth year of Numa's reign a terrible pestilence overspread the whole of Italy. Rome was greatly afflicted by it, and the citizens became dreadfully despondent. To rouse their drooping spirits, Numa called them together and showed them a brazen target, which he declared had fallen from heaven into his hands, while his mountain nymph and the Muses had assured him that it was sent to stop the pestilence and save the city. In gratitude he commanded that the spot where he had received the target, as well as the surrounding fields and the spring which watered them, should be hallowed to the use of the vestal virgins, who were to wash their temple and holy vestments with the waters of the spring. In a short time the pestilence disappeared.

Fearing that the wonderful target might be stolen, Numa ordered eleven others to be manufactured exactly like the one he had received from heaven, and so perfect were they that it was impossible to distinguish the original. It was to guard the twelve targets that the order of the Salii was founded. In the month of March each year, these priests, clad in short purple frocks, with broad brass belts at their waists, and helmets on their heads, danced through the city, carrying the sacred targets, and beating time on them with short daggers.

Near the temple of Vesta, Numa built a house, where he spent much of his time performing divine services, instructing the various orders of priests, and conversing with them on sacred topics. Whenever there was to be a public procession, criers went along the streets through which it was to pass, to give notice to the people, who were expected to lay aside whatever occupations they were engaged in, and turn their attention wholly to religion. On such occasions the streets were cleared to make way for the priests, all signs of labor disappeared, and profound silence was observed. Such discipline had the effect of making the people look up to Numa with a feeling of awe and reverence. They honored him for his great virtue, and had such confidence in him that whatever he said, no matter how fabulous it might appear, was received with perfect faith. Nothing seemed impossible to them where Numa was concerned.

NUMA POMPILIUS

There is a story told of how he invited a great number of citizens to an entertainment. When they assembled, they were surprised to find a meal spread out for them consisting of the poorest and plainest food, and the table appointments of the roughest and ugliest sort. No sooner were they seated than Numa entered, and announced that the goddess with whom he always consulted had just made him a visit. While he spoke, presto, change! the humble table disappeared, and was replaced by one loaded with the choicest viands, served on gold and silver dishes, costly wines, and all sorts of magnificent drinking vessels.

There are many other such wonderful tales related about Numa, but none are more absurd than his conversation with Jupiter. Before Mount Aventine was enclosed within the city walls, it was inhabited by two demi-gods named Picus and Faunus, who are said to have wandered among its shady groves unmolested. These demi-gods were skilled in drugs and magic, and went about in different parts of Italy astonishing the people with their remarkable tricks. By mixing wine and honey in the fountain from which they drank, Numa caught them. Then they changed themselves into various forms, some of them most strange and terrible; still they could not escape. At last, in despair at being held imprisoned, they took Numa into their confidence, and taught him a charm for thunder and lightning, composed of onions, hair, and a kind of fish called pilchard. But some historians say that Picus and Faunus did not teach this charm to Numa themselves, but that they used their magic to bring Jupiter down from heaven, and the god was so angry when he found himself on earth that he ordered the charm to consist of heads. Numa, who had been instructed by his mountain nymph what to say, asked, "Heads of onions?"

"No, human—" began Jupiter, but, anxious to avoid so cruel a charm, Numa interrupted, and said, "Hairs."

"No," exclaimed Jupiter, "with living—"

"Pilchards," suggested Numa, quickly.

Finding that he could not have his own way, the god went off, and so the charm remained onions, hair, and pilchards.

Though superstition led the Romans to believe all such fabulous tales about their king, he nevertheless exerted a most wise and healthy influence over them in many respects. Numa placed his confidence in the Almighty, and wished them to do the same. Once when word was brought to him that the enemy was coming, he only smiled, and said, "And I am sacrificing." He meant by this that while he was engaged in religious exercises no harm could come to him, nor could he turn his attention to other matters. Numa built temples to faith, and taught his subjects that to swear by faith was the greatest of all oaths, because he wished them to consider their word as binding as any contract in writing could be. He was the first person who marked out the boundaries of Rome by stones, so that no man could trespass on the land that belonged to his neighbor. Thus the poor, as well as the rich, felt that their rights were protected. They therefore devoted themselves to agriculture, anxious to make their land as profitable as possible. In this way too, Numa increased their desire for peace, because, of course, they had no wish to fight with neighboring tribes, who would be sure to destroy the crops they had taken pains to cultivate.

The land was divided into portions, and over each was placed an overseer or governor. Sometimes Numa would inspect them himself, and praise and reward those farmers who were thrifty and industrious, while he would severely censure those that were indolent and careless. But of all his institutions, the one which had the best effect was the division of his people into companies, according to their occupations. The musicians formed one company, the carpenters another, the shoemakers another, and so on, each having its own separate court, council, and religious observances. Before these companies were formed there had been two parties, who were always quarrelling about their rights, the Sabines and the Romans not being willing to unite in any movement. By the new institution party distinction was lost sight of, and harmony was the result.

The law which gave fathers the power to sell their children was changed; for Romulus had permitted a master to sell his slave but once, while a father could sell his son three times. It seemed unjust that a woman should marry a man whom she considered free, and then have him sold if his father so determined. Therefore Numa ordered that any man marrying with his parents' consent should thenceforth be considered free.

Another reformation that Numa attempted was the making of a calendar, in which he displayed a great deal of skill, although he was not quite correct. During the reign of Romulus some of the months had contained twenty-five days, others thirty-five, and others even more; and the year was made to contain three hundred and sixty days. Numa first observed that there was a difference of eleven days between the lunar and the solar year; of these he disposed by introducing an extra month of twenty-two days after the February of every second year. He likewise changed the order of the months, making March the third,—it had been the first,—

January and February, which had been eleventh and twelfth, becoming first and second.

Romulus had placed the month of March first, because it was dedicated to the god Mars. April is derived from a Latin word which means to open, it being the spring month when blossoms unfold. May and June take their names from two words meaning old and young. The succeeding months were called by their number, according to the order in which they stood, but later July was named in honor of Julius Cæsar, and August in honor of Augustus, the second emperor of Rome.

Numa preferred January for the first month of the year, because its name was derived from the god Janus, who was called the god of a "good beginning." Janus was represented with two faces, because it was thought he had altered the rude state of the world and had given life a new aspect by establishing peace and cultivating society. The Romans never took an important step without asking Janus to bless the beginning. There was a temple with two gates, called the gates of war, dedicated to this god. While peace reigned these gates were closed, and in time of war they were kept constantly open. Numa's reign being distinguished for peace, the temple of Janus remained shut for a space of forty-three years; for not only were the people of Rome influenced by their just and wise king, but their neighbors too began to improve, and all Italy was benefited. Holidays were observed, friendly visits were interchanged, the love of justice and virtue grew day by day, and all plots and conspiracies ceased. There had never been known so long a season of harmony and prosperity. But it lasted only as long as Numa lived, for peace and good-will vanished at his death, the temple of Janus was opened, and Italy was again drenched with blood.

NUMA POMPILIUS

Numa was eighty years of age when he died. The neighboring states united with the Romans in doing honor to his memory, all taking part in the funeral rites. The senators carried the bier on which lay the corpse, and the priests followed in solemn procession, while men, women, and children walked behind, weeping as though each had lost a near and dear relation. Numa had ordered two stone coffins to be made, in one of which his body was enclosed, and in the other all his sacred books. He desired his writings to be buried because the priests knew them by heart, and he feared that if they were ever permitted to circulate freely they would cease to be regarded with the mysterious awe and reverence that had helped to impress them on the minds of his disciples.

SOLON

This philosopher was descended from a noble stock. His father was Execestides, a man whose power was great in Athens, though his means were small. So generous was he in the benefits he conferred on others that he actually ruined his own estates thereby. When this happened, his son Solon resolved to leave home and become a merchant. He had friends enough who would have been pleased to assist him, but as he came of a family who were in the habit of conferring favors, he would not consent to receive any. Besides, Solon lived at a time when the merchant's was considered a noble calling, on account of its bringing different nations in contact with each other, encouraging friendship between their kings, and serving as a means for increasing one's experience.

Solon was always anxious to gain knowledge, and when he grew old he used to say that "each day of his life he learned something new." There can be no doubt of this, for he made excellent laws, and became one of the seven sages of Greece. His reputation for wisdom extended so far that learned men from other parts of the world often sought his acquaintance. Once Anacharsis, a Scythian philosopher, who was on a visit to Athens, knocked at Solon's door and announced that he wished to become his friend.

"It is better to make friends at home," said Solon.

SOLON

"Then you that are at home form a friendship with me," replied Anacharsis.

Solon was so pleased at the readiness of this answer that he admitted the stranger and kept him in Athens for several years.

At that time Solon was engaged in writing his code of laws, and often asked the advice of Anacharsis as he proceeded. The Scythian laughed at him for supposing that men could be restrained from acts of dishonesty by written laws, which he likened to spiders' webs, that might catch the weak and poor, but would be easily broken by the powerful and rich. Solon's argument against this was that men would certainly keep their promises if nothing could be gained by breaking them, and he meant so to frame his laws that the citizens of Athens would find it to their advantage to observe them. Anacharsis was nearer the truth in his judgment of men than Solon was, as later events proved. And he further showed his discernment when, after attending an assembly, he said that "the wise men pleaded causes, and the fools decided them."

Once when Solon was visiting Thales of Miletus, one of the seven wise men of Greece, he asked Thales why he had no family. Thales did not answer immediately, but a few days later he introduced to Solon a stranger, who said that he had returned from Athens ten days before. Solon inquired what news he had brought. "None," replied the man, in accordance with the instructions he had received from Thales, "but I saw the funeral of a young man, which the whole city attended. They said he was the son of an honorable person of high standing who was travelling."

"What a miserable man is he!" exclaimed Solon. "But what was his name?"

"I heard his name, but do not recollect it," said the stranger; "all I remember is, that there was much said about his wisdom and justice."

Solon's fears were aroused, and becoming extremely anxious he at last mentioned his own name, and asked the stranger in a trembling voice whether it was his son that was dead. On hearing that such was indeed the case, the philosopher gave way to a transport of grief. Then Thales took his hand and said, "These things which strike down so firm a man as Solon have kept me from marrying and having children; but take courage, my good friend, for not a word of what has been told to you is true." No doubt Solon thought, as all sensible people must think, that Thales gave proof of great weakness; for a man ought to be reasonable enough to arm himself against misfortune, and to remember that he may be deprived of wealth, glory, or wisdom as well as of objects of affection, yet he would not on that account object to having them. It is not excess of feeling, but lack of moral strength, that causes men to sink under affliction.

Solon was not so successful with his writings as many of the ancients, but his poem called Salamis is considered very beautiful, and he wrote it under peculiar circumstances. After the Athenians had grown tired of the war they had carried on in vain for so long a time with the Megarians for the island of Salamis, they made a law condemning any one to death who should write or speak in favor of the renewal of hostilities. Solon was vexed at their failure, and knew that there were thousands of young men ready to fight if only somebody would lead them on. So he pretended to be insane, and his own family spread the news of his misfortune throughout the city. He then composed his verses urging his fellow-citizens to renew the war, and learned them by heart. Having done this, he proceeded to the market-place, mounted the herald's stand, and sang his composition to the crowd that gathered to hear him. Pisistratus, his kinsman, was in the secret, and went about urging people to obey Solon's directions; the result was that the law was repealed, and the war began again.

Solon himself took the command, and with five hundred Athenian volunteers, a number of fishing-boats, and one thirty-oared ship, anchored in the bay of Salamis. As soon as the Megarians heard of this they began to prepare for battle, but meanwhile sent out a ship to ascertain whether the report they had received was true. Solon captured the ship, secured the Megarians on board of it, and replaced them with his own men, who had orders to sail to the island as privately as possible. At the head of the rest of his soldiers Solon marched against the Megarians by land, and whilst they were fighting those from the ship took possession of the city. The battle was a furious one, and many were killed on both sides, but the Athenians claimed the victory, and dedicated a temple to Mars in honor of it.

This achievement made Solon famous throughout the land, and his glory was heightened still more by the part he took in the Sacred War in defence of the Delphic oracle against the people of Cirrha. Cirrha is a town on the Bay of Corinth. The inhabitants, coveting the riches contained in the Temple of Apollo, besieged the city of Delphi, where it stood, in order to get possession of them. Solon pronounced this an infamous deed, and persuaded the Amphictyons, who were the representatives of the various nations of Greece, to declare war against the Cirrhæans. They did so, and the army laid siege to Cirrha for a long time, but without success. At last, becoming greatly discouraged, they consulted the oracle. The answer was that they should not be able to reduce the place till the waves of the Cirrhæan Sea washed the territories of Delphi. As that seemed impossible, the soldiers were struck with surprise; but Solon helped them out of the dilemma by advising them to consecrate the whole territory of Cirrha to the Delphic Apollo, when the sea would be sure to wash the sacred soil. Thus was the problem solved, and victory was the result.

Now, there was a strong party in Athens opposed to the government and anxious to have their ancient system of laws restored. Cylon, a man of quality, and son-in-law of the tyrant of Megara, headed this party, being himself ambitious for power. Accordingly, he formed a conspiracy to seize the fortress on a certain day when many of the citizens had gone to the Olympic games. Megacles, who was chief magistrate, immediately called those Athenians who had remained at home to arms, and proceeded against the conspirators. Cylon managed to escape; but his men, finding themselves likely to be overcome, sought refuge in Minerva's Temple. Megacles dared not pursue them into the holy place; but he ordered them to come forth like men. At first they refused; but it suddenly struck them that if they fastened a string to the shrine of the goddess and kept hold of it, they would still be under divine protection. So they left the temple; but as Megacles and his men rushed upon them the string broke, and the butchery that followed was kept up to the very altar; for some of Cylon's men returned to the temple, and both sides were too excited to remember that they were on sacred soil.

The conspirators who were fortunate enough to escape won many over to their side and kept up a constant quarrel-

SOLON

ling with the Megacles faction. Thus two parties were formed, and the disturbances became so serious that Solon advised the magistrates who had polluted the Temple of Minerva to submit to a public trial, hoping thereby to appease the indignation of the populace and restore quiet.

The magistrates were accordingly tried, found guilty of sacrilege, and condemned to death. Still Athens was in a state of tumult, which the priests increased by announcing that the sacrifices gave proof of divine displeasure.

Solon knew that reforms were needed; but, not feeling powerful enough to produce them alone, he entreated his countrymen to call in the aid of Epimenides of Crete, another of the sages of Greece, who was supposed to have intercourse with the gods.

So Solon and Epimenides worked together, and the result was the establishment of a more sensible form of religious worship, as well as of funerals and mourning ceremonies. Various barbarous customs were abolished, and the Athenians were taught to purify themselves, their houses, and their roads. They were encouraged to build shrines and temples, and to live together in harmony by dealing honestly with one another.

The good effect of the Cretan sage's visit was felt by all, and when he returned home valuable presents were offered to him; but he would accept nothing but a branch of the sacred olive, which he took as a memento. Much work still remained for Solon to do, because no sooner were the troubles springing out of Cylon's conspiracy settled than new ones arose among the political parties.

The people of the mountains, those of the plains, and those of the sea-coast represented these parties, and each desired a separate form of government. The state was in a dangerous condition, because the poor suffered so severely at the hands of the rich. Bad times and disasters had tended to increase poverty and to render the aristocrats tyrannical. So deeply were the poor in debt to the rich that they were compelled to pay a sixth part of the produce of their land or to engage their persons for the debt. In the latter case their creditors had the power to make slaves of them or to sell them to foreigners. Some parents were even forced to sell their own children and fly from the country to escape the cruelty of their oppressors.

The time came when the bravest of these poor people resolved to bear imposition no longer. They declared themselves ready to stand by one another, to liberate their friends, and to alter the government. But first of all they needed a leader; they were eager for a change, and preferred to be ruled by one despot rather than be tyrannized over by a great number of lords.

After a great deal of discussion, Solon was unanimously chosen by both parties as mediator. The rich favored him because he was nobly born and wealthy; the poor, because he was honest. Under the title of Archon, he was invested with full authority to frame a new set of laws. He did not abuse his power, nor did he go to extremes; he merely made such alterations as were just and expedient, and afterwards, when he was asked if he had left the Athenians the best laws that could be given, he replied, "The best they were capable of receiving."

First of all Solon relieved the poor by diminishing the rate of interest; next he raised the value of their money so that they might with greater ease pay off their debts; then he

SOLON

abolished the law which enabled a creditor to enslave his debtor, and recalled those unfortunate creatures who had been sold into slavery merely because they were not rich. Everybody was dissatisfied,—the wealthy because they had not been specially favored, and the poor because the land had not been divided as they had hoped it would be, and all men placed on an equality, as the Lacedæmonians had been under the laws of Lycurgus.

However, as time rolled on, the good results of Solon's laws began to be felt, and grumbling gradually ceased. Indeed, such a change took place in the feelings of the people towards the sage that they chose him to govern their magistracies, their assemblies, their courts, and their councils.

Draco had made statutes for the Athenians, but they were so severe that Solon found it necessary to repeal a great many of them, and that was the next task to which he devoted himself. According to Draco, a man convicted of idleness was to be punished with death, and one who stole a cabbage or an apple was made to suffer as severely as a villain who had committed the most heinous crime. It was said, long after, that Draco's laws were written not with ink but with blood. When he was asked why he made death the punishment for most offences, he said, "Small ones deserve death, and I have no worse punishment for greater crimes."

Solon did not agree with him, however, and preferred milder measures. He also desired to give all the people a share in the government, and this is how he managed it: Those who were worth five hundred measures of fruit he placed in the first rank of magistrates; those who could afford to keep a horse or were worth three hundred measures of fruit constituted the second class; those who had two hundred measures, the third; and all others, though not admitted to office, could go to the assembly and act as jurors. At first this seemed a trifling matter, but it proved to be a great privilege, because almost every subject of dispute was brought before the jurors. Any man who considered himself injured might appeal to the courts, and this tended to make the citizens resent one another's abuses. When Solon was asked what city was best modelled, he answered, "That where those who are not injured are no less ready to punish the unjust than those who are."

He next re-established the court of Areopagus, which had lost much of its power under Draco. This council had always consisted of men noted for wealth, power, and honesty, but Solon made it a more imposing body by stipulating that it should consist only of those who had borne the office of Archon, and he himself became a member. The Archons stood so high in the public estimation that their decrees were never questioned, so it is easy to understand how powerful the Areopagus must have been. But, besides, there was a council of four hundred, selected from four different Greek tribes, whose duty it was to consider all matters previous to their being placed before the people, and to take care that nothing but what had been first examined should be brought up in the general assembly. Thus one council acted as a check upon the other, and neither could have absolute power. One of the most remarkable of Solon's laws was that which pronounced a man unfit for the privileges of citizenship if he failed to take a decided stand when disputes arose. For the law-giver would not permit any one to be so absorbed in his own personal affairs as to lose sight of the public good or fail to fight in defence of justice.

With regard to marriages, the new laws required that an heiress who chanced to lose her husband should marry one of his relations, so that the money might remain within the family. No bride was permitted to have a dowry, and her trousseau was allowed to consist of three suits of clothes only. She brought to her husband's home, besides, a few inexpensive household utensils, merely to signify that she would do her part towards providing for the family. Solon desired marriages to be contracted out of pure love, and not for the sake of gain; hence the laws that governed them.

It was forbidden to speak ill of the dead, for, as they could no longer defend themselves, it was not considered just to do so, nor was it wise to encourage the unkind feelings of others towards those that were no more. One dared not speak evil of the living, either, in public, without paying a fine; for Solon pronounced it ill bred and a proof of great weakness not to be able to bridle one's tongue and temper.

The laws regarding the making of wills were regulated, as well as those that appertained to journeys, feasts, and funerals. When we consider the reforms instituted for mourning ceremonies, we shall see how necessary they had become, for the women were forbidden to tear themselves, as they had previously done, for the purpose of exciting pity. Mourners could no longer be hired to weep and wail at the funeral of a person for whom they cared nothing. Only three garments might be buried with the corpse, and the sacrifice of an ox at the funeral was prohibited.

Women were required to dress modestly, to behave in a quiet, decent manner, and to go out at night only in a chariot, before which a torch was to be carried to show that they were entitled to respect.

As Attica was rather a barren country, a husbandman's labors scarcely rewarded him; therefore Solon turned the attention of the citizens towards manufactures, and no son was called upon to support his father unless he had taught him some sort of trade. Laziness was regarded as a crime and considered the mother of mischief. So the council of the Areopagus inquired into every man's means of support, and severely chastised the idle.

Solon's laws controlled even matters that at first sight appear trifling, such as the digging of wells, the planting of trees, the money value of sacrifices, and the raising of bees; but they were important, for they influenced the welfare and comfort of the citizens, and were not made without a great deal of knowledge and forethought. They were written upon wooden tables, which could be turned around in the oblong cases that contained them, and the whole council bound themselves by oath to observe them. Each man swore that if he should be guilty of breaking one of them he would place a golden statue of the same weight as himself at Delphi. This would have been no trifling penalty, for gold was very scarce in Greece.

It must not be supposed that all these new laws were put into practice without considerable annoyance to the founder of them, for such was not the case. Solon was daily interviewed by visitors, who sought him to condemn or to criticise certain points that happened to affect their interest. Many praised the laws, it is true, but so much explanation was called for, that Solon found himself likely to incur the ill will of a great number of people whom he could not possibly satisfy. He therefore resolved to seek relief in flight. So, making an excuse for a journey, he bought a trading vessel, and obtained leave of absence for ten years, hoping that by

SOLON

the expiration of that period his code of laws would be firmly established.

He went first to Egypt, and then to Lydia, where he was received by Crœsus, the king, by whom he had been invited. The magnificence Solon beheld at this wealthy court surprised him; but he did not betray this to Crœsus, who made the most gorgeous display in honor of his visitor, nor did he compliment and flatter the grand monarch. He seemed rather to despise such gaudy display, and when asked by Crœsus, "Have you ever known a happier man than I?" he answered, boldly, "Yes, Tellus, a fellow-citizen of mine, who died on the battlefield, bravely fighting for his country, and left behind him a family of good children."

Crœsus was much vexed at this reply, and considered his visitor a very ill-bred fellow; however, he ventured another question:

Besides Tellus, do you know another man as happy as I?"

"Yes," again returned Solon, "Cleobus and Biton, two loving brothers and most dutiful sons, who, when the oxen were late, harnessed themselves to the wagon and drew their mother to the temple of Juno, amid the blessings of all the people who beheld the act. Then, after sacrificing and feasting, they went to rest and never rose again, but died in the night, without sorrow or pain, in the midst of their glory."

"What!" cried Crœsus, angrily, "and do you not then rank me among the number of happy men at all?" Not wishing to excite his anger further, Solon replied, "The gods, O king, have given the Greeks a moderate proportion of everything, even of wisdom, and we have no taste for the splendors of royalty. Moreover, the future carries in its bosom various and uncertain events for every man. The good fortune of to-day may change; therefore he who is blessed with success to the last is in our estimation the happy man. He who still lives and has the dangers of life before him appears to us no better than the champion before the combat is decided." Then Solon departed, leaving the king displeased, but no wiser than before.

Æsop, who wrote the famous fables, happened to be on a visit to the court of Crœsus when Solon was there, and felt very unhappy at the unkind feeling Crœsus showed towards that sage. He therefore ventured to give a little advice. "Solon," he said, "you should either not converse with kings at all, or make it a rule to say only what is agreeable to them." Whereupon Solon replied, "No; I should either not speak to kings at all, or say only that which ought to benefit them."

When Crœsus was defeated in his wars with Cyrus, his city taken, and himself made prisoner and bound upon a pile to be burned, he cried aloud in the presence of all the Persians, "Oh, Solon, Solon, Solon!" "What god or man is that upon whom he calls when on the eve of so great a calamity?" asked Cyrus. "He is one of the wise men of Greece," answered Crœsus, "for whom I sent, not for the purpose of learning anything, but that he might witness my glory and increase my reputation for wealth. But the loss of what I once possessed is a misfortune for which the pleasure it gave me did not compensate. My miserable end must have been foreseen by that great man, for he warned me not to rely on uncertainties, or to call myself happy until the day of my death." Cyrus, who was a much wiser man than Crœsus, was so impressed by what he heard that he at once set his prisoner at liberty and honored him with his protection as long as he lived. Thus Solon was instrumental in saving the life of one king while teaching a useful lesson to another.

When Solon's leave of absence expired, he returned to Athens. He found his laws still observed, but the citizens were clamoring for a change of government, because there had been quarrelling among the leaders of the Plain, the Seaside, and the Hill parties. Now Solon was an old man, and could no longer take so active a part in public affairs as he had done. However, he was distressed at the disturbances, and did all in his power to reason with the leaders privately. Pisistratus, who headed the Hill party, seemed the most tractable and moderate of men to an ordinary observer, but Solon was a good judge of human nature, and it did not take him long to find out that Pisistratus only pretended to yield to argument, though he was really obstinate in his desire for absolute power. He had gained the good will of the multitude by his smooth, persuasive language, adroitly concealing the ambition which prompted all his actions and speeches.

At this time Thespis began to act tragedies, which became so popular that the people flocked in crowds to witness them. Solon was leading a life of comparative leisure, but, with his innate desire to learn anything new that presented itself, he too went to see the play. After it was over he asked Thespis whether he was not ashamed to tell so many lies before such a number of people. Thespis answered that since it was all in jest there could be no harm in it. "Ay," said Solon, striking on the ground with his staff, "that is all very well, but if we encourage such jesting we shall soon find it entering into our contracts."

Not long after, Pisistratus appeared at the market-place in a chariot, with a wound on his body that he had inflicted with his own hand. His object was to inflame the minds of the populace against his enemies, who, he declared, had attacked and wounded him on account of political differences. Great indignation was expressed on all sides, but Solon was not deceived. He approached Pisistratus and said, "Son of Hippocrates, you act Homer's Ulysses but indifferently, for he wounded himself to deceive his enemies, but you have done it to impose upon your countrymen."

In spite of this, the rabble were ready to fight for Pisistratus, who was immediately supplied with a guard consisting of fifty clubmen. Solon was very much opposed to this, but, finding that he could not alter the determination of the citizens, he retired, declaring that he was wiser than those who did not see through the design of Pisistratus, and stronger than those who did understand it, but were afraid to oppose the tyranny. Solon was right; for, not satisfied with fifty clubmen, Pisistratus increased the number until he could control a powerful body, and then took possession of the Acropolis. Great consternation was the result, and Megacles, who headed the Seaside party, fled with his whole family.

Then Solon appeared once more in the market-place, and pointed out to the populace how misfortune had overtaken them because they had not acted with proper decision and spirit. They listened attentively, for they knew that he was right. After making a lengthy speech, he concluded by urging them to stand up like men for their liberty, and not tamely submit to a tyrant. Still they were afraid to act, and Solon was too aged a man to take the lead; he therefore returned to his own home, and placing his weapons at the street-door, wrote over them, "I have done all in my power to defend my country and its laws."

SOLON

His friends begged him to leave Athens, but he refused to do so, and wrote poems in which he thus reproached his countrymen:

> "If now you suffer, do not blame the Powers.
> For they are good, and all the fault was ours.
> All the strongholds you put into his hands,
> And now his slaves must do as he commands."

People assured Solon that the tyrant would certainly put him to death for daring to express himself so plainly, and asked him to what he trusted for protection. "To my old age," he replied.

Instead of condemning Solon, however, Pisistratus had no sooner established himself firmly in power than he sent for the law-giver, treated him with the greatest consideration and respect, and asked him to become his adviser. Not only did Pisistratus do this, but all his actions were guided by the laws which Solon had made, and he obliged his friends to observe them also.

It is said that Solon lived only a couple of years after Pisistratus usurped the government, and that when he died his ashes were strewn over the island of Salamis, as he had ordered; but neither of these statements is to be received as positive fact, though some very reliable authors vouch for the latter one.

PUBLICOLA

PUBLICOLA'S real name was Publius Valerius; but we shall see why the surname, which means "Protector of the People," was given to him. At an early age he was noted for his eloquence, which he used in defending the injured, and his father left him a large fortune, which was employed by Valerius in relieving the wants of the needy.

He was a young man when Tarquinius Superbus, by an illegal act, placed himself on the throne. The Romans groaned under the tyranny and brutality of Tarquinius; but they did not revolt until Lucretia, one of their matrons, killed herself because of the shameful treatment she had received from a member of the royal family. Then they rose in arms, and, with Lucius Brutus and Valerius to lead them, drove out the cruel king with his whole family.

Brutus succeeded to the throne, and Collatinus, husband of the injured Lucretia, was elected consul. Valerius was disappointed at not having the latter office himself; but the Romans were so much in fear lest the Tarquins might return, that they preferred one who could not help hating them.

Valerius then left the senate, and for a while took no part in public affairs. This gave rise to the suspicion that he might be induced to act in the interest of the banished royal family. There were others, besides, whom Brutus had cause to fear, so he appointed a day for solemn sacrifices, and when the people were assembled made them swear allegiance to the state. On that occasion Valerius was one of the first to take the oath to defend the Roman liberty with his sword.

Not long after, when ambassadors came from Tarquinius with proposals that sounded fair, it was Valerius who stood up against the senators, most of whom were disposed to favor them, for he feared the effect upon the populace should they hear what Tarquinius offered.

A second time ambassadors arrived at Rome to announce that Tarquinius was willing to give up his crown and lay down his arms if only he and his friends might have their money and estates restored to them. Many were inclined to consent, Collatinus being of the number; but Brutus would not hear of such a thing. He rushed into the Forum and pronounced the consul a traitor for so much as thinking of allowing supplies which might be used for war, to enemies who ought not even to be allowed means of subsistence in their exile. All the citizens were assembled, and great excitement prevailed. At last it was decided that Brutus was too harsh, and that it was better, since they had secured the liberty for which they had fought, to let the treasures go to the tyrants who owned them.

Now, Tarquinius had not sent his ambassadors because he set any particular store by his effects; what he wanted was to sound the people, and to prepare for an act of treachery that he had planned. After it was decided that he should have his property his men took their time about collecting it, pretending that some was to be sold and the rest to be sent away. This gave them an opportunity to move about freely among the people, and to carry their scheme into effect.

They took pains to worm themselves into the good graces of two of the best families in Rome,—the Aquilii, of whom three were senators, and the Vitellii, of whom there were two members in the senate. These families were relations of Collatinus, the consul, and, as Brutus had married a sister of the older Vitellii, some of the younger ones were his own sons. Two of these were persuaded to join in a plot for the re-establishment of the Tarquins, hoping that if they met with success they would have more freedom, because Brutus was very harsh and strict with them, as well as with all his subjects.

A meeting was held at an out-of-the-way building which belonged to the Aquilii, for the purpose of perfecting the arrangements. There, in a dimly-lighted apartment, each conspirator bound himself, by a dreadful and solemn oath, to do his part of the work, touching the entrails and tasting the blood of a murdered man as he swore. The room in which this scene was enacted was seldom used, but it happened that just before the conspirators arrived a slave named Vindicius had entered it. He was so awed by the mysterious manner of the men that he dared not make his presence known; so, hiding behind a large wooden chest that stood in one corner, he saw and heard all that happened. Having declared their determination to kill the consuls, the conspirators wrote letters giving all the details of their intentions to Tarquinius and placed them in charge of the ambassadors.

When Vindicius was left alone he stole out of his hiding-place and began to reflect upon what he had heard. To go to Brutus and Collatinus with the intelligence that their relations had planned to kill them seemed impossible, for it would be difficult to get a private audience, and perhaps more difficult to make himself believed. Suddenly he remembered

Valerius, whose gates were always open to those who sought him, and who was ever ready to advise and aid the poor and helpless. Fully alive to the fact that not a moment ought to be lost, Vindicius hastened to the house of Valerius and told him all about the dreadful discovery he had made.

Valerius was amazed; but, without losing his presence of mind for a moment, he locked the slave in a room, and, placing his wife to guard the door until he had ascertained the truth of the story just related to him, he ordered his brother, Marcus, to surround the palace that Tarquinius had occupied, seize all the letters to be found there, and secure the servants.

Meanwhile, Valerius, with a large number of friends and attendants, repaired to the house of the Aquilii. None of them were at home, and an entrance had to be forced through the gates. Papers containing a full account of the conspiracy were found upon a table in the ambassadors' apartment. These were rolled up and taken in charge, and the party had reached the outer gate just as the Aquilii returned. A desperate fight took place, and after several moments, Valerius's men, at a given signal, took off their gowns, threw them over the heads of their opponents, and, twisting them tightly about their necks, dragged them to the Forum. While this scene was being enacted, another, almost as exciting, took place at the king's palace, which Marcus, in obedience to orders, had attacked. Having possessed himself of all the letters to be found there, Marcus, with his men, made prisoners of the royal servants, whom he marched to the Forum just in time to meet Valerius as he came up with his victorious party.

The tumult caused by the assembling of the prisoners was so great that all the efforts of the consuls were required to restore quiet; but when that was accomplished, an order was given for Vindicius, the slave, to be brought forth. Standing erect upon the platform, he made his accusation in a loud, clear voice. The confiscated papers were next produced and read, the traitors standing with bowed heads, while the people present listened with amazement and sorrow. Collatinus shed tears; Valerius remained silent, and whispers of banishment passed among the crowd, whose eyes were fixed on Brutus. That unhappy father looked stern and unforgiving as he rose, and, drawing himself up to his full height, thus addressed his sons: "Canst not thou, O Titus, nor thou, Tiberius, speak out boldly and defend thyself against this shameful charge?" There was a painful silence; the question was repeated, but still there was no answer. Brutus spoke once again; then turning to the lictors, or executioners, he exclaimed, "What remains is your duty!"

The lictors thereupon seized the youths, stripped off their clothes, bound their hands behind them, and scourged them with rods. The scene was so horrible that strong men turned aside, unable to witness it, but Brutus showed no signs of weakness or pity; he watched the agony of his children until the bitter end, when the lictors laid them on the ground and cut off their heads with an axe. Then, leaving the punishment of the other traitors to Collatinus, Brutus rose and walked away.

For a long time after Brutus had left the Forum horror and astonishment kept the people silent. Seeing that Collatinus inclined towards forbearance, the Aquilii gained confidence, and requested that their servant Vindicius should be delivered up to them, and that they should be granted time to answer the charge against them. Collatinus was disposed to consent, and began to dismiss the assembly, but Valerius

PUBLICOLA

would not listen to such a thing, and declared against the injustice of allowing any of the traitors to escape punishment, particularly as Brutus had set them a terrible example by witnessing the death of his own sons. Then the consul lost his temper, and ordered Vindicius to be removed. The lictors pushed through the crowd prepared to obey, but the friends of Valerius attacked them, and surrounded the slave, determined that he should not be lost sight of. During the conflict loud cries arose for Brutus, and some people ran to fetch him. His reappearance acted like magic: the fighting ceased, silence ensued, and every eye was directed towards his face. All he said was that he had been able to pass sentence upon his own sons, supposing that the free citizens would see justice done with regard to the other traitors, and added that any one might plead for them who chose. No man spoke until it was decided to put it to the vote, when, with one voice, the traitors were condemned to death. They were beheaded on the spot.

Collatinus had been suspected for some time of favoring the royal family, particularly as Tarquinius Superbus was his second cousin: he had therefore become unpopular, and this last affair had not tended to make him less so. Finding such to be the case, he resigned his consulship and retired from the city. Valerius was elected to succeed him, and his first act was to reward Vindicius, by making him a free man and a citizen of Rome, with the privilege of voting. The king's palace was torn down, and all his valuables were taken by the state.

Tarquinius Superbus, though disappointed at the failure of the conspiracy, by no means abandoned hope. On the contrary, he interested the Tuscans in his cause, to such an extent that they raised a great army for the purpose of restoring the kingdom to him. The Romans, headed by their consuls, collected their forces on the battlefield ready to resist the enemy. In the first action Aruns, the son of Tarquin, and Brutus, the Roman consul, sought each other out, and engaged in a terrible hand-to-hand encounter. They fought until they fell dead together. The rest of the warriors on both sides engaged with similar fury, and the loss was very great. A tremendous storm put an end to the fighting at last. When night came on, neither army knew which was victorious, but each was dismayed at the number of dead that lay upon the field. Valerius was greatly perplexed, for he could not find out how the enemy regarded the conflict, nor could he guess what they would do when day dawned. While he pondered, a strange thing happened. It was midnight, and both camps were hushed in silence and repose. Suddenly the grove shook, and a loud, clear voice was heard, announcing that the Tuscans had lost one man more than the Romans. No one was to be seen, but every living soldier heard the voice. From the Roman camp arose shouts and cheers, while the Tuscans were filled with fear and disappointment, and at once began to desert their camp. About five thousand of them, less fortunate than the rest, were taken prisoners by the Romans, who lost no time in renewing the battle. After plundering the Tuscan camp, the victors set about the task of numbering the dead, when it was discovered that the Tuscans had lost eleven thousand three hundred, and the Romans just one man less, as the mysterious voice had declared.

Then Valerius made a triumphal entry into Rome in a magnificent chariot drawn by four horses. He was the first consul who had ever done this. The citizens gathered in crowds to welcome the return of their victorious army, whom they received with cheers and exclamations of delight. While

PUBLICOLA

receiving these honors, Valerius did not forget Brutus, who had fought so nobly for his country, but assisted at his funeral and delivered an oration filled with praises of the dead warrior. The Romans were so well pleased with this idea that from that time they adopted the custom of having speeches made by their best men at the funerals of remarkable citizens, setting forth their virtues and great deeds. Among the Greeks funeral orations were not in use until the battle of Marathon, sixteen years after the death of Brutus. They honored in this manner only those heroes who fell on the battlefield, but the Romans publicly eulogized a man who had served his country in any capacity.

After a while Valerius gave offence by assuming too much authority. The Romans remembered that Brutus, whom they regarded as the father of their liberty, would not consent to rule alone, but had always associated some other consul with himself. "What is the use," they asked, "in this man's praising Brutus as we all heard him do, and then imitating Tarquinius? He walks about with all the stateliness and pomp of that tyrant, and occupies a house not less magnificent than his was." It is true that Valerius's house was a very handsome one. It was situated on the Velian Hill, overlooking the Forum, so that when the consul descended he could be seen nearly all the way. At that time his insignia were those of the kings, except the crown, and he was preceded by twelve lictors, who walked one by one in a line, carrying axes. This procession made a very imposing show, and the citizens began to question whether they had not again placed their heads in a tyrant's yoke.

Valerius heard their murmurings, but said nothing. One morning, when a crowd assembled at the Forum, great was their surprise to find that the beautiful mansion on the

Velian Hill had vanished. It was soon made known that Valerius had engaged workmen to destroy it during the night. Now the citizens felt heartily ashamed to think that their grumblings and jealous fears had caused their consul to leave himself without a roof to cover his head. They immediately set to work to select another piece of land, and put up a less pretentious house, Valerius meanwhile being dependent on the hospitality of his friends.

His power was not diminished in the least, but Valerius thought best to have it appear as if it were, and for that reason ordered his lictors to lay aside their axes, and for the future to carry the long poles only to which they had been attached. These they were instructed to lower whenever Valerius went to a great assembly, as a sign that supreme power was lodged in the citizens, and not in the consul; that is, the consul wished to intimate that he no longer had the power of life or death.

Valerius declared that any citizen was free to apply for the consulship, but before any one had the chance of doing so he made his most important regulations. First, he supplied the vacancies left by the senators who had been put to death by Tarquinius, or had perished in the late battle with the Tuscans. Then he made several laws which increased the liberty of the people, lightened their taxes, and encouraged them to work.

All the new laws were popular and moderate except one, which was very severe. It declared that any man who should attempt to set himself up for a king might be killed without trial or hearing of any sort, and the person who took his life should be excused, providing he could prove the intended crime.

PUBLICOLA

Money for purposes of war had to be raised out of the estates of the citizens, and Valerius made an excellent arrangement for this fund. He would not take charge of it himself, nor would he permit any of his relations to do so, but ordered it to be placed in the Temple of Saturn, and chose two worthy young men for Quæstors, or treasurers. Their position was considered a very lofty one, and they were required to give a yearly account of the funds.

It was at this period that Valerius was called Publicola, "protector of the people," and so we shall henceforth designate him.

Having regulated affairs of state, Publicola appointed Marcus Horatius to share the consulship with him.

Tarquinius now began to prepare for another war against the Romans, but it was abandoned for a very strange reason. While he was king of Rome it suddenly occurred to him that a porcelain chariot would look well on the top of the Jupiter Capitolinus Temple, and the artists of Veii, in Tuscany, who excelled in such work, were ordered to mould one. It was not completed when Tarquinius lost his crown, but the artists did not abandon their task. They made the chariot and put it in the furnace to bake. Instead of contracting by the evaporation of moisture the clay used on this occasion swelled, until the chariot became so large and so hard that it could only be removed with difficulty even after the furnace was pulled to pieces. The soothsayers believed that power and success would attend the possession of this wonderful chariot, so the Tuscans determined not to let the Romans get hold of it. But a few days later there was a race at Veii, with all the usual ceremonies, and when the victorious charioteer, with his garland on his head, was quietly driving out of the ring, his horses took fright, from no apparent cause, and dashed at full speed towards Rome. The driver pulled the reins and called to the animals in vain; they whirled along until they came to the Capitol, where he was thrown out by the gate called Ratumena. This occurrence so surprised and terrified the people of Veii that they forthwith sent the chariot Tarquinius had ordered to the Romans. It was placed on top of the Temple of Jupiter Capitolinus, when Publicola desired to dedicate it, but certain of the nobles were so jealous of him that, taking advantage of his absence with the army, they procured an order from the people for Horatius to do so instead. Accordingly, he was conducted to the spot, and the usual ceremonies were performed. Just when Horatius took hold of one of the gate-posts to pronounce the prayer of consecration, Marcus, the brother of Publicola, hoping even at the last moment to interrupt the ceremony, cried out, "Consul, your son lies dead in the camp!" "Then cast out the dead where you please; I admit of no mourning on this occasion," answered Horatius, who showed great presence of mind, for the statement was, as he suspected, a falsehood. And so the first temple to Jupiter Capitolinus was dedicated, and Publicola had no share in it.

Let us return to Tarquinius Superbus. When his son was killed in single combat with Brutus he fled to Clusium and sought aid from Lars Porsenna, a man of worth and honor, and one of the most powerful princes of Italy. Porsenna was interested in the Tarquins because they were countrymen of his, being of Tuscan descent, as he was; so he immediately sent word to Rome that Tarquinius was to be received as king. A prompt refusal was the only reply he got, whereupon he declared war, proclaimed the time and place of his intended attack, and approached with a powerful army.

PUBLICOLA

Publicola, who had been re-elected consul, and Titus Lucretius, who shared the government with him, took command of the Roman army. Porsenna made such a spirited assault that he drove his opponents back to their city, which they entered in such haste and confusion that the enemy came very near getting beyond the gates also. It was Publicola who prevented such a catastrophe by rallying his men and giving battle to the enemy on the banks of the Tiber. He fought until, being dangerously wounded, he was carried out of the battle. The same fate overtook Titus Lucretius; and the Romans, finding that both their consuls were disabled, lost courage and retreated to Rome. The city would certainly have been taken had it not been for the heroism of Horatius Cocles. This surname was given to Horatius because he had only one eye, having lost the other in the wars. Those who named him so meant Cyclops, but miscalled the one-eyed giants and made it Cocles instead. With the aid of Herminius and Lartius, two of the first men in Rome, Horatius Cocles defended the wooden bridge over the Tiber and kept back the enemy until his own party cut it down behind him. Then he plunged into the river with his armor on and swam back, although he had been wounded in the hip by a Tuscan spear.

Publicola was so pleased at the courage shown by Horatius on the bridge that he at once proposed that every Roman should present him with one day's provisions. Afterwards he gave the hero as much land as he could plough around in one day, and erected a statue in his honor in the Temple of Vulcan. Horatius Cocles could never be made consul, because of his lameness and of his having only one eye.

While Porsenna besieged Rome, another body of Tuscans laid the country waste. Fearing they would produce famine, Publicola marched against them without giving warning, and killed five thousand. A Roman warrior named Mucius, who was distinguished for his valor, resolved to go quite alone and kill Porsenna. Disguised in the Tuscan attire and speaking the Tuscan language, Mucius went to the enemy's camp and made his way straight to the spot where the king sat among his nobles. On arriving there he was at a loss to decide which was Porsenna; and, fearing to betray himself by making inquiries, he drew his sword and slew the man who he thought had most the appearance of king; but he made a mistake and was seized on the spot. During the examination which followed, Porsenna threatened Mucius with torture by fire, in order to make him name his accomplices. Thereupon, to show how indifferent he was to pain, Mucius thrust his right hand into a blazing fire prepared upon a portable altar for purposes of sacrifice. While his flesh was burning he kept his eyes fixed on the face of Porsenna without once flinching. The king was lost in admiration of such fortitude, and graciously returned to the prisoner the sword that had been taken from him. Mucius received the weapon with his left hand, and said to Porsenna, "I regarded not your threats, but I am conquered by your generosity, and will now tell you what you could never have forced from me. There are three hundred Romans who have taken an oath, as I did, to kill you; they are now walking about your camp, waiting for an opportunity. It was my lot to make the first attempt; but I am not sorry that I failed, for so brave and good a man as you ought to live to be a friend to Rome rather than an enemy." Porsenna did not fear the three hundred who wanted to take his life, but he was so favorably impressed by the example of courage Mucius had shown that he was willing to come to terms, and soon ceased to have any regard for Tarquinius. Indeed, so kindly disposed was he towards the Romans that he ordered his forces to quit camp with nothing but their arms, and to leave their tents full of provisions as a gift to them. This generous act was rewarded by the senate with a present to Porsenna of a throne adorned with ivory, a sceptre, a golden crown, and a superb robe. A brazen statue was also erected near the senate-house in his honor.

Publicola was made consul a third and a fourth time. Then the Sabines threatened a war, and preparations were made to oppose them. Among that race was a man named Appius Clausus, noted for his wealth, his excellent character, and his great eloquence. Clausus did all he could to prevent the war, and thus came to be suspected of favoring the Romans. He did not care to stand a trial when this accusation was made, because, although he knew that many would be delighted if peace could be preserved, the army would be angry. However, he had numerous friends and allies, who helped him in disputing the question of war, thus causing a delay. Meanwhile, Publicola sent messengers to tell Clausus that he was assured of his honesty and good intentions, and that if he pleased to secure himself against his enemies and come to Rome, he would be most cordially received. Clausus considered the proposition seriously, and concluded to accept it. Five thousand of the best Sabine families determined to accompany him, and all set out together for Rome.

On being informed of their approach, Publicola went out to meet them, and gave them a hearty welcome. The advantages of citizenship were bestowed on them, and each family was presented with two acres of land. But Clausus received twenty-five acres and an invitation to become senator. He soon rose in political power, and established such a fine reputation that the Claudian family, of which he was the founder, became one of the most illustrious in the city.

The Sabines who remained at home would have settled down quietly after the departure of Clausus with his party, but their leaders were determined upon war, and told them it was disgraceful not to resent the desertion of so large a number of their race. A grand army was therefore equipped and gathered at Fidenæ, not far from Rome. Then an ambuscade of two thousand men was stationed in a wood on the outskirts of the city, with this design: as soon as day dawned a few horsemen were to set forth and ravage the country up to the very gates, and then suddenly to retreat and draw the enemy, who would be sure to follow into the ambush. But Publicola was informed of this by deserters, and so prepared his forces. The night before the attack was to be made, Posthumius Balbus, son-in-law of Publicola, went out with three thousand men, and stationed them on top of the hills beneath which the Sabines were hidden, for the purpose of watching their movements. Lucretius, with a body of the boldest and most active Romans, was appointed to meet the Sabine cavalry, while the consul himself, with the rest of the forces, surrounded the enemy in the rear. Taking advantage of a fog that settled at dawn, Posthumius, with loud shouts, assailed the enemy from the hills, Lucretius cut off the retreat of the cavalry, and Publicola attacked the camp itself. The Sabines were completely taken by surprise, and the slaughter was tremendous. There was so much confusion among them that those in the camp ran to the ambuscade, and those in the ambuscade flew to the camp, each expecting protection from the other. Had not the city of Fidelæ been so near, all the Sabines would have been killed or captured, but, as it was, some of them escaped. The plunder and the sale of the prisoners brought great wealth to the Romans, who gave all the credit of the victory to their general.

PUBLICOLA

While at the height of his glory Publicola resigned his office. He lived only a short time after that, and when he died he did not leave money enough to pay the expenses of his funeral, a good proof that he had honorably used the public funds. Each citizen contributed a piece of money towards paying for the funeral, and the women mourned a whole year for Publicola, one of the greatest generals and the most popular consul Rome ever had.

CAIUS MARCIUS CORIOLANUS

CAIUS MARCIUS CORIOLANUS belonged to the noble Marcii family, and was early distinguished for his courage and for his deep interest in all that pertained to war. So when Tarquinius Superbus tried to replace himself on the throne, as has been related in the life of Publicola, young Marcius gladly embraced the opportunity of appearing on the battlefield. In one of the engagements he distinguished himself by stepping into the place of a Roman soldier who had been disabled and killing his assailant. For this brave deed he was crowned after the battle with a wreath of oak-leaves, it being the custom in Rome so to adorn any soldier who saved the life of another. This crown could be worn whenever the owner chose, and entitled him to marked respect.

After that Marcius performed so many exploits that there was scarcely a battle from which he did not return crowned. This only fired his ambition to do better, and his mother's warm embrace as she received him crowned with laurels delighted his heart. His father had died when Marcius was an infant, so all his love was bestowed on his mother, from whom he never lived apart, even after he was married and had a family of his own.

Marcius added much to his glory during the war between the Romans and the Volscians. Cominius, the consul, surrounded Corioli, the principal city of the Volscians, whereupon the rest of the nation sent all their forces, so that an attack might be made upon the enemy from within and without the walls at the same time. But Cominius would not risk such an encounter; he therefore divided his army, and leaving part under the command of Titus Lartius, one of the bravest Romans of his time, to continue the siege, he led the other part out to meet the approaching Volscian troops.

Those within the walls of Corioli thought they could easily manage the small army that remained, and so gave them battle, and drove them into their trenches. Then Marcius, with a few selected warriors, flew at the Volscians, and cut to pieces all that he encountered, calling at the same time on his countrymen to renew the battle.

Encouraged by his voice and example, the Romans rallied and fought the enemy to their very gates. Thousands of darts rained down upon the besiegers from the walls, and they were on the point of retreating, when Marcius cried out, in tones remarkable for their power, "Fortune has opened the gates of Corioli to receive the conquerors!" Followed by a handful of brave men, he pushed his way through the crowd into the city. A combat followed which resulted in victory for Marcius. Some of the citizens of Corioli sought refuge in the interior, while the rest laid down their arms. Then Lartius led in the rest of the Romans, who at once began their work of pillage.

But Marcius was not satisfied. He reproached the soldiers, and told them that it was disgraceful for them thus to spend their time when the consul and his troops were perhaps engaged with the other Volscians; drawing about him the few who were willing to sacrifice the booty that lay before them, he hastened along the road Cominius had taken, praying to the gods as he went that he might arrive before the fight was over.

It was the custom among the Romans just before going to battle, while girding on their bucklers, to make a verbal will in the presence of three or four hearers. The army of Cominius was thus engaged, with the enemy in sight, when Marcius entered the camp all besmeared with blood, and attended by his small train. All thought that he had come to report defeat, but when after a moment's conversation Cominius embraced and saluted him, they knew that Corioli had fallen, and cried out to be led to battle.

Marcius inquired where the best soldiers among the enemy were stationed, and on being told in the centre, said, "Let me be granted the favor of being posted against them." He had his wish, and wherever he went he broke the Volscian ranks. Once he was completely surrounded, when, seeing the danger, the consul sent some of his choicest men to the rescue. These fought so hard that they drove the enemy from the field. Marcius was then urged to retire to the camp and rest, for he was faint from loss of blood, but he said, "Weariness is not for conquerors," and joined in the pursuit of the Volscians until part were killed and the rest captured.

The next day, when Marcius Coriolanus presented himself at the tent of Cominius, he received a hearty welcome and loud praise for his remarkable achievements. The consul then told Marcius to choose a tenth part of the booty, the horses, and the captives as his reward before the regular division was made among the soldiers, and presented him with a fine horse covered with rich trappings and ornaments. The whole army applauded; but the hero only accepted the horse, and, after thanking Cominius for his approval of his deeds, refused any other reward except what fell to his share.

"I have one special favor to ask," he added, "which I hope will not be denied me; it is that one of the prisoners, a worthy man, whose hospitality I have enjoyed, now reduced from wealth and freedom to captivity, may not be sold as a common slave."

Applause louder and longer than before greeted this request, for the men were more impressed by Marcius's refusing the rich reward offered to him and by his kind remembrance of his friend than they had been by his bravery on the battlefield. As soon as quiet was restored, Cominius said, "It is useless, fellow-soldiers, to force gifts upon one who is unwilling to receive them; but let us offer him that which he cannot reject: let us pass a vote that he shall henceforth be called Coriolanus, on account of his actions at Corioli." This is how he came by his third name.

When the war was over there was such a scarcity of provisions in Rome that a famine was feared, and great disturbance was the consequence. There had been frequent quarrels between the rich and the poor, and now the orators stirred up the latter to the belief that the Patricians, as the noble class was called, had brought about the scarcity of food out of revenge. The senate did not know what to do, but Marcius did not wait for them to decide. He secured as many volunteers as possible, marched into the territory of the Antiates, and returned to Rome with a rich supply of corn, cattle, and slaves, no part of which he kept for himself.

Those who had stayed quietly at home were filled with envy when they saw Marcius again victorious, and began to talk about the danger of his growing power.

Not long after, he presented himself in the Forum as a candidate for consul. This was a period of purity, a golden age, when bribery had not been resorted to, and a man solicited the votes of his fellow-citizens on account of his merit. So Marcius appeared in the Forum wearing only a loose gown, or toga, and no tunic. Thus attired, the scars he had received during his seventeen years' service in battle could be plainly seen, and the people told one another that they could not help creating him consul when he displayed such marks of merit. If the election had taken place then and there, Marcius would have received the office he desired, but he made this mistake: when election-day came he appeared not displaying his scars, but handsomely clad and attended by a train of senators. The other Patricians made such efforts to secure his election that the common people rejected him merely for the sake of opposition.

Coriolanus was so indignant that he burst into a violent fit of rage, which the angry remarks of his friends among the young noblemen encouraged. He vowed that he would be avenged, and they promised to uphold him in all he did.

His time came when grain was brought in large quantities to Rome from various parts of Italy and from the King of Sicily, who sent it as a present. The senate assembled to distribute it, and the people flocked in crowds, expecting to buy very cheap, and to get what the king had sent without charge.

Then Coriolanus stood up and declared boldly that he was opposed to any favors being shown the Plebeians, as the common people were called. He said that they were no longer to be trusted, since they were unwilling to obey magistrates not of their own class; that they were traitors whose insolence ought to deprive them of any favors whatsoever. He added much more, but the most aggravating part of his speech was the proposition to keep the price of corn as high as ever, and thus prevent the people from becoming independent.

When the crowd heard what Coriolanus had said, they were so angry that they wanted to break in upon the senate. Thereupon the tribunes assured them that the offender should be punished, and that they should be fairly dealt with regarding the price of food. After a short consultation, Sicinius, the boldest of the tribunes, announced that Marcius Coriolanus was condemned to die, and ordered the magistrates to take him to the top of the Tarpeian rock and throw him down the precipice.

Even his enemies were shocked at such a sentence; but his friends closed around him and would not allow the officers to come near, while he stood prepared to make a desperate resistance. Finding that he could not be taken without a great deal of bloodshed, the tribunes decided to leave his fate to the people, and let them say what should be done with him. Sicinius then turned to the Patricians and asked, "What do you mean by rescuing Marcius when he is on the eve of punishment?" They answered, "What do you mean by thus dragging one of the worthiest men in Rome, without trial, to a barbarous execution?" "If that be all," returned Sicinius, "the people grant you what you desire: the man shall have his trial. As for you, Marcius, we request you on the third market-day to appear and defend yourself; the Roman citizens will then decide your case by vote."

Several charges were brought against Coriolanus, some just, some unjust, when the trial took place, and he was condemned by a majority of votes to perpetual banishment.

This sentence was received by the Plebeians with loud expressions of joy; but the Patricians felt and looked sad and depressed. Marcius alone appeared unmoved, because he was too indignant to show what he suffered. He went to his own home, bade farewell to his mother and his wife, and then left Rome, being accompanied to the city gate by the Patricians in a body. The next few days he spent at one of his farms in the neighborhood, turning over in his mind the best method of revenging himself. At last he decided to stir up some nation to a cruel war against the Romans, and fixed upon the Volscians as most likely to favor his plan. They had been defeated, but they were still strong in men and money, which they would, he did not doubt, be ready to use against Rome.

So one evening he went secretly to the town of Antium in disguise, and made his way to the house of Tullus Aufidius, a man of wealth, influence, and noble birth among the Volscians. He entered without speaking to anybody, proceeded straight to the hearth, seated himself there, and covered up his head.

As the household gods of the Romans were always placed on the hearth, it was considered a sacred spot, and any person desiring assistance, no matter of what character, went there for refuge. Something impressive in the appearance and the silence of Coriolanus prevented the people of the house from disturbing him; but they went to Tullus, who was at supper, and told him that a stranger had come who probably desired to speak with him. Tullus rose from the table, and, going towards the visitor, asked who he was, and upon what business he had come. Uncovering his face, Coriolanus looked for a moment at the Volscian, and spoke thus: "If thou dost not know me, Tullus, I must be my own accuser. I am Caius Marcius, who have brought so many misfortunes on your people; and as a proof of that I bear the additional name of Coriolanus, which is all the reward I have for the labors and dangers I have undergone. Of everything else I am robbed by the envy of the people on the one hand and the cowardice and treachery of the magistrates on the other. Driven from Rome as an exile, I come as a suppliant to thy household gods,—not for protection, for were I afraid to die I should not come here, but for vengeance on those who have wronged me. I begin by putting myself in thy hands. If thou art disposed to attack the enemy, brave Tullus, take advantage of my misfortunes; let my personal distress be the happiness of thy countrymen, and be assured that I shall fight much better for thee than I ever fought against thee. But if thou hast given up all thoughts of war, I neither desire to live nor is it fit for thee to preserve one who has been thine enemy and is not able to do thee any sort of service."

Tullus was delighted with this address; taking the hand of the Roman in his, he said, "Rise, Marcius, and take courage. The present you make us of yourself is of great value, and you may be sure that the Volscians will not prove ungrateful." He then feasted him, and the two men spent several of the following days consulting together about the war. They took the principal men of Antium into their confidence also, and all felt the difficulty of invading Rome because of a treaty of peace which had been sworn to for two years.

Coriolanus was not a man to stop at trifles; having resolved to fight, he managed in this way to make the Romans themselves furnish a pretext. He sent a message to the consuls that it was the intention of the Volscians residing in Rome to fall upon the citizens during the public games and set the city on fire. The consequence was a proclamation ordering the Volscians to depart before sunset. That was enough; such an indignity was not to be borne patiently, and Tullus did what he could to work on the feelings of his countrymen until he persuaded them at last to send ambassadors to Rome to demand that the land taken from the Volscians during the late war should be returned. The reply they received was "that the Volscians were the first to break the treaty and take up arms, but the Romans would be the last to lay them down."

Then Tullus called an assembly, and the majority voted for war. By his advice Marcius was chosen to share the command of the army with him, and so impatient was the latter to begin operations that before all the arrangements were completed he marched with part of the troops to the confines of Rome, and created such a panic by his unexpected appearance that the Volscians took more booty than they could carry away or use in camp. But this was not all that Marcius desired. He had wickedly made up his mind to increase the ill feeling that existed between the Patricians and the Plebeians, so he ordered his soldiers to destroy right and left everything that they could not carry away, but on no account to lay hands on a Patrician estate. The consequence was that the people accused the rich of encouraging Coriolanus to attack Rome because they knew that he would offer them no injury.

While disorder reigned and the two parties in Rome quarrelled and disputed, Coriolanus was marching about from city to city, plundering, killing, and increasing the wealth and number of his army. At last he laid siege to Lavinium, where the images and sacred things of the gods were kept. Then the Romans became so terrified that they demanded the recall of Coriolanus.

At first the senate refused, but when the enemy advanced to within five miles of Rome they sent ambassadors to ask Coriolanus to forget the past and return.

He received them seated in state, surrounded by Volscian officers, and replied, "As general of the Volscians I demand all the territory seized by the Romans in the late war, also the same rights and privileges for the people I command as are granted to the Latins, otherwise peace cannot be lasting. I give you thirty days to decide."

The Volscian forces were then led out of the Roman territory, but attacks were continued on other cities in Italy, and Coriolanus took possession of seven important ones. When the thirty days had passed, the ambassadors were sent again, not to agree to the terms proposed by Coriolanus, but to ask him to withdraw the Volscian army, and then to make any proposals he thought best for both parties. He refused, but granted to the Romans three days more for consideration of the matter. The senate were in despair, for the city was in a perfect uproar, and with a powerful enemy at their very gates ready to pounce down upon them at a moment's notice, nobody had the heart to engage in regular pursuits.

Here was a case that called for extraordinary measures: so a decree was issued that the whole order of priests, soothsayers, and priestesses should go in full procession, attired in their sacred robes and carrying all the emblems of their holy offices, to see what impression they could make on the now terrible Marcius. They were admitted to the camp, received with mildness and patiently listened to, but nothing was granted to them. They were sent away with this choice: either to yield to the terms proposed or to fight. So much had been expected from the intercession of the holy ambassadors that their failure made matters worse than before. In their despair the Romans resolved to remain within their walls, and merely defend themselves when the attack should be made, trusting to the friendliness of the gods to put off the evil day.

In this dreadful season of uncertainty the women of Rome daily congregated at the various temples to pray for the safety of their homes and families. Those of the highest rank met at the altar of Jupiter Capitolinus, and it was one of their number who hit upon a plan that no member of the senate would ever have thought of. Her name was Valeria, and she was sister of the great Publicola, whose services were of so much value to his country. "Come," said she to her companions, as though suddenly seized with divine inspiration, "let us go to Volumnia, the mother of Marcius; she and Vergilia, his wife, may succeed where all others have failed."

On arriving at the house, they found the mother sitting with her daughter-in-law and her grandchildren. Valeria stepped forward from amidst the score of ladies who accompanied her, and spoke thus: "We have come to you, Volumnia, and you, Vergilia, as women to women, not by the direction of the senate or an order from the consuls, but prompted by the Divine Being himself, to entreat you to do a thing that will save us and raise your glory above that of the Sabine women, who won over their fathers and husbands from mortal enmity to peace and friendship. Arise and come with us to Coriolanus; help us to bear testimony in behalf of our country, that in spite of the many wrongs that have been put upon her she has never once done you an injury, but now restores you safe into his hands, though she may not on that account obtain better terms for herself."

Volumnia made answer: "Vergilia and I, my countrywomen, not only share with you the common misery, but we have the sorrow besides of knowing that Marcius is lost to us, his glory dimmed, his virtue gone, for we behold him surrounded by the arms of the enemy, not as their prisoner but as their commander. It is the greatest of all misfortunes that our country has become so weak as to rest her hopes upon us, for since Marcius has no regard for the country which he used to love better than mother, wife, or child, we can scarcely hope that he will listen to us. However, lead us, if you please, to him; if we can do nothing else we can at least expire at his feet pleading for Rome."

Having thus spoken, she took Vergilia and the children by the hand, and, after gaining the approval of the senate and consuls, proceeded with the Roman matrons to the Volscian camp. Their appearance touched the sympathies of the enemy, and when they approached the general he was overcome at the sight of his dear ones, who headed the line. He came quickly forward, embraced his mother, then his wife and children, and burst into tears. After a few moments Volumnia spoke as follows, in the presence of the Volscian counsellors, who had drawn near: "You see, my son, by our attire and miserable looks to what a forlorn condition your banishment has reduced us. Now ask yourself whether we are not the most wretched of women,—Volumnia who beholds her son and Vergilia her husband in arms against Rome. Even prayer, whence others gain comfort in misfortune, only adds to our distress, for we cannot ask the gods at the same time for our country's victory and your preservation. Your wife and children must see either Rome or you perish. As for myself, I shall not wait for war to decide, for if I cannot prevail with you to prefer peace to hostility and become the benefactor of

CORIOLANUS AND HIS MOTHER

both parties rather than the destroyer of one, rest assured that you shall never reach your country unless you trample upon the dead body of her who gave you life. It would ill become me to wait for the day when my son should come into Rome as the conqueror of his fellow-citizens, or be led into it as their captive. If I desired you to save your country by ruining the Volscians the case would be hard, for it would be quite as dishonorable to betray those who have put their trust in you as to destroy your countrymen. All we ask of you is a deliverance that will be most to the honor of the Volscians, though equally beneficial to them and to us. We ask of them the blessing of peace and friendship, which their superiority enables them to grant. If our petition meets with favor, you will be regarded as the chief cause of it; if we are repulsed, you alone must expect to bear the blame from both nations. The chances of war are uncertain. If you conquer Rome, you will have the reputation of having undone your country, but if the Volscians are defeated under you, all the world will say that to satisfy your revenge you brought misfortune to your friends and benefactors."

Marcius listened to his mother, but said not a word. Wondering at his silence, she spoke again: "My son, why are you silent? Is it an honor to yield everything to revenge, and a disgrace to grant your mother so important a petition? Does it become a great man to remember injuries done him, and to forget the reverence he owes his parents? Surely you, of all men, should take care to be grateful who have suffered so much from ingratitude. Yet you have not made your mother the least return for her kindness and devotion. The most sacred ties of nature and religion require you to indulge me in this reasonable and just request, but if it must be so, this only is left." She fell on her knees at his feet, and Valeria and his children did the same.

"Oh, mother, what is it you have done?" cried Coriolanus, as he raised her from the ground and tenderly pressed her hand. "You have gained a victory fortunate for the Romans, but ruinous to your son! By you alone am I defeated."

Although he knew that the Volscians would never forgive him for granting a favor to their enemies, he broke up the camp the next morning and led them homeward.

When the Roman matrons returned home all the temples were thrown open, and people crowned themselves to prepare for the sacrifices, as it was their custom to do when news of a great victory was brought to them. The extent of their rejoicing showed how great their misery had been. The senate passed a decree that the women who had saved their country should have any honor or favor granted them that they chose to ask.

They simply demanded that a temple should be erected to Female Fortune, offering to pay for it themselves if the city would furnish the cost of sacrifices and other matters necessary to do honor to the goddess.

The senate praised their generosity, but ordered the temple to be built at the public expense. Then the women set up a second statue of Fortune, which was said to have uttered these words when placed: "O women! most acceptable to the gods is your pious gift." We need not believe that an image spoke, but the ancient Romans had so much superstitious faith that they accepted many improbabilities as facts.

CAIUS MARCIUS CORIOLANUS

When Marcius returned to Antium he was accused of treachery by Tullus, who was jealous of his victories and his fast-growing popularity. So when he stood up before the public assembly to defend himself, Tullus and his party cried out, "We will not listen to a traitor! Volscians want no tyrant!" Amidst such exclamations they set upon Marcius and killed him on the spot.

In a subsequent battle with the Romans Tullus was slain, and the Volscians became their subjects.

THEMISTOCLES

As a boy Themistocles was remarkably bright and intelligent, and showed such deep interest in everything pertaining to public affairs that his master often said to him, "Boy, you will certainly make your mark, either as a blessing or a curse to your country." He was not disposed to study those branches that most of his companions preferred, and when they jeered at him for not desiring accomplishments he would get angry and say, "I may not know how to tune a harp or play upon a lute, but I understand the art of raising a small and unimportant city to glory and greatness." Most of his leisure moments were passed in imagining cases of dispute among citizens, and composing orations bearing upon them.

He could not be taught graceful manners, for they seemed of little consequence to him, though his countrymen attached great importance to the art of pleasing. Themistocles was an unruly boy, and carried on his mad pranks without much restraint. When taken to task for them he said, "The wildest colts make the best horses when they come to be properly trained." So ambitious of power and position was he that as he grew older he became involved in many quarrels with people of high rank and influence. Among these was Aristides, a man of mild disposition and unusual honesty, who was frequently annoyed by the way Themistocles would stir the people up to enterprises that seemed unjustifiable.

THEMISTOCLES

The great battle of Marathon, in which the Athenians had won such a magnificent victory, was ever in the mind of the young man, and he burned to crown himself with glory, as Miltiades had done by entirely defeating the grand Persian army. Ambition rendered him sleepless by night and absorbed his thoughts by day. He became absent-minded and reserved, and lost interest in the recreations he had before enjoyed. His friends questioned him as to the cause. He said, "The trophies of Miltiades will not suffer me to sleep."

Few supposed that an opportunity would arise for him to gain such trophies, for it seemed as though the signal defeat of the Persians had put an end to the war. But Themistocles advised the Greeks to prepare their ships for an attack which he foresaw Darius, the Persian king, would make by sea, with the hope of restoring the fortunes lost at Marathon. This wonderful foresight proved that Themistocles had at least one of the qualifications of a great general, and we shall see that he had others besides.

The most flourishing people in all Greece were the Æginetans, and Ægina, their city, situated on an island near Attica, was one of the principal seaports. An old feud had existed between the people of Athens and Ægina, the effect of which was felt for many years. Taking advantage of this feeling of enmity, Themistocles found little difficulty in persuading his countrymen to make war on their powerful neighbors, whose ships rendered them masters of the sea. His real object was to prepare a navy to resist the Persians, but he thought best not to say so, knowing that little attention would have been paid to him if he had. The Persians at a distance did not seem formidable, nor was there much probability that they would so soon recover from Marathon as to make another attack. So long as he accomplished his desire, Themistocles was satisfied to keep his opinions to himself.

A large sum of money was required for ship-building, and this is how Themistocles managed to raise it. In the public treasury there happened to be an ample surplus that had been accumulating for many years from the rich silver-mines of Larium. A proposition was on foot to distribute this fund among the Athenians; but Themistocles used his utmost efforts in order to persuade them to appropriate it for the purpose of increasing their maritime power. He succeeded, and in a very short time had at his command a formidable fleet of two hundred ships, well equipped to resist any invaders.

There was at that time no other man in Greece who could have accomplished so much. Themistocles loved his country, and possessed all the brilliant qualities of a great statesman, yet he had his faults. His passion for distinction has never been surpassed, and he was so avaricious that he would accept bribes, and stoop to various other dishonest actions from mere love of gain. Most of his countrymen were displeased at his fondness for display, which in a man of humble birth was regarded as an evidence of bad taste. On the other hand, he won the hearts of the lower classes by the pains he took to salute each person by name, as though he were deserving of special consideration. Besides, he was just in his decisions when business transactions were submitted to him, and generally settled them satisfactorily. So anxious was he for notoriety, that long before he became famous he prevailed upon a young musician who played well upon the lyre to practise at his house, that people might inquire who lived there, and seek for admittance. Later, he appeared at the Olympic games in a splendid equipage, furnished his tent gorgeously, and gave the most sumptuous entertainments, all for the purpose of making himself the observed of all observers.

At this period the Athenians had great taste for tragedy, which had been brought to a high standard. Prizes were given to those who produced the best, and no pains was spared to make them attractive. Themistocles competed for one of these prizes, produced the play entirely at his own expense, and won. In memory of his success he put up this inscription: "Themistocles exhibited the tragedy; Phrynichus composed it; Adimantus presided."

We have said that Themistocles and Aristides frequently quarrelled. Two men, so entirely opposite in character, could scarcely be good friends. Aristides was the inferior in ability, but vastly superior in honesty and integrity. His one desire was to benefit his country, regardless of party or self-interest, and for this very reason he gained enemies among those who managed public affairs. His uprightness and justice were acknowledged by all who knew him, and he received the surname of "the Just." But he always opposed Themistocles, and in the course of three or four years they became such bitter enemies that he was banished by ostracism, his rival being so popular as to influence the multitude to this end.

Banishment by ostracism was managed in this way: every citizen took a piece of pot or shell, on which he wrote the name of the person he would have banished. These were collected and counted by the magistrates; if the number amounted to six thousand they were sorted, and the man whose name appeared the greatest number of times had to leave Athens within ten days and remain in exile ten years.

Xerxes had succeeded Darius as king of Persia by this time. He was not a man of much ability or experience, but he was anxious for military glory, and so resolved to invade Greece, as his father would have done a second time, had he lived long enough. It was fortunate for the Greeks that Xerxes was such an inferior general as he proved himself, for he came with a mighty army, the sight of which spread terror among the enemy. But he passed the winter at Sardis, and during that season gave the Greeks a chance to prepare for resistance.

Themistocles undertook the command of the Athenian forces, and tried to persuade the people to go out on the ships and fight the Persians as far away from the coast of Greece as possible; but this plan met with so much opposition that he joined his army with that of the Lacedæmonians and marched to the Pass of Tempe, which forms the entrance to northern Greece. This was found to be an unsafe position, being open to attack from the rear, so the army returned without having accomplished anything; and then the Thessalians and all the northern Greeks as far as Bœotia, being left to themselves, went over to Xerxes.

Thus the proposition of Themistocles to fight by sea gained favor, and he was sent to guard the Straits of Artemisium, which form the entrance to the Gulf of Thessaly. When the forces assembled there arose a dispute as to who should take the lead. The Lacedæmonians wanted to command, and to have Eurybiades for their admiral. Themistocles showed his wisdom by persuading his countrymen to yield, and assured them that if in this war they behaved like men they need not fear, but all the Greeks would be willing enough to submit to them for the future.

THEMISTOCLES

Eurybiades was astonished when the Persian armada hove in sight, for he had never seen such an array of ships; but when he was informed that two hundred more were coming around the island of Sciathus his heart misgave him, and he determined to retire to a position where the land army and the fleet of the Greeks could unite. The fights that took place in the Straits of Eubœa were not so important as to decide the war, but they served as experience to the Greeks, which proved of great benefit to them. They had shown themselves brave soldiers on land, but it remained to be seen what sort of seamen they would become.

While defending the Eubœan straits the Greeks resolved to make a stand at Thermopylæ also. This was a narrow pass, about a mile in length, lying between the lofty mountains of Œta, and considered, after Tempe, the most convenient point for defence against an invading army. A small band of Spartans under Leonidas was sent there. History tells us of the brave resistance they made against the mighty hosts of Xerxes, and how they were overcome at last by the treachery of a Malian, who led the Persian army by a secret path across the mountains.

When the dreadful news was brought to Artemisium that King Leonidas and all his soldiers were slain, and that Xerxes was master of the passages leading into Greece, a panic seized upon the army, and they returned to the interior of the country.

Xerxes advanced, burning and ransacking the cities of the Phocians without mercy. The Athenians were desirous that the northern Greeks should unite with them and make a stand at Bœotia for the protection of Attica; but they were intent upon defending Peloponnesus, and resolved to gather all their forces within that district, and build a wall from sea to sea across the narrow isthmus which connects it with central Greece, and thus defend themselves. The Athenians were very angry at being deserted by their confederates, because they knew how useless it would be to attempt to fight the numerous army of Xerxes alone. There seemed nothing left for them but to leave their city and take to their ships; but this plan met with opposition from the majority, who declared that they could not hope for success if they forsook the temples of their gods and exposed the tombs of their ancestors to the fury of the enemy.

All the arguments that Themistocles brought to bear were of no avail, so he employed oracles to convert the people to his opinions. The Dragon of Minerva suddenly disappeared from her temple, and, at the suggestion of Themistocles, the priests made it known that the offerings set before the holy place remained untouched, and that the goddess had forsaken the city and preceded the army to the sea. The voice of the oracle constantly urged the people to trust to walls of wood, which meant ships, and pronounced the island of Salamis divine, which was interpreted as meaning that the Athenians would meet with good fortune there. Superstition prevailed, and it was soon settled that all who were old enough to fight should embark, and that the women, aged men, children, and slaves should be removed for protection to Trœzene.

It was heart-rending to see the whole city of Athens deserted, and the cries and sobs of the women and children who were leaving their husbands, brothers, and fathers, perhaps forever, filled the air. Even the domestic animals were objects of pity, as they ran about the town, and in their dumb way showed their eagerness to be carried along with their masters. One poor dog jumped into the sea, and swam beside the ship all the way to Salamis, falling dead from sheer exhaustion as he reached the shore. In spite of these pathetic scenes the Athenians, who were going forth to fight, stood firm and resolute.

The Trœzenians offered a hearty welcome to those who were placed in their care, and passed a vote that they should be maintained at the public expense. The children were free to gather fruit wherever they pleased; they had many other privileges besides, and school-masters were provided to attend to their education.

Themistocles showed himself wise by recalling Aristides at this time. He had been banished before the war, but it was clear that the people wanted him back, and even feared that to revenge himself he might be induced to join the Persian army, which would have been a dreadful blow to the cause of Greece. A decree was therefore proposed recalling all those who were banished, so that they might give aid to their fellow-citizens in this trying period.

Now when the fleet had assembled off Salamis, Eurybiades grew faint-hearted, and wanted to set sail for the Isthmus, where the Peloponnesian army was encamped, but Themistocles would not listen to such a thing, and his opposition led to a serious quarrel. Some sided with one commander, some with the other, but Themistocles boldly maintained his ground, and while he spoke an owl was seen, which after flying to the right of the ship came and perched on top of the mast. This was considered a happy omen, for the owl was sacred to Minerva, the goddess of the Athenians, and everybody eagerly prepared at once to fight. The enemy's fleet advanced and covered the neighboring coasts, while Xerxes himself was observed marching towards the shore with his land forces. Such a prodigious armament struck terror to the hearts of the Greeks, and many of them gave orders to their pilots to steer that very night for the Isthmus.

Determined to retain the position he held in the straits, and not to allow any of his confederates to desert, Themistocles contrived a stratagem for carrying out his plans.

There was in the Athenian army a Persian captive named Sicinus, who was warmly attached to Themistocles and ready to obey any of his commands. Themistocles sent him secretly to Xerxes, with the assurance that the commander of the Athenians desired to join the Persian army, and was therefore the first to inform him of the intended flight of the Greeks. He begged the king not to let them escape, but advised him to take advantage of their confusion to attack and destroy their whole navy while they were at a distance from the land army. Of course Themistocles did not intend to turn traitor to his country, but Xerxes was completely deceived by his message, and ordered the commanders of his fleet to set out at once with two hundred ships, and so surround all the islands as to prevent the Greeks from escaping, and added that the rest of the ships would follow at their leisure.

Aristides was one of the first to observe this movement of the enemy, and at great personal risk made his way to the tent of Themistocles to inform him of it. The Athenian commander was touched by the generosity of the man whom he had long regarded as an enemy, and told him of the message he had sent to Xerxes, at the same time urging him to entreat the Greeks to stay and fight. Aristides approved of the stratagem, and went among the different officers of the navy

THEMISTOCLES

with words of encouragement and hope; but they would not believe that the enemy's vessels were upon them until a galley deserted from the Persians and came in to confirm the report that all the straits and passages were threatened. Then the Greeks were forced to fight whether they would or not, and this was just what Themistocles had striven for.

As soon as day dawned, Xerxes had a golden throne placed on an eminence, and seated himself thereon to watch the movements of his army. Secretaries stood near to write down all the details of the fight which was to decide the fate of Greece. Xerxes and the princes who were with him felt sure of victory; but there was one person present who saw at what a disadvantage the large Persian ships would be in the narrow straits of Salamis, and that was Artemisia, the Queen of Halicarnassus, who tried to dissuade the king from engaging; but her arguments had little weight, and the order for attack was given.

Meanwhile, Themistocles had not only chosen the most advantageous place, but he also managed not to begin the fight until the time of day when the fresh breeze from the open sea began to blow and produce breakers in the channel. They were not inconvenient to the Greek ships, but rendered the cumbrous Persian ones quite unmanageable. The Greeks kept their eyes fixed on their commander, not only because they were eager to follow his lead, but because at the very beginning of the battle Ariamenes, brother and admiral to Xerxes, began to oppose his ship and to shower down darts and arrows upon it, as though he had been stationed on a castle. After a time the Persian and the Athenian galley stuck their prows into each other so that they were fastened together. Then Ariamenes attempted to jump on the Greek vessel, but he was run through the body with a pike and thrust into the sea. His corpse was recognized and picked up by Artemisia, who commanded one of the ships.

Although the Persians had a tremendous fleet, only a part of it could enter the narrow arm of the sea at a time, and their ships fell foul of one another. We need not follow all the details of the battle of Salamis, one of the most memorable in history; it is only necessary to say that when the day declined the Greeks had gained a complete victory. The Queen of Halicarnassus distinguished herself by such daring deeds of bravery that day that Xerxes, indignant at his defeat, contemptuously exclaimed, "My men are become women, and my women men!"

Now Themistocles and Aristides had a consultation, and decided that the best thing they could do was to try to get Xerxes and his army out of Greece, for if permitted to remain there they would certainly seek to avenge their recent defeat. The sagacity of Themistocles was again brought into play to accomplish this object. Among his captives was one of the king's slaves, named Arnaces, who was sent to his master with this message: "That the Greeks, who were now victorious, were determined to sail to the Hellespont and destroy the bridge of boats there; but that Themistocles, being a friend to Xerxes, sent to reveal this secret to him in order that he might hasten to his own dominions before it was too late, promising that he would cause delays and hinder his confederates from pursuing him."

Xerxes was so frightened that he hurried out of Greece with all the speed in his power, never for a moment doubting that Themistocles was really his friend.

The city of Ægina was considered to have done the best service in the war, and to Themistocles was awarded the prize among the commanders. The Lacedæmonians took him with them to Sparta, where they rewarded Eurybiades, their commander, for bravery, but crowned the Athenian general with an olive-wreath for his wisdom and good management. They also presented him with the best chariot in the city, and sent an escort of three hundred young men with him to the border of their country. The next time he appeared at the Olympic games everybody stared at him, and he was pointed out to the strangers present as a hero. He was so gratified by the clapping of hands that greeted his appearance that he confessed to his friends he then reaped the fruit of all his labors for Greece.

Many anecdotes are told of Themistocles which prove how fond he was of having honors shown him. When he was chosen admiral by his countrymen he would not quite arrange anything until the day of sailing, so that he might appear full of important business and seem powerful to those who stood about him. When he saw the bracelets and necklaces on the dead bodies cast ashore by the sea after the battle of Salamis, he said to a friend, "You may take these things, for you are not Themistocles." To Antiphates, a handsome young man, who had once treated him with disdain, but was ready to court him when he became famous, he said, "Time, young man, has taught us both a lesson." He declared that the Athenians did not honor or admire him, but made a sort of plane-tree of him, under which they would shelter themselves in a storm, and which they would rob of its leaves and branches when fine weather appeared again.

An officer who thought he had done the state some service boastingly compared his actions with those of Themistocles, whereupon the latter answered him with this fable: "Once upon a time a dispute arose between a feast-day and the day after the feast. Said the latter, 'I am full of hurry and bustle, whereas with you folks enjoy quietly everything already provided.' 'Very true,' returned the feast-day; 'but if I had not been before you, you would not be at all.' So if Themistocles had not come first, where would you be now?" When his own son persuaded his mother, and through her means himself also, to grant a favor, Themistocles said, laughingly, "You, child, are greater than any man in Greece; for the Athenians command the Greeks, I command the Athenians, your mother commands me, and you command your mother."

When two young men courted his daughter at the same time, he preferred the worthy man to the rich one, saying, "I would rather have you marry a man without money than money without a man."

Some one offered to teach Themistocles the art of memory, but he answered, "Ah, teach me rather the art of forgetting; for I often remember what I would not, and cannot forget what I would."

There are many more anecdotes related of this great general, but we have quoted enough to show that his ready wit equalled his military skill.

Having secured Athens from all danger of an immediate attack, Themistocles next devoted himself to rebuilding and fortifying it. He did the same to the harbor of Piræus, which provided sea-coast accommodations for the city. Then he had another scheme, which shows the immoral side of his character. He alluded to it before a large assembly of the citizens, but said at the same time that he could not explain it in detail before so many people. "Then communicate it to Aristides alone," they said; "and if he approve, we agree to carry it into execution." This is a proof of the confidence still reposed in Aristides, in spite of the injustice and ingratitude that had been shown him. Themistocles took him aside and told him that what he wished was to destroy the whole Greek fleet that had gone into harbor for the winter, his object being to make the Athenians stronger on the sea than their neighbors. Aristides was shocked at such a shameful proposition, and told his fellow-citizens "that the enterprise which Themistocles had in view would indeed be advantageous, but most dishonorable." The Athenians then ordered it to be abandoned at once.

After that Themistocles was guilty of accepting bribes and of resorting to other dishonorable deeds, which made him so unpopular that he was publicly reprimanded; thereupon he haughtily reminded the citizens of the numerous services he had performed in the interest of his country, and of the gratitude due him. At length his pride and vanity became unbearable, and he was banished by ostracism.

He proceeded to Argos, and shortly after his arrival there certain papers found among the effects of one Pausanias, who had been put to death for the crime of treason, cast suspicion upon the banished general. He was accused, and his enemies were so eager for his punishment that they refused to listen to the defence which he made by letter, and despatched officers to fetch him back to Athens to stand a trial. But he had been warned in time to make his escape, and, after wandering about under an assumed name in disguise, he at last reached Persia in safety.

By that time Xerxes was dead, and his son Artaxerxes had succeeded him on the throne. Themistocles first sought an interview with Artabanus, a military officer high in command, to whom he said, "I am a Greek, and have travelled a great distance on purpose to speak with your king about matters of the greatest importance to Persia." The officer replied that if he was willing to conform to the customs of the country, and to prostrate himself before the king, he might be permitted to see him and speak to him. Themistocles promised to do so. "But," returned Artabanus, "who shall we say you are?" "Nobody must know that before the king himself," answered Themistocles. Thereupon he was introduced to the royal presence, and upon being questioned, answered through an interpreter in the following contemptible manner: "The man who now stands before you, O king, is Themistocles, the Athenian, an exile, persecuted by the Greeks. The Persians have suffered much by me, but it must not be forgotten that after I had saved my own country I did them a service. I come to you now prepared to receive your favor and to offer my submission. Believe what my enemies have said of the services I have done the Persians, and make use of the opportunity my misfortunes afford you to show your generosity rather than to satisfy your revenge. If you save me, you save your suppliant; if you kill me, you destroy the enemy of Greece."

The king made no answer, but he congratulated himself upon his good fortune, and prayed secretly that the gods might always influence his enemies thus to drive off their ablest men. In his sleep that night he was heard to exclaim three times, as in an ecstasy of delight, "Themistocles, the Athenian, is mine!"

The next day the exile was ordered to appear before the king and his council. After graciously saluting him, Artaxerxes spoke thus: "I owe you two hundred talents, for that is the price I set upon your head, and, as you have delivered yourself up to me, it is but just that you should receive the reward. In addition I promise you my protection. Now speak freely, and let us hear what you have to propose with regard to Greece."

"A man's discourse is like a piece of tapestry, which when spread out displays figures that were concealed among its folds; therefore let me have time," returned the Athenian. This flowery, mysterious manner of expressing one's self was customary among Oriental nations, and the king was so pleased with the bearing of Themistocles that, although he did not understand him, he granted him all the time he desired. Themistocles demanded a year, and during that period he studied the Persian language until he could converse without an interpreter. He won the king's favor besides, and became so popular at court that the nobility grew jealous of the favors that were shown him. The king took him hunting, talked with him freely, and introduced him to the queen-mother, who honored him with her confidence.

Once he was sent on business of importance to the sea-coast, and stopped at a city called Leontocephalus, or Lion's Head. The governor of Upper Phrygia hated him, and engaged some men to kill him; but he was saved in this way: he was taking a nap one afternoon, when the mother of the gods appeared to him in a dream and said, "Beware, Themistocles, of the Lion's Head, lest the lion crush you. For this warning I require your daughter for my servant."

Themistocles awoke in terror, devoutly returned thanks to the goddess, and left the place of danger. As he travelled on, one of his horses that carried his tent happened to fall into a river, and at night the servants spread out the wet hangings to dry. The would-be assassins mistook these hangings in the moonlight for the tent of Themistocles, and advanced with drawn swords, expecting to kill their victim while he slept. But they were repulsed by his servants, who killed some and captured others. In honor of the goddess who had saved his life Themistocles built a temple at Magnesia, and appointed his daughter priestess of it. After that he behaved with great prudence, and lived for a long time at Magnesia in peace and security.

This was not to continue, however, for Egypt revolted, the Athenians took sides with her, and Cimon, the great general, was master of the seas. Then the King of Persia called on Themistocles to make good his promise and help him to oppose Greece. That he could not do, for he still loved his country too well to fight against her. He resolved, therefore, to put an end to his existence. Having offered sacrifices to the gods, he assembled his friends, bade them farewell, took a dose of poison, and expired almost immediately.

The people of Magnesia erected a handsome monument to his memory, and the king's admiration was excited to such a degree by the cause and manner of his death that special honors and privileges were granted to his descendants.

ARISTIDES

IN the life of Themistocles there is a great deal said concerning the character of Aristides, and comparing the traits of the two Greek statesmen. They were never friends. Some historians say that the first ill feeling between them arose on account of a love-affair, both, when very young, forming an attachment for the same girl. She died, but the rival lovers never forgave each other.

When they grew older and took prominent parts in public affairs, Aristides was so honest and Themistocles so tricky that they could never agree on any point. Once when Aristides had carried a case against Themistocles, who had fought hard for it, he said, "The affairs of the Athenians can never prosper unless they throw Themistocles and me into the Barathrum." This was a deep pit into which criminals were thrown headlong. Aristides did not mean to call himself or his opponent a criminal, but it was his belief that so long as two men guided by such different principles controlled Athenian politics there could be no peace or prosperity.

He was a thoroughly conscientious man, and always put himself and his personal interests out of the question in the cause of right. Even when one of his enemies was about to be condemned for a criminal action, Aristides stood up and begged the judges to give the man a chance to defend himself. When he was called upon at one time to settle a quarrel between two private citizens, one of them tried to influence him by telling him what injurious things the other had done to him. "Tell me rather, good friend," he said, "what wrong he has done you; for it is your cause, not my own, that I am judging."

Aristides, upon being appointed treasurer of the public funds, accused those who had held the office before him of having stolen some of the money. Thereupon Themistocles, who was among the accused, turned the tables upon him, and got him condemned. But the Court of the Areopagus defended him, and not only secured his release from the fine imposed, but had him chosen treasurer again. He then changed his tactics, and allowed those who were under him to steal the public money without appearing to know it. This made him very popular with the few who were benefited, and when his term of office expired they begged that he might be reappointed. When this was about to be done he thus addressed the Athenians: "While I managed your money like an honest man I was loaded with abuse, but now when I suffer a lot of thieves to rob you I become a good citizen; but I assure you I am more ashamed of the present honor than I was of the former disgrace, for I see that you prefer to oblige bad men rather than to take proper care of the treasury." Thus he turned the dishonest men against him, but gained the praise and confidence of the worthy ones.

It was about this time that a Persian fleet arrived at Marathon and began to destroy all the neighboring country. Miltiades was appointed first in command of the Athenian forces to oppose the enemy, and Aristides second. It was the custom for the generals to serve in turn, but Aristides cared so much more for the welfare of his country than he did for personal glory that, feeling Miltiades to be a more able general than himself, he gave up his right, and showed the inferior officers that he considered it no disgrace to submit to the directions of wise and able men. His example was followed by the other generals, and Miltiades took the whole command. Themistocles and Aristides fought together with such success that the Persians were driven back to their ships. The Greeks then hurried to Athens, fearing an attack there while the city was not properly defended. Aristides was left at Marathon to watch the prisoners and the spoils, and although there was much gold and silver scattered about, as well as rich garments and other booty, he neither touched them himself nor permitted his men to do so.

In course of time Aristides was called "the Just," because it was his love of justice that had more weight with the common people than any of his other virtues. Strange to say, this very surname which added to his popularity at first caused his unhappiness later, for Themistocles became envious of the weight attached to his decisions, and raised a report that Aristides was trying to abolish courts and get supreme power in his own hands. This made the Athenians so uneasy that Aristides was banished by ostracism, a proceeding that we have explained in the life of Themistocles.

When the people were inscribing their names on the shells for the ostracism, an ignorant countryman, who did not know Aristides and could not write, handed his shell to him with the request that he would write 'Aristides' upon it. "Has Aristides ever injured you?" asked the good man. "No, and I do not even know him," answered the countryman, "but it annoys me to hear him called 'the Just' all the time." Without another word Aristides wrote his name upon the shell. As he quitted Athens he raised his hands towards heaven, and prayed that his countrymen might never see the day which should force them to remember Aristides.

Three years later he was recalled because Xerxes marched into Attica, and it was feared that Aristides might go over to the enemy and induce many of his countrymen to do likewise. But he was incapable of so base a deed, and after his recall he risked his life one night by going to the tent of Themistocles with a piece of important news. "Let us lay aside our childish enmity now," he said, "and work together to save Greece. You may rule, but let me advise you to engage the enemy in the straits without delay, for the sea all around us is covered with their fleet; we cannot escape, so let us fight and prove ourselves men of courage." Themistocles replied, "I would not be outdone by you in generosity, Aristides; my future actions shall be as noble as this one of yours." He then revealed to him the stratagem he had planned, which was to send a messenger to inform the Persians that the Greeks were going to quit the straits of Salamis, and if they desired to crush them there was no time to lose. Aristides gave his hearty approval, and did all he could to aid Themistocles.

Perceiving a body of the enemy collected on a small island in the straits near Salamis, he selected the bravest of his countrymen, and went there in small boats. Challenging the Persians to battle, he slew all except a few distinguished persons, whom he took prisoners and sent to Themistocles. He received high praise for this great service, and Themistocles sought his advice still further as soon as the battle was over. He said, "You have performed a remarkable deed, Aristides, but much more remains to be done. If we sail quickly to the Hellespont and destroy the bridge there, the enemy will not be able to escape, and we can conquer them completely."

"Let us not think of such a thing," returned Aristides; "it will be better for us to devise some means of driving the Persians out of Greece without delay; for should we destroy their only means of escape, they will fight so desperately that we shall be made to suffer no end of misery." Themistocles saw the wisdom of this advice, and his busy brain soon conceived a plan not only for getting rid of the enemy, but at the same time for placing himself in a favorable light before the king. This is what he did. He sent one of the prisoners secretly to Xerxes, to inform him that the Greeks were preparing to advance to the Hellespont and destroy the bridge, but that out of regard for his royal person Themistocles was doing the very best he could to prevent it. The message had the desired effect, for Xerxes was so terrified that he hurried home, leaving Mardonius, his commander-in-chief, behind, with a force of three hundred thousand of his best troops.

Now, although the king was out of the way, the Greeks still had much to fear, for with such an army at his command Mardonius was very powerful, and constantly made his presence felt by the threatening messages he sent the various Greek tribes. By the king's advice he tried to win over the Athenians, and offered, if they would take no further share in the war, to provide them with plenty of money, rebuild their city, and make them sole rulers of Greece.

The Lacedæmonians were so afraid they might accept the tempting proposal that they sent ambassadors to offer protection and support to their wives and children so long as the war should last. It is true that the Athenians were in dire distress, having lost their city, but they understood the offer, and were so indignant that they sent the following reply: "We could forgive the Persians, who worship gold, for supposing that we might be bought, but we are offended that Lacedæmonians, who are, like ourselves, Greeks, should imagine us capable of deserting our country under any pretext whatsoever. We are poor and wretched, but we would not exchange all the treasures either above or under ground for the liberty of Greece." This was dictated by Aristides. To the Persians he said, pointing to the heavens, "As long as that sun shines, so long will the Athenians carry on war with the Persians for their country, which has been ruined, and for their temples, which have been profaned and burnt."

When Mardonius entered Attica the second time, Aristides met him with an army, and in the first skirmish that ensued Masistius was killed. This was a terrible blow to the Persians, because Masistius was their cavalry general, and a man of remarkable courage, strength, and personal beauty. When he fell and they saw that he was mortally wounded, they fled and left the Greeks masters of the field. Their loss had not been great in numbers, but they could have spared many in place of their general, for whom they mourned very deeply. They filled the air with their lamentations, and as a sign of mourning cut off their hair, as well as the manes of their horses and mules.

After this engagement there was no fighting for a long time, because both the Persian and the Greek priests announced that all the omens promised victory to the side that stood ready for defence, but defeat to the one that made the attack. At length Mardonius felt obliged, in spite of the omens, to fall upon the Greeks, because his stock of provisions was getting very low, and he saw fresh troops joining the enemy every day and increasing their strength. So one night he gave orders for an attack to be made at break of day, thus expecting to take the Greeks unawares; and he would have succeeded had it not been for the warning the Athenians got in this way: at midnight a man approached the Grecian camp on horseback, and bade the sentinels call Aristides, to whom he had something important to say. Aristides came immediately, and the man spoke thus: "I am Alexander, King of Macedon, who for the friendship I bear you have exposed my life to save you from a surprise; for Mardonius will give you battle to-morrow, not because he expects to succeed, but because his provisions are scarce. The soothsayers give him no encouragement, but he must either risk a battle or see his whole army perish from want. Prepare yourself, but do not reveal what I have said to you."

Aristides thanked the king, and promised to tell nobody until after the battle except Pausanias, who was commander-in-chief.

As Alexander rode off, therefore, he hastened to the tent of Pausanias, who, on receiving the warning, summoned his captains and gave orders for the army to be put in battle-array.

The Athenians felt certain of victory. "Let us fight," they said, "not only in defence of our country, but that the trophies of Marathon and Salamis may belong to the people of Athens, and not to Miltiades alone." The first day passed without decisive action, and during the night the Grecian camp was removed to a spot that offered greater advantages. The Lacedæmonians made no alteration in their position, and they were the first to be attacked. For a while they allowed themselves to be slain without offering resistance, because Pausanias, who was sacrificing at a distance, could get no favorable signs, though he prayed aloud and entreated the gods with tears in his eyes. Suddenly the soothsayers announced a change and gave promise of victory. Then, with shouts and yells of delight, the Lacedæmonians rushed to the fight like wild beasts, so furious were their actions. They struck their pikes into the breasts and faces of the enemy, and killed many, though they, too, fought desperately.

Meanwhile, the Athenians, hearing of the engagement, marched back to assist the Lacedæmonians just as they were beating off the Persians. A Spartan named Arimnestus killed Mardonius by a blow on the head with a stone, the Persian camp was taken, and their men were slain by thousands.

The Greeks had gained a splendid victory, but it nearly caused their ruin, because both the Athenians and the Spartans claimed the honor of the day, and would have settled the question at the point of the sword. But Aristides did all he could to pacify the generals, and at last persuaded them to leave it to the judgment of the whole country. A council was called, and it was decided that in order to prevent a civil war the honor should be conferred neither on the Spartans nor on the Athenians, but on the Platæans. Aristides yielded at once, and Pausanias followed his example.

Both the Spartans and the Athenians built temples in honor of the victory, and sent to consult the oracle at Delphi as to what sacrifice they should offer. The answer directed them to build an altar to Jupiter, the Deliverer, but not to offer any sacrifice upon it until all the fires in the country had been put out, because they had been polluted by the barbarians. Pure fire was then to be brought from Delphi. The Greek generals visited every part of the country, and caused the fires to be extinguished, while a man named Euchidas hastened to Delphi for a fresh supply. On arriving there he purified himself with water, put a crown of laurel on his head, took fire from the altar, and hurried back to Platæa, where he arrived before sunset. But he had exhausted himself by travelling so fast, and had only time to salute his fellow-citizens and deliver the sacred fire, when he fell down dead. A monument was erected to him in the Temple of Diana, on which was inscribed, "Here lies Euchidas, who went to Delphi and back in one day."

When the first general assembly of the Greeks was called after peace had been restored, Aristides proposed that priests from all the states should meet at Platæa each year to offer sacrifices to the gods, and that every fifth year the Eleutheria, or Games of Freedom, should be celebrated there; also that ships, men, and horses should be annually supplied for war against the Persians, but that the Platæans should devote themselves to religious services, and never again stain their hands with human blood. This became a law, and the yearly procession for the sacrifice began at break of day. First a trumpeter appeared sounding the advance; then followed chariots loaded with myrrh and garlands; next a black bull, followed by young men carrying wine and milk in large vessels, jars of oil, and precious ointments. No slaves could appear in this procession, because it took place in honor of men who died fighting for freedom. Last of all came the chief magistrate of Platæa. It was considered unlawful at other times for this dignitary to touch iron or to wear any but a white garment, but on this occasion his robe was purple, and he carried a sword and a large jug. Drawing water from a spring, he washed with his own hands the little pillars of the monuments over the dead, and rubbed them with essences. Then he killed the bull upon a pile of wood, brayed to Jupiter and Mercury, and invited the brave men who had fallen in the cause of Greece to the banquet, at the same time filling a bowl with wine, and saying, "I present this bowl to the men who died for the liberty of Greece." This was the ceremony observed by the Platæans.

Another law that Aristides caused to be passed was that the Archons should be chosen from among all the Athenians, because he thought that the commons should have a voice in the government as well as the upper classes. As we have said, the people had great regard for the judgment and honesty of Aristides, and were always willing to refer to his decision. Once when Themistocles told the assembly that he had a plan to propose for the benefit of Athens, which ought to be kept secret, he was requested to tell it to Aristides. It was to burn the whole fleet of the other Greeks, so that the Athenians might become supreme rulers. Aristides was shocked at such a dishonorable proposition, and assured his countrymen "that nothing could be more advantageous than the project of Themistocles, nor anything more unjust." So the matter was dropped without the particulars being given, simply because Aristides had pronounced against it.

Eight years later Aristides was sent again to fight the barbarians, sharing the command with Cimon. His gentle, courteous manners formed such a striking contrast to the harshness and severity of the Spartan commanders, that in course of time several of the Greek nations placed themselves under him and joined the Athenians.

Aristides made himself more popular still by lessening the taxes all over the country. Notwithstanding his great influence and power, he was always poor, but he was prouder of poverty than of his trophies.

ARISTIDES

He died at Athens, well advanced in years and greatly lamented by his countrymen. Great honors were shown to his memory, and a monument was erected to him after his death.

CIMON

CIMON had the misfortune to lose his parents at so early an age that his education was seriously neglected, and he became in consequence a very immoral young man. But he was blessed with a noble, generous disposition, besides other good qualities, which led to his becoming later in life the ablest general of his day. He was as brave as Miltiades, his father, his judgment was considered as good as that of Themistocles, and he was more upright and honest than either. Cimon was a handsome man, being tall and well built, and he possessed what was looked upon as a great adornment among the Greeks of his time, a profusion of thick curls that covered his head and fell around his neck.

Miltiades left an unpaid fine, which his son felt bound in honor to settle, but he had not the means, and was sorely puzzled where to turn for them. It was his sister Elpinice who helped him out of the difficulty in this way. Callias, a rich Athenian, wanted to marry her, but could not get Cimon's consent; however, he secured it by promising in return to pay the fine, and so it was arranged.

When the Medes and Persians invaded Greece, Themistocles urged his countrymen to carry all their arms on shipboard and meet the enemy in the straits of Salamis. The Athenians were amazed at this advice, but Cimon immedi-

CIMON

ately went to the citadel with a bridle in his hand, which he offered to the goddess, to show that seamen were needed, not horsemen. Then, taking a shield, he proceeded to the seashore, and thus inspired his fellow-soldiers with so much confidence that they did not hesitate to follow him. He distinguished himself at the battle of Salamis, and ever after his countrymen loved and admired him very much, and when he became interested in politics he was preferred to Themistocles. Aristides prized him highly, and did what he could to advance him to the highest offices in the state, knowing that his honesty would prove a safeguard against the deceit and boldness of Themistocles.

When the Medes were driven out of Greece, Cimon was elected admiral, when he immediately set to work to make his seamen superior to all others. He was so kind and good to the allies that without fighting for it he gained the command of all Greece. He then sailed for Thrace with the forces, because the Persians had seized the city of Eïon and were giving the Greeks in the neighborhood a great deal of annoyance. He defeated the Persians in battle, shut them up within the walls of the town, then set upon the Thracians and drove them out of the country to prevent their lending supplies to Eïon. Thereupon Butes, who commanded the Persians, set fire to the town, and burned himself, his property, and all his relations.

So Cimon did not get much booty, but he put the Athenians in possession of the country about, and it was so rich and fertile that it was a good place for them to settle. The people of Athens were so pleased with what Cimon had done that they permitted him to erect three marble monuments, with appropriate inscriptions, in honor thereof. He next went to the island of Scyros, which was inhabited by the Dolopes, a nation of pirates, and took possession of it. That done, he recollected that Theseus, the ancient hero of Athens, had been treacherously killed on the island of Scyros by King Lycomedes, and that an oracle had requested the Athenians to take back his remains and to honor him as a demi-god. So Cimon set to work to search for the tomb, which he found after a long time. He put the remains of Theseus on his own vessel, and took them back to the home that hero had left eight hundred years before.

The Athenians were so gratified to have the bones of Theseus among them that they prepared games to celebrate the return. One feature of the entertainment was the reading of tragedies by Sophocles and Æschylus, two of the best composers of their day. These tragedies were written for this occasion, and it was universally agreed that Cimon should award the prize, though heretofore it had been decided by lot. Sophocles was the fortunate competitor, and Æschylus felt so distressed because he was not successful that he went to Sicily, where he spent the rest of his life.

An interesting story is told of Cimon by an ancient author, who chanced to meet him at a supper given at the house of Laomedon. After the meal Cimon was asked to sing; he amiably complied, and was much praised for his musical talent. Then the guests went further and recounted the various public actions he had performed, until, interrupting them, he said, "You omit the very exploit for which I give myself most credit." "What is it? tell us," urged one after another. Cimon then told the following story:

"When our Grecian allies had secured the prisoners at Sestos and Byzantium they gave me the privilege of dividing the booty. I therefore placed the prisoners in one lot, and their jewels, rich clothing, and arms in another, telling the allies to take their choice, and assuring them that we Athenians would be contented with what they left. Thinking that I had made an absurd division, they naturally chose the pile of costly chains, bracelets, rich gold collars, and robes of scarlet and purple, laughing in their sleeves at me for being satisfied with a lot of slaves, who, being unaccustomed to work, seemed perfectly useless. Not long after, the friends and countrymen of my prisoners offered large sums for their ransom; then I appeared in a more favorable light, for I got money enough for my slaves to purchase at least four months' provisions for my ships and to send a quantity besides to the Athenian treasury." The guests acknowledged that Cimon's management on that occasion was indeed worthy of praise.

In course of time Cimon became a rich man, and he deserved it, for he used his means, as every man of wealth ought to do, in giving pleasure to others. He ordered the fences of his fields and gardens to be removed, so that strangers, as well as his own countrymen, might help themselves to all the fruit and flowers they wanted. A supper of plain but good and plentiful food was spread at his house every evening, and all the poor citizens were invited to partake of it, so that instead of devoting time and thought to money-making they might turn their attention more to public affairs. When he took a walk, Cimon was always attended by a party of young men well clothed, and if they happened to meet an aged citizen in mean attire, one of them was ordered to exchange with him. They carried money besides, which was slipped into the hands of the better class of poor citizens who stood about in the market-place. This was done as privately as possible, so as not to give offence. It was said of the generous-hearted Cimon that he got riches that he might use them, and used them that he might get honor by them. This was the more remarkable, because all the men of his day, except Aristides and one or two others, enriched themselves out of the public money, but to the very end of his life Cimon's hands were clean, and he was never known to do or say anything for the sake of private gain. Once, when a certain Persian revolted from his king and fled to Athens, he sought the protection of Cimon and placed in his doorway two cups, one filled with gold and the other with silver coin. Cimon cast his eyes upon them, and then asked, with a smile, "Do you desire my hired services or my friendship?" "Your friendship, without doubt," was the reply. "Go, then, and take these things back," ordered Cimon; "for if I be your friend, your money will be mine whenever I need it."

Now the time came when the allies objected to furnishing more ships or men for the navy. They said that they were tired of war, and that as they were no longer troubled by a foreign enemy, they preferred to turn their attention to agriculture. But the Athenian generals would not listen to them, and tried to compel them to supply their quota by fines. Cimon, as soon as he was in power, adopted a different course; he took ships and money from the Grecian allies, but forced no man to serve in the army or to pay fines. The consequence was that in course of time they were more fitted for manufacturing and tilling the soil than for war. The Athenians, on the other hand, were compelled to serve on the ships, and became so thoroughly disciplined and so powerful that, instead of being their fellow-soldiers as before, the allies, by their own mistaken short-sightedness, became their subjects. This was when, on account of certain changes, they were forced to pay a tribute or fight, and they had lost all taste for the latter occupation.

No man ever did more than Cimon to humble the pride of the Persian king; for he was not content with driving him out of Greece, but followed him to Asia Minor, and in one day gained a victory by sea that surpassed Salamis in glory, and one by land that outdid Platæa. The Persian army was completely routed, and the king was so humbled that he made the celebrated treaty of peace by which he promised that his army should approach no nearer the Grecian Sea than a day's journey on horseback, and that none of his ships of war should appear between the Cyanean and the Chelidonian Isles.

The spoils of this war were publicly sold, and yielded so much that, besides raising the south wall of the citadel of Athens, the conquerors were able to lay the foundation for the long walls called the Legs. And this was no trifling matter, for they were built on soft, marshy ground, and it was necessary to sink great stones before a firm support could be attained. All this was done out of the money Cimon supplied, and he adorned the city besides. He laid out the fine places of exercise and resort, which became much frequented spots, he planted trees in the public parks, and made of the Academy, a barren, dirty field about two miles north of the city, a delightful grove, with shady walks and an open race-course. Later, the Academy became a favorite resort for philosophers, who pursued their studies there.

The Persians still kept possession of the Thracian Chersonese, but Cimon was sent to drive them out, which he did so successfully that he made the whole of the Chersonese the property of Athens; also the gold-mines on the island of

Thasus. This opened a passage for him into Macedon, but that nation being at peace with the Athenians, he returned home without following up his advantage; therefore he was accused of having been bribed by Alexander, the king of Macedon, but he made such an able defence of his conduct that he was acquitted.

His public life after that was devoted to keeping the common people in check, for they wanted to put down the nobility and get the government in their own hands. So long as his power was felt, all went well, but when war broke out again, and he was sent in command of the army, the ancient laws and customs were overthrown, and the populace, with Pericles at their head, insisted upon trying offenders themselves, instead of leaving them to the Court of Areopagus. This state of affairs grieved Cimon when he returned to Athens, but with the leaders to oppose him he was powerless to make any improvements. Besides, he had openly expressed admiration of the simplicity and temperance of the Spartans, and that had, for the moment, rendered him unpopular with his own countrymen.

Just then a most fearful earthquake visited Sparta. The ground opened in great chasms, and every house in the city except five was destroyed. It happened that the boys and young men of the city were exercising in the Portico at the time, but many of them had started in pursuit of a hare an instant before the shock occurred. The building fell, and killed all who were in it.

Archidamus, the ruler of Sparta, foreseeing a still greater danger, ordered the trumpets to be sounded to give an alarm to battle. At this all the citizens flocked about him armed, and it was well they did, for, taking advantage of the dreadful tumult, the Helots flocked in from the fields, bent on murdering the Spartans whom the earthquake had spared. Finding them armed, however, they repaired to the neighboring villages and declared open war. Thereupon the Lacedæmonians sent to Athens for aid, and Cimon was sent with an army. After restoring peace he returned home, but the Spartans had occasion to ask again for the assistance of the Athenian army. But when the Athenians arrived, instead of being received with open arms, they were accused of dishonorable designs, and sent back. Of course they were very angry at such an affront, and declared that they would have nothing further to do with the Spartans. Part of their indignation they vented on Cimon, because he had openly expressed admiration of their new enemy, and so banished him by ostracism for ten years. He soon had an opportunity, however, to prove that he preferred his country to all others, for when the Athenians went to fight the Lacedæmonians at Tanagra he joined them.

The Council of Five Hundred, on hearing that Cimon had joined his tribe, commanded the officers not to receive him: so he retired, after enjoining his companions to fight bravely. They were a hundred in number, and fought in a body until all were killed. The Athenians regretted the loss of such a brave set of men, and began to believe that they had perhaps wronged Cimon; for had he been so good a friend to the Spartans as they suspected, his tribe would scarcely have fought them so desperately. The following spring, therefore, when there was a prospect of another war, Cimon was recalled, because the Athenians loved their country so much that their first consideration always was the public good. He put an end to the war and restored peace between the two cities.

After a while the Athenians became restless, and, fearing that they might begin another war at home, Cimon fitted out two hundred galleys to make an attack on Egypt and Cyprus, wisely concluding that if his countrymen must fight it had better be against their natural enemies. When everything was ready, and the army on the point of embarking, Cimon dreamed that a furious dog barked at him, and mixed with the barking was a horrible kind of human voice, that uttered these words:

> "Come on, for thou shalt shortly be
> A pleasure to my whelps and me."

This dream was hard to interpret, but a man skilled in the art said that it presaged Cimon's death. "A dog," he said, "is the enemy of him he barks at, and one is always most a pleasure to one's enemies when one is dead; the mixture of the human voice with the barking signifies the Medes, whose army is made up of Greeks and barbarians."

Cimon had another bad omen. When he was sacrificing to Bacchus, and the priests were cutting the animal in pieces, a number of ants took up little congealed particles of blood and laid them about Cimon's great toe. He observed this only at the moment when the priests called his attention to the fact that the part of the liver known as the head was missing,—another very bad sign. Nevertheless, he could not withdraw, and so he set sail.

On arriving at Cyprus, Cimon sent messengers to consult the oracle at the Temple of Jupiter Ammon about some secret matters that have to this day never been made known. It is not known what their question was, but they got for answer "that Cimon was already in the land of the gods."

CIMON

Without understanding the meaning of what they had heard, the messengers returned to the army, and were surprised to hear that their general had died before they could have reached the temple.

Cimon's remains were carried to Athens and buried with honors, a monument being afterwards erected to his memory.

PERICLES

PERICLES was fortunate in being the son of people who were not only nobly born, but who knew the advantages of a good education for their child. They therefore took pains to have him well taught, and engaged learned masters for that purpose. It seems strange that a philosopher should give music lessons, but one who bore the name of Damon actually taught Pericles to play upon the lyre. To be sure, he was something besides a musician, for he gave his pupil instruction in politics as well, and in course of time he came to be regarded as such a dangerous meddler in state affairs that he was banished for ten years by ostracism.

Zeno, another learned man, taught Pericles natural philosophy, but it was Anaxagoras who did him the greatest service by developing the noblest traits of his character and instilling into his mind the best of principles. He taught his pupil how to find natural causes for events which frightened the ignorant, and showed him the absurdity of putting faith in anything supernatural.

The superiority of Pericles was felt by all who came in contact with him, and he had the gift of oratory, which was an immense advantage. He was so eloquent, and his voice was so well trained, that he could hold the attention of his hearers by the hour, and never failed to produce the effect he desired.

PERICLES

For many years Pericles took no decided stand in state affairs, but proved himself a brave soldier on the battlefield. When Themistocles was banished from Athens, however, and Aristides was dead, he came forward as the leader of the common people in opposition to Cimon, who headed the nobles.

He had never been a member of the Areopagus, which we know was composed of Archons, and he had not been appointed to that position. He lessened the power of that court, and had more trials conducted by the people. This was all very well so long as Pericles lived, but the effect was bad, because it encouraged bribery, and as those who had not been accustomed to power gained wealth in this way, they became extravagant and luxurious; this led in time to the downfall of the Athenian commonwealth.

We have mentioned the eloquence of Pericles and the influence it had on his hearers. Thucydides was once asked which was the better wrestler, Pericles or himself. He answered, "When I throw him, he says he was never down, and persuades the very spectators of his fall to believe him." His power was so great that he caused the banishment of Cimon, by accusing him of treasonably favoring the Lacedæmonians, though he had won several glorious victories, had filled Athens with money and spoils of war, and had made an able defence when the charge was brought.

Cimon was banished by ostracism, as we have seen in his life, but before the ten years expired a war broke out between the Athenians and the Lacedæmonians, and he entered the ranks with his countrymen, anxious to prove his loyalty. The friends of Pericles forced him to retire, but when the Athenians were defeated the majority clamored so loudly for the recall of Cimon that Pericles was obliged to gratify them. Besides, Cimon was so popular with the Lacedæmonians that he induced them to make peace, which Pericles, whom they hated, could not have done.

Cimon died at the isle of Cyprus while conducting a fleet, and then Thucydides, a near relation of his, was chosen to lead the opposition, partly because a wise politician was needed to prevent the power of Pericles from becoming absolute. Thucydides did not possess Cimon's talent for war, but he was an able statesman, and preserved the balance of power in the government by composing his party of men superior in rank and dignity. So there were two distinct parties in Athens, one called the people, the other the nobility.

The former was headed by Pericles, who did his best to retain his popularity by means of shows, games, feasts, and processions. His aim was to keep the populace amused and occupied. He sent out six vessels every year on an eight months' voyage, manned with a large number of citizens, who were paid for their services and were given this opportunity to become experienced seamen. Many colonies were established in the neighborhood by him, not only to keep foreign nations in awe, but to get rid of those Athenians who had no occupation and were likely to become mischievous in consequence.

The name of Pericles will be remembered forever in connection with the magnificent temples and public buildings he caused to be erected. In this way he gave employment to a vast number of mechanics and trades-people, who vied with one another in producing beautiful and good work. Thus money circulated freely among persons of every rank and condition, and a taste for magnificent designs was encouraged. The work was done well, and at the same time with marvellous rapidity.

The Thucydides party saw Athens daily growing in beauty, but they complained of the expense, and accused Pericles of wasting the public funds simply for the sake of opposing him. When the charge was brought, he rose in the open assembly and asked the people whether they thought he had laid out too much money. "A great deal too much," they replied. "Then let it be charged to my account," said Pericles, "and let the inscription on the buildings stand in my name."

He was a good judge of human nature, and knew perfectly well that the vanity of the Athenians would not let them submit to his having the glory alone, so he was not surprised when they exclaimed, "No, spend on; use what you please of the public treasure; spare no cost until the work is done!"

A final contest took place between Thucydides and Pericles to see which should be banished by ostracism. It resulted in the defeat of the former and the breaking up of his party, leaving Pericles in absolute command, which continued during forty years. He governed wisely, never stooped to a bribe, and influenced his people, often against their will, to take steps that he knew to be of advantage to them. With all his power, he did not enrich himself, yet he knew the value of money, and was careful that the sum his father had left him should not be wasted or lessened. He had a valuable servant, named Evangelus, who managed his private purse excellently, took care that the proper economy was practised in his household, and superintended the cultivation of his lands.

Pericles gave proof of a good heart once when his old tutor, Anaxagoras, fancying himself neglected, determined to put an end to his life. It was the custom among the ancients when they resolved, for one reason or another, to die, to cover up their heads and starve themselves. When Pericles heard of the resolution of Anaxagoras, he hastened to his house, entreated him to change his mind, and used every argument he could think of to make him do so. At last he asked what would be the fate of his administration if he should be deprived of so valuable a friend and counsellor. Then the old man uncovered his head, and said, "Ah, Pericles! those that have need of a lamp take care to supply it with oil." The ruler never forgot to provide for the sage after that.

Pericles gained confidence by the caution he displayed in military matters, for he would never engage in a fight unless sure of success, and he made so many expeditions with his powerful fleet that the kings and chiefs of the various barbarous nations in the neighborhood of the Euxine Sea were forced to feel the power and greatness of the Athenians. He was wise in restraining his countrymen from seeking foreign conquest, and always told them that they would find occupation enough at home if they would keep the Lacedæmonians in check. They were soon convinced that he was right, for various Greek nations invaded their territory, but they were so successful in repulsing them all, that the Lacedæmonians consented to a truce with them for thirty years.

As soon as this was done, Pericles ordered an expedition against Samos. The pretext he gave was, that when he had commanded the Samians to put an end to the war with the Milesians they had not obeyed; but it is probable that he was persuaded to take this step by Aspasia, who was a Milesian woman.

PERICLES

Aspasia was a very remarkable woman, and Pericles was in love with her. She was noted for her wisdom and political ability, and the most learned Athenians flocked to her house with their wives, considering it a privilege to be allowed to listen to her discourse. Socrates was one of her visitors, and Pericles often sought her advice.

He was victorious as usual, established a popular form of government in the island, and then returned to Athens, taking with him fifty of the principal men and fifty children as hostages. But the Samians revolted again, and by some secret means recovered their hostages. Then Pericles went to fight them a second time, gained another victory, took possession of their harbor, and laid siege to the city of Samos. But he made a mistake, as even the wisest will at times, and, leaving a small part of the fleet to guard the harbor, he sailed out to give battle to the Phœnicians, who were coming to the relief of the enemy. While he was gone, Melissus, a distinguished philosopher, persuaded his countrymen not to wait quietly and merely defend themselves when an attack came, but to rise and give battle to the Athenians. They did so, and gained the victory, taking many prisoners and destroying the greater part of the enemy's fleet.

No sooner did the sad news of defeat reach Pericles than he returned with eighty ships, completely routed the Samians, and blocked up their town by building a wall around it. But his men murmured at the waste of time, and it was so difficult to keep them from making an assault, that Pericles divided his army into eight parts, and ordered them to draw lots to see which should fight. The division that drew a white bean were to feast and enjoy themselves while the others fought. In allusion to this custom, a day of happiness and festivity was called a white day by the ancients. The siege lasted nine months before the Samians surrendered.

On his return home, Pericles had a very imposing ceremony performed in honor of those Athenians who had fallen in the Samian war, and delivered a remarkable funeral oration, which certain chroniclers state was composed by Aspasia.

Some time after this the Peloponnesian war broke out, and there can be no doubt that Pericles was the author of it. Many causes are given for this war, but it is not easy to discover the real one. Some historians say it was connected with Phidias, the great sculptor, who superintended the splendid buildings for which Athens is indebted to Pericles. They tell us that when the sculptor was engaged upon a statue of Minerva, he was accused by a rival who was envious of him of stealing some of the gold intended for the adornment of the statue. Pericles was a good friend to Phidias, and knew that the charge was false; he therefore ordered the gold to be weighed, and Phidias had so disposed of it around the figure of the goddess, which was of ivory, that the task was easy. The innocence of the sculptor was proved; but then fault was found with him for introducing a likeness of himself and of Pericles in a prominent position among the figures that adorned the walls of the Parthenon, or temple of Pallas, which was built under his supervision. The principal objection was made to a figure of Pericles, who is represented fighting an Amazon, because it gave a false idea of history, and took from Theseus, the founder of Athens, the glory of having combated with that race of warlike women.

Phidias was thrown into prison, where he died. Aspasia was accused of impiety, because she believed in one God and

PERICLES

had formed new opinions about the appearance of the heavenly bodies. Pericles pleaded for her, and she was acquitted, but he knew that he could not succeed so well in the case of his old tutor, Anaxagoras, who also believed in the unity of God, so he caused him to leave the city. Pericles now began to fear that, as his friends were attacked one after another, his turn would come next, and therefore to engage the public attention in a different quarter he hurried on the war. This he did by refusing certain demands made by the Lacedæmonians, who soon showed themselves resolved upon violating the Thirty Years' Truce in consequence.

They invaded Attica with a tremendous army under the command of Archidamus, and the Athenians would have given them battle on their own territory if Pericles had been willing, but we know that he never went into any engagement unless he felt sure of success. He did not feel so on this occasion, and said to his countrymen when they urged him, "When trees are trimmed they will grow again, but when men are cut off the loss is not easily repaired."

It required great firmness to withstand all the unjust charges that were brought against him, but Pericles would not move until he felt sure that he was right. He fitted out a hundred ships, and sent them against Peloponnesus, but he chose to stay and keep the reins of government in his own hands until he was rid of the enemy. However, after the fleet had gained some victories, he attacked Megara and laid the whole country in ruins. The war would soon have come to an end had it not been for the breaking out of a terrible pestilence, which carried off no less than a fourth of the population. It was a strange disease introduced from Asia, and the Athenian physicians did not know how to treat it. Those who were fortunate enough to recover from an attack were often entirely deprived of memory, and while the fever lasted many raved against Pericles, who they declared had brought on the epidemic by crowding such an immense number of people together during the summer. Of course those who lived outside the walls had flocked to the city for protection when the war began, and were penned up in huts and cabins, there not being houses enough to accommodate them. These had no occupation, and it was believed that their mode of life, which encouraged laziness and kept them indoors instead of in the pure open air to which they had been accustomed, had gone far towards increasing the plague.

Hoping to remedy the evil, and at the same time to annoy the enemy, Pericles manned a hundred and fifty ships, and when all were ready went on board his own galley prepared to lead them. Suddenly there was an eclipse of the sun. This was regarded by the superstitious soldiers as a bad omen, and caused the greatest consternation. Observing that his pilot was affected like the rest, Pericles took off his cloak, held it over the man's eyes, and asked him whether he found anything to terrify him in that, or considered it a bad omen. The pilot answered in the negative. "Then what is the difference between this and the other darkness, except that something bigger than my cloak has caused that one?"

Nothing remarkable resulted from this expedition, and the Athenians were so disappointed on account of it, and so many of them died of the epidemic, that Pericles was requested to resign his command. This was decided by vote, as well as the fine he was required to pay. Cleon, who afterwards became general, opposed Pericles more than any one else.

After a time the people began to see the importance of the policy of Pericles, and he was reelected general. But he was not long to enjoy his return to favor, for the loss of many friends by the epidemic, as well as of several members of his family, besides other serious domestic troubles, kept him at home for a year, and at last he was struck down with the disease himself. When he was dying, some of the principal citizens who sat by his bed spoke of his virtues, his exploits, his victories, and the splendid buildings he had erected in Athens while he was commander-in-chief. After listening in silence to all they said, he replied, "I am surprised that while you praise me for acts in which Fortune did her share, you take no notice of the greatest and most honorable thing of all, *that no Athenian through my means ever put on mourning.*"

This great general died in the third year of the Peloponnesian war, and his loss was greatly felt by his countrymen. Even those who chafed under his authority when he was alive were forced to acknowledge after he was gone that where severity was required no man had ever been more moderate, and that in cases where mildness would answer no man had better preserved his dignity. What had been termed tyranny had supported the state, and, after the death of Pericles, wickedness and corruption set in, which there was no one capable of checking. All historians do not agree that he was a great politician, but none can deny that he was a man of genius, and a liberal patron of the arts and of literature.

NICIAS

ON the death of Pericles the rich and powerful men of Athens exerted themselves to place Nicias at the head of the government, feeling convinced that he would be the best person to keep Cleon, an insolent, daring politician, in check. Cleon was in high favor with the common people, who liked his off-hand, familiar way of addressing them, and he had won the good will of some of the poorest of them by liberal presents. Nicias was favored by them because he always treated them with due consideration. This being the case, he was likely to prove an offset to Cleon. But he had one serious fault for a statesman, and that was excessive timidity, which often prompted him to shirk responsibility and remain in retirement instead of taking a decided stand. In one sense this weakness was a drawback to Nicias, but it rendered him popular, because no one felt awed in his presence.

Nicias was noted for his piety, and made offerings of the most costly character to the gods. This he was enabled to do because he was a very wealthy man, being the owner of some rich silver-mines. Once a handsome slave of his represented the god Bacchus at a religious ceremony, and the audience applauded him loudly. Thereupon Nicias rose and said, "I should think it impious to keep a slave whom the public voice seems to consecrate to a god; I therefore give him his freedom."

NICIAS

It was the custom for the principal cities of Greece to send a select band of musicians to Delos every year to sing praises to Apollo. The procession was called Theoria, and it was considered a great honor to have the management of it. When the musicians landed, the people of the island would flock to the shore and press them to sing, so that they were forced to do so even while putting on their robes and garlands, and otherwise preparing for the ceremony. In order to prevent the disorder which this caused, Nicias, when taking charge of the Theoria, landed first on the isle of Rhenia, in the Ægean Sea (now called Sdili), with the choir, the victims for the sacrifices, and all the other necessary matters. Then during the night he had a bridge, which he had brought from Athens, thrown across the narrow channel to Delos. This bridge was gayly decorated and hung with garlands and tapestry; at break of day he marched over it at the head of the choir, who, dressed in the costliest of robes, sang hymns to the gods as they moved decorously along. After the sacrifices, games, and feasts were over, Nicias consecrated a palm-tree of brass and a large open field to Apollo, and arranged that the interest on the sum of money he paid for the field should be used in purchasing sacrifices, and that the Delians should always pray for the blessings of the god on himself as the founder.

Nicias was so sensitive about what people might say of him that he kept aloof as much as possible. He would never attend parties of pleasure, nor would he stop to converse with anybody in the street. When he was Archon, he was the first to enter the court and the last to leave, and if he had no public business on hand, he would shut himself up at home and refuse to see any one. If persons came to his gate and demanded to see him, his friend Hiero, who was brought up in his house, would go out and say that he was occupied with important public affairs, and had no time for repose or pleasure. Whether this was true or not, it had its effect; the people honored a man who was so occupied for their welfare, and did nothing to prevent his advancement to glory.

Nicias possessed great military talent, and when he took command of the army he proved this by making it his study to do nothing rash. For this reason he was generally successful, and though the Athenians met with many misfortunes in those times, Nicias was not to blame for them. He won some very important victories, and gained a large amount of territory, but once, when at war with the Lacedæmonians, he prolonged a siege until his soldiers lost all patience. Then Cleon undertook it, and within the time he had fixed for victory came back with all the Spartan soldiers who had not fallen in the field as captives. This threw some disgrace on Nicias, and made Cleon more arrogant than ever, but when Cleon was killed in battle some time afterwards, Nicias worked so hard to bring about a peace between the Lacedæmonians and Athenians that he became famous. Then nothing was talked of but Nicias, who was said to be beloved of the gods on account of his great piety. It was decided that the long-wished-for blessing should bear his name, and so the peace agreed to for fifty years was called the "Nician Peace."

All Athens rejoiced at the return of peace, but it was not to be enjoyed very long, for it was soon broken by those who wanted to be always engaged in war. Alcibiades was the principal of the war party, because he was not willing to form an alliance with the Lacedæmonians, being angry with them for having once treated him with neglect. So, taking advantage of Nicias's absence when he was sent on a public errand

NICIAS

to Sparta, he had himself appointed general, and then did not rest until the war broke out again.

When Nicias returned, he and Alcibiades kept up such a constant quarrelling that it was proposed to banish one of them by ostracism, which process we have already explained. The younger men, who were for war, wanted Nicias banished, while the older ones, who had learned the value of peace, desired to get rid of the warlike Alcibiades.

While this matter was under discussion, one Hyperbolus, a wicked wretch, who hoped to gain influence with one of the generals as soon as the other should be removed, went about Athens secretly abusing both, because it made little difference to him which got the number of votes that were necessary for banishment. Nicias and Alcibiades heard of the man's doings, so they had a private interview, and agreed to work together to turn the ostracism against him instead of themselves. This was a punishment that had fallen on some of the greatest patriots, such as Thucydides and Aristides, but it was a great deal too easy for a creature who deserved the gibbet, and no one was more surprised than Hyperbolus himself when he found that his name was to appear among those of good and honest men. He was the last person ever banished by ostracism; Hipparchus had been the first.

Then Alcibiades persuaded the Athenians to join other Greek nations and undertake the Sicilian expedition, and this was considered very important, because he told them it would open the way to Carthage and to all Africa. Such a glorious picture did he paint of the victories that awaited them that very few, either of the commons or the nobility, openly sided with Nicias, though many of the more sober-minded Athenians did so privately.

Nicias worked for peace even after the decree for war was passed, but he worked in vain, and he was appointed to command with Lamachus and Alcibiades. The priests were opposed to the expedition, but Alcibiades had his own diviners, who promised great glory for the Athenians in Sicily, and those who were sent to consult the oracle of Jupiter Ammon returned with the answer that the Athenians would surely capture the whole Syracusan nation. It is true that there were some unfavorable signs, but those who knew of them tried to conceal them, not thinking it worth while to object to an expedition that nearly all their countrymen were determined upon. One of these unfavorable signs was that during a certain night all the statues of Mercury had their heads cut off. This was the more remarkable because there was one in the gateway of each temple and before most of the private houses in Athens. Another bad omen was this: the golden statue of Pallas, which had been put up to celebrate the victory of the Athenians over the Medes, had been pecked at by crows for several days. There were other signs that made the cautious shake their heads when they thought of the splendid army fitted out at so great an expense and likely to come to grief. Socrates, the learned philosopher, said that the expedition would prove fatal to Greece, and he probably had reasons for his opinion grounded on a more important basis than bad omens; but Alcibiades and the majority of the Athenians would listen to no objections, and so the army started.

Before anything had been accomplished, Alcibiades was called home to stand his trial, an account of which is given in his life. Lamachus was killed on the battlefield shortly after, and Nicias was left to command alone. Meanwhile, he had astonished the Syracusans by building a wall almost

NICIAS

around their city in a very short space of time, and when this was done his success seemed sure, for the inhabitants began to send messages offering terms of peace, and ceased to show themselves outside their walls. Then if Nicias had been active and energetic he would soon have brought the war to a close, but he delayed until his troops lost confidence in him.

Meanwhile, Gylippus, the Spartan commander, went to the relief of the Syracusans with a large force, and soon brought about such a change in the condition of affairs that the Athenians found themselves besieged instead of being the besiegers. Nicias became so much discouraged, and his health was so bad, that he wrote home desiring to be recalled. This was refused, but large reinforcements were sent to Sicily under Demosthenes and Eurymedon. Before they arrived, Nicias had lost a naval battle, which proved that the Athenian fleet was not so powerful as it had been.

Demosthenes came with fresh troops and plenty of energy, but he too was defeated again and again, and then preparations were made for the Athenian army to depart secretly. But on the very night when this was to be carried into effect there was an eclipse of the moon, and the soothsayers said that the army must not leave its position for three times nine days. Of course Nicias obeyed, because he was too pious and superstitious to do otherwise, so he gave up all thought of war, and passed his time in prayer and sacrifices, while the enemy took possession of the walls and forts, and filled the harbor with their vessels. Not only the men from the ships, but the boys from the fishing-boats challenged the Athenians to come and fight, and offered them every kind of insult they could think of.

At last the Syracusans made an attack, and a furious sea-fight took place, which resulted in the defeat of the Athenians, who, as it was out of the question for them to escape by sea, wanted to do so by land, but their force was still large, and Hermocrates, the Syracusan general, fearing that if they escaped they might make a stand in some other part of Sicily and renew the war, resorted to this stratagem: he sent persons whom he could trust, bidding them to pretend friendliness for Nicias, and to warn him not to march in the night, because the Syracusans had laid several ambushes for him and had seized all the passes. Nicias believed them, and stayed where he was. The next morning the enemy got off before he could do so, and then really did take the passes, break down the bridges, and place their cavalry everywhere, so that the Athenians could scarcely advance a step without fighting. They were in a dreadful condition, and, what was worse, they were forced to leave their sick and wounded friends and comrades behind them. Nicias was more to be pitied than any one, for not only was he ill and suffering bodily, but he had to bear the disgrace of defeat after having hoped for honor and success. He had opposed the war with all his might, it is true, but when fighting was to be done, he had shown the spirit and energy of a true hero. In spite of all difficulties, he strove hard to conceal his sufferings from his soldiers, and during an eight days' march, with frequent attacks by the way, he kept his division of the army in good order until Demosthenes was taken prisoner. Then he offered to pay the Syracusans the whole cost of the war if they would suffer his army to quit Sicily; but they indignantly refused to treat with a man who had entered their country to take possession of it.

NICIAS

Nicias reached the river Asinarus the next day with his men in a state of exhaustion; for the enemy's troops had galled them all the way. When they came to the banks of the river, some plunged into the water to quench their burning thirst, but they were butchered while they drank, and a cruel scene of bloodshed followed. At last, throwing himself at the feet of Gylippus, Nicias spoke in heart-rending tones, "Gylippus, let pity move you in your victory; I ask nothing for myself; what is life to a man who has had so many misfortunes? But for the other Athenians I ask your mercy; you should remember that the chances of war are uncertain, and that my countrymen treated you with mildness and moderation when they were prosperous."

Gylippus was touched by the words and appearance of Nicias, for he remembered that he had been friendly to the Lacedæmonians; besides, to capture two generals alive would be great glory; so, raising the conquered Nicias from the ground, he bade him take courage, and ordered the fighting to cease. Then the prisoners were collected, and, adorning themselves and their horses with garlands, the Syracusans returned to their city in triumph.

A general assembly was called, and it was resolved that the Athenian servants and allies should be sold as slaves, the freemen, and those Sicilians who had sided with them, should be sent to work in the quarries, and the generals should be put to death. But Hermocrates sent a messenger to inform Demosthenes and Nicias of what their fate was to be, and they both committed suicide.

As for the other Athenians, many of them died of disease and poor food in the quarries, for they were allowed only a pint of barley and half a pint of water a day. Those that were sold as slaves had the figure of a horse branded on their foreheads, but they behaved so well that they were either soon set free, or won the love and respect of their masters, with whom they continued to live. Several were pardoned because they were able to recite the poems of Euripides, the Sicilians being great admirers of his writings, and the captives were often released from slavery merely because they remembered and could teach something that poet had written.

Once a ship pursued by pirates ran into the harbor of Syracuse for protection, and was only received because the seamen, on being questioned, were found capable of repeating the poems of the favorite bard of the citizens.

ALCIBIADES

ALCIBIADES was noted for his beauty as well as for his charming manners, which attracted everybody who came in contact with him. He talked very rapidly, and with a little lisp that seemed rather to add to the grace of his speech, and to give it a certain power when he was persuading people to do what he desired. He was an Athenian, with a character made up of such opposite traits that while he was praised for his talent as a statesman and his skill and courage as a commander, he was condemned for his lack of principle, his extravagance, and his dissipation.

He was a disciple of Socrates, the celebrated philosopher, for whom he felt great admiration and affection. Socrates did not flatter his pupil, as most people did, but always told him the truth, even though it was not agreeable, and tried to instill in him the best of principles. Alcibiades was often rude to his companions, though many of them were noble and wealthy, but to Socrates, whom he loved and admired, he was ever mild and courteous, and never lost an opportunity to be with him. The philosopher loved his young companion too, and when, at various times, he was led away by the youths of Athens and took part in their vicious pleasures, Socrates would seek him and bring him back to the proper path. He could do this, for he was feared and respected by Alcibiades as no one else was.

This young Athenian chose Pericles for his model in public life, and was ambitious to rise to the position that illustrious statesman had held. Even as a child the thought of ever being defeated or opposed in anything was most painful to him, and he would resort to any trick to prevent it. Once, when engaged in a wrestling-match, finding himself on the point of being thrown, he bit the hand of his opponent with all his might. "You bite like a woman, Alcibiades," cried the boy, angrily, letting go his hold. "Oh, no," returned our hero; "I bite like a lion."

Another time, when he was playing at dice, a loaded cart came along just when it was his turn to throw. He called to the driver to stop, but the latter paid no attention and drove on, the boys making way for him to pass. But Alcibiades would not yield; so he stretched himself across the road and cried out to the carter, "Now drive on if you will!" The man was so startled that he drew back his horses, and the child gained his point.

At school Alcibiades obeyed all his masters pretty well, except the one who tried to teach him the flute. That instrument he declared he would never learn, because it was not becoming in a free citizen so to disfigure himself with the blowing. He was willing to play upon the harp, because he could speak or sing at the same time, and was not obliged to make ugly faces. "Let the Theban youths pipe," he would say, "because they do not know how to talk, but we Athenians, who have Minerva for our patroness and Apollo for our protector, cannot stoop so low." This decision of his had so much weight among his companions that not one of them would play on the flute, and that instrument fell into disuse.

ALCIBIADES

Socrates saved the life of Alcibiades when he was a soldier, in this way. They fought side by side, and the latter was wounded so seriously that he must have received further injury had not the philosopher defended and rescued him from the enemy. Such being the case, Socrates might have claimed the prize for valor, but he was so anxious to encourage in his young friend a thirst for glory that he used his influence to have him rewarded with a crown and a complete suit of armor. Many years later, when the Athenians were defeated at the battle of Delium, and Socrates was retreating on foot, Alcibiades, who was on horseback, placed himself between him and the enemy, and, in his turn, became a shield.

He had a very fine dog, for which he had paid a large sum of money. It was a beautiful animal, remarkable for its handsome tail, which everybody noticed. Alcibiades had this ornament cut off. Thereupon his friends exclaimed at such a piece of inhumanity, and told him that all Athens was talking about it. "That is exactly what I wanted," replied the young man, "for if the Athenians had not this to talk about, they might say something worse of me." Unfortunately, his conduct was often so shameless that he gave ample opportunity for scandal.

Few men have had greater advantages for entering public life than Alcibiades, but he was determined to owe success to nothing but his own eloquence, and he became a most accomplished speaker, always using the right word in the right place and expressing himself in the choicest language.

We have alluded to his extravagance. He spent enormous sums of money for horses, of which he owned the finest breed, and he is the only person who ever sent seven chariots at one time to the Olympic games. He carried away the first, second, and third prizes, and two others were won by his horses. This was considered so remarkable that the representatives of the various Greek cities, who witnessed his success, made him handsome presents, and after the games were over he entertained all the spectators at a magnificent repast.

When Alcibiades entered public life, he had two rivals; one was Nicias, a man advanced in years, and one of the best generals of his day, the other Phæax, a youth just beginning to make his way. Phæax was of high birth, but inferior to Alcibiades as an orator. It was said of him that he could talk, but was no speaker.

Not only was Nicias esteemed by the Athenians, but he was in high favor with the Lacedæmonians on account of the care he had bestowed on their soldiers who were captured at Pylos, and the peace he had afterwards brought about. This aroused the jealousy of Alcibiades, and he was bent upon the downfall of Nicias, so he accused him of having neglected his opportunities when he was commander for the express purpose of currying favor with the Lacedæmonians. His eloquence won the day, as usual, and he was declared general.

His first step was to unite three other Greek nations with his own, and combine an immense force against the Lacedæmonians. At the same time he removed the seat of war so far from the Athenian territory that should the enemy conquer they would gain little, and in case of defeat Sparta would not be safe. This was a fine stroke of policy, and showed great genius on the part of Alcibiades.

Shortly after the first battle the officers of the Argive army desired to have an independent government, and the

ALCIBIADES

Lacedæmonians offered to assist them in accomplishing this. But their object was soon found to be a desire to form an aristocracy like that of Sparta, and so get a foothold among the nobility themselves. This made the people of Argos so angry that they took up arms against the Lacedæmonians, and with the aid of Alcibiades gained a great victory over them. He then persuaded the people of Argos to build their wall down to the sea, so that they might always be in condition to receive aid from the Athenians, and sent carpenters and masons from Athens to do the work. He advised the people of Patræ to build a similar wall, whereupon somebody suggested that the Athenians would one day swallow them up. "That may be so," answered Alcibiades, "but they will begin at the feet and do it by little and little, whereas the Lacedæmonians will begin at the head and gobble you up all at once."

Alcibiades made his countrymen love and hate him at the same time. They felt that they could not do without him, and were fascinated by his speech as well as by some of his worthy deeds, but they hated his luxurious habits, and were disgusted with the contempt he showed for the law. They made apologies for him on the score of youth and good nature, and were won, in spite of themselves, by his liberality, his courage, and his attractive manners. Once when a whole assembly went to congratulate him upon an unusually brilliant oration he had made, Timon, an Athenian philosopher, who was given to making disagreeable remarks, took him by the hand and said, "Go on, my brave boy, and increase your popularity as much as you can, for you will one day bring calamities enough upon these people."

Alcibiades next turned the attention of his countrymen to the conquest of Sicily, a place they had long coveted as being the surest stepping-stone to Carthage. Nicias did not approve of the expedition, and pointed out the innumerable difficulties that would attend it, but Alcibiades worked with so much success upon the minds of the young men of Athens that they were all eagerness to depart, and preparations were begun. Much against his will, Nicias was appointed to command with Alcibiades, because it was expected that his experience and judgment would act as a check on the younger and rasher general.

When everything was ready, a damper was put upon the expedition by many unlucky omens. Among others, all the images of Mercury in Athens were disfigured during one night, and this excited great terror in the minds of the populace. Several reports were circulated to account for this strange occurrence, and at last Alcibiades and his friends were accused of having mutilated the images when in a state of intoxication. It was further stated that, disguised as a highpriest, he had on the same night acted the sacred mysteries, his companions playing their parts in the profane farce also.

The people were very angry with Alcibiades, and would have brought him to trial at once, but the young men who were ready for war declared that they would be led by no one else, so it was decided that he should set sail at once and be tried on his return. No sooner was the fascination of his presence removed than the enemies of Alcibiades circulated false reports concerning him. These, added to the suspicion (for it could not be proved) that he had mutilated the statues of Mercury, increased the popular feeling against him to a perfect fury, and the belief gradually gained ground that he was engaged in a conspiracy to betray Athens to the Lacedæmonians. It is hard to understand what connection there could be between this charge and the others; but such

ALCIBIADES

was the feeling against Alcibiades that the people were ready to believe whatever they heard, no matter how improbable it might appear.

Every relation and friend of the unfortunate general was put into prison unheard, and such great regret was felt that Alcibiades himself had not been tried and punished, that a vessel was sent to fetch him back. The soldiers objected to his leaving them, for they thought that the war would never end under the management of Nicias, but they were not heeded, and their general was forced to go. However, he took the precaution to embark on a vessel of his own, and not the one that was sent for him. On landing at Thurii, in Italy, he made his escape and hid himself. Some one, who happened to recognize him in his hiding-place, asked him if he was afraid to trust his country. "As to anything else I will trust her," he replied, "but with my life I would not trust even my own mother, lest by mistake she should throw in a black bean for a white one."

We know that one black bean was sufficient to banish a man by ostracism; but a severer punishment was ordered for Alcibiades, for the republic condemned him to die. When he heard of this, he said, "But I will make them feel that I am alive." As he failed to appear, his property was confiscated, and all the priests and priestesses were ordered to curse him. Theano was the only priestess who refused, saying, "It is my duty to pray for sinners, not to curse them."

Meanwhile, fearing that he was not safe at Thurii, Alcibiades had made his way to Argos. Thence he sent a message to Sparta, asking permission to live there, and adding a promise that he would serve the state faithfully. An escort was provided to take him to Sparta, where he immediately began to work in opposition to his country, never ceasing until it was almost crushed.

Of course such a service made Alcibiades exceedingly popular in Sparta, traitor though he was, and he gained many friends in private life by the way he adapted himself to their customs. This man, who had been so luxurious in his habits as to have his meals prepared by a professional cook, to employ a perfumer, and to clothe himself in flowing robes of regal purple, now wore his hair closely cropped, bathed in cold water, ate coarse meal, and dined on black broth. He was not changed really, but he had the gift of entering into the habits and ways of the people he was with, and of appearing to be one of them. Therefore when, at a later period, his life was in danger because of the jealousy of some ambitious Spartans, he placed himself under the protection of Tissaphernes, satrap to the king of Persia, and immediately became of great importance in the new field. Although Tissaphernes hated the Greeks, he was an admirer of Alcibiades, whose underhanded ways were rather to his taste than otherwise; so he received him with many marks of hospitality, and honored him by giving his name to one of the most beautiful of his parks.

Alcibiades now turned against the Lacedæmonians, and advised Tissaphernes not to assist them in ruining the Athenians, but to let the two nations fight on and gradually consume each other. His influence was so great that he was obeyed, and in consequence of his power he rose high in the esteem of his own countrymen, who now began to regret the sentence they had passed on him, particularly as they had suffered on account of his absence.

ALCIBIADES

At this time the whole strength of the Athenian army was stationed at Samos. They were in great dread of Tissaphernes and the Phœnician fleet; so when Alcibiades sent them word that he would make the Persian their friend, it was an immense relief. But he did not propose to do this, he said, unless a change in the government of Athens could be brought about. He wanted the power vested in the hands of a few aristocrats, doubtless thinking it probable that he would then be recalled to Athens; but he did not let this selfish aim appear.

The change really did take place, and the government was assumed by a body of four hundred chosen citizens, called the Five Thousand to give it an appearance of strength; but nobody ever knew of more than the four hundred, who established themselves by force and dismissed the ancient senate. This was an end of the Athenian democracy, which had lasted nearly a century.

Any man who dared to oppose the four hundred was put to death, and when the Athenians at Samos heard of this deposition they became so indignant that they sent for Alcibiades, declared him general, and urged him to lead them on to put down the tyrants. But he refused, for he saw clearly that such a step could only lead to harm and involve Athens in a civil war. He performed a still greater service by using his influence with Tissaphernes to prevent the Phœnician fleet from joining the Lacedæmonians.

Soon after this the four hundred usurpers were driven out of Athens, and then Alcibiades was commanded to return. But he would not do so until he had distinguished himself in some service. He, therefore, sailed from Samos with a few ships and proceeded to the Hellespont, where there was to be a battle between the Spartans and Athenians assembled there. He gained a great victory, of which he felt so proud that he was anxious to show himself to Tissaphernes, and he went to visit him with some handsome gifts. Much to the astonishment of Alcibiades, the Persian, who had displeased the court by showing him favors, had reason on that account to fear the displeasure of his king, and so had the Athenian arrested and sent to Sardis a prisoner.

But Alcibiades had his revenge, for he made his escape before the month was out, and publicly announced that the Persian satrap had helped him to do so. Then he hastened to join the Athenian fleet, and was greeted by loud cheers when he made his appearance. He went to the Hellespont again, fought a desperate battle, and completely overthrew the Lacedæmonians. Elated with this great victory, the Athenian soldiers began to believe that no power could resist them, led by Alcibiades, so they attacked many important places along the coast of Asia Minor, and took possession of them all.

Then, crowned with glory, Alcibiades turned towards Athens, longing once more to appear before his countrymen. So he set sail with a fleet of two hundred vessels laden with spoils. It was not without misgivings that he entered the harbor, but he was reassured by his relations and friends, who flocked to the shore and invited him to land. As soon as he did so the multitude crowded around him, some crowning him with laurel-wreaths, while others, who could not get near, shouted with delight, and followed in his train, satisfied with an occasional glimpse of the great hero.

Afterwards, in a public assembly, gold crowns were placed upon the head of Alcibiades, he was created general both of the land and sea forces, his estates were restored to him, and the priests were ordered to absolve him from the curses they had pronounced against him.

It was believed by the majority that Alcibiades could fail in nothing that he attempted; and this belief caused his ruin. For after a while, when he fought a battle with the Lacedæmonians and was defeated, it was said that he had commanded carelessly, and had spent his time in dissipation and pleasures while in sight of the enemy, leaving the management of the fleet to incompetent people. There were other charges brought against him besides, and ten generals were appointed in his place to lead the Athenian army and navy.

It was Lysander who commanded the Lacedæmonians when they gained this victory, and he then took formal possession of Athens, burnt her ships, and demolished the long walls. Alcibiades, fearing the new masters, retired to Asia Minor, carrying a large amount of treasure with him. But he was robbed, and then determined to seek refuge at the court of Artaxerxes, the Persian king.

Meanwhile, a reign of terror was established in Athens by the thirty despotic rulers whom Lysander had set over the people. Then there was talk of recalling Alcibiades. No one could tell precisely how one man could counteract the outrages of the thirty despots, but it was the general belief that Alcibiades, were he on the spot, could effect some change.

Lysander thought so too, and therefore sent people to assassinate him. They went to the village in Phrygia, where he was then living, and set his house on fire in the middle of the night. Alcibiades was on the alert because of a remarkable vision he had had; so when he discovered the flames he looked out and beheld the men who surrounded his house. Wrapping his cloak tightly about him, he rushed through fire and smoke, drawn sword in hand, and would have made his escape, for the assassins were afraid to approach him, had he not been hit by their darts, which, like cowards, they fired from a safe distance.

He fell covered with wounds. Thus, in the fortieth year of his age, perished one of the most remarkable, though by no means one of the greatest or best, men of Greece. His qualities were such as ought to have made him a benefactor to Athens; but his judgment was at fault, and no man ever inflicted greater misery on his native land.

LYSANDER

LYSANDER was a Spartan, and inherited, as all the children of that nation did, a passion for glory and a keen sense of praise or blame. He was poor, and cared little for money, but, strange to say, he enriched Sparta and made her people love wealth. When Alcibiades increased the power of the Athenians at sea, the Lacedæmonians resolved to continue the Peloponnesian war, which had been going on for a long time, and selected Lysander to take charge of their navy.

He went to Ephesus, and finding the people friendly but in danger of being corrupted by the Persians, many of whom were living there, he made that city his headquarters and proceeded to build ships of war. This improved trade by land and water, and from that moment Ephesus began to grow, and in course of time became a great and powerful city.

On hearing that Cyrus, the king of Persia's son, had arrived at Sardis, Lysander went to see him, and they became such good friends that at a banquet which the prince gave in honor of his guest he asked him to oblige him by requesting a favor. "As you are so kind," answered Lysander, "I will ask you to increase the seamen's pay from three to four pence." Cyrus was so pleased with this generous request that he gave Lysander ten thousand pieces of gold. With this money the wages of his men were increased, and many from the enemy's ships deserted to the side where they would get better pay. Still Lysander did not dare to risk a battle with the Athenians; but when Alcibiades left Samos, Antiochus, commander in his absence, sailed with only two ships to the harbor of Ephesus, and shouted out insulting remarks to the Lacedæmonians to show his contempt of them.

Then Lysander ordered a few ships under sail and gave them chase, but when Antiochus was strengthened by more Athenians, he called out extra vessels, and the battle became general. Lysander gained the victory, and took fifteen ships, whereupon the people of Athens were so angry with Alcibiades that they took the command from him. This was not an important battle, except as it affected the future of Alcibiades.

Lysander made himself so popular at Ephesus that great regret was felt when he left, and Callicratidas, who succeeded him, although an honorable, generous, high-spirited Greek, was unsuccessful in whatever he attempted. This was not just, for Lysander was by no means an honest, straightforward man; his policy was that it was excusable to resort to any degree of deceit in order to gain one's point. He would laugh at those who thought otherwise, and say, "Where the lion's skin will not reach, you must patch it up with the fox's."

Cyrus did not forget his friendship for Lysander, but sent for him to Sardis, where he presented him with large sums of money. Nor was this all: when he went to visit his father in Media, he ordered that Lysander should receive the tribute of the towns and govern in his stead until he returned, begging him not to fight the Athenians during his absence, because he meant to bring back a powerful fleet from Phœni-

LYSANDER

cia and Cilicia for that purpose. Lysander promised, and Cyrus departed on his journey.

But it was impossible for the Spartan commander to keep still with a fleet at his command and his Athenian enemy still powerful. So he cruised about, reduced several islands, pillaged some important towns, and then, sailing to the Hellespont, captured the city of Lampsacus. This was a great loss to the enemy, who proceeded at once to give battle to Lysander. He refused to accept their challenge, however, because he feared that his fleet was not powerful enough to destroy theirs, and so he kept them at bay for two or three days, until, having made up their minds that they had nothing to fear from a cowardly commander, they ceased their watchfulness. It was for just such an opportunity that the Lacedæmonians waited; so on the fifth day, when many of the Athenians were enjoying themselves on land, others were asleep, and the rest preparing their dinner, Lysander rushed on to an attack, and took them so completely by surprise that three thousand of their number were captured and their whole fleet was seized. Thus within one hour, and with little bloodshed, Lysander put an end to a conflict that had lasted twenty-seven years, and caused the death of more generals than all the wars of Greece combined.

The three thousand prisoners were condemned to die, and Lysander asked Philocles, one of their generals, what punishment he thought he, who had given his countrymen bad advice, deserved. "Do not start a question where there is no judge to decide it," answered the brave general; "but now that you are a conqueror, proceed as you would have been proceeded with had you been conquered." He then bathed, dressed himself in a rich robe, and led his countrymen to execution, he being the first to suffer.

Lysander next sailed among the various seaport cities, and ordered all the Athenians to go to Athens. His object was so to overcrowd the city as to produce a famine, and save the trouble of a long siege. In each place he left a Lacedæmonian governor, thus increasing his control of Greece, for it was his own friends whom he appointed, and they had power of life and death. The famine that Lysander had worked for really did visit the Athenians, so that when he entered their harbor, called the Piræus, they were obliged to surrender. He then wrote to the Ephors, or magistrates of Sparta, "Athens is taken." Thereupon they issued this decree: "The Athenians must destroy the Piræus and pull down the long walls; they must give up all the cities they possess, and live within the bounds of Attica. On these conditions they shall have peace, provided they pay what is reasonable and recall their exiles. As to their ships, we will give orders as to the number they may be allowed to keep."

Lysander took all the Athenian ships except twelve, and finding that at the end of the time he had granted they had not destroyed their walls and harbor, he did it himself. Then he changed their form of government, placed thirty tyrants over the city and in the harbor, and garrisoned the citadel under the command of a Spartan.

Now, since Lysander's power was so absolute, of course he had a great deal of wealth, and all the gold and silver that he had taken or had been presented with he sent to Sparta. This was a source of uneasiness to the wisest of the citizens, who said some hard things about Lysander for introducing an evil that would be sure to increase crime. A council was therefore called, who decreed "that no coin of gold or silver should be introduced into Sparta, but that only their old money should be used." Their money, being of iron, had little value, because it was so bulky and heavy that a whole cart-load was not a large sum. Lysander's friends would not have his gold and silver sent away, but proposed by way of compromise that it should be considered public treasure, and that to use it for private purposes should be accounted a crime. This was not wise, for it only made gold and silver coin appear more valuable, and encouraged a desire to possess it.

Lysander was the first Greek to whom altars were erected and sacrifices offered as though he had been a god. Not that he was beloved or honored, but that he was feared, and people superstitiously believed that the gods might thus avert the cruelty from themselves which Lysander showed towards others. So much flattery made him vain and haughty; in return for friendship or hospitality he graciously bestowed government positions, and any man who was so unfortunate as to arouse his displeasure was put to death.

He was not above resorting to dishonesty in order to gain a point: thus, when he had conquered Miletus, fearing that the plebeian party might escape, he swore to do them no harm if they would leave their hiding-places. They did so, and were handed over to the opposite party, by whom eight hundred of them were put to death. Such shameful scenes were repeated in various cities, for Lysander knew no law but his own wicked passions, and he was remarkably cruel and revengeful.

Many complaints were made, but the Lacedæmonians paid little attention to them until Pharnabazus, whose country Lysander had pillaged and destroyed, despatched a messenger to Sparta to inform against him. Then the Ephors sent him a scroll commanding his return. The scroll was made in this way: when the Ephors sent an officer on an expedition they had two round pieces of wood cut of precisely the same length and thickness; one they kept, the other they gave to the person who went away. These pieces of wood were called scytales. When the Ephors wanted to send a secret communication, they took a long, narrow strip of parchment and rolled it from end to end on the scytale like a bandage; they then wrote upon the parchment following the direction of the wrapping, took it off, folded it, and sent it to the possessor of the corresponding scytale, who could read the message only after the parchment was bound as it had been when it was written upon.

As soon as Lysander received the scroll he hastened to wind it, and found out what order it contained for him. He was not only distressed, but alarmed, when he read it. He knew that he had incurred the anger of Pharnabazus; nevertheless he sought an interview with that monarch, hoping to soften him and to have the charges against himself withdrawn. He used all the eloquence he could bring to bear, and the result was that Pharnabazus consented to write to the Ephors and acknowledge that he had been hasty and unjust in the complaints he had made against Lysander. After showing the letter to his visitor, Pharnabazus replaced it by another containing even more serious complaints, which he had prepared secretly. This he sealed in the presence of the unsuspecting Lysander, who felt greatly relieved at having, as he supposed, the dreadful charges against his conduct removed, and hastened with the sealed packet to Sparta. His surprise and indignation must have been great when he was shown the letter of which he had been the bearer, particularly as the Lacedæmonians were exceedingly friendly towards Pharnabazus, and were not likely to order light punishment to any one who had wronged him.

LYSANDER

Two or three days elapsed, when Lysander asked and received permission of the Ephors to go to the temple of Jupiter Ammon, there to offer sacrifices that he had vowed to the god before the war. This temple was in Libya, for which place Lysander set sail at once. While he was gone, the various Greek nations resolved to drive out his friends and re-establish popular government. The Athenians were the first to revolt, and attacked and defeated the thirty tyrants; then Lysander returned and persuaded the Lacedæmonians to support him and punish the people. So they gave large sums of money to the tyrants to carry on the war, and appointed Lysander their general. Then Pausanias marched into Attica, pretending that he wished to support the thirty tyrants against the people, but his real object was to put an end to the war and prevent Lysander from becoming master of Athens again. This he managed by making the Athenians friendly with each other, and, as they worked together, quiet was soon restored.

It was through the influence of Lysander that Agesilaus, the great soldier and statesman, was placed upon the throne of Lacedæmon. Having done him this service, he persuaded him to undertake an expedition to Asia, assuring him that he might easily conquer the Persians and add much to his own glory. Lysander accompanied him. He was so well known in Asia that he was applied to for everything, and the people stood at his door or followed him in crowds to receive his orders. This made Agesilaus angry, and the more attention Lysander received the less would he show him favors, until at last it became generally known that if any one asked for a thing through Lysander the king would be sure to refuse. Then people applied directly to Agesilaus, but still showed deference to Lysander, and joined him in the public walks and other places of resort.

The king's envy and jealousy became so great at last that he appointed Lysander his carver at table, and said to the people, "Now go, if you please, and pay court to my carver."

Lysander sought the presence of the king, and said, "Truly, Agesilaus, you know very well how to tread upon your friends."

"Yes, when they want to be greater than myself," was the reply; "but it is just that those who increase my power should share in it."

"Perhaps this is what you say, rather than what I have done. I beg of you, however, for the sake of those strangers who have their eyes on us, to put me in some post where I shall be least offensive and most useful to you."

Accordingly, he was sent as ambassador to the Hellespont, where, though still angry with Agesilaus, he performed his duty faithfully. After a time he returned to Sparta, with the intention of making certain changes in her government. For this purpose he pretended that the oracles had given him instruction, and offered the priests and priestesses large sums of money to make answers that would suit his purpose. But they were not to be bribed, and he was found out. Nevertheless, the Spartans brought no charge against him.

Before Agesilaus returned from Asia, Greece was engaged in the Bœotian war, during which Lysander was surprised and killed by the Thebans. His burial was conducted with the usual honors, and his poverty at the time of his death raised him very much in the estimation of his countrymen, for they then saw that he had desired wealth and power only for them.

CAMILLUS

Furius Camillus was a very celebrated Roman, who did so much service for his country that he was called a second Romulus. He filled many important offices, and early distinguished himself in a great battle against the Aquians and Volscians. On that occasion he received a wound in the thigh which would have driven most men from the field, but Camillus pulled the javelin from the wound and then engaged with the bravest of the enemy until he put them to flight.

One of the most wonderful of his achievements was the taking of the city of Veii, after it had been under siege for ten years. Veii was the chief city of Tuscany, and equal to Rome in the number of her soldiers, as well as in her wealth, luxury, and refinement. The Veientes, after many fights with the Romans, in which they were generally defeated, became discouraged, and contented themselves at last with building strong walls, filling their city with warlike provisions, and then waiting an attack. As soon as the Romans saw their intention, they laid siege to Veii, but as years passed by and the city did not succumb, the generals were blamed for not showing sufficient energy, and many of them were removed. Among those put in their places was Camillus, who was then tribune for the second time.

In the midst of the war a remarkable occurrence aroused the superstition of the Romans. It was this: Alban lake lies embedded in the midst of hills, from the springs of which it is fed. Now, in the autumn succeeding a long, unusually dry summer, when all the lakes, brooks, and springs of Italy were dried up and the rivers ran low, Alban lake began suddenly to rise without apparent cause. It rose and rose until its surface was nearly on a level with the tops of the hills. Such a size and depth it had never attained before, and everybody was amazed. But the increased bulk and weight of the lake broke away the earth which had held it in place like a great dam, and the water flowed in a torrent over the ploughed fields and plantations below until it found its way to the sea. Not only the shepherds and herdsmen, but all the Italians, were stricken with terror. They felt sure that some extraordinary event was pending. Those in the camp before Veii thought that this omen had been sent to them by the gods, but whether its portent was good or evil they could not even guess.

One of the warriors who, during the long siege, had had opportunities for conversation with the enemy, had made the acquaintance of a man of Veii who was versed in ancient traditions and supposed to be uncommonly skilled in the art of divination. Finding this man inclined to rejoice at the strange behavior of Lake Alba, the Roman hit upon a scheme for getting his opinion of it without asking questions. So, pretending to treat the matter with the utmost indifference, he said, "Oh, I could tell you of many prodigies that have happened of late to the Romans, some of which are far more wonderful than the rising of Lake Alba."

Thinking to gain some personal benefit, the man urged the Roman to communicate freely with him, and became so

CAMILLUS

absorbed in the stories invented to deceive him that he suffered himself unconsciously to be led far away from the gates of the city. Suddenly, as the two approached the camp, the Roman snatched up his companion in his arms and held him fast until two or three others came up and carried him before the commanders. He was ordered to declare the secret oracles of Veii. Knowing that he would be forced to speak if he refused, he wisely decided to do so at once. "The city of Veii shall never be taken," he said, "until the waters of Alban lake, which have found new passages, be turned back, and not allowed to mingle with the sea."

The senate held a consultation, and decided to get the opinion of the oracle of Delphi also. For that purpose three persons of distinction were selected. On their return from the voyage they reported, among other answers, that some of the ceremonies relating to the Latin feasts had been neglected. With regard to the lake, the oracle had said that it should be shut up in its ancient bed, if possible, but, if that could not be done, canals and trenches should be dug, through which it was to be drained off. Without a moment's loss of time, the priests set to work to offer sacrifices, and the people to dig new channels for Alban lake.

This happened in the tenth year of the siege, and then Camillus was made dictator. He selected Cornelius Scipio for his general of horse. After making a vow to the gods that if they would grant a happy termination to the war he would celebrate the great games to their honor, and also dedicate a temple to the goddess Matuta, or Mother, Camillus resolved to try a new plan for the capture of Veii. The soil about the city being easy to work, he ordered mines to be dug, and this was done in such a secret manner as to remain unnoticed by the enemy. Then Camillus began an assault which drew the

Veientes to the walls, and enabled part of his army to make their way under ground to the citadel close to the Temple of Juno, the most important one in the city.

At that moment the Tuscan general was offering a sacrifice. The priest who stood by exclaimed, "The gods promise victory to him who shall finish this sacrifice." No sooner were the words out of his mouth than the Romans, who had heard them, burst through the floor with loud shouts and the clashing of arms, which so frightened the Tuscans that they fled, leaving the entrails of the animal they were offering. These were gathered up and carried to Camillus.

Thereupon the city was taken by storm, and while the soldiers were occupied in gathering the spoils, Camillus raised his hands on high and offered a prayer of thanksgiving to Jupiter. At its conclusion he turned to the right, which was the Roman custom after prayer, but in doing so he fell. His friends were uneasy at this, and regarded it as a presage of evil, but Camillus reassured them by saying that it was just what he had prayed for,—a small mishap as a counterbalance to his great success, lest the gods should become jealous of his uniform good fortune.

Veii was sacked, and the dictator resolved to carry the statue of Juno to Rome. Workmen were employed to remove it, but, before they began, Camillus sacrificed to the goddess, and asked her if she would be pleased to accept of his devotion, and if she would vouchsafe to consent to be placed among the gods that presided at Rome. It is said that the statue answered in a low voice that she was ready and willing to go. This is one among innumerable circumstances mentioned by ancient historians for which we of the present day can easily account by a natural course of reasoning. Words

CAMILLUS

uttered by persons who had no concern in their affairs were interpreted by the heathens as good or bad omens if they happened in any way to apply, and they were so superstitious as to believe that statues really did speak, groan, and give other signs on occasions. A bright flame from an altar was always considered a good omen, as was also a sneeze from a person standing at the right hand of the priest engaged in sacrificing.

Like many a hero before and since his time, Camillus was so puffed up by the praise he received on all sides, on account of his having conquered so famous and important a city as Veii, that it turned his head somewhat and made him very haughty. On his return to Rome he drove through the city in a triumphal chariot drawn by four white horses. No general had ever done such a thing, that sort of conveyance being considered sacred to the king and father of the gods, and the Romans were therefore shocked and displeased.

Their disfavor was still further increased when a plan was proposed for dividing the city. The tribunes desired the senate and people to be divided into two equal parties, one to remain at Rome and the other to remove to the newly-taken city. This was a very popular project, for it promised great advantages to the poor, but the senate and the nobler of the citizens feared that in time the two cities might become so independent of each other as to go to war, and thus fall into the hands of their common enemies. They therefore opposed it, and applied to Camillus for assistance, but, fearing the result of a decision, he managed to occupy the people with other matters, and so gain time. Such underhanded behavior was displeasing, and still more so was the manner of disposing of the spoils of Veii. For Camillus had vowed, before undertaking the siege, that if he conquered the city he would dedicate to Apollo one-tenth of the spoils. Instead of doing so, he had permitted the soldiers to divide everything they could lay hands on among themselves.

Some time after, the senate and priests announced that their sacrifices showed signs of divine anger, and that something must be done to satisfy the gods. So the soldiers were required to give up a tenth of the treasure they had appropriated. This decree created a great deal of dissatisfaction in the army, but Camillus excused himself by saying that he had forgotten all about his vow. The soldiers had to submit, therefore, and when the spoils were gathered it was decided to make a bowl of massive gold to be sent to Delphi. But there was a scarcity of gold in the city, and the bowl could not have been manufactured at all had it not been for the Roman matrons, who nobly came forward and gave up their ornaments to supply the required amount. As a reward for this act of self-denial the matrons were granted leave to ride in chariots at the public games and sacrifices, and in open carriages on other occasions. As soon as the golden bowl was ready, three of the prominent citizens were sent in a large, well-manned ship to carry it to Delphi and place it on the altar of Apollo with all due ceremony.

Before the division of the city could be completed, the Falerians declared war, and Camillus was appointed to command the Roman forces. He marched at once to the enemy's territory, and laid siege to Falerii, their chief city. Trusting to the strength of their fortifications, the Falerians did not trouble themselves much about the siege, but left the guarding of their walls to those whose duty it was during times of peace, and continued their usual occupations.

CAMILLUS

Now, it so happened that in Falerii there was a schoolmaster who had under his charge a large number of boys, and after their lessons were finished he would take them daily to the outskirts of the town for play and exercise. He constantly assured them that they had nothing to fear from the enemy at their walls, and they followed their master with perfect confidence wherever he chose to lead them. One day he approached the Roman advance-guard, surrounded by all the boys, whom he delivered up to be carried to Camillus. When questioned by the commander, he told who he was, and said "that he preferred the favor of Camillus to the obligations of duty, and that he had come to hand over to him the Falerian children, and through them the whole city."

The commander was shocked at such base treachery. "War is at best a savage thing," he said, "but it has its laws from which men of honor will never depart; though desirous of victory, they do not avail themselves of acts of villany." So saying, he ordered the lictors to tear off the wretch's clothes and tie his hands behind him, then to furnish each boy with a rod and a scourge, with which to whip the traitor back to the city.

Meanwhile, the Falerians had heard of the fate of their boys, and men and women crowded to the gates in a state of distraction, filling the air with their lamentations. Suddenly they beheld the school-master running towards them pursued by his pupils, who did not spare their blows, but shouted and yelled with delight, while they proclaimed the Roman commander "their God, their Deliverer, their Father." The citizens were so struck by the generosity of Camillus that it was decided in council to send deputies to the noble commander to surrender the city to him. Camillus took time to consult the senate of Rome, who advised him to demand a sum of money of the Falerians, but on no account to accept anything more. Peace was then restored, and the Roman army returned home.

But the soldiers were disappointed at being forced to go back empty-handed when they had expected rich spoils, and determined to vent their anger on Camillus. So before many days, while he was mourning over the death of a dearly-beloved son, they accused him of having appropriated more than his share of the Tuscan spoils. His indignation at such a shameful charge may be better imagined than described, but he was in no mood to defend himself, so he summoned those of the citizens who were friendly and requested them to do it for him. They decided that it was impossible to prevent sentence from being passed, but offered to club together to pay whatever fine might be imposed. Camillus was too proud and upright a man to submit to such an indignity, and therefore resolved to absent himself from Rome at once. So, after bidding farewell to his wife and his only surviving son, he went into voluntary exile.

In course of time misfortune overtook the Romans, and they felt the loss of Camillus most keenly. This was when the Gauls, in tremendous numbers, marched through Italy, splendidly equipped for battle, and spread terror right and left, never stopping until they reached the very gates of Rome. The tribunes led out the army, but it happened to contain at that time many men who had had no experience in the field; the consequence was a total defeat and flight of the Romans in the very first engagement, which took place on the banks of the river Allia.

Had the Gauls followed up their advantage they might have taken possession of Rome itself, but, not being aware of the full extent of their victory, they contented themselves with gathering and dividing the plunder of the deserted camp. Thus the Roman citizens who desired to escape had ample time given them, while those whose duty it was to defend the city lost not a moment in making the necessary preparations. The latter assembled in the Capitol, which they fortified and supplied with arms; but their first care was for the holy things, which were hidden in a safe spot, while the Vestal Virgins fled with the sacred fire and vestments.

Some of the priests and older senators could not bear to leave the city of their birth, so they put on their holy robes, made their vows to the gods, and sat down in the ivory chairs in the Forum, prepared to sacrifice themselves to their country.

When the Gauls arrived, they were surprised to find the gates unguarded. After placing a strong force about the Capitol, Brennus, their leader, went down to the Forum, where the priests and senators had placed themselves. There they sat, perfectly motionless, and apparently unconscious of the approach of the enemy. The Gauls gazed and wondered, but for a long time were afraid to touch the men, who they thought must be superior beings of some sort. At last one of them ventured up to a senator named Papirius and timidly stroked his long beard, whereupon Papirius struck him on the head with his staff. The Gaul drew his sword and killed him on the spot. That was a signal for the rest, who forthwith despatched all who came in their way, pillaged the houses, and finally set fire to the city. When provisions failed they foraged the country mercilessly, laying waste the towns and villages. It so happened that the best disciplined part of their army went against Ardea, where Camillus had been living in retirement ever since his exile. The noble Roman forgot the ingratitude of his countrymen, and burned to relieve them from the hands of so formidable an enemy. So he interested the young men of Ardea in the Roman cause, and then, with the consent of the magistrates and senate, armed all those who were of the proper age, and drew them together within the walls, that the enemy might not suspect what he was about.

The Gauls, elated with their success, became careless, and encamped upon the plains in a most disorderly manner. Night found many of them intoxicated with wine, and so soundly did they sleep that the Ardeans, led by Camillus, were in their very midst before they were aware of it. Most of them were killed that night, and those who were sober enough to make their escape were overtaken and despatched the next day.

When the neighboring cities heard of this action, their warriors agreed to send for Camillus and place themselves under his leadership. Among these were many Romans who had escaped from the battle of Allia. But Camillus answered that he could not command them unless he should be appointed to do so by those of their countrymen who were shut up in the Capitol. Though Rome lay in ashes, he would take no step against the constitution of his country.

To get a messenger to the Capitol while the enemy held the city seemed impossible; however, a young man named Pontius Cominius undertook the difficult task. He carried no letters, that in case he should be seized would betray Camillus, but, dressed in mean attire, he travelled without fear by day and entered Rome after dark. He could not cross the bridge, because it was guarded by the Gauls, but he swam across the river unobserved, walked through deserted streets, and climbed up to the Capitol on the side of the hill which is steepest and roughest. He called out to the guards, told them his name, and was received with great joy, and conducted to the magistrates.

The senate were speedily assembled and informed of the victory of Camillus. They were then asked to appoint him commander, as the citizens out of Rome would obey none but him. This was done, and Pontius returned by the same road by which he had come. When Camillus joined the Romans at Veii he found twenty thousand of them in arms; to these he added a still larger number, and marched out against the Gauls.

Meanwhile, the marks that Pontius had made with his feet and hands when he clambered up the precipitous rock to the Capitol were discovered by the Gauls, and their leader urged them to follow the example set by their enemy and make an attack from that side. The nimblest of them were selected, and they began the ascent at midnight, with great difficulty, but in silence. The Romans would certainly have been taken by surprise had it not been for some sacred geese kept near the Temple of Juno. These creatures, not being so well fed as in time of peace, had grown restless and watchful; the slight noise made by the Gauls excited them, and they ran up and down cackling so loudly that the whole camp was roused. Each man seized the nearest weapon he could lay hands on, while the Gauls, finding themselves discovered, boldly advanced to the assault.

Manlius, a powerful, courageous Roman, distinguished himself on this occasion. He fought two Gauls at once, cut off the right arm of one just as it was raised to strike, and, running his target full in the face of the other, pitched him headlong down the steep rock; then he mounted the rampart, and, with the assistance of others, drove off the rest of the enemy. A reward of half a pound of bread and one-eighth of a pint of wine from each citizen was voted to Manlius after the fight. The captain of the guard was punished for allowing danger to come so near by being flung down the rock on the heads of the enemy. Thus was the Capitol saved from falling into the possession of the Gauls.

After the siege of the Capitol had lasted seven months, the condition of both the contending armies was so dreadful, and suffering, disease, and death had increased to such an alarming extent, that it was agreed to propose a treaty. For this purpose Sulpicius, one of the military tribunes, had an interview with Brennus, and agreed that the Romans should pay a thousand pounds of gold to the Gauls on condition that they would at once quit the country. After the necessary oaths were taken, the gold was brought, but the Gauls used false weights. The Romans soon detected the cheat, and openly expressed their indignation. Thereupon Brennus, with an insulting remark, took off his sword and belt and threw them into the scale with the gold. Sulpicius asked what that meant. "What should it mean," returned Brennus, with an air of contempt, "but woe to the conquered?" The Romans were so angry that some of them wanted to take back their gold and endure the siege to the bitter end, while others argued that since it was a disgrace to settle their quarrel with gold, it was better, in consideration of their necessities, to submit to the insult offered by the Gaul.

It must be remembered that Camillus had not yet made his way to Rome, but he arrived at the gates with his army just at the right moment, before the gold question was decided. As soon as he heard about it he ordered the main body of his

CAMILLUS

army to advance slowly and in good order, while he, with a select few, hastened to join the Romans, who received him with all the respect due their dictator. He advanced towards the scales, took out the gold, which he handed to the lictors, and ordered the Gauls to begone with their weights, saying, proudly, "It is the custom of Romans to deliver their country with steel, and not with gold."

Brennus flew into a rage, and declared that he had been unjustly dealt with. His men drew their swords, and a fight ensued, but it was conducted in such a disorderly manner that, after a few had fallen, the Gauls were ordered back to their camp. During the night they marched away, and returned to their own country.

Thenceforth Camillus was regarded as the deliverer of Rome, and this time, when he made his triumphal entry, he was followed by a long train of men, women, and children, while those who had been shut up in the Capitol and almost starved to death went out to receive him, weeping for joy, and embracing the friends and relations whom they had feared they should never behold again. The priests brought back all the holy things that they had hidden or carried out of the city at the approach of the enemy, Camillus offered sacrifices, and then set to work to rebuild the temples where they had stood before the entrance of the Gauls.

As the city lay in ruins, it became necessary to rebuild it also, and Camillus effected this only with constant words of encouragement to the people and incessant exertion on his own part. The walls and buildings were all completed in one year, but in consequence of the hurry and confusion the streets were narrow and crooked, and the houses were badly planned and huddled together without order or design, each man pitching on any plot of ground that happened to strike his fancy.

No sooner was the work of rebuilding Rome finished than a new war broke out. This time it was three hostile tribes that invaded the Roman territory. Camillus was appointed dictator for the third time, and crowned himself with additional glory by the victory he gained. The citizens acknowledged his ability, but some of them were envious of his success; among these, the one who made himself most notorious was Marcus Manlius, surnamed Capitolinus, on account of his heroic conduct when the Capitol was surprised by the Gauls. He was ambitious to be considered the greatest man in Rome, and it galled him to see honors heaped on another. So he gradually drew the poorer class of citizens about him, defended them against their creditors, and encouraged them to such lawless acts that he made himself obnoxious to the magistrates, and was sent to prison. The people put on mourning for their leader. This was never done except in times of great public calamity, so the senate, fearing an insurrection, ordered Manlius to be set at liberty. Instead of profiting by the lesson he had had, he became more troublesome than ever, and incited the populace to riots. He was again arrested, and condemned to be thrown headlong from Capitol rock, the scene of his former glory. Then his house was pulled down and a temple erected in its place.

At this period Camillus was appointed tribune for the sixth time, but he was in ill health and declined the honor. However, the Romans declared that they could not do without his advice, particularly as a new enemy was just then laying waste their territory, so he consented to go into camp, without intending to take an active part in the fight. But Lucius Furius, who was in command, acted so rashly in leading on his forces that he was driven back. Thereupon Camillus jumped from his bed, old and feeble though he was, fought his way to the battlefield, urged his countrymen on, and soon regained for them the ground they had lost. The next day he killed nearly all of the enemy and took possession of their camp. Then he marched to Satricum, overcame the Tuscans, and returned to Rome with great spoils.

A Roman named Licinius Stolo created a disturbance between the senate and the people, by urging the latter to insist upon having one of their consuls chosen from among the Plebeians, and not both from the Patricians, as they had always been. In order to settle this matter, Camillus was chosen dictator for the fourth time, but, finding that he was a better soldier than politician, he resigned his office on the plea of illness. Before the election for consuls took place, news came that the Gauls were again advancing upon Rome. Everybody was terrified; nobles, senate, and people all relied on Camillus to save them, and he was unanimously chosen dictator for the fifth time. Although nearly eighty years of age, the noble Roman would not desert his country in her hour of need, but at once undertook the command of the army. He proved that his military genius was not yet on the wane, for he had the honor of beginning the attack, and won a glorious victory.

The conflict with regard to the consuls had yet to be settled, and to that matter the people turned their attention as soon as the army returned. As dictator, Camillus presided in the senate, where there were lengthy debates and various opinions on the subject. At last it was decided that one of the consuls should be a Plebeian; this satisfied the populace; but at the same time the Patricians had a new officer appointed, called Prætor, who was to be next in dignity to the consuls, and this was an offset to the point they had yielded. The military tribuneship was at this period abandoned forever.

It was Camillus who announced to the multitude the decision of the senate. Loud shouts of applause greeted his welcome speech, and he was conducted to his home in triumph.

The next day it was unanimously agreed that the temple Camillus had vowed to Concord should be built in commemoration of the victory the people had gained over the senate instead. One more feast-day, in honor of the victory, was added to the list, and at the sacrifices offered on each anniversary the Romans were ordered to appear adorned with garlands.

The election was held at the regular time, when Marcus Æmilius was the consul chosen from among the nobles, and Lucius Sextius from among the commons. The latter is to be remembered as the first Plebeian who held the position of consul in Rome.

We have nothing further to relate of Camillus, except that during the following year he fell a victim to the dreadful pestilence that visited Rome, and his death was much lamented by his countrymen.

ARTAXERXES

THE Artaxerxes about whose life we are going to tell was the second Persian king of that name. The first one was son of Xerxes, and reigned thirty years; the second was son of Darius, and ascended the throne on the death of his father. He was surnamed the Mindful, because of his extraordinary memory.

Darius had four sons,—Artaxerxes, Cyrus, Oxtanes, and Oxathres. Cyrus was his mother's favorite, and when the king was dying she tried very hard to have him named successor. The argument she used was that Cyrus had been born after his father began to reign, whereas Artaxerxes, having been born before that period, was therefore not the son of a monarch. But the dying father insisted that his eldest child should succeed him, and he was therefore proclaimed king. Cyrus, who had always been a headstrong, ambitious boy, was very much disappointed; but his brother made him governor of Lydia, and commander-in-chief of all the cities along the coast of Asia Minor, thinking that such an important post ought to satisfy him. We shall see, however, that it did not.

Artaxerxes, according to the custom of his country, went to a place called Pasargada, to be crowned by the priests in the temple of the goddess of war. The ceremony was conducted in this way: the royal person on entering the holy place had to take off his own robe and put on the one which Cyrus I. wore before he became king; he had also to eat a cake of figs, chew some turpentine, and drink a cup of sour milk.

Artaxerxes was just on the point of going to the temple, when Tissaphernes, one of his highest officers, brought in a priest who had come to say that Cyrus was hidden in the sacred building, ready to kill his brother when he was changing his robe. Cyrus was seized and brought before the king; but Parysatis, the mother, came with him, and, throwing her arms about his neck, implored her eldest son to pardon him for her sake. He did so, and Cyrus went back to Lydia; but he was not grateful for his escape, and hated his brother because of the indignity he had suffered in being brought before him in chains.

Artaxerxes was a very mild, gentle king at first, with affable manners towards the lowly as well as the lofty in station, and always ready to reward liberally any deserving person. No matter how trifling a present offered to him might be, he received it graciously. A subject once brought him an uncommonly large pomegranate. He said, "By the light of Mithra, this man, if he were made governor of a small city, would soon make it a great one." As he passed through the country, his people would present a variety of things; a poor man, on such an occasion, having nothing to offer, ran to the river and brought some water in his hands, and the king was so pleased that he sent him a gold cup and a liberal sum of money. One day when he was hunting, a courtier pointed out a tear in his robe. "What shall I do with it?" asked the king. "Give it to me," was the reply. "It shall be so," returned Artaxerxes; "I give it thee; but I charge thee not to wear it." The courtier, being a vain, silly fellow, put on the robe, and, adding to it some costly jewels, made a display of himself thus adorned. The courtiers expressed great indignation at seeing a royal robe worn by one who had no right to it, but the king only laughed, and said, "I allow him to wear the trinkets as a woman, and the robe as a madman." So by attaching the proper weight to trifles Artaxerxes made his reign popular, and Statira, his wife, did her share towards it, for she always rode in her chariot with her curtains open, that people might see her, and she was so gracious in her manners that women were not afraid to approach and salute her. Of course, there were those who did not approve of the king, for there are always fault-finders in every age and country; they thought that Persia required a more dignified, ambitious, despotic ruler.

Knowing such to be the case, Cyrus resolved to make war upon his brother, and collected an army of more than a hundred thousand fighting-men, at whose head he began his march.

Tissaphernes was the first person to hear of the approach of Cyrus, and lost no time in communicating the dreadful intelligence at court, where it aroused the greatest consternation. Parysatis was taken to task for the danger that threatened, because it was she who had saved the life of her son Cyrus when he would otherwise have forfeited it. Statira reproached her more than any one else for bringing war and all its calamities on the country, and this made the queen-mother so angry that, later, she had the queen assassinated when Artaxerxes was at the war.

Cyrus and his army were amazed when they beheld the magnificent array the Persian king brought into the field. He had nine hundred thousand well-armed, well-disciplined men, who advanced slowly and in perfect order. The two armies met at a place called Cunaxa, about sixty miles from Babylon, and the battle fought there was so fierce and so remarkable that many ancient historians have written descriptions of it. It is therefore only necessary for us to recount the result.

Mounted on a high-spirited horse, Cyrus fought with great fury, and routed the king's guard. He then engaged with the monarch himself, pierced his cuirass with his javelin, and gave him such a terrible wound that he fell in a swoon.

This event caused disorder among the king's troops, and before they recovered their presence of mind the animal which bore Cyrus became excited and dashed in among the ranks of the enemy. It was growing dark at that time, and the prince was not at once recognized; but he was so elated with victory that he spurred on his horse, shouting, "Make way, ye slaves, make way!" The ranks opened at his command, but his helmet happened to become loose and fall from his head, whereupon a young Persian named Mithridates, who chanced to be riding by, struck a dart deep into one of his temples. The blood gushed forth, and Cyrus fell senseless to the ground. When he recovered consciousness a couple of slaves tried to lead him away, but he was so dizzy that he could with difficulty reel along supported on both sides. As one by one whom he met began to recognize and salute him as king, begging at the same time for grace and mercy, Cyrus knew that victory was his. But he was not long to enjoy his triumph, for a party of men employed to do camp-work for the royal army fell into his train, under the impression that he was not an enemy. However, they soon discovered their mistake when they observed that the coats over the breastplates of Cyrus and his attendants were red, while those of the king's men were white. One of them, without recognizing Cyrus, struck him in the leg with a dart. He fell, and, dashing his wounded temple against a stone, died on the spot.

Presently an officer of the king came along and asked the slaves over whom they were weeping. "Do not you see, O Artasyras," asked one of them, "that it is my master, Cyrus?" "Be of good cheer, and keep the body safe," said Artasyras, as he rode off in all haste to carry the news to the king.

Artaxerxes, who had given up his cause for lost, and was suffering from his wound, could scarcely believe the good news. He started up, and ordered Artasyras to lead him to the spot where his dead brother lay. Thirty messengers were sent forward to make sure that Cyrus was really dead, and when the king came into the plain they met him with torches, and held up the head and right hand of Cyrus, which, according to the Persian custom, had been cut off.

Taking the head in his hand and holding it up by the long, thick hair, Artaxerxes showed it to the soldiers, all of whom flocked to him as soon as they heard of his good fortune. He returned to the camp followed by seventy thousand men, who only a short hour before had been prepared to desert to the victorious Cyrus.

The king then rewarded every man who had been in any way instrumental in causing the death of the prince, as well as the messenger who brought him the good news and those who confirmed it. But the two who had struck the fatal blows, the one in the temple and the other on the leg, went about boasting of their exploits, which made the king so angry that he ordered both to be executed. This was not because he felt any sorrow on account of his brother's death, but because he wanted all the credit among the enemy of having caused it himself.

Parysatis, as we know, had always loved Cyrus more than her other sons. She was a cruel, vindictive woman, who would stop at nothing in order to satisfy her revenge. So she begged that the condemned men, as well as the slave that had cut off the head and hands of her son, might be left to her for punishment. Artaxerxes gratified her, and the barbarous torture to which she subjected them before death came to their relief is too horrible for description.

Now, a large number of Greeks had followed Cyrus into Asia, and Artaxerxes had been most anxious to conquer them, because such a feat would add greatly to his reputation. But he failed in this, and they made a remarkable retreat through more than two thousand miles of the enemy's country, followed and harassed all the way by a victorious army. They reached their cities on the Euxine Sea, feeling contempt for the barbarous Persian king, with all his wealth, luxury, and display, and great eagerness for new conflicts with him.

Artaxerxes was now the peaceable possessor of the throne, and immediately set about preparations for another war. The Lacedæmonians had offended him by giving aid to Cyrus, and he resolved to punish them. For that purpose he joined Conon, the Athenian general, and made him, with Pharnabazus, admirals over his fleet. The Lacedæmonians were so badly defeated that they lost their control of the seas, and Artaxerxes gained so much power over Greece as to be permitted to dictate his own terms of peace.

It was called the peace of Antalcidas, being named after the Spartan who, acting in the interest of the Persian king, induced the Lacedæmonians to let him govern all the Greek cities in Asia. The terms of this well-known treaty were so humiliating that they cast more disgrace on the Greeks than any defeat had ever done. Artaxerxes showed Antalcidas special favors when he went to Persia, and continued to do so until the battle of Leuctra was fought; then the Spartans were again defeated, and lost their lofty position among the Greek nations. They were in such distress after this battle that they were obliged to send Agesilaus, their commander, to Egypt to borrow money.

Antalcidas then entreated the Persian king to assist his wretched country, but he met with nothing but insults and a harsh refusal. Fearing to return to Sparta after being so treated by a monarch whose cause he had favored, he starved himself to death in despair. Then all the Greek cities of Asia fell under the sway of Artaxerxes.

A revolt in Egypt next attracted the attention of the Persians, and was followed by one in Upper Asia. The king attended his army in person, and showed that he could endure danger and fatigue in spite of the splendor and luxury by which he was always surrounded when at home.

He was now growing old, and his sons began to dispute among themselves as to which should succeed him. The eldest one, who was named Darius, would probably have been appointed; but he was so impatient for the exalted station that he formed a plot against his father's life. It was discovered, and the king had barely time to escape through a door concealed behind a piece of tapestry when the would-be assassins entered his bedchamber. He gave the alarm, and they were captured. The proof that Darius was at the head of the plot was too strong to be questioned, and he was put to death.

Artaxerxes died at the age of ninety-four, and his son Ochus, a cruel, blood-thirsty prince, succeeded him.

AGESILAUS

AGESILAUS, being a Spartan, was brought up with the severe discipline that formed so large a part of the education of that race. He was a younger brother, with little prospect of becoming a ruler, so he was trained to obey the laws strictly, and, being of a yielding, gentle, sensitive nature, anxious to do right, and distressed at the slightest rebuke, he was easily controlled.

According to the custom with Spartan youths, he was bred in one of the flocks or classes, and so orderly and well behaved was he that Lysander took a fancy to him. He was a handsome boy, in spite of a slight deformity, which consisted in one leg being shorter than the other; but that did not inconvenience him much, for he was high-spirited and eager to distinguish himself. When he grew to manhood he was undersized and insignificant-looking, but his good humor, cheerfulness, and kindliness made him attractive to the end of his life.

By the death of his brother he became king of Sparta, and grew into great power and popularity. In the life of Lycurgus there is an account of how that statesman instituted two bodies to act as a restraint upon the power of the kings. These were the Ephors, who were chosen annually, and the Elders, who held their offices during life. The idea which

AGESILAUS

Lycurgus had in this change in the government was good, but it was a constant cause of disturbance, because the kings did not like to share their authority.

Agesilaus was wise enough to court favor with both the Ephors and the Elders; he asked their advice on every point, and was always ready to go to them when they needed him. Besides, he treated them with great respect, and made them so fond of him that they were satisfied with everything he did, and thus he became powerful almost without their suspecting it. By seeming to obey he ruled them and Sparta, and by justice to his enemies and attachment to his friends he won many hearts.

Agesilaus had not been long on the throne when news came that the king of Persia was preparing a great fleet to overthrow that of the Spartans. Lysander then wanted to be sent to Asia to support his friends, who were governors of the Greek cities there, so he persuaded Agesilaus to enter Asia at once with his forces, in order that the war might be carried on at a distance from home. Agesilaus consented, and called an assembly of the people, before whom he agreed to undertake the war on condition that they would supply him with thirty Spartans for captains and counsellors, two thousand chosen men of the newly-freed Helots, and six thousand of the allies. This request was granted, and Agesilaus started, with Lysander for his chief. Both were glad to go upon this expedition, because it seemed to offer an opportunity for them to win laurels.

While the army was collecting at the sea-shore, Agesilaus went with his friends to Bœotia, and the first night he slept there he dreamed that a man approached him and said, "O King of the Lacedæmonians, you know that since Agamemnon nobody has been appointed captain-general of all the Greeks but yourself. Therefore, since you command the same people, go against the same enemies, and depart from the very place that he did. You ought to please the goddess by offering the sort of sacrifice he offered before he sailed."

Now, Agesilaus knew that Agamemnon had sacrificed his daughter Iphigenia in obedience to the oracle, but he meant to do no such thing with his own daughter; so, when relating his dream next morning, he said, "I will not imitate the savage ignorance of Agamemnon, for I do not believe that would give pleasure to so reasonable a being as the goddess; I will offer another sacrifice, however." He thereupon put a crown of flowers on a hind, delivered her to his private soothsayer, and ordered him to perform the ceremony. This gave offence to the chief magistrates of Bœotia, who said that if their own soothsayers were left out of the sacrifice, which they could perform only according to the laws and customs of their country, the ceremony should not take place at all. So the thighs of the hind were thrown from the altar, and Agesilaus, highly offended at such treatment, departed in anger. He was distressed also, for the omen seemed to warn him of failure, and he dreaded to undertake the expedition against the Persian king.

He then joined Lysander at Ephesus, where he found that officer in such high favor that the greatest honors were being shown him. All sorts of applications were made to him, so that the importance of Agesilaus was lessened, and he became ruler only in name. He was not naturally a jealous man, but this he could not stand, and determined to change it. The method he chose was to oppose everything Lysander said or did. If a man applied to Lysander for anything, Agesilaus made it a point to refuse, so that even the friends of the former knew they must go straight to the king if they wanted to be heard. Agesilaus went further: he appointed his chief officer to the position of carver in the royal household, and, when he did so, said before several guests, "Now let the people who want favors pay their court to my carver."

Lysander was very much hurt, and said, "Agesilaus, you know well how to humble your friends." "I know those who want more power than I have," answered Agesilaus. "But perhaps," returned Lysander, "that has been so represented to you rather than tried by me. However, all I ask is that you will place me in a position where I may serve you without displeasing you." He was sent as lieutenant to the Hellespont, and was killed in the war not long after.

Agesilaus then proceeded with an army to Persia, and on his approach Tissaphernes, the Persian commander, was so frightened that he proposed a treaty by which the Greek cities in Asia were to be governed by their own laws; but when his forces were collected, they proved to be more numerous than he had expected, and so he took courage and declared war.

To punish him for breaking his word, Agesilaus pretended to march with his whole army to Caria, and as soon as the Persians were drawn to that quarter he turned about and entered Phrygia, where he took many cities and immense treasure. But he found his cavalry to be weak, and retired to Ephesus to increase it. The plan he adopted was to insist that every person of means who did not wish to serve should provide a man and a horse, and thus he got together quite a respectable body.

One day he ordered that all the prisoners should be stripped and sold at public auction. Their clothing was offered separately, and brought a large price, but, the prisoners being for the most part small, and their skins being white and soft, it was not thought that they could make valuable slaves, and the bids for them were low. Agesilaus, who stood by with his soldiers at the auction, said, in a tone of contempt, "These are the persons with whom ye fight;" then, pointing to the rich spoils, he added, "Those are the things for which ye fight."

Agesilaus then gave out that he would invade Lydia, but Tissaphernes, who had been deceived before, now made up his mind that Caria was to be the next scene of battle, and led his forces there. When the Greeks spread out on the plains of Sardis, the Persians had to march there in such haste, that, taking advantage of their disorder, Agesilaus gave them battle, put them to flight, took their camp, and killed great numbers. The king of Persia was so displeased with his general on account of this defeat, which opened the country to the enemy, that he sent Tithraustes to cut off his head and take the command instead. That general was also instructed to offer Agesilaus large sums of money on condition that he would go back home. "The making of peace belongs to the Lacedæmonians, not to me," answered Agesilaus. "As for wealth, I would rather see it in the hands of my soldiers than in my own; we Grecians do not think it honorable to enrich ourselves with bribes from our enemies; we prefer to carry home spoils." But, to show his gratification at the way in which Tissaphernes had been disposed of, he retired into Phrygia. While on the march he received *a staff*, or "scytale," from Sparta, appointing him commander of the navy as well as of the army, an honor that had never been given to any one else; but he was considered the greatest and most illustrious man of his time, more on account of his virtue and real merit than of his power.

The Grecian army did great damage in Phrygia, which was ruled by Pharnabazus. The latter did not feel strong enough to oppose the enemy, but moved about with his valuables from place to place to avoid a battle, and at last requested an interview with Agesilaus which was granted. Agesilaus reached the appointed place first and threw himself down upon the grass under a tree. Pharnabazus came with soft skins and rich rugs to recline upon, but when he beheld Agesilaus he grew ashamed of such luxury, and, in spite of his fine clothing, sat on the grass also.

After the usual salutations, Pharnabazus explained that he had just cause of complaint against the Lacedæmonians, they having ravaged his country, although he had done them great service at the time of the Athenian war. The Spartans who were present knew that they had wronged this man, who had indeed been their friend, and felt so ashamed that they hung their heads and blushed. Their general answered as follows: "While we were friends to the king of Persia, we treated him and his in a friendly manner; now that we are at war with him, we treat him as an enemy. As for you, we must look upon you as part of his property, and wound him through you. But whenever you prefer to be a friend to the Grecians rather than a slave to the king of Persia, you may count upon this army and navy to defend you, your country, and your liberties." To this Pharnabazus replied: "If the king send another governor in my place, I will certainly come over to you, but as long as he trusts me with the government I shall be just to him, and shall not fail to do my utmost to oppose you." Agesilaus was so struck by this noble reply that he took the hand of Pharnabazus, and said, "Heaven grant that so brave a man may be our friend rather than our enemy."

As Pharnabazus was going away, his son went up to Agesilaus, and saying, with a smile, "Sir, I extend to you the rites of hospitality," handed him a javelin. Agesilaus received it, and was so well pleased with the youth that he stripped a horse near by of its magnificent trappings and presented them in return. Many years later, when this same Persian was driven from his home by his brothers, he fled to Greece, and Agesilaus befriended him. One of the most marked traits in the character of Agesilaus was his loyalty to his friends, which sometimes led him to injustice. Thus, when Nicias was on trial, he wrote to the Prince of Caria, "If Nicias be innocent, acquit him; if he be guilty, acquit him on my account; but in any case acquit him."

By the time Agesilaus had been at the head of the army for two years he was so renowned that he was able to restore order in the governments of the various cities of Asia that had revolted from the Persians. He then resolved to remove the seat of war and attack the king in his own home, but before he could do so he was summoned to Sparta on account of the civil war which had broken out in Greece. Though at the very height of his glory, Agesilaus did not hesitate for a moment; his country needed him, and he must go, even though his work remained unfinished.

Some countries allowed him to pass as a friend, through others he was obliged to fight his way, and before he arrived home he was stopped by an Ephor, who came with a message that he was to go at once to Bœotia. He obeyed, and met the Thebans in battle, gaining a splendid victory after one of the most desperate fights ever known.

AGESILAUS

At last he returned to Sparta, and settled down to his former simple habits, just as though he had never seen a foreign country, and this made his fellow-citizens love and admire him more than ever. He was wise enough to make a friend of Agesipolis, the king who ruled Sparta with him, and by so doing got his half-brother, Teleutias, chosen admiral. Then, with his assistance at sea, Agesilaus made an expedition against the Corinthians, and took possession of their long walls. He was engaged in several other wars, being sometimes victorious and sometimes defeated, but always ready to fight the Thebans, whom he hated exceedingly. Indeed, this hatred was so well known that the Thebans complained of it, and said, "We are wearing ourselves out by going in such numbers on this or that expedition every year at the will of a handful of Lacedæmonians."

But Agesilaus convinced them that he had more warriors in the field than they had; for, as the Lacedæmonians were forbidden to learn trades, they were all warriors, whereas the Theban army was composed of mechanics of all sorts.

The Spartans were not always successful, but met with several defeats both by sea and by land, and at last, tired of so many wars, the various Greek states sent ambassadors to Lacedæmonia to arrange a treaty of peace. By the advice of Agesilaus, Thebes was left out when the treaty was signed, and war was declared on the spot against that city.

All the signs were opposed to war, but Agesilaus was determined to gratify his dislike of the Thebans, and the defeat of Leuctra was the consequence. In that battle four thousand Spartans were killed, and they were the flower of the army, brave young men, who fell sword in hand. From that time Sparta lost the superiority she had held in Greece for nearly five hundred years. The Thebans lost only three hundred men at Leuctra, and won the most glorious success that one Greek tribe could ever boast of over another.

The Spartans knew how to bear adversity with dignity, and showed in this case how truly brave they were. For when the news of their defeat reached Sparta a solemn feast was being celebrated, and many strangers from foreign countries were present. The Ephors gave orders that the rejoicings should not be interrupted, and privately sent the names of the slain to each family that had lost a member. The next morning the relations of those that had died fighting for their country appeared in public with cheerful countenances and congratulated each other, while those whose sons and brothers had survived hid themselves and looked troubled.

The reason of this was that among the Spartans those of their warriors who escaped death when their army was defeated were called runaways, and as such the laws against them were very severe. They had no honors of any sort shown them; no woman wanted to marry them; it was permitted to any one who should meet them in the street to beat them, and they dared not resist. They were in such disgrace that they were obliged to go about unwashed and poorly dressed, with patched clothes and unshaven beards.

At this time, when soldiers were needed, it was unfortunate for so many to be in disgrace, and it was feared that they might commit some desperate deed, so Agesilaus was requested to decide what was best to do. He would not take it upon himself to change any part of the laws, but, appearing in the public assembly, he proclaimed "that the law should sleep for to-day, and from this day forth be rigorously executed." So the young Spartans preserved their honor, and, in order to encourage them, Agesilaus led them at once into Arcadia, ravaged the country, and took the town of Mantinea. This success was balm to their wounded honor.

In the southern part of Greece is a district called Laconia, which, at the time we speak of, was inhabited by the Dorians. So powerful were these people considered that no man dared to invade their territory, and for six hundred years they had not seen the face of an enemy within its limits. But now the Thebans were aroused, and would stop at nothing, so with Epaminondas, a learned and virtuous statesman and soldier, to lead them, they invaded Laconia with a tremendous army, and ravaged and plundered the country to the very outskirts of Sparta.

Agesilaus stayed in Sparta to strengthen the fortifications and guard the exposed places. He was constantly taunted by the Thebans, who called him the author of all the trouble in his country, and bade him defend himself as best he could. Besides, he had to bear the reproaches of the old men and the women of Sparta, who were almost out of their senses on account of the enemy being so near, for hitherto it had been the proud boast of his countrymen that their wives and daughters had never beheld the smoke of the enemy's fire. This was changed now, and Agesilaus felt that he was to blame for it; his reputation was tarnished, and he had the pain of knowing that the country, which had been in a most flourishing and powerful condition when he mounted the throne, was now laid low; her glory had departed, and his own boasts had come to nothing.

While the disturbance lasted, several conspiracies were formed among the bad citizens, but, as soon as they were discovered, Agesilaus consulted with the Ephors and had the offenders put to death privately. This was a new proceeding, for Spartans had never before been punished without trial. Many of the Helot soldiers deserted to the enemy, thereby causing great alarm to the inhabitants, which Agesilaus sought to remedy by having the soldiers' quarters searched regularly before daylight and the arms of the deserters hidden, that it might not become known how many of them there were.

No historian gives a reason for the departure of the Thebans from Laconia, but certain it is that it took place after three months, and all agree that Sparta was saved from complete ruin by the wisdom of Agesilaus. He could not restore her glory or her ancient greatness, but he could and did sacrifice all personal feelings for her safety in time of peril.

Although Agesilaus had now grown old, he could not be satisfied with inactivity. So he entered the service of Tachos, the Egyptian chief, though it was regarded as unworthy for such a man to hire himself out as captain of a band of mercenary or paid soldiers to assist a rebel in opposing his sovereign. But he did this nevertheless, and fitted out a fleet with the money Tachos had sent him, and then set sail with thirty Spartans for counsellors, as he had done at the very beginning of his career.

On his arrival in Egypt, all the great officers of the kingdom flocked to the shore, anxious to behold a hero who was looked upon as the first commander in all Greece. When they saw only a little old man in mean attire seated on the grass, they laughed, and said, "The old proverb is now made good; the mountain has brought forth a mouse."

Tachos was preparing for the war, and Agesilaus expected to be put in command of all the forces, but he was disappointed in this as well as in other matters. The Egyptians were haughty and insolent towards him, and he soon began to regret having joined them. Therefore, an opportunity offering for him to desert, he did it, although even the most partial of his biographers cannot acquit him of base treachery in doing so. But he was growing old, and longed to return to Sparta, which was again engaged in war. It was winter when he set sail, and he was overtaken, by a storm, which drove him upon a desert shore of Africa called the Haven of Menelaus, where he died at the age of eighty-four.

It was a Spartan custom to bury ordinary persons in the land where they ceased to breathe, but their kings were carried home. So the attendants of Agesilaus embalmed his body with melted wax and conveyed it to Sparta, where it was buried with all due honors.

DION

WHEN Dionysius the Elder was tyrant or ruler of Syracuse, he had two wives, whom he loved very much. Their names were Doris and Aristomache. Aristomache had a brother Dion, who is the subject of this chapter.

Dion was well received at court, and his brother-in-law, Dionysius, liked him so much that he ordered his treasurer to supply him with all the money he wanted. Dion was too virtuous to take undue advantage of such generosity, but it enabled him to devote his time to study, and he became a very talented man.

Plato, the great Athenian philosopher, instructed him, and under such good influence Dion improved in every particular. He was considered one of Plato's most distinguished scholars, and so impressed was he by the doctrines of the philosopher that he wanted Dionysius to get the benefit of them too. So he persuaded him to attend some of the lectures; but Dionysius was not pleased to hear virtues lauded for which he cared nothing. Plato told him that only the just could be happy, and that the unjust were sure to be miserable. This was a new idea to Dionysius, whose actions were governed entirely by his passions, and it was an unwelcome one, particularly as he could find no good argument to bring forward on the other side.

DION

So he became angry, and asked Plato, roughly, "What business have you here in Sicily?"

"I came to seek an honest man," answered the philosopher.

"Then you have lost your labor, it seems," returned the tyrant.

His anger did not end with words, and at last Dion persuaded Plato, for his own safety, to leave Sicily. Accordingly, he embarked on board a vessel to return to Greece. Dionysius ordered the captain either to drop him into the sea or to sell him as a slave. "For," said he, "according to his own teachings, this man can never be unhappy; a just man, he says, must be happy in a state of slavery as well as in a state of freedom."

The captain took his passenger to Ægina, and sold him there for twenty pounds, for the people of that place, being at war with the Athenians at that time, had decreed that any of them who were taken on their shore should be so disposed of.

Dionysius continued to be fond of Dion, and sent him on several important embassies. During his absence on one of these occasions the tyrant died, and was succeeded by his son of the same name.

The younger Dionysius was a less able man than his father, and had neither his judgment nor experience, so he allowed himself to be ruled by courtiers, who led him into all sorts of gayety and dissipation, against the advice of Dion, who, having returned to Syracuse, did what he could to direct the young man properly.

Dionysius wondered at the wisdom of Dion, and might have been influenced by him if the courtiers had been out of the way, but they were determined to keep the upper hand in the government and to control the young king. So they encouraged him to spend his life in enjoyment, and made up stories that put Dion in a bad light.

With a tyrant whose time and attention were devoted to pleasure the government became very weak, and this so grieved Dion that he persuaded Dionysius to invite Plato to Sicily and place himself under his guidance. At first he paid little heed to what Dion said, but as time went on and the maxims of Plato were repeated and made clear to him, he became impatient to see the man who set forth such novel and wonderful ideas. So he wrote two or three letters urging the philosopher to come to Syracuse. Dion and other wise men added their entreaties, and Plato, with the hope of doing good to the young tyrant, at last consented.

One of the royal chariots, richly ornamented, stood on the sea-shore to receive him when he landed, and after welcoming him, Dionysius sacrificed to the gods in acknowledgment of the great happiness, as he called the arrival of Plato, which had overtaken his government.

For a while all went well, and the citizens were delighted with the changes that were made, for their tyrant became kind and gentle, paid attention to matters of business, gave banquets that were decent and respectable, and no longer spent days at a time in intoxication, as he had frequently done. Everybody began to reason and argue about questions of public interest, and even the palace itself was filled with students.

But this state of affairs was not to last, for the greater Plato's influence became, the more were the courtiers alarmed at the effect it might eventually have on their tyrant. So they talked against Dion openly, and declared that through Plato he had bewitched Dionysius for the purpose of destroying in him all desire for power, riches, or pleasure, and of inducing him to settle his government on the children of Aristomache, Dion's sister.

At last they brought matters to a climax by showing Dionysius a letter which they said Dion had written the Carthaginians, advising them when they wanted peace to ask it through him, because he would promise to obtain for them whatever terms they proposed. Dionysius said nothing about this to Dion for a long while; but one day, having invited him to take a walk, he led him to the sea-side, and there produced the letter, and accused his companion of having conspired with the Carthaginians against himself. Dion was completely taken by surprise, and made such a lame defence that the tyrant resolved to get rid of him on the spot. He therefore ordered his attendants to carry him to a vessel which lay at anchor in the harbor close by, and bid the seamen to sail at once, and set their prisoner ashore on the coast of Italy.

Now Dion was a great favorite in the royal household, and there were loud lamentations when his fate was made known; but Dionysius declared that he had not been banished, but only sent away for a limited time and for his own good. He did not reveal his true reason for his conduct with regard to Dion, but pacified his relations by giving them permission to load two vessels with the servants and effects of the exile and send them to him.

Dion was a man of wealth, and the number of costly and luxurious articles his friends shipped to him enabled him to fit up his house with royal splendor. In course of time he settled himself at Athens, and the people wondered what must be the power of a tyrant when an exile from his kingdom could make such a display of riches.

Dionysius removed Plato to the castle under pretence of doing him honor, but in reality to set a guard over him, lest he should follow Dion and tell the world how he had been banished. Dionysius had another reason for wishing to keep Plato with him, and that was that he had grown fond of him and of the study of philosophy under his guidance; but a war soon broke out, and he was forced to let him go.

Meanwhile, Dion was becoming very popular in Athens as well as in other Grecian cities, and public honors were often bestowed on him merely because of the love and admiration he inspired. This made Dionysius so angry that he confiscated the estates of the exile, and no longer sent him a supply of money. Then, fearing that Plato might speak ill of him among the philosophers, he collected a number of wise men at his court and tried to appear very learned before them. He soon found, however, that he needed Plato to help him to sustain his arguments, so he sent a messenger to beg him to return to Sicily, and wrote a letter in which he said that Dion might expect no favors from him unless Plato consented. The wife and sister of Dion also wrote, imploring Plato, for their sakes, to gratify the tyrant.

Therefore Plato set sail for Sicily the third time, and his arrival was hailed with joy, no less by Dionysius than by the citizens. Before long Plato began to speak of his friend Dion, and tried to make the tyrant say what he meant to do for him;

but Dionysius always changed the subject, hoping that in time Plato would cease to think of Dion altogether.

While matters stood thus, one of Plato's followers foretold an eclipse of the sun, and as it happened just when he said it would, the tyrant rewarded him with a talent of silver. Thereupon a philosopher jestingly said, "I, too, can predict something extraordinary." On being questioned, he replied, "I foresee that in a short time there will be a quarrel between Dionysius and Plato."

Soon after this the tyrant sold Dion's estate, but refused to send him the money. Plato was so indignant at this that he resolved to leave Sicily forthwith, and one of his friends provided a vessel for him. But Dionysius, desiring to soften Plato's feelings towards himself, gave him some grand entertainments before he left. At one of these he said, "No doubt, Plato, when you are at home among the philosophers, you will often make my faults the subject of your conversation." "I hope we shall never be so much at a loss for subjects in the Academy as to talk of you," returned Plato.

Not only did the tyrant confiscate the absent Dion's estates, but he compelled the unfortunate man's wife to marry one of his favorite courtiers. When Dion heard of how he had been wronged he determined to make war on Syracuse. Many friends declared themselves ready to help him, and soldiers to the number of eight hundred were raised. They met on an island in the middle of summer, and Dion prepared a magnificent sacrifice to Apollo. Afterwards there was an eclipse of the moon, which frightened the soldiers dreadfully, but Dion, who understood the natural causes of such an event, made one of his soothsayers explain it as meaning that the splendid reign of Dionysius should be eclipsed as soon as they arrived in Sicily. So they were encouraged, though there were several other unfavorable omens, which even the most ingenious failed to turn to account.

Dion sailed with all his men in two ships, and had the good fortune to land at Syracuse when Dionysius was absent in Italy. There was great excitement in the city when his arrival was known, but he took care to preserve quiet as much as possible. Timocrates, who had married Dion's wife, despatched a messenger to Italy with a letter informing the tyrant of what had happened. While passing through Rhegium the messenger met an acquaintance who was carrying home part of a sacrifice. A piece of the meat was offered to him; he accepted it and proceeded on his journey. He travelled a good part of the night, but towards morning, being overcome by fatigue, he entered a wood just off the road and lay down to rest. He fell asleep, and a wolf, smelling the meat, came and seized it, and carried it away with the letter-bag, to which it was tied. When the man awoke he looked everywhere for his bag, and was dreadfully distressed at not being able to find it. Of course he did not dare to go before the king without the letter, so he decided to hide himself and keep out of the way of the royal displeasure.

Thus it happened that Dionysius heard nothing of the arrival in Syracuse of Dion for a long time. When at last the news reached him, he hastened home by sea and got safe into the citadel. But this took place a whole week after Dion had declared the Sicilians free from the yoke of the tyrant, and had liberated the state prisoners and armed the citizens.

Dionysius despatched agents privately to Dion to see what terms could be made, but the answer he received was that he must treat with the people. So the tyrant sent one messenger after another with the fairest and most flattering promises; but the Syracusans had no faith in him, and would scarcely listen to his proposals. At last he asked them to offer terms themselves, or to send some representatives to the citadel to discuss what it was best to do. The Syracusans consented, but their agents were seized and locked up by the tyrant, who, having freely distributed wine among the soldiers in the citadel until they were intoxicated, made an attack on the city by break of day.

Dion was unprepared for such a surprise, but he resisted at first with the hired soldiers, whom he led on in person, and fought a fierce and bloody battle. He was wounded in the hand, but mounted a horse, rallied the citizens as they fled, and at the same time brought up his Greek soldiers, who drove Dionysius and his army back to the fortress after a great number of them had been killed. The Syracusans rewarded the foreign soldiers for their service, and put a gold crown on Dion's head.

The tyrant made another trial to regain his kingdom; this time by letter. He wrote Dion begging him not to destroy the government and give freedom to his enemies, but to proclaim himself king, if only for the protection of his family and friends. Dion was honest enough to show this letter to the Syracusans, but instead of admiring him for so doing, they became suspicious that he might really take some desperate step for the sake of his wife and son. So they began to look about for another leader, and heard with joy that Heraclides, a soldier then under banishment, who had once held an important command in the service of Dionysius, was on his way home.

As soon as he arrived an assembly was called, and he was chosen commander of the navy. Heraclides pretended to be a friend to Dion, but secretly he was an enemy, and tried in every possible way to injure him in the minds of the citizens. So Dion's unpopularity increased, but he worked so hard to keep order that no attack was made on him.

In course of time Dionysius made his escape from the citadel, and then Heraclides, who had charge of the navy, was openly blamed. He did not know how to excuse himself, so he turned people's attention in another direction, by causing one of the public speakers to go among them and excite them to rebel against Dion's laws, and to urge them to insist upon a redivision of land, on the ground that so long as they remained poor they would be slaves. He spoke to them also, and advised them to get rid of Dion's oppression. The idea of freedom was so new to the Syracusans that they did not quite understand it, but they hated Dion, and were willing to be led by any other person who seemed to be on their side.

So they called an assembly and elected twenty-five captains, among whom was Heraclides. They tried to win over Dion's men by offering to make them citizens of Syracuse if they would desert him. But they would not listen to anything so base; they went to Dion, and, with their swords in their hands, placed him in their midst and conveyed him out of the city. He went to Leontium, where he was received with honors. But the time came when the Syracusans were glad enough to get him back again. It happened in this wise.

Dionysius sent a fleet commanded by a Neapolitan, named Nypsius, with provisions and pay for those he had left in the citadel. Nypsius was attacked by the Syracusans, who took four of his ships, but, as they had no person to guide them and had not learned to control themselves, they celebrated their victory by feasting, rioting, and drunkenness, in which their twenty-five commanders joined. Taking advantage of the disorder, Nypsius broke through the walls in the night and let his soldiers loose upon the city. They tore down the fortifications, set fire to the houses, killed the men, and dragged the women and children shrieking and screaming to the citadel. The Syracusan officers gave up all for lost. Suddenly, in the midst of the terrible scene, a voice from the cavalry was heard crying, "Send for Dion and his Peloponnesians from Leontium."

The very mention of his name inspired hope; the people shouted for joy, and half a dozen of the cavalry immediately rode off towards Leontium. They arrived just after sunset, and, throwing themselves at the feet of Dion, told him of the deplorable condition of their city. He summoned an assembly, and the Leontines and Peloponnesians soon gathered about him. Then, at his request, the soldiers repeated the sad news, and added entreaties that he, with his foreign soldiers, would go to the assistance of the unfortunate people, who had suffered so much because of their ingratitude and ignorance. For several minutes Dion was so overcome with grief that he could not speak, but at last, wiping away his tears, he said, "Men of Peloponnesus and of the confederacy, I asked for your presence here that you might consider your own interests. For myself, I have no interests to consult while Syracuse is perishing, and, though I may not save it from destruction, I will hasten thither and be buried in the ruins of my country. Yet if you can find it in your hearts to assist us, you may, to your everlasting honor, save the unhappy city. But if the Syracusans are to have no more pity or relief from you, may the gods reward you for what you have done for them, and for your kindness to Dion, of whom speak hereafter as one who did not desert you when you were injured and abused, nor his fellow-citizens when they were afflicted."

Before he had ended, the soldiers shouted out their readiness to go with him, and begged him to lead them at once to the relief of Syracuse. When quiet was restored, Dion gave orders that all should go to their quarters and prepare to march. That night they set forward.

Meanwhile, another attack had been made on the city by Nypsius, who seemed determined to lay it in ruins and leave not a living human being within its walls. In this dreadful strait, messenger after messenger met Dion on the road, and begged him to hurry forward. He made his arrangements that he might attack from several quarters at once, and, having offered vows to the gods, rode into the city at the head of his men, while a confused sound of shouts, congratulations, and prayers was raised by the people. They called Dion their deliverer, and his soldiers their friends, brethren, and fellow-citizens.

Heaps of dead bodies lay in the streets through which Dion passed with his men, and houses were blazing on all sides, which made it both difficult and dangerous for them to advance. When they came near the enemy, the road was so narrow and uneven that only a few could engage at a time, but they beat off Nypsius's men and put them to flight. Many got into the castle, but those who did not were put to the sword.

The Syracusans could not spare time to rejoice, for they were too busy in trying to put out the flames, at which they worked the entire night. All of the captains, except two, escaped from the city, well knowing that they deserved punishment for what had happened.

The two who remained were Heraclides and Theodotes. These went to Dion and surrendered themselves. They acknowledged that they had been wrong, but begged him to treat them more kindly than they had treated him, and to be generous to men who were absolutely in his power.

Dion's friends advised him on no account to pardon men who had been so active in bringing about the ruin of the city, but he said, "My studies under Plato and other wise men have taught me to subdue my passions, and not to give way to anger and revenge. There would be no merit in showing kindness to men of virtue; it is those who have injured us that we must pardon. If I have excelled Heraclides in ability, I must not be inferior to him in justice and clemency. Heraclides may be treacherous, malicious, base; but must Dion therefore sully his glory by indulging his anger? There is no man so wicked but that he may be influenced by kindness and softened by favors."

Having spoken thus, Dion pardoned the guilty men and sent them away.

But Heraclides proved himself unworthy the mercy that had been shown him, for, although Dion even restored him to his position as admiral after having pardoned him, he excited the sailors to rebellion and led them against Syracuse. Dion went out to sea with an army to meet him, and defeated him. Then it was decided to lay by the fleet, because it was not really needed at that time, and was only an expense and trouble to the Syracusans.

Attention was next turned to the citadel, and the son of Dionysius, who had been left there in command, agreed to deliver up the fort, with all the soldiers and ammunition, to Dion. It was a happy day for Syracuse when the prince sailed away with his five vessels, leaving them free from the most tyrannical rule that had ever existed.

Dion now settled himself in his house, and lived in very plain, frugal style, notwithstanding his high position. He knew that the eyes of the whole world were upon him, and he was anxious to show that prosperity did not make him foolish.

It was not long before Heraclides gave trouble again by interfering with political affairs, and opposing everything that Dion attempted. Then some of the citizens, feeling that there could be no peace while Heraclides lived, broke into his house and murdered him.

Dion had a friend named Calippus, in whom he placed a great deal of confidence; but Calippus only pretended friendship, while all the time he was going around among the lower classes talking against Dion, and trying to make them hate him. When Dion heard what Calippus said of him, he believed, as he had been told by the false friend, that it was done merely for the sake of finding out who were true to him, and that Calippus spoke so freely on purpose to draw others out.

But he soon found his mistake, for Calippus was forming a plot against his life. Just then his only son threw himself from the top of a house in a fit of temper and broke his neck. While Dion was mourning the loss of this youth, whom he had loved very dearly, Calippus hurried on his conspiracy by announcing that the son of Dionysius was going to be sent for to become their ruler. This aroused the people to such a degree of indignation and terror that a great number were added to those already in the plot. So when Dion sat at supper one evening with several of his friends, the conspirators surrounded the house and guarded the windows and doors while a few entered, and, falling upon Dion, threw him to the ground and endeavored to stifle him. His friends thought only of their own safety, and did not attempt to assist him. Presently a sword was handed in at one of the windows, and with it the almost exhausted Dion, who had made a desperate resistance, was quickly despatched.

Calippus then took the government of Syracuse in his own hands, but he was hated and despised by everybody. No city that he visited would receive him, and at last he was killed by his own soldiers with the very sword that had been used to put Dion to death.

PHOCION

NOTHING positive is known about the birth of Phocion, except that it took place in Athens. His parents were supposed to be of high standing, because he was well bred and well educated, which would probably not have been the case had they been ordinary people.

Phocion had a gentle, humane disposition, but the expression of his face was so severe that only those who knew him well dared to approach him. His conversation was full of wisdom and instruction, but he wasted no words, for he spoke briefly and always to the point, so that a philosopher of his day said, "Demosthenes is the best orator, but Phocion is certainly the most powerful speaker in Athens."

So reserved was Phocion that the Athenians never saw him either laugh or cry or use a public bath. If he made an excursion to the country, or marched out to war, he always went barefooted and without his cloak, unless it happened to be intensely cold, and then his soldiers used to laugh and say, "It is a sign of a sharp winter; Phocion has got his clothes on."

In his youth he served as a soldier under Chabrias, a general with whom he became such a favorite as to be selected from among the whole army to conduct enterprises of importance and trust.

PHOCION

Strange as it may seem, Phocion had great influence over his commander, who was many years his senior, and often kept him in check when he was rash, or urged him on when he was inclined to postpone a battle. In return, Chabrias gave his young friend opportunities to distinguish himself, and at the sea-fight of Naxos he behaved with so much valor that he won a great reputation in Greece.

After Chabrias was killed, Phocion continued to be friendly with his family, and tried very hard to improve his son, who was a stupid, badly-behaved fellow. Once he lost patience with the boy because he asked so many silly rude questions, and exclaimed, "O Chabrias, Chabrias! what a return do I make thee for thy favors, by bearing with the impertinence of thy son!"

The Athenians had so much confidence in the military genius of Phocion that whenever they were about to engage in a war they turned to him for aid, and he was elected general of their army forty-five separate times, though he never asked for the office, and was seldom present when the elections took place.

Phocion had the moral courage to do what he thought right, and no amount of ridiculing or fault-finding on the part of others could change him. On a certain occasion his countrymen insisted that he should lead them against an enemy, and, when he refused, called him a coward, whereupon he answered, "Do what you will, I shall not be brave; and do what I will, you will not be cowards; however, we know one another very well."

At a time of danger to the country the people once became angry with him, and demanded an account of how he had used the public money. All he said was, "My good friends, first get out of your difficulties."

While war lasted they were always humble and submissive, but as soon as it was over they were apt to find fault with their general. Once they declared that he had robbed them of victory at the very moment when it was in their hands. "It is well for you," he said, "that you have a general who knows you; otherwise you would have been ruined long ago."

There was a quarrel between the Athenians and Bœotians, which the latter refused to settle by treaty, and proposed to decide by the sword. Phocion told them, "Good people, you had better try the method you understand best; and that is talking, not fighting."

Demosthenes, the orator, who belonged to the opposite party, said to him, "Phocion, the Athenians will certainly kill thee some day." "They may kill me if they are mad, but it will be you if they are in their senses," was his ready answer.

A very fat man was one day urging on a war with Philip of Macedon, and got so hot and excited while speaking that he stopped several times to swallow a little water. "Here is a nice fellow to lead us to war," exclaimed Phocion, "for what may we expect of him loaded down with a suit of armor, when he is ready to choke under a speech that he has composed at his leisure?"

When Lycurgus took him to task for opposing the demand which Alexander made for ten Athenian orators to be sent to him, he answered, "It is true I have given my countrymen much good counsel, but they do not follow it."

PHOCION

There was a citizen named Aristogiton, who always pretended to be in favor of war; but when the lists came to be made out, he appeared with his leg bound up and a crutch under his arm. "Here comes Aristogiton," cried Phocion, aloud; "put him down a cripple and a coward."

It seems strange that a man who could say such severe things should have been surnamed the *Good*, but such was the case with Phocion, for he could be both rough and gentle, sweet-tempered or cross, according as he was affected by different circumstances. He never did harm to a fellow-citizen from personal feelings, but he was severe against those who worked not for the public good, and he was always ready to assist an unfortunate person, even though he chanced to be an enemy. His friends finding fault with him one day for pleading the cause of a man who was undeserving, he said, "Surely the good have no need of an advocate."

Although Phocion always desired peace, yet he distinguished himself frequently in battle, and he was so popular among the nations allied to Athens, that they treated every other commander sent to them as an enemy, though they always welcomed him and received him with honors.

He defeated the forces of Philip of Macedon in Eubœa, and afterwards saved Byzantium from that monarch, and recovered several cities that had been guarded by his forces. Thus King Philip was driven quite out of the Hellespont, where, until then, he had been greatly feared.

Upon the news of Philip's death, which happened not long after, Phocion would not allow sacrifices or public rejoicings, for he said, "Nothing shows greater meanness of spirit than expressions of joy on the death of an enemy. After all, the army we fought with is lessened only by one man, so there is no great reason to rejoice."

When Alexander of Macedon marched against Thebes and took possession of the city, he demanded that Demosthenes and three others who had opposed a treaty should be delivered up to him. The people did not know what to do, but turned to Phocion for advice. As usual, he spoke out boldly, and said, "The persons whom Alexander demands have brought the commonwealth into such a miserable state, that even if he had named my most intimate friend as one of them, I should vote to deliver him up. For my part, I should think it the greatest happiness to die for you all. At the same time I am not without pity for the Thebans who have taken refuge among us; but it is enough for Greece to weep for Thebes, let her not weep for Athens too. The best thing we can do is to intercede with the conqueror for both, but by no means to think of fighting."

Acting upon this advice, the Athenians sent Phocion himself to confer with Alexander, and he was so successful that not only was peace restored, but he became the friend and guest of the great monarch, who showed him more respect than he did any other person at his court. Later, Alexander sent him a hundred talents for a present. When the money was brought to him, Phocion asked the ambassadors, "Why, among all the citizens of Athens, am I singled out as the object of this bounty?"

"Because," said they, "Alexander looks upon you as the only honest and good man."

"Then let him permit me always to continue so," returned Phocion, as he returned the money.

PHOCION

The men were invited to go home with him, and when they saw how simply and plainly he lived, his wife baking bread, himself drawing water to wash his feet, they urged him again to accept the gift, saying, "It is a shame for a man whom Alexander calls friend to live so poorly."

"There would be no use in my having money which I would not spend, and if I did make use of it I should get a bad name both for myself and for Alexander from my countrymen." So the treasure went back; an evidence that the man who could afford to refuse it was richer than he who offered it.

Alexander was displeased because Phocion would not accept his gift, and wrote him, "I cannot number among my friends one who refuses my favors." Still Phocion would not take the money. But he did ask a favor of the king, which was immediately granted, and that was the release of six prominent persons whom he held as prisoners. Afterwards, Alexander wanted to present him with one of four cities of Asia, which he named, but again he refused, and a few months later Alexander died.

Phocion had a son named Phocus, who gave him a great deal of trouble, because his habits were disorderly and he drank to excess. Once he asked permission to take part in the games at the great feast of Minerva; his father granted it, not because he valued the victory, or even supposed that Phocus would gain it, but because he hoped the training and discipline would make a better man of him. Phocus won the race, and many of his friends invited him to banquets in honor of it. One of these Phocion attended, and when he saw the costly preparations, for even the water which was brought to wash the guests' feet contained wine and spices, he was disgusted, and took his son to task for permitting his friend to spoil his victory thus. With the hope of weaning Phocus from such company and such luxurious habits, he sent him to Lacedæmon, to be placed among the youths under a course of Spartan discipline. The Athenians took offence at this, thinking that Phocion did not appreciate home education. One of them said to him in public, with a sneer, "Phocion, suppose you and I advise the Athenians to adopt the Spartan constitution. If you like, I am ready to introduce a bill to that effect and to speak in its favor." "Indeed," returned Phocion, sarcastically, "you, with that strong scent of perfumes about you, and that costly mantle on your shoulders, are just the very man to speak in honor of Lycurgus and Spartan simplicity, are you not?"

When the news of Alexander's death reached Athens it caused so much excitement that Phocion said, "Well, then, if Alexander be dead to-day, he will be so to-morrow and the day after, so we may make our arrangements quietly and at leisure."

Immediately after this the Lamian war began. This was a war between all the Greeks, except the Bœotians and the Macedonians; it received its name from the fact that Antipater was besieged in the town of Lamia.

It was Leosthenes who raised the forces for this war; for Phocion was very much opposed to it, and used every argument to prevent it. Thereupon one young man asked him, "Tell us, then, what will be the proper time for the Athenians to go to war?" He answered, "When the young men keep within the bounds of order and propriety, the rich become liberal in their contributions, and the orators stop robbing the public."

PHOCION

Leosthenes was victorious at first, and there was great rejoicing in Athens, particularly when an embassy came from Antipater to sue for peace. But the victors would listen to nothing but an unconditional surrender. Leosthenes was killed at the siege of Lamia, and from that moment victory favored Antipater, until he had defeated all the Greek states except Athens. Then a treaty was agreed upon, and Phocion, who was highly esteemed by Antipater, was made ruler of the city.

But there was a Macedonian garrison stationed there and commanded by Menyllus, a man who was friendly to Phocion, and did no sort of injury to the citizens. Once he offered Phocion a sum of money as a token of friendship. It was refused, with this remark, "Menyllus is not a greater man than Alexander; nor have I greater reason to receive a present now than I had when the latter offered me one." "Take it for your son Phocus," urged Menyllus. Phocion answered, "If Phocus becomes sober, his father's estate will be sufficient for him; and if he continues to drink nothing will be so."

Although Phocion commanded the Athenian armies so many times, it is to his credit that he remained poor to the end of his life. The Athenians were constantly begging him to ask Antipater to withdraw his garrison, but he saw no reason for doing so, and refused. All went well until the death of Antipater, and then new troubles arose.

Polysperchon had been nominated general-in-chief of the army, and Cassander commander of the cavalry, before Antipater died. Cassander immediately sent Nicanor to take the place of Menyllus, because that would give him more power, the former being his friend. This made the Athenians very angry, and they accused Phocion of having kept the death of the king secret until the change was made. He did not take the trouble to defend himself against the charge, but made it a point to visit Nicanor, until he succeeded in gaining his good will for the Athenians. He also persuaded him to seek theirs by presiding at their public games.

Meanwhile, Polysperchon, who had the care of the young king, Alexander's son, was determined that Cassander should not have his way in Athens, so he wrote letters to the citizens telling them that the king restored them all their liberties. The result was that at a general assembly death or banishment was voted for any man who had held office while the Macedonians were stationed at Athens. This of course included Phocion, who had been highest in office.

Now Polysperchon was not really acting in the interest of the Athenians, though he made it appear so. His object was to get possession of their city, and he knew that in order to do so it was necessary to put Phocion out of the way. This could only be brought about by the offer he made of freedom to the citizens.

Nicanor knew what Polysperchon's intention must be, and, trusting his person to Phocion, for he did not feel safe during the excitement that prevailed, he entered the assembly to explain the case to the Athenians. Then a commander of the Macedonian king tried to seize him, but he was warned in time to defend himself, though he resolved to have his revenge. The Athenians found great fault with Phocion because he let Nicanor escape when he had him in his power, but he said, "I have no reason to believe that Nicanor means us harm; but even though he should, I had rather suffer wrong than do anything unjust."

PHOCION

Phocion was very honorable, but he made a mistake in the confidence he placed in Nicanor; for that general no sooner found himself safe among his soldiers than he ordered an attack on Athens. Phocion would have gone to oppose him, but his countrymen had lost confidence in him and would not obey his commands. The son of Polysperchon, whose name was Alexander, arrived just at that period and pretended that he meant to assist the city against Nicanor. Instead of that, he wanted to get hold of it himself; so, collecting about him the exiles who had returned with him, besides the foreigners and the citizens who were for one reason or another in disgrace, he made himself so powerful that he was able to turn Phocion out of office and appoint his own men instead. The city would not have escaped this snare had Alexander been more prudent; but he had several secret meetings with Nicanor, which were discovered by the Athenians and aroused their suspicion.

Phocion and several others of the most respectable and distinguished citizens who had been publicly accused of treason went over to Polysperchon for safety. They arrived at the same time with an embassy from Athens that had been sent to accuse them and to insist that they should be compelled to return.

Polysperchon basely gave them up to stand their trial, as he said, though he knew perfectly well that they were as good as sentenced to death already. It was Clitus who took the prisoners back to Athens and shut them up until he could call an assembly of the people. Having read a letter from the Macedonian king, in which he said, "I find the prisoners guilty of treason, but leave the Athenians, as freemen, to pass sentence upon them," Clitus led forth the unfortunate men.

Many covered their faces and shed tears when they beheld Phocion so humbled. One man tried to say a word in his behalf, but he was silenced by the excited crowd. At last Phocion desired to speak; and although he could scarcely raise his voice enough to make himself heard in the tumult, he asked, "Do you wish to put us to death lawfully or unlawfully?"

"According to law," was the answer.

"How can you do that unless we have a fair hearing?" was the next question. No one replied. Then, advancing a few steps, Phocion said,—

"Citizens of Athens, I acknowledge I have done you injustice, and pronounce my public conduct to deserve sentence of death; but why will you kill these men, who have never injured you?"

"Because they are your friends," cried out the populace.

Phocion had hoped to save them by declaring himself deserving of death, but he now drew back and said no more.

The sentence was then read and put to the vote, and there was scarcely one negative. Some of the people even crowned themselves with flowers, as though they were at a festival.

After the assembly separated, the doomed men were carried back to prison, all weeping and lamenting except Phocion, whose expression and bearing were just the same as when he was in command of the army. Some of his enemies abused him as he went along, and one man spat in his face, upon which he turned to an officer and said, "You should stop this fellow's rudeness."

PHOCION

One of the prisoners bemoaned his hard fate when he saw the executioner preparing the poison. "Dost thou not think it an honor to die with me?" asked Phocion.

One of his friends inquired whether he had any commands for his son. "Yes," said he; "tell him, from me, by all means to forget the ill treatment I have had from the Athenians."

The execution took place on the day when there was a solemn procession in honor of Jupiter, and many of the horsemen threw away their garlands and wept as they passed the prison. But Phocion's enemies were so numerous that they would not allow his body to stay within the borders of Attica, nor any Athenian to furnish fire for his funeral pile. A man whose business it was to bury people for pay carried the body to Megara, and a woman who, with her maid-servants, assisted at the ceremony of burning gathered up the bones carefully in her apron and carried them by night to her own house. She buried them under her hearth, and thus addressed the gods as she did so: "Ye guardians of this place, to you I commit the remains of a good and brave man, and I implore you to protect and restore them to the tombs of his fathers when the Athenians return to their senses."

And indeed it was not long before they began to feel what an excellent, just governor they had lost. Then a statue in brass was erected to his memory, and his bones were interred with honors at the public expense.

PELOPIDAS

NOW we come to a great man, who was also such a kind, benevolent one, that the fortune of which he got complete control when he was still a youth was all used for the relief of others. Many a Theban had cause to rejoice on account of the liberality of Pelopidas. Indeed, he devoted so much time to affairs of state that he neglected his money matters, and his friends took him to task for it. He replied, "What care I for money? it is only necessary for such as Nicodemus there," pointing to a man who was both lame and blind.

All of Pelopidas's friends felt the benefit of his wealth except one; that was Epaminondas, who could never be persuaded to accept any of it. But Pelopidas loved him so much, that he spent his money on others, and for his own part preferred to live humbly, to dress plainly, and to work as Epaminondas did. This united the two friends very closely. Their tastes differed somewhat, for Pelopidas spent his leisure hours in wrestling or hunting, while the other was reading and studying. But no feeling of envy ever marred the affection of one for the other, and both had the same aim, which was to raise their country to the very highest point of glory. So they worked together to accomplish this, and their friendship lasted to the end of their lives.

PELOPIDAS

During the Peloponnesian war, the Spartans appeared friendly towards the Thebans, though in reality they were jealous of their power. There were two political parties in Thebes, the liberal one, headed by Ismenias and Androclides, to which Pelopidas and Epaminondas belonged, and the opposite one headed by Leontidas. The liberals made themselves so much feared that Leontidas even became a traitor to keep them from getting the government in their hands. Once, when the Lacedæmonian troops were marching past Thebes, he actually helped them to seize the fortress. This gave them authority to govern the city, and left the liberals no chance whatever. Ismenias was taken prisoner, and soon after murdered in Sparta. Pelopidas and others escaped this fate by running away, for which they were sentenced to banishment. Epaminondas was too poor and too much of a student to have much power, so he was not disturbed.

All the exiles went to Athens, where they were kindly received. There seemed little hope of being able to shake off the Spartan tyranny, but Pelopidas gathered his countrymen around him, and constantly told them how shameful it was for them to submit tamely, until he aroused in them a determination to strike a blow for liberty. Then they sent messages to their friends in Thebes, telling them of their plans, and Charon, a prominent citizen, offered his house for a meeting-place.

Meanwhile, Epaminondas had not been inactive, for he took pains to lecture about bravery to the young Thebans, and encouraged them to organize wrestling-matches with the Lacedæmonians, and when they were victorious he would tell them "that they ought to be ashamed of their meanness of spirit in remaining subject to those to whom they were superior in strength."

When the day fixed for action came, it was agreed by the exiles that twelve of the younger men should go forward and get into the city, if possible, while the rest should stay at the plain of Thriasian. Pelopidas was the first to offer himself for the dangerous expedition, and all those who joined him were men of noble families, who rivalled one another only in courageous exploits. Clad in short coats, such as hunters wore, carrying hunting-poles, and followed by dogs, the twelve brave Theban exiles set out over the fields towards their native city. Their friends who were in the plot met them and provided each with the dress of a peasant; then they separated and entered Thebes at different points. All proceeded to Charon's house, which they reached in safety. When the exiled twelve and their friends had assembled, their number was forty-eight.

Phillidas, who was in the plot, had managed meanwhile to get the position of secretary to the tyrants Archias and Philip. On the night of the meeting, at the house of Charon, the secretary had invited the two tyrants to his house to an entertainment, telling them that they should be introduced to some ladies of distinction. They accepted the invitation, and, while waiting for the ladies they expected to meet, drank a great deal of wine, which Phillidas supplied liberally.

While thus engaged, a messenger entered to tell Archias that there was a report about town of the presence of some conspirators in Charon's house. Phillidas ridiculed the report, and Archias was enjoying himself so much that he did not wish to be disturbed, so he sent one of his guards to bring Charon before him at once.

The conspirators were just in the act of girding on their armor, when they were startled by a loud knocking at the door. One of them stepped out to see what was the matter, and when he informed the others that an officer had been sent to fetch Charon they felt sure that their cause was lost without their having had a chance to prove their valor. It was agreed among them that Charon should obey the summons, and if possible deceive the tyrants and put a stop to their suspicion. But Charon was placed in a very unpleasant position with his friends, for he feared that they might think it was he who had let out the secret and played the part of a traitor. So before leaving he brought his little boy to Pelopidas, and said, "If you find me a traitor, treat this child as an enemy, and show him no mercy."

Many wept, and begged Charon not to think them so base and mean-spirited as to suspect or blame him; they therefore requested him to put the child beyond the reach of danger, so that he at least might escape the tyrants and live to avenge the city and his friends. "No," said Charon; "what life, what safety, could be more honorable than to die bravely with his father and such generous companions?"

When Charon was announced, Archias came out of the house, followed by Phillidas. The former said, "I have just heard, Charon, that certain suspicious-looking men have come to town and are concealed by some of the citizens." Seeing that he had no positive information, Charon was immensely relieved, and, assuming an air of innocence, asked, "Who are they? Who conceals them? Do not disturb yourself on account of a mere rumor. I will go and make all the inquiries I can, for it is perhaps not prudent to disregard anything of that sort." Phillidas praised him for being so ready to watch the interests of his country, and then led Archias back to his bottle, telling him that neither he nor Philip must go until the ladies arrived.

Not long after, a letter was handed to Archias from a friend in Athens. On the outside was written, "Urgent business; to be read at once." It contained a full account of the conspiracy; but Archias was too intoxicated by that time to care for anything; so, pushing the letter under his cushion, he said, with a drunken smile, "Urgent business to-morrow," and tried to turn his thoughts to what his host was saying, for Phillidas worked hard to hold the attention of his guests.

The return of Charon was greeted with cheers, and the friends of liberty prepared to act without delay. Pelopidas, taking half under his direction, went against two of the nobles in the neighborhood, whose names were Leontidas and Hypates, while Charon and the rest, having put on women's clothes over their armor, and wreaths of pine and poplar upon their heads to conceal their faces somewhat, undertook to dispose of the tyrants who were being entertained by Phillidas.

The make-believe women were allowed to enter the house without the least resistance. Three or four of them walked straight to the table at which Archias and Philip sat, and while Phillidas persuaded the rest of the company not to interfere, they drew their swords and killed the intoxicated tyrants without much trouble.

Pelopidas and his party had a more difficult task, for Leontidas was not only brave, but he was sober. His house-door was found locked, for he had gone to bed, and the conspirators had to knock loud and long before they could make themselves heard. At last a servant unbarred the door, but before he could ask what was wanted he was knocked down, and a rush was made for the bed-chamber. The noise aroused Leontidas, who, always on the alert for treachery,

PELOPIDAS

jumped up and seized his sword. If he had remembered to put out his lamp, he might have escaped; but, as he did not, his chances were few. However, with one stroke he laid the first man who entered dead at his feet. Pelopidas was the second. The narrow door-way and the dead body that lay across it made the fight long and doubtful, but Pelopidas was victorious at last; and no sooner had he slain Leontidas than he hastened to the house of Hypates, who had been warned just in time to seek refuge with a neighbor; but he was followed and killed also.

By this time the whole city was aroused, and all was terror and confusion. Men ran to and fro trying to find out what had really happened, for all sorts of wild rumors were afloat, and the citizens watched eagerly for day to dawn, that they might find out the truth. Now there were fifteen hundred Spartan soldiers in the garrison, and many people had joined them during the night, but they were so alarmed and so unable to find out the true state of affairs that they contented themselves with merely guarding the citadel, instead of falling upon the conspirators as they ought to have done.

By the time the longed-for day did at last dawn, those of the exiles who had remained outside the city had joined the others. Pelopidas had sent Phillidas to the jails to release those brave Thebans who had been imprisoned by the Spartans, and Epaminondas, with a large body of armed men, young and old, had marched to the market-place, where an assemblage of citizens was soon summoned.

Pelopidas stood surrounded by priests, who carried garlands in their hands and called aloud to the people to exert themselves for their gods and their country. Loud cheers rent the air, and the excited assembly shouted the names of the conspirators in turn, calling them their preservers and deliverers.

Pelopidas was chosen chief captain of Bœotia, and his first action was to blockade the citadel. With the assistance of Charon and Melon he stormed it on all sides and drove the Spartans out. A good many skirmishes were fought between the Spartans and the Thebans after that, but the former could not again get the upper hand. From the night when the Theban exiles fought so desperately for liberty and put an end to the tyrants who ruled them, the Spartans lost their power.

Pelopidas, with his company of three hundred foot-soldiers, called the *Sacred Band*, won victories at every turn. This *Band of Lovers*, as it was sometimes termed, was the very flower of the Theban army, a brave, resolute set of young men who had vowed eternal friendship for one another, and had bound themselves by the strongest ties to stand by one another to the last drop of blood. These warriors showed themselves superior even to the Spartans, who had never before been beaten by a company smaller than their own, and proved that the bravest and most formidable opponents are those who fear disgrace more than danger.

The Thebans gained so many victories that they won over to themselves the greater part of those nations that had formed the Spartan confederacy. The army was led by Pelopidas and Epaminondas, both so popular that the peoples they conquered were glad to be placed under their protection and to follow wherever they led. This being the case, they did not stop until many towns of Lacedæmonia had been taken, and the whole country to the very sea-shore had been laid waste.

PELOPIDAS

Then Alexander, the tyrant of Pheræ, made war against the Thessalians, and they sent to Thebes for assistance. Pelopidas offered himself, and he was so successful in Thessaly that Alexander became frightened and stole away with his guards. Having relieved the Thessalians of their tyrant, Pelopidas went to Macedonia, because his reputation for justice was so well known that he had been sent for to settle a dispute between Ptolemy of Egypt and the king of Macedonia. He made peace between the two monarchs, and received for hostages Philip, Prince of Macedonia, and thirty children of noble birth. These he sent to Thebes, to show the Greeks what confidence was felt in the only one of their colonies that still had a popular government.

Again were the Thessalians forced to seek aid of the Thebans. Pelopidas and Ismenias went to them, but took no troops of their own this time, and were therefore obliged to make use of the Thessalian forces.

But just then there was fresh trouble in Macedonia, for a new quarrel had arisen, and Ptolemy had killed the king. Thereupon the friends of the dead sovereign called on Pelopidas to help them, and having no troops of his own, as we have said, he hastily raised some mercenaries or paid soldiers, and marched with them against Ptolemy. It must be remembered that these mercenaries were foreign soldiers who received money for their services; consequently, as they were not prompted by patriotism, they fought for the highest bidder. Such being the case, Ptolemy bribed them liberally and got them over to his side. But even then he was so much afraid of Pelopidas that, not knowing what steps he might take next, he went to pay his respects to the Theban general, and tried very hard to pacify him by promising to keep the kingdom in trust for the brothers of the dead king, and to take sides with Thebes against her enemies. As a guarantee of honesty, he delivered his son and fifty of his companions as hostages. These also were sent to Thebes.

Pelopidas next turned his attention to the mercenaries, whose treachery he determined to punish. They had lodged themselves, with their effects, their wives and children, at Pharsalus, and thither, with some troops from Thessaly, Pelopidas proceeded. Much to his surprise, it was the tyrant Alexander with his army who met him there. Supposing that he desired to apologize for his former conduct, Pelopidas and Ismenias went to him together. They speedily found their mistake, for they were seized and shut up in the fortress at Pheræ.

As soon as the Thebans heard of this outrage, they ordered their troops to Thessaly without delay. Epaminondas was acting as a private soldier then, because he had been accused of not pursuing all his advantages in a late battle against the Spartans, and, in consequence, deprived of his command.

The tyrant Alexander did not prevent his prisoner from seeing people while he was in the fortress; he rather encouraged visitors to go there, because he wished to make a display of the way he had humbled Pelopidas. But the Pheræans were so distressed when they saw the situation of so brave a general that he had to comfort them. One day he sent word to the tyrant "that he was very wrong to put to death so many of his innocent subjects and spare him, who, he might be sure, was determined to punish him as soon as he was free."

"Why is Pelopidas in such haste to die?" asked the tyrant. When this question was repeated to the prisoner, he said, "It is that Alexander, being more hated by the gods than ever, may the sooner come to a miserable end."

This Alexander was such a wicked wretch that he often buried people alive, and some he would have dressed in the skins of bears and wild boars, and then either drive dogs at them or fire darts at them, merely to amuse himself. Many such horrible deeds are related of him, and, knowing what a cruel tyrant he was, it is astonishing that Pelopidas should have been so daring. But he probably knew that tyrants are nearly always cowards, and Alexander proved the truth of this saying when Epaminondas was placed at the head of the Theban army again. This change was made because the other generals who had gone to Thessaly were either incapable or unfortunate. As soon as Alexander heard that Epaminondas was coming, he began to tremble, and sent ambassadors forward to meet him and offer satisfaction.

Epaminondas would enter into no treaty with such a man, nor would he listen to any propositions. He made a formal demand for the return of Pelopidas and Ismenias; they were conducted to him, and he marched away with his army.

About this time the Spartans and Athenians sent to the Persians for assistance, and as soon as the Thebans heard of it they despatched Pelopidas on the same errand. This was a wise choice, for Artaxerxes had heard of the wonderful victories of the Theban, and of his having beaten the Lacedæmonians by sea and land, and he was proud to receive such a distinguished person with honors. He offered him costly presents too, but Pelopidas would accept nothing; all he asked was "that Greece should be free and independent; that Messenia should be repeopled; and that the Thebans should be considered the king's hereditary friends."

These terms being granted, greatly increased the popularity of Pelopidas at home. The other ambassadors met with no favors whatever.

Soon after Pelopidas got back to Thebes, the Thessalians were obliged to send for him again, because the tyrant Alexander had seized many of their cities, and was threatening others. The army was just ready to move, when an eclipse of the sun took place at noonday. We know with what superstitious awe the ancients looked upon this event, and how they always considered it an ill omen. Pelopidas was not more advanced in this regard than his countrymen, but he was ready to march, and nothing could deter him. But he understood the objections made by the seven thousand citizens who were under arms, and sympathized with them, so with a body of only three hundred volunteer horsemen he set forward.

At Pharsalus more troops joined him, and the two armies met at Thetidium. "The tyrant meets us with a great army," said one of the soldiers to the general on beholding Alexander with his numerous troops. "So much the better," he replied, "for then we shall conquer the more."

When the battle began, Pelopidas commanded his cavalry to charge the enemy. They did so, and routed them. Then Alexander took to the hills near by, and killed many of the Thessalians as they tried to climb after him. But Pelopidas sounded a retreat to his cavalry, and, leading his foot-soldiers to the attack, drove the enemy back in their turn. By this time the Thessalians had got on a hill above the enemy, and, observing a good deal of disturbance among them, Pelopidas ordered a charge, rushing first himself headlong and calling on Alexander to come and fight him single-handed. The

PELOPIDAS

tyrant did not obey the challenge, but retreated and hid himself among the guard. The foremost of the mercenaries that attacked Pelopidas were driven back, and some were slain; but many at a distance aimed their darts at him and killed him before the Thessalians could run down the hill to save him. The cavalry then came on again, drove the enemy before them and strewed the country with three thousand of their dead and wounded.

The Thebans showed deep grief at the death of Pelopidas, and called him their father and deliverer. They gathered about his body, and would neither put off their armor, dress their wounds, nor unbridle their horses. They were silent and sad, and any stranger seeing them would not have supposed that they had just gained a great victory over a tyrant. As soon as the death of Pelopidas was known in the cities, the magistrates, priests, and youths marched out to meet the body, carrying crowns, garlands, and suits of golden armor. The Thessalians begged that they might give the funeral, and said to the Thebans, "Friends, we ask this favor of you, that will be an honor and a comfort in this our great misfortune. We can never again wait on the living Pelopidas, never give honors that he can know of, but if we may have his body, adorn his funeral and inter him, we hope to show that we have met with a heavier blow than you have. You are deprived of a good general, while we have lost both a general and our liberty. For how shall we dare to ask of you another captain, since we cannot restore Pelopidas?"

The request was granted, and never was a more splendid funeral seen in Greece. The death of the tyrant Alexander occurred not long after, in this way: he had a wife named Thebe, who had been witness to many of his wicked and cruel actions. Besides, he had not been a faithful or a good husband, and so year by year she hated him more and more. This was the cause of her laying a conspiracy to kill him, though of course it does not excuse her. She took her three brothers into her confidence and sought their aid, though the palace was filled with the tyrant's guard. Besides, a ferocious dog kept watch before his chamber-door every night, and would allow no one to approach but Thebe and Alexander himself; he had to be disposed of before anything could be done. Having made her plans, Thebe concealed her brothers all day in a room not far from the one in which the tyrant slept, so that their presence in the palace was not suspected. In the night, after her husband was in bed, she made some excuse for entering his room, and, finding him fast asleep, took the sword that hung at his head, concealed it under her gown and carried it to her brothers. Then she called a servant and requested him to take the dog, which she had led out, saying that Alexander was disturbed by the movements of the animal and had ordered his removal. The concealed brothers were next brought forth and led by the treacherous wife to her husband's bedside. The young men hesitated before performing the horrible deed, but Thebe urged them on, and, holding a lighted lamp that there might be no mistake, directed them in their movements. Two of them seized the sleeping tyrant, while the third plunged the sword Thebe had provided through his body. So occurred the death of one of the most sinful, hard-hearted wretches that ever lived.

TIMOLEON

SICILY was in a dreadful state of disorder about 350 B.C., because each of her cities had in turn declared its independence and elected a ruler of its own. The Carthaginians heard of the disturbance, and took advantage of it to invade the island, and they were such a powerful nation that success seemed certain to them. Their city was Carthage, of which nothing now remains but a mass of ruins; but in ancient times it was the metropolis of Africa, and celebrated for its wealth and magnificence. Some historians tell us that it was built by Dido, one hundred and sixteen years before Rome was founded; but this is not certain.

When the great Carthaginian fleet appeared off the coast of Sicily, the inhabitants were so terrified that they sent ambassadors to Greece to ask the Corinthians for help, This race was chosen because Syracuse, the chief city of Sicily, had been founded by them, and because they often engaged in wars, not for the sake of gain, but for independence, and for the purpose of putting down tyrants.

The ambassadors were kindly received, and a vote was passed granting them the aid they sought. The next thing to be considered was who should command the troops. The magistrates named several citizens who had distinguished themselves, but somebody proposed Timoleon, and, although he had up to that time taken no part in the business of the commonwealth, he was unanimously elected, and soon proved himself a patriot of no ordinary stamp.

But we must go back and tell something of his early life. The parents of Timoleon both belonged to the best families of Corinth. They had another son besides the one we have mentioned, whose name was Timophanes. The two brothers were as totally different in character as it was possible to be, for Timoleon had a remarkable love for his country and a disposition as mild as his extreme hatred of tyrants and wicked men was deep. He was prudent, courageous, and capable of conducting a war. Timophanes, on the other hand, was rash, dishonorable, and anxious for power. In time of war he seemed to give so little thought to danger that he was considered courageous, and often intrusted with the command of the army. But it was his brother who kept him in check, found excuses for his faults, and made the most of his good qualities.

Once when his horse was wounded on the battlefield and threw him within reach of the enemy, he would have been killed had not Timoleon shielded him with his own body, and, after receiving several wounds, by vigorous efforts repulsed the assailants, and so saved his brother's life.

Some time after this, when Timophanes had command of the army, he put to death a number of the principal inhabitants of Corinth, and tried to become absolute ruler of the city. This was exceedingly unjust and dishonorable, and Timoleon felt so ashamed of his brother's conduct that he went to him and urged him to give up the idea of enslaving his country, and to think of some means by which he could atone to his fellow-citizens for the crimes he had committed.

TIMOLEON

Timophanes laughed at his brother and treated the matter with ridicule. A few days later, Timoleon, accompanied by two friends, went to him again. At first Timophanes laughed, as he had done on the previous occasion, but as the three men continued to reason with him he flew into a violent passion. Then Timoleon stepped aside and covered his face with his hands, while the other two drew their swords and killed the older brother on the spot.

There were those among the people of Corinth who approved of this deed, and admired the greatness of soul which prompted Timoleon to prefer his country to his kindred. He had saved his brother's life when he was fighting for his country, but had killed him when he became a traitor. There were others who, while rejoicing at the tyrant's death, pronounced Timoleon guilty of a horrible, unnatural crime. Among these was the mother of the slayer and the slain. She cursed Timoleon, and in the bitterness of her grief ordered her doors to be shut against him, declaring that she would never again look upon his face. Overcome with sorrow and remorse, he resolved to starve himself to death, but his friends, after much argument and entreaty, prevailed upon him to live. He then withdrew from all public affairs, and removed to the country, where he lived in solitude for twenty years.

It was at the close of this period that he was appointed to the command of the Corinthian army, and when he was informed of it, the messenger, a man of influence and rank, said to him, "Behave well, and be brave; for if your conduct be good, we shall consider you as the destroyer of a tyrant; if bad, as the murderer of your brother."

Timoleon accepted the post, and while preparing to set sail with his forces he received letters from Hicetes, Prince of the Leontines, telling him that he need not go to the expense and trouble of leading his men to Sicily, because the Carthaginians would not allow them to land. He added, besides, that he had joined the Carthaginians, and would aid them in the attack on Syracuse.

Such treachery aroused even the most indifferent of the Corinthians to action, and they supplied Timoleon with whatever he wanted, so that he might lose no time in sailing. When all was ready, he made a visit to Delphi to offer sacrifices to Apollo, and when he went down into the place where the oracles were pronounced, a crown embroidered with images of victory slipped from among the offerings that hung over the altar right upon Timoleon's head. That was a good omen, for it appeared that Apollo sent him on the expedition crowned beforehand. He set sail with ten ships of war, and a prosperous wind soon brought the fleet to the coast of Italy. But on arriving there Timoleon received bad news. It was that Hicetes had beaten Dionysius, the tyrant of Syracuse, in battle, and shut him up in the citadel. Before Timoleon could decide what steps to take, twenty Carthaginian galleys arrived, bringing ambassadors with a message from Hicetes to the effect that if Timoleon would send his ships and troops back to Corinth, he might, if he chose, go to Syracuse and share the government, for the war was almost finished, and the Carthaginians would not let his army proceed.

The Corinthians were very indignant at this message, but Timoleon soon calmed them by explaining what he intended to do. After that he had an interview with the Carthaginian ambassadors and commanders, and said to them, "I will submit to your proposal on condition that you will go ashore with me and make it before the people of Rhegium, a Grecian city friendly to both of us, for that will render the compact more binding." They agreed and the magistrates of Rhegium, who really wished to see Sicily in the hands of the Corinthians, entered heartily into Timoleon's scheme. So they summoned an assembly of the citizens, and then closed the gates and began one after another to make long speeches. The Carthaginians suspected nothing wrong, for Timoleon was present, and they were waiting for his turn to make an address. Meanwhile, in obedience to their commander's instructions, the Corinthian fleet put to sea, and the enemy, believing that since one vessel was left for Timoleon the others were returning to Corinth, let them go quietly. Being informed by a signal that his fleet was off, Timoleon pressed through the crowd, his retreat being covered by the Rhegians, got down to the shore, and set sail full speed for Sicily.

He landed with his whole fleet at a place called Tauromenium, because Andromachus, the ruler, was friendly, and had given permission for him to do so. No sooner did Hicetes hear of the landing of the Corinthians than, although terribly alarmed, he set out with a force of five thousand fighting-men to prevent their advance. Timoleon had only twelve hundred soldiers, but he advanced until he heard that Hicetes was approaching Adranum; then he pitched his camp before that place, and, without giving his army time for rest or refreshment, placed himself at their head and led them, as he told them, to victory. The bravery of such a leader was contagious, and his men followed him with so much spirit that the enemy were thrown into confusion; three hundred of their number were slain, and twice as many taken prisoners. Those that fled had no time to think about their camp or baggage, of which the Corinthians took possession. Such a victory induced the people of Adranum to throw open their gates and take sides with Timoleon. Then they assured him, with a mixed feeling of awe and admiration, that they had felt confident he would triumph, because just as the battle began the doors of their temple flew open without being touched by any one, and the spear which their god held in his hand trembled, while drops of sweat ran down his face. Those, they declared, were omens that always foretold victory.

Such an impression was made by Timoleon and his army that the neighboring cities, one after another, sought his friendship and offered their services. At last Dionysius himself sent a messenger to say that he was ready to deliver to the Corinthians not only the citadel, but his own person. Timoleon immediately despatched two of his captains, with four hundred men, to seize the castle, and directed them how to proceed so that no trick could be played on them.

They found a magnificent supply of horses, war-engines, and weapons in the palace of Dionysius, all of which, besides two thousand soldiers, were handed over for Timoleon's service. Then the tyrant himself, with his treasure and a few friends, embarked on a vessel secretly, so as not to be stopped by Hicetes, and sailed to the camp of Timoleon. In the attire of a humble citizen this prince, who had been born and educated in one of the most splendid of courts, now presented himself before the victorious Timoleon, worn out with wars, contests, and some of the greatest misfortunes that ever fell to the lot of man. For the present we shall say no more about Dionysius, except that he was sent to Corinth with a small sum of money; a fuller account of him is given in the life of Dion.

TIMOLEON

Within fifty days after his landing in Sicily we find Timoleon's men in possession of the fortress of Syracuse. This was a splendid beginning; but Hicetes was still in the city, and continued to besiege the castle, so that those who were shut up in it could receive no provisions. Besides, he filled the city with soldiers, and there was every prospect that the Carthaginians would soon make themselves its sole rulers. Not only did the besieged Corinthians suffer from want of provisions, but they were constantly attacked about the walls of the castle, and had to divide themselves for defence. The harbor was blocked up by the Carthaginian fleet, of which Mago was admiral; but during a storm, when the ships got separated, Timoleon managed to send a quantity of corn to his besieged soldiers by little fishing-boats that slipped in unnoticed.

Timoleon was then at Catana, and Hicetes was determined to stop all further supply of provisions from that quarter; so he selected the best of his troops, and, with Mago to manage the ships, sailed from Syracuse.

Leo, the Corinthian commander in the citadel, saw the departure of the fleet, and soon observed that those of the forces that were left behind kept guard very carelessly: so he made an attack upon Achradina, the strongest quarter of Syracuse, and took possession of it. It must be borne in mind that, unlike other cities, this one was divided into four parts, each separated from the other by a strong wall, so that Syracuse might be called an assemblage of towns. Achradina, which was quite near the citadel, was the strongest quarter, and had suffered least from the enemy, so Leo found plenty of provisions and money there. He knew the value of what he had, and determined to keep it, so he fortified it and joined it to the citadel. As Mago and Hicetes approached Catana a messenger met them and informed them of the dreadful misfortune that had overtaken them at home; whereupon they hurried back. Shortly after Mago sailed to Africa, though there seemed to be no reason for thus allowing Sicily to slip out of his hands.

Meanwhile, Timoleon had received reinforcements from Corinth, and with these he took the city of Messina, and then went on to Syracuse, where he beat off the forces of Hicetes and put them to flight. He next ordered the town-criers to call on all the Syracusans to come with their tools to help to tear down the fortifications of the tyrants. They came, one and all, and worked with a will for liberty. Not only did they destroy the citadel, but the palaces and monuments near by, and whatever else there was to remind them of their former tyrants, were demolished.

When the spot was cleared, Timoleon built a hall of justice, to show the citizens that a popular government was to be established on the ruins of tyranny.

But now so many people had been killed in the wars, and so many more had run away, that Syracuse looked deserted, and there was danger that the soil would not be properly cultivated. To avoid this evil, Timoleon wrote to his countrymen, urging them to send people to settle there. He had another reason for desiring to populate Sicily. It was this: Mago had killed himself after he returned to Africa, because he could not bear the reproaches he received for leaving Sicily, and after his death his countrymen began to collect forces for a second invasion of the island.

When Timoleon heard this, he knew that he ought to be prepared with an army; so, besides the message to Corinth, he invited all the Syracusans who had fled to return, and offered them protection on the voyage. In a short time ten thousand people sailed from Corinth for Syracuse, and sixty thousand more flocked there from Italy and other places.

The land Timoleon divided freely among the new citizens, but he sold them the houses, and thus raised a fund which was much needed; for not only was the public treasury exhausted, but it had even been found necessary to sell the statues to defray the expenses of the war.

After restoring order and establishing reforms in Syracuse, Timoleon marched to other parts of Sicily, and compelled the tyrants of the various little towns to destroy their palaces and take their places among the private citizens. Hicetes was one of these, and he was forced, besides, to promise to interfere no further in the affairs of the Carthaginians. Then Timoleon returned to Syracuse to see how the new laws were working.

Meanwhile, the Carthaginians had landed an immense army in the territory that still belonged to them on the island of Sicily. They were drawn together on the banks of the river Crimesus; and as soon as this was known to Timoleon he hastened to meet them with the small army that he could get together. It was composed of paid foreigners for the most part, because the citizens of Syracuse were so frightened when they heard how great was the number of the enemy's forces that they would not follow Timoleon, and of the four thousand whom he hired nearly a quarter grew faint-hearted by the way and deserted.

As Timoleon was climbing a hill overlooking the river Crimesus, whence he expected to see what the Carthaginians were about, he met a train of mules loaded with parsley. The soldiers looked upon this as an ill omen, because parsley was used to adorn tombs. But among the Corinthians it was at that time made into garlands to crown the victors of the public games. So, to remove all forebodings of evil, Timoleon turned this to account, and assured his soldiers that victory was certain, the garlands being already theirs. Then he crowned himself with a wreath made of the parsley; all his captains and soldiers followed his example, and marched on.

When they reached the top of the hill, they beheld the enemy crossing the river with their formidable four-horse chariots of war, followed by thousands of foot-soldiers bearing glittering arms. Timoleon called his first cavalry officer to his side and gave him orders to fall at once upon the enemy, while part remained on one side of the river and part on the other, and before they were drawn up in line of battle. This was done; and after watching the action for a while, Timoleon saw that his soldiers were harassed by the armed chariots of the enemy, which ran to and fro in front of their own army, and not only prevented the Greeks from coming to close quarters, but forced them continually to wheel about to escape having their ranks broken. So, taking his shield in his hand, he cried out to the foot-soldiers to follow him, and amidst the blasts of trumpets rushed down the hill with drawn sword into the thickest of the fight.

With their stout armor, the Carthaginians had not found it difficult to repel the spears of the horsemen, but when it came to swords, which required more skill than strength, they were at a disadvantage. Then, too, the onslaught of Timoleon was attended by a terrific thunderstorm, and the enemy were so placed that the rain, wind, and hail beat right into their faces and almost blinded them. Added to this, the thunder prevented them from hearing the commands of their officers, and their armor was so heavy that when once the Greeks got them down in the mud they could not rise,

TIMOLEON

and there was plenty of it, for the river had overflowed its banks a short time before. The Carthaginians rolled and tumbled about in the ditches, where they were cut to pieces without being able to offer much resistance.

The Greek armor was light, the storm was at their backs, and they made such havoc in the first ranks that the whole Carthaginian army began to fly. Great numbers were overtaken in the fields and killed, many were drowned, and those who tried to escape into the mountains were stopped by the Greeks. Ten thousand Carthaginians lay dead upon the plain at the close of the battle, among whom were many men of rank, wealth, and reputation. The booty the Greeks collected was so rich that they did not take the pains to reckon the brass or iron, gold and silver being so plentiful. Then there were two hundred chariots of war, besides all the camp-equipments. Timoleon's tent was resplendent with the military ornaments, and thousands of rare and beautifully wrought breastplates and shields.

The Carthaginians, encouraged by Hicetes, sent another army, but were again defeated. Hicetes was captured alive, tried, and condemned to death. Then the Carthaginians sued for peace, and it was granted to them under certain conditions, to which they were glad to yield in consideration of all they had suffered. A few more battles put an end to all the tyrants of Sicily and converted the island into such a happy, civilized home that even strangers went there in great numbers to settle. Timoleon was loved and honored by all, and the Sicilians looked upon him as the founder of their government. He was presented with one of the best houses in Syracuse, and there he lived contentedly and comfortably with his wife and children, who came to him from Corinth when the wars were at an end.

As he grew old his sight began to fail, and at last he became totally blind. He bore this misfortune meekly and patiently, and the people of Syracuse continued to show him every mark of respect and gratitude. They went constantly to pay their respects to him, and took every stranger who visited the city to see the man whose brave exploits had brought about so much happiness. In honor of Timoleon, they passed a vote that whenever they should be engaged in war with a foreign nation none but a Corinthian general should lead them. When an important question was to be decided, the blind old commander was always consulted, and for that purpose he was carried to the marketplace in a litter. When he appeared, the people saluted him by name, then he would listen to the debate and deliver his opinion. That done, he was escorted back to his house.

This respect and tenderness were shown to the old hero until he died, and when that event occurred a great concourse of people assembled to do honor to his memory. The bier was borne by young men, followed by thousands of people robed in white and crowned with garlands, many of them shedding tears as they moved along.

When the bier was placed upon the pile of wood to be burned, one of the public criers read the following proclamation in a loud, clear tone of voice: "The people of Syracuse inter Timoleon, son of Timodemus, the Corinthian, at the common expense. They propose to honor his memory forever by establishing annual prizes for horse-races, music, and wrestling, because he overthrew the barbarians, destroyed tyrants, repeopled desolate cities, and restored to the Sicilian Greeks their laws and privileges."

TIMOLEON

A monument was erected on the spot where the body was interred; near by was a place where the young men exercised, to which they gave the name of the Timoleonteum. For thirty years the Sicilians lived in peace and prosperity under the laws which Timoleon had left them.

DEMOSTHENES

THE father of Demosthenes was an Athenian citizen of rank. He owned a sword-factory, in which he employed a large number of people, but he did not work himself, because that would have been beneath the dignity of a man of his position. He died when his son was only seven years of age, leaving a large fortune, which went to young Demosthenes; but he was too much of a child to attend to it properly, so his guardians robbed him to such an extent that even his teachers were cheated of their salaries. This was one reason why his education was limited, but another reason was, that, being a weak, delicate boy, his mother would not let him study hard. Thus several years passed in idleness, until the boy reached the age of sixteen. Then his future was decided in this way: he had often heard of an orator named Callistratus, of whom men of learning spoke in the highest terms, and felt great curiosity to hear him. An opportunity offered on the occasion of an important trial, which was conducted in open court. Demosthenes begged the doorkeeper for a seat where he might hear without being seen. He listened with profound attention to the orator's eloquent pleading, and when he won the case, the boy was so impressed by the applause and honors he received that he resolved on the spot to become a public speaker.

DEMOSTHENES

He employed an orator named Isæus to teach him, but much of his rich, grand style of speaking he learned from Plato. He was only seventeen years old when he appeared before the public courts and made an attempt to get back his father's estate. He was successful in that, but not in his oratory, for his style was not yet sufficiently cultivated, his voice was weak, he had a peculiar way of catching his breath, and he stammered. The public ridiculed him so much that he could scarcely make himself heard at times, and he was so mortified at being laughed at that he was on the point of giving up the profession he had chosen. It was Satyrus, the actor, who inspired him with new hope, in this way:

He was going home one day in deep distress when he met Satyrus, who, being an old acquaintance, joined him and went along with him. Then Demosthenes told him the cause of his sorrow. "I am the hardest worker among all the orators, and have almost injured my health by study, yet I can find no favor with the people, though they listen with pleasure to the low, drunken, uneducated fellows who address them."

"What you say is true, Demosthenes," replied the actor, "but if you will recite to me some speech in Euripides or Sophocles, I will show you a remedy."

Demosthenes did so; Satyrus repeated the same speech, but it seemed to have a different meaning as it came from his lips, and Demosthenes saw how much he had yet to learn before he could gesticulate and pronounce correctly. But he did not lose courage; he built himself a study under ground, and there he would stay for three and four months at a time to exercise his voice. He shaved half his head, so that he might feel ashamed to go out even if he desired to do so, and thus his studies were not interrupted.

When he began to speak in public again, he always went to the study he had built to compose his orations, and scarcely ever delivered one unless he had prepared it with the utmost care. Even after it was over he would reconsider it, and decide what more he might have said and what left unsaid, which was his way of constantly improving himself.

Demades was another orator who lived in Athens at the same period with Demosthenes; but he was one of those gifted men who are always ready, and he was frequently known to rise quickly and support Demosthenes when he faltered. A wise man was once asked to pass judgment on the two orators. He said, "Demosthenes is worthy of the city of Athens." "What do you think of Demades?" was asked. "I think him above it," was the reply. A politician of the day expressed this opinion: "Demosthenes is our greatest orator, but Phocion is the ablest, for he expresses the most in the fewest words."

When Phocion stood up to plead against him, Demosthenes often said, "Here comes the pruning-knife of my periods." Whether this referred to Phocion's style of delivery, or to his superior character, which gave him weight and influence, is not known.

Demosthenes cured his stammering by speaking with pebbles in his mouth, he strengthened his voice by reciting some piece of prose or poetry while running up a hill, and he regulated his gestures before a large looking-glass, which he had placed in his house for that purpose. To cure a habit which he had of raising his left shoulder while speaking, he suspended a naked sword over it whenever he practised, and

DEMOSTHENES

he would stand on the sea-shore during a storm to declaim, that he might accustom himself to the tumult of a public assembly. In short, he worked exceedingly hard to perfect himself in his art, and his enemies, who knew that he never made a speech over which he had not worked many hours, maliciously said they "smelt of the lamp."

Demosthenes first took part in public affairs soon after the Phocion war, and then he set himself the task of defending the Greeks against Philip of Macedon. This he did so well that he at once became famous for his eloquence and courage.

His courage was not displayed on the battlefield, it was more in his bold manner of addressing a crowd, for he freely told them of their faults, and would never grant an unreasonable demand. Once he was called upon to accuse a certain person; he refused, and the assembly was at once in an uproar, whereupon he rose and said, "A counsellor, ye men of Athens, you shall always have in me, whether you will or not; but a false accuser I will never be, no matter how much you may wish it."

At another time, one Antiphon, who was on trial, was acquitted by the general assembly, but Demosthenes carried him before the Areopagus, in spite of the offence he gave to the people by so doing. Before that court he proved that Antiphon had promised Philip of Macedon to burn the arsenal; the accused was condemned to death. He also pronounced a priestess guilty of several misdemeanors; she was found guilty and executed on his charges. These incidents go to prove that he had the moral courage to do what he thought right in spite of public opinion.

We have said that Demosthenes set himself the noble task of defending his country against Philip of Macedon. This was at a period when the Athenians had become so luxurious and indolent that they had ceased to take part in public affairs. At heart they were really patriotic, but they needed some one to arouse them from their apathy and to make them look out for the safety of their liberty. Demosthenes knew this; he also knew that Philip of Macedon was trying to get power in Greece; so he set to work to awaken the enthusiasm of the people and to oppose Philip. The fourteen years which preceded the downfall of Grecian freedom form the brightest portion of the history of this wonderful orator, and so powerful were his speeches that Philip looked upon him as a person of the greatest importance in Athens. It was his eloquence that aroused the Athenians to action at last, and when, after several engagements, their cause seemed almost hopeless, again did his eloquence save them, for he won over the Thebans, who had for many years been firm allies of the Macedonians. Then Philip sent ambassadors to Athens to sue for peace. Meanwhile, Greece recovered from her depression, and the various assemblies waited for directions from Demosthenes, whom they now loved and respected.

But fortune seemed suddenly to turn against Greece, and all the oracles foretold that she was on the point of losing her liberty. Demosthenes had so much confidence in her arms, and was so encouraged by the spirit of the brave men who came forward in her defence, that he would not pay attention to the oracles. He was bravery itself in his speeches, but he threw away his arms and fled in a most shameful manner at the next battle, which was fought at Chæronea. Some of his enemies took that opportunity to bring grave charges against him, but the people acquitted him of them all,

DEMOSTHENES

invited him to continue to take part in public affairs, and when the bones of those who had fallen at Chæronea were brought home to be interred, he was chosen to deliver the funeral oration.

After that Demosthenes mounted the rostrum every day and made speeches in the interest of his country, but he could not save it from Alexander, who had by that time succeeded Philip as king of Macedon. Alexander spread terror wherever he went, and when the Athenians lost their city he sent to demand ten of their orators, Demosthenes heading the list.

But Demosthenes feared Alexander so much that he made one of his most eloquent appeals to the people, and told them the fable of the sheep, in which the wolves promised to leave them at peace if they would give them their dogs. He meant to show that he and the other orators were the guardians of the people as the dogs were of the sheep, and that Alexander was the great wolf they had to treat with.

The Athenians did not know what to do, so they called a general assembly to consider the matter. Demades, one of the orators, offered to go entirely alone to the king of Macedon on condition that the other orators would each pay him five talents, nearly five thousand dollars. They agreed, and he was so successful in pleading for their release that Alexander became reconciled to the city.

Then for a while Demades was regarded as the greatest orator of the day, and Demosthenes sank into obscurity. But this did not last long, for at his own expense Demosthenes rebuilt the walls of Athens, whereupon a crown of gold was voted for him, which was considered the most splendid reward a Greek citizen could receive. This excited the envy of

Æschines, who did all he could to prevent the Athenians from presenting the crown. It was on that occasion that Demosthenes made one of the most celebrated of all his orations. While the two orators were discussing the point, immense crowds assembled to hear them. Then it was put to the vote, and, as Æschines did not get one-fifth of the number of votes, the law compelled him to pay a fine and to go into exile. It was a law in Athens that if an accuser got less than a fifth of the votes cast, he should be so punished.

A short time after this splendid victory Demosthenes stooped to a shameful action. Harpalus, a Macedonian governor, was then in Athens, where he had sought protection, because he had stolen a large sum of money from Alexander's treasury in Babylon. One day Demosthenes was looking over some of the rich vessels that Harpalus had, and particularly admired the workmanship of a gold cup; he was surprised, too, at its weight, and asked Harpalus how much it might bring. "It will bring you twenty talents," was the reply of the governor. That night he sent the cup filled with the sum he had named, and Demosthenes could not resist the temptation. He received the treasure as a bribe, and immediately went over to the interest of Harpalus. The next day he appeared in the assembly with his throat bandaged, because he feared he might betray himself if he spoke, and made signs, when called upon, to signify that he had lost his voice. But he had been found out, and a man near by said, "It is no common hoarseness that came to Demosthenes in the night; it is a hoarseness caused by swallowing gold and silver." When it became generally known that he had been guilty of taking a bribe he wanted to defend himself, but nobody would listen to him, and Harpalus was sent out of the city.

Then Demosthenes moved that the affair be brought before the Areopagus. This was done, and he was found guilty. His sentence was to pay a fine of fifty talents and be imprisoned until it was paid. He made his escape, however, and fled to Ægina, whence he could behold the shores of his beloved country, and whenever he looked that way he shed tears.

During the exile of Demosthenes Alexander of Macedon died, and a new league was formed among the Grecian cities against the Macedonians. Then Demosthenes was recalled, and as the galley which had been sent to fetch him came into port the citizens flocked to meet him with loud cheers and joyful greetings. On landing, the orator raised his hands to heaven and said, "Happier is my return than that of Alcibiades. The Athenians were forced to restore him, but me they have recalled from a motive of kindness."

The fine had not been paid, and as there was no way of releasing Demosthenes directly, this plan was adopted: It was the custom to give a certain sum of money to those who were to furnish and adorn the altar of Jupiter, the Preserver; so Demosthenes was appointed, and fifty talents, the amount of his fine, ordered for him.

He did not enjoy his home long, for when the report reached Athens that Antipater and Craterus were coming he and his party escaped, some going in one direction, some in another. Antipater's soldiers followed them, and found Demosthenes on the island of Calauria, where he had hidden himself in the temple of Neptune. It was Archias, an actor, who led the party of soldiers that entered the temple. Archias spoke mildly, and tried to persuade the orator to go with him to Antipater, as though no harm would come to him if he did so. Demosthenes looked into his face while he spoke, without answering; at last he said, "O Archias, I am as little affected by your promises now as I used formerly to be by your acting."

That made Archias so angry that he began to threaten, whereupon Demosthenes said, "Now you speak like the true Macedonian oracle; before you were only acting a part. Therefore leave me for a few moments, while I write a word or two home to my family." Feeling sure of his victim, Archias complied. Demosthenes then took out a scroll, as if he meant to write, but put the reed into his mouth and began biting it, as he often did when composing one of his speeches. Then he bowed his head and covered it. The soldiers who stood at the door of the temple suspected nothing but that Demosthenes was a coward, and so they made fun of him. Presently Archias went up to him and repeated the promises he had made of good treatment from Antipater. Demosthenes had been sucking poison out of his reed, and now began to feel its effect. He uncovered his face, and, looking up at Archias, said, "Now you may act the part of the tragedian in the play, who cast out the body of his victim unburied. For myself, O gracious Neptune! I quit thy temple with my breath within me; but these Macedonians would not have scrupled to profane it with murder." By this time he could scarcely stand, and in attempting to walk out he fell by the altar and with one groan expired.

It was not long before a brass statue was erected in his honor at Athens; but the inscription it bore sounds more like a disgrace than an honor to his memory. It was this:

"Divine in speech; in judgment, too, divine;
Had valor's wreath, Demosthenes, been thine,

Fair Greece had still her freedom's ensign borne,
And held the scourge of Macedon in scorn."

ALEXANDER

ALEXANDER was the son of Philip, King of Macedon, and at a very early age showed that he had the spirit of a warrior. His father won many brilliant victories, but, instead of rejoicing at them, Alexander would say to his friends, "My father will go on conquering until nothing extraordinary be left for you and me to do." He never cared for pleasure or riches, but thirsted for glory, and therefore hoped to inherit a kingdom that was plunged in wars, so that he might be able to exercise his courage.

The care of his education was given to several instructors, but Leonidas, a kinsman of his mother, presided over them all. Lysimachus was his chief preceptor, but he was neither a good nor an able man. Philip therefore soon secured the services of a great philosopher, because the following circumstance convinced him that his son was worthy of every advantage.

A horse, Bucephalus by name, was offered to Philip for the sum of thirteen talents, or about thirteen thousand dollars of our money, and the king, with the prince and many others, went to the field to see him tried. He proved to be so vicious and unmanageable that none of the grooms dared venture to mount him. Philip was displeased at any one's having brought him such an animal, and angrily ordered him to be taken away. Alexander was, on the contrary, so delighted with the fine points he observed in the horse that he exclaimed, "What a horse are they losing for want of skill and spirit to manage him!" Philip did not at first notice the boy, who made several such remarks. At last he said, "Young man, you find fault with your elders, as if you knew more than they, or could manage the horse better." "I certainly could," answered the prince. "If you should not be able to ride him; what will you forfeit for your rashness?" "I will pay the price asked for him." Everybody laughed; but, having gained his father's permission, Alexander ran to the animal, and, laying hold of the bridle, turned his head to the sun. He did this because he had observed that the continually-moving shadow of himself annoyed Bucephalus. Then he spoke softly to the animal, and stroked him gently until he grew calm; after which he leaped lightly on his back and seated himself. Having accomplished that much, he jerked the bridle gently, and Bucephalus started forward without the use of whip or spur. Philip and his courtiers looked on in anxious silence; but when the prince turned the horse and rode straight back to the spot whence he had started, he was received with loud shouts, while the father, with tears in his eyes, embraced him and said, "O my son, seek another kingdom worthy of thy abilities, for Macedonia is too small for thee."

It was immediately after this that Aristotle, the most celebrated and learned of all the philosophers, was engaged to instruct Alexander. The boy soon learned to love his master almost as much as he did his own father, and in after-years he would say, "From my father I derived the blessing of life, but from Aristotle the blessing of a good life." Alexander was born with a love for study, which never left him to the very

OUR YOUNG FOLKS' PLUTARCH

ALEXANDER TAMING BUCEPHALUS

end of his life. He was only sixteen years old when his father went from home on an expedition and left him regent of Macedonia, and keeper of the royal seal. He did not remain idle, but reduced a rebellious tribe, took their chief town by storm, planted a mixed colony there, and called the place Alexandropolis after himself. At the battle of Chæronea this young prince charged and broke the Theban *Sacred Band*, and had the glory of being the first who had ever done that.

King Philip was preparing for a war against Persia, B.C. 336, when he was assassinated. Alexander, who was just twenty years of age, succeeded to the throne. The kingdom he was called upon to rule was in a most unsettled condition; for, by his numerous victories, Philip had subdued Greece, but she had not become accustomed to the yoke, consequently the whole country was in a tumultuous state.

Alexander's counsellors advised him to give up Greece entirely, but he would not listen to them, particularly as several of the states, thinking they had nothing to fear from so young a sovereign, showed signs of rebellion. He marched without delay as far as the Danube, where he fought a great battle with the Triballi and defeated them.

Shortly after he was informed that the Thebans and the Athenians had revolted, so he advanced immediately through the pass of Thermopylæ, saying, "Demosthenes called me a boy while I was among the Triballi, a stripling when in Thessaly; but I will show him before the walls of Athens that I am a man."

The Thebans made a desperate resistance, and the war began with great fury; but the Macedonians had such a large army that they surrounded Thebes on all sides and completely destroyed it. Among the inhabitants, the priests and the poet

Pindar were spared, but thirty thousand were sold as slaves, and more than six thousand were killed in the battle.

Some of the scenes enacted are too horrible to recount, but an anecdote about Timoclea, a woman of rank and wealth, is worth repeating. A party of Thracians entered her house and carried off all the valuables it contained, but, not satisfied with that, the captain asked whether she had not some gold and silver hidden away. "Oh, yes," she said, leading him to a well in her garden; "when the city was taken I threw all my jewels and money down there." The captain stooped to examine the well, whereupon Timoclea pushed him in and threw all the heavy stones she could find on top of him. The soldiers seized her, bound her hands, and led her before Alexander, to whom they told what she had done.

"Who are you?" asked the king.

"I am the sister of Theagenes, who, as general of our army, fought Philip for the liberty of Greece and fell in the battle of Chæronea," she replied, boldly.

Alexander could not help admiring her bravery, nor could he blame her action, seeing that she was dealing with an enemy, therefore he commanded her and her children to be set at liberty. The rest of the Greek nations were so impressed by the fate of Thebes that they gladly came over to the Macedonian party, and soon after chose Alexander for their general when their war with Persia began.

They were assembled at Corinth for this election, and most of the public officers and philosophers of the neighborhood went to visit Alexander and offer their congratulations. But there was one who took no notice of him whatever, and that was Diogenes of Sinope, then living at a little place just outside of Corinth called Cranium. So Alexander went to see the philosopher, whom he found lying in the sun. At the approach of so many people he looked up, and the king in a friendly tone asked, "Is there any way in which I can serve you?"

"Yes; I would have you stand from between me and the sun," replied the philosopher.

Alexander was struck with surprise, for he did not suppose there was a man in the world so contented as to require no service at his hands. His courtiers were annoyed and called Diogenes a monster, but the king said, "If I were not Alexander I should wish to be Diogenes."

After consulting the oracle and receiving for answer, "My son, thou art invincible," Alexander set out with an army of four thousand five hundred horse and thirty thousand foot-soldiers. On his arrival at Troy, he sacrificed to Minerva, anointed the tomb of Achilles with oil, then put a garland on it, and congratulated the dead hero on his good fortune in having such a friend as Patroclus and such a poet as Homer to sing his praises.

Alexander moved so rapidly that he took the army of Darius by surprise, and got as far as the river Granicus, in Asia, without meeting any opposition. He advanced under showers of darts thrown from the steep opposite banks, which were covered with the enemy's troops, and having climbed the muddy, slippery paths, engaged in a hand-to-hand fight, and won a decisive victory. Alexander was attacked several times, and had a horse killed under him, but, although he was easily known by his waving white plumes, he escaped without a wound.

The loss on the Persian side was very heavy, while their conqueror had no more than sixty horse and thirty foot-soldiers killed. Among these were twenty-five of Alexander's personal friends, and to do honor to their memory he erected a brass statue to each. The Grecians got a share of the spoils, particularly the Athenians, to whom he sent three hundred bucklers. Upon the rest he ordered this inscription to be placed: "Alexander, the son of Philip, and the Grecians, except the Lacedæmonians, won these from the barbarians who inhabit Asia." All the plate, purple garments, and ornaments that he took from the Persians, except a small quantity that he kept for himself, he sent as a present to Olympias, his mother.

Alexander was so elated with this victory that he did not rest until he had freed all the Greek cities in Asia Minor from the Persian yoke. Then, on hearing of the death of Memnon, the principal commander of Darius, he determined to march to the upper part of Asia. A serious and dangerous illness, caused by a cold bath in the river Cydnus, detained him, however. Possibly he might have been cured in a few days if he had not been a king, but his physicians were afraid to try severe remedies, lest they might not have the desired result and thus subject themselves to suspicion and probably punishment. Philip, one of the physicians, who loved Alexander exceedingly, thought it shameful when his master was in danger not to risk something, so he took upon himself the cure, and set to work to prepare the medicine.

Before it was ready, one of his commanders sent the king a letter bidding him beware of Philip, who had been bribed by Darius to poison him. Having read the letter, Alexander put it under his pillow without showing it to anybody. He had perfect confidence in Philip, of which he gave proof when the medicine was brought; for, placing the cup to his lips, he swallowed the dose even while the physician read the letter which he handed him. Philip was indignant at the unjust charge, and threw himself down by the bedside, entreating his master to have courage and trust to his care. In about three days the invalid was so much better as to be able to show himself to the Macedonians, whose anxiety had been very great on his account.

Darius did not know that illness detained Alexander, and he made up his mind that it was fear; he therefore marched forward to Cilicia with his army. This was a mistake, because he had to fight in narrow passages, where his immense forces were so cramped that they could scarcely obey orders, whereas had he remained in Assyria he would have met Alexander on wide, open plains; but he paid dearly for his error, and suffered a signal defeat. He lost over a hundred thousand men, and came very near being captured himself. However, he escaped, though his chariot and bow fell into the hands of the conqueror, who returned with them in triumph to his soldiers.

The Persian camp was filled with rich armor and clothing, of which the Macedonian soldiers took possession; but they did not touch the tent of Darius. That they reserved for Alexander, who found in it richly-clothed officers of the royal household, magnificent furniture, and great quantities of gold and silver.

Having laid off his armor, the conqueror said to those about him, "Let us go and refresh ourselves after the fatigue of the battle in the baths of Darius." "Nay, rather in the baths of Alexander," said one of his friends, "for the goods of the conquered are and should be called the conqueror's."

When Alexander looked about and beheld the basins, boxes, vials, vases curiously wrought in gold, the splendid and luxurious lounges and cushions, and smelled the fragrant essences, he turned to his friends and asked, "Can it be possible that a king finds happiness in such enjoyments as these?"

At that period Alexander had not been spoiled by Persian luxury, and his tastes were extremely simple. His table was always splendidly and plentifully supplied, but he did not care for delicacies, and frequently left them untouched, though he was careful to see that his guests were treated to the very best the market afforded. Some historians have accused him of drinking to excess, but this is a mistake arising from his habit of sitting a long time at table. This arose from his fondness for conversation, for with every cup of wine he would discourse at length on some subject or other, and never indulged in this pleasure unless he had ample leisure. When he was busy he would neither eat, sleep, nor drink; otherwise he could not in his short life have performed so many great actions. Much of his leisure was spent in hunting, throwing the javelin, and otherwise exercising, or reading and writing. As his fortune increased his feasts became more magnificent, until each cost no less than ten thousand drachmas. These feasts always lasted many hours, because they were lengthened out by conversation, in which art Alexander surpassed most other princes.

He showed great kindness of heart in his treatment of Darius's family after the defeat of that monarch in Cilicia. As he was sitting down to dine, when the battle was over, he was told that among the prisoners were the mother, wife, and two daughters of Darius, all of whom were bowed down with grief because, as they saw the royal chariot among the spoils, they concluded that the king was dead. Alexander felt very sorry for the poor captives, and after a few moments' thought sent Leonatus to them with this message: "Assure them that Darius is not dead; that they have nothing to fear from Alexander, for his dispute with Darius was only for empire, and that they shall find themselves provided for in the same manner as when Darius was in his greatest prosperity."

He kept his promise in every particular, and not only were the captives allowed to do funeral honors to what Persians they pleased, but they were furnished for that purpose with all the necessary robes and other decorations out of the spoils. Besides, they were provided with as many domestics as they needed, and all the comforts and luxuries they had ever enjoyed; no soldier dared to obtrude upon their privacy, and they soon lost sight of the disagreeable fact that they were in an enemy's camp.

Alexander did not follow the Persian monarch, but took possession of Damascus, which contained a large portion of the royal treasure, and conquered all the towns along the Mediterranean Sea. Tyre refused to submit, and was therefore besieged. While the siege lasted, Alexander dreamed that Hercules offered him his hand from the wall and invited him to enter, which was considered a favorable sign. Some of the Tyrians dreamed that Apollo told them he was displeased with their behavior, and was about to leave them and go over to Alexander. So they seized the statue of the god, loaded it with chains, and fastened the feet to the pedestal, to prevent his becoming a deserter. At the end of seven months the siege was suddenly brought to a close in this way: One of Alexander's soothsayers, after offering sacrifices, examined the entrails of the victim, and proclaimed, "The city shall be taken this month." "How can that be," asked the soldiers, "this being the very last day of the month?" Thereupon Alexander answered by ordering that it should be called the twenty eighth, not the thirtieth, and so sounded the trumpets for an onslaught. It proved the most violent attack that had been made, and the soothsayer's prophecy came true, for the city of Tyre fell that day.

Then Alexander proceeded on his victorious march through Palestine until he reached Gaza, one of the largest cities of Syria which, after a siege, shared the fate of Tyre. From there he sent presents to his mother and all his friends. To Leonidas, his early tutor, he forwarded a great load of frankincense and myrrh, because once when offering sacrifices he had been so extravagant with those spices that Leonidas had said, "Alexander, when you have conquered the country where spices grow you may be thus liberal of your incense; but, in the mean time, use what you have more sparingly." So, when he sent the present from Gaza, Alexander wrote, "I have sent you frankincense and myrrh in abundance, that you need no longer be stingy with the gods."

One day a magnificent casket that had belonged to Darius was brought to him, and he asked his friends what they thought the most worthy thing to place in it. One suggested one article, another something else; but he said, "No, Homer's Iliad most deserves such a case," and from that time his copy of that work was kept in the costly box.

In Egypt, Alexander was received as a deliverer, because the inhabitants were tired of the Persian yoke and glad of a chance to throw it off. Alexander restored their former customs and religious rites, and founded Alexandria, which became one of the most important cities of ancient times.

Thence he made a journey through the desert of Libya to consult the oracle, Jupiter Ammon. Few men would have started upon so long and dangerous a journey without misgivings, for there was likely to be scarcity of water, and violent winds that would blow about the poisonous sand of the desert and cause the death of those who inhaled it. But Alexander was not to be turned from anything he was bent upon; besides, he had known nothing but good fortune all his life; he was therefore bold. The gods seemed to favor him as usual, for plentiful rains fell, which not only relieved the soldiers from fear of drought, but made the sand moist and firm and purified the air. Besides, some ravens kept up with the Macedonians in their march, flying before them and waiting for them if they fell behind; but the strangest part of all was, that if any of the company went astray in the night, the ravens never ceased croaking until they were guided to the right path again.

When Alexander had passed through the wilderness and arrived at the place, the high-priest of Ammon bade him welcome in the name of the god, and called him son of Jupiter. "Have any of the assassins of my father escaped me?" asked Alexander. "Do not express yourself in that manner," said the priest, "for your father was not a mortal."

"Well, then, are all the murderers of Philip punished? and am I to be the conqueror of the world?" asked Alexander. "That high distinction you shall have, and the death of Philip is fully revenged," was the answer.

Alexander was so pleased at what he had heard that he made splendid offerings to Jupiter, and gave the priests presents of great value. But he put on a lofty bearing after being addressed as the son of Jupiter. Some people think that he did this among the Persians only to make them honor and respect him, for once, when he was wounded with an arrow, he said to those about him, "This, my friends, is real, flowing blood, not such as the immortal gods shed."

In course of time Darius wrote to Alexander proposing terms of peace, and offering ten thousand talents as a ransom for his captives, all the countries on this side the river Euphrates, and one of his daughters in marriage. Parmenio, a friend of the Macedonian king, said, "If I were Alexander I would accept those terms." "So would I if I were Parmenio," replied the king. At the same time he sent this message to Darius: "If you will come to me, you shall find the best of treatment; if not, I must go and seek you." And so he began his march. But he had gone only a little way when news was brought to him of the death of Darius's wife. He felt very much grieved at this sad event, and returned to bury the dead queen in a style befitting her rank. Tireus, one of the slaves of the bed-chamber, was at once sent to carry the news to Darius, who, in the midst of his lamentations, was somewhat comforted at the assurances Tireus gave him of the care, respect, and attention that had been shown his family. After hearing all that the Macedonian king had done for them, he raised his hands towards heaven and said, "Ye gods, grant that I may reestablish the fortunes of Persia and leave them as glorious as I found them; grant that victory may put it in my power to return to Alexander the favors which my dearest ones have received from him. But if the time determined by fate and the divine wrath is now come for the glory of the Persians to fall, may none but Alexander sit on the throne of Cyrus!"

When spring returned, Alexander, having subdued all the country on this side the Euphrates, began his march against Darius, who had collected an army of a million of men. The Macedonians did not number half so many; nevertheless, Alexander felt no doubt of his success. But when some of his chief officers beheld the Persian troops covering a vast field, they felt so anxious that they begged their monarch to attack Darius by night. "Oh, no," he replied; "I will not steal a victory." This answer did not imply any trifling with danger, for Alexander knew there was much to fear; but he foresaw that in case Darius was overcome in the darkness of night it would afford him an excuse for trying his fortune again.

After giving this answer, Alexander went to bed in his tent, and slept so soundly that Parmenio was obliged to give the soldiers orders to take their breakfast and then to arouse Alexander, for there was not much time to lose. "How is it possible for you to sleep so soundly when you are on the point of fighting the most important of all our battles? One would suppose that we were already victorious." "And are we not so indeed," asked Alexander, "since we are at last relieved from the trouble of wandering in pursuit of Darius?"

So, with a display of eagerness for the fight, the great warrior buckled on his armor and left his tent. This is how he appeared: he wore a short coat of Sicilian cut that fitted close to his figure, and over that was a thickly-quilted breastplate of linen, which had been taken among the spoils of the last battle. His helmet was of iron, beautifully wrought, and so highly polished that it shone like silver; to this was fitted a piece of armor called a gorget, that protected the neck and throat, set with precious stones. His sword was of the best tempered steel and very light, and his belt of the most superb workmanship. When drawing up his army and giving orders before a battle, Alexander never rode Bucephalus, because he was getting old and had to be saved for battles; but he always charged upon that fiery steed, and gave the signal as soon as he was mounted.

Alexander made a long speech to the Greeks, who answered with loud shouts and begged him to lead them on. Then, raising his right hand towards heaven, he exclaimed, "If I be really the son of Jupiter, defend and strengthen the Greeks, ye gods!" Just then his chief soothsayer, who rode by his side in a white robe with a crown of gold upon his head, pointed to an eagle that soared above and directed his course towards the enemy. This was a favorable omen: the cavalry charged at full speed, and the phalanx rushed on like a torrent.

That day witnessed one of the most furious battles that ever was fought in the world, and in the very face of danger Alexander showed the same coolness, courage, and good judgment throughout. The Persians fought bravely too, and fortune favored them at times; but it so happened that Alexander threw a dart at Darius, who, being the tallest and handsomest man in his army, could easily be distinguished. The dart missed him, but killed his charioteer on the spot, whereupon some of the guards raised a loud cry, and those behind, thinking the king had been killed, fled. The troops in front were driven back, and the wheels of the royal chariot became so entangled among the dead bodies that the horses plunged and darted without being able to move forward or back. Throwing down his arms, Darius jumped from the chariot, mounted the nearest horse, and fled for his life. But he would not have escaped, for Alexander was anxious to capture him, and might have done so had it not been for Parmenio, who at that moment sent for his assistance.

Alexander was vexed at being stopped, but when he was riding to the part of the army that had called for him, he was informed that the enemy were totally defeated and put to flight. So the Persian army, baggage, tents, and immense treasures, fell into the hands of the victor. Alexander was now proclaimed king of Asia, and the first thing he did was to make magnificent sacrifices to the gods and presents of large sums of money and offices to his friends.

Indeed, Alexander was always noted for his generosity to his friends, and he carried this trait so far that his mother wrote him, "You make your friends equal to kings by giving them the power of getting any number of friends of their own, while you leave yourself destitute." He took no notice of this remonstrance, for he never allowed his mother to meddle in matters of state or war, although he always showed her great respect, and treated her with even more generosity than he showed to others.

Alexander seated on the throne of Darius was a gratifying spectacle to the Greeks, but from that time the warrior's glory grew dim, for no sooner was he master of the greatest empire in the world than he began to indulge his passions, and gave himself up to all sorts of dissipation. It was in a fit of intoxication that he set fire to the magnificent palace of the Persian kings, which was filled with valuable treasures, and burned it to the ground. But when he became sober, he was so ashamed of this act that he set out at once with his cavalry in pursuit of Darius.

He made a long and painful march of eleven days, during which his soldiers suffered so much from want of water that they were loath to continue. About noon one day a party of Macedonians came up to Alexander. They were on mules, and carried vessels filled with water. One of them, seeing the king almost choking from thirst, filled a helmet with water and offered it to him. He took it in his hands, then looked about at the faces of his suffering soldiers, who wanted refreshment just as much as he did, and said, "Take it away, for if I alone should drink, the rest will be out of heart, and you have not enough for all." So he handed back the water without having touched a drop of it, while the soldiers applauded the hero, jumped on their horses, and demanded to be led forward.

Alexander had heard that Darius was kept a prisoner by Bessus, and hoped to save him, but when Bessus found himself in danger from the approaching army, he ordered the king to be assassinated. Polystratus was the first officer who beheld the dying monarch, as he lay on a chariot by the roadside, covered with wounds. He asked for water, which was handed to him, then he said, "It has become the last extremity of my ill fortune to receive benefits and not be able to return them. But Alexander will recompense thee, and the gods will reward Alexander for his humanity to my mother, my wife, and my children. Tell him I give him my hand, for I give it to thee in his stead." So saying, he took the hand of Polystratus and expired. When Alexander came up, he shed tears, and, taking off his own cloak, threw it over the body, which was afterwards laid in state.

Somewhat later Bessus was captured, and this is how he was punished: two straight trees were bent, and one of his legs was made fast to each, then the trees were allowed to return to their former position, and the body was torn in two.

Once a party of barbarians fell upon some Macedonians who had Bucephalus in charge, and captured him. Alexander was so provoked at this that he sent a herald to tell them that if they did not immediately return the horse he would kill every man, woman, and child in their country. Bucephalus was brought back, and the barbarians surrendered their cities, but they were treated with great kindness.

Alexander next marched into Parthia, and in order to gain the affection of the people he dressed like a Persian and adopted their manners, though at the same time he introduced to them some of the Macedonian customs. Besides, he married Roxana, an Asiatic lady of great beauty, whom he loved devotedly. This added more to his popularity in Persia than anything else.

Parmenio, who has been mentioned several times, was Alexander's principal general and a man of great ability. He had a son named Philotas, who for valor and endurance in time of war was next to the monarch himself. But Philotas had fallen into the habit of boasting so much of his exploits that his father took him to task for it several times, and his friends became envious not only of his deeds, but of the favors that were constantly shown him at court. So when a plot was discovered against the life of the Macedonian king, any trifling word or sign that might tend to cast suspicion on the favored officer was eagerly repeated to Alexander. As nothing could be proved, it was decided to put Philotas to the torture, the monarch hiding himself behind a tapestry to hear what might be forced from his lips. The victim lamented so much, and begged so hard for his life, that Alexander cried out, "O Philotas, with all this unmanly weakness, how didst thou dare engage in so great and dangerous an enterprise?" He was put to death and Parmenio also, although the latter had been the prime mover in the expedition into Asia, and had been a loyal, valiant soldier for many years. This unjust deed made Alexander terrible to his friends, and the fate of Clitus was not less shocking to them.

Clitus had been one of Alexander's bravest officers and most faithful friends, and this is what happened to him. Some very fine fruit had been brought from Greece to the king, who was so pleased with it that he invited Clitus to supper that he might enjoy it also. The company drank freely, and became quite lively as the meal proceeded; but towards its close one Pranicus began to sing a song that had been written in ridicule of the Macedonian officers, who had recently been beaten by the barbarians. The older men present felt offended, and condemned both the poet and the singer; but Alexander laughed and bade Pranicus repeat the song. Clitus, who was under the influence of wine, said, angrily, "It is not well done to make a jest of Macedonians among their enemies, for, though they have met with misfortune, they are better men than those who laugh at them."

"Clitus pleads his own cause when he gives cowardice the soft name of misfortune," said Alexander.

Clitus started up as if he had been stung, and cried, "Yes, it was cowardice that saved you, son of Jupiter, as you call yourself, when you turned your back to the sword of Spithridates. It is by the blood of the Macedonians and these wounds that you are growing so great as to disown Philip for your father and pass yourself off for the son of Jupiter Ammon."

Irritated at these bold words, Alexander replied, "Thou shameless fellow! dost thou think to say such base things of me, and stir the Macedonians up to sedition, and not be punished for it?"

ALEXANDER

"We are already punished," rejoined Clitus. "What reward have we for all our toils? Do we not envy those who do not live to see Macedonians bleed under Median rods, or sue to Persians for access to their kings?"

Thus one word led to another, until, unable longer to control his drunken rage, the king picked up an apple and threw it in the face of Clitus, who then looked about for his sword. But one of his guards had prudently removed it, while the older men gathered about the irate king and begged him to compose himself.

Meanwhile, Clitus had been dragged out of the room, but he returned by another door, singing loudly some insulting verses. Then it was impossible to restrain the king any longer; he snatched a spear from one of his guards, rushed towards Clitus just as he raised the curtain to enter, and ran him through the body. He fell to the ground, groaned, and expired.

Then Alexander felt very sorry for what he had done, for he had loved Clitus, and he became sober as soon as he beheld him dead at his feet. For a moment he gazed in silence, then hastily drawing the spear out of the body was about to run it into his own throat, when the guards seized it and led him by force to his chamber. He passed that night and the next day plunged in grief, uttering now and then a pitiful moan, but speaking to no one. Several philosophers sought to console him, but failed. At last Anaxarchus entered, and exclaimed in a loud tone, "Is this Alexander upon whom all the world is looking? Can it be he who lies on the ground crying like a slave, in fear of the law and the tongues of men? He himself should be the law to decide right and wrong. What did he conquer for but to rule and command? Know you not, Alexander, that Jupiter is represented with justice and law by his side to show that all the actions of a conqueror are right?"

The king was pacified by these soothing words, and his conscience ceased to be disturbed, but he became more unjust and haughty than ever, for he was only too ready to believe, as the philosopher had said, that whatever he might choose to do was right. Thus was this great hero thoroughly spoiled by the flattery of those who surrounded him.

But he was not yet prepared to rest; he had made up his mind to conquer India, a country little known at that time. After he had passed the Indus he formed an alliance with Taxilus, who ruled the region beyond the river and furnished troops and a hundred and thirty elephants for the Macedonian king. With this addition to his army Alexander marched against King Porus, who defended the river Hydaspes with his troops. A bloody battle ensued, and Alexander came off victorious.

While fighting, King Porus rode on one of the largest of his elephants, but he was such an enormous man that the proportion was about the same as between a man of medium height and a horse. The elephant that Porus rode was an intelligent animal, that took great care of his master during the battle, several times preventing him from falling off when he was hit, and at the close kneeling down slowly and with his trunk pulling out every dart that stuck in his body.

Porus was taken prisoner and led before Alexander. "How do you desire to be treated?" asked the latter.

"Like a king," was the reply.

"And have you nothing else to ask?"

"No; everything is included in the word king," said Porus. Alexander was pleased with his bearing and his replies, and not only restored to him his kingdom, but added extensive territories to it besides.

It was in the battle with Porus that Bucephalus received wounds which caused his death soon after. Alexander showed much regret at the loss of this faithful friend, and built a city where he was buried, which he called Bucephalia.

Seventy Greek towns were founded by Alexander as he marched along, and he was so elated by success that he resolved to go as far as the river Ganges; but his army refused to march farther, and he was forced to return. He built a fleet on the Hydaspes, and as he travelled with his troops met several Indian princes in battle. He laid siege to the town of Malli, where he was the first to mount the scaling-ladder; but it broke, and he was left on the wall alone, a target for the darts which were showered at him from below. He hesitated for a moment, then jumped down in the midst of the enemy. Fortunately, he fell on his feet, and the flashing of his armor so frightened the Mallians, who thought it was lightning proceeding from his body, that they turned and fled. That gave time for some of his guard also to jump down from the walls; but the enemy recovered from their astonishment and returned. A hand-to-hand attack ensued, and Alexander was wounded through his armor, although he fought desperately. Other wounds brought him to his knees, and he would have been despatched had it not been for his two guards, who placed themselves before him. One of them was wounded and the other killed. A tremendous blow with a bludgeon on the back of the neck struck Alexander senseless, but the Macedonians, who by that time had flocked within the walls, gathered about him and carried him to his tent. It was reported that he was dead, but in course of time he recovered, and there was great rejoicing in his army when he again appeared among them. After offering sacrifices to the gods he continued down the river, and subdued a vast deal of country as he coasted along.

Among other prisoners, he took ten philosophers called Gymnosophists, who had urged a prince named Sabbas to revolt against the Macedonians. These Gymnosophists always went naked, differing in this as well as in other particulars from the ordinary philosophers. One of their customs was to discuss learned subjects while they dined, and when they assembled not only they, but all their pupils, even the youngest, were questioned as to what good they had done during the day, and those who had not some kind action or some useful occupation to tell of, were allowed no dinner.

Well, on hearing that the ten philosophers he had captured were remarkable for the answers they always gave, even to the most obscure questions, Alexander determined to try them, first announcing that he would put to death the one of them who answered worst, and after him all the rest. The oldest man among the Gymnosophists was appointed judge.

"Which are more numerous, the living or the dead?" he asked of the first. "The living; for the dead no longer exist," was the answer.

"Does the earth or the sea produce the largest animals?" the second was asked. He answered, "The earth; for the sea is part of it."

Alexander's question to the third was, "Which is the cunningest of beasts?" "That which men have not yet found out," he said.

ALEXANDER

He ordered the fourth to tell him what argument he used to persuade Sabbas to revolt. "No other," he answered, "but that he should either live or die nobly."

Of the fifth he asked, "Which is the older, night or day?"

The philosopher replied, "Day is older, by one day at least;" and noticing that Alexander was not satisfied, he added, "You ought not to wonder if strange questions draw forth strange answers."

"What should a man do to be exceedingly beloved?" asked the king of the sixth. "He must be very powerful, without making himself too much feared," was the reply.

"How may a man become a god?" was the question to the seventh philosopher. "By doing that which is impossible for me to do."

"Which is stronger, life or death?" the eighth was asked "Life, because it bears so many evils."

"How long is it good for a man to live?" "As long as he does not prefer death to life," said the ninth philosopher.

Then turning to the judge, Alexander ordered him to pass sentence. The old man said, "In my opinion each has answered worse than the other."

"Then thou shalt die first for giving such a sentence," said Alexander.

"Not so, O king, unless you said falsely that he should die first who made the worst answer," returned the oldest Gymnosophist. The king was so amused that he gave them a great many presents, and sent them away.

Alexander spent seven months on the rivers, and at the end of that time war, illness, caused by bad food and excessive heat, and famine had destroyed three-quarters of his army, and he was glad to return to Persia. When passing through that country he had about him everything that was beautiful and luxurious, and spent much of his time in feasting. At one of his suppers he promised that the man who drank most should be crowned with victory. Promachus won the crown, for he drank about fourteen quarts of wine, but he lived only three days afterwards, and forty-one others died from the quantity they drank on that occasion.

When Alexander reached Susa he married Statira, the daughter of Darius, and his officers followed his example, each marrying a Persian lady. Then he gave a grand entertainment in honor of these events. He had no less than nine thousand guests, and presented each with a golden cup, and everything was arranged with such magnificence as had never been seen at a feast before.

After that Alexander offered splendid sacrifices, and gave a number of sumptuous banquets; but there were repeated bad omens, both in the appearance of the victims of the sacrifices and in other circumstances, all of which made Alexander so superstitious that he was ready to listen to any interpretation made by his numerous soothsayers, even of the most trifling and natural events. He became sad and dejected, but one day he roused himself and gave another feast, then took a bath and went to bed. The next day and night he drank so hard that a fever came on, and the more he drank the more ill he became, until delirium ensued, and at the end of thirteen days he died.

ALEXANDER

This great conqueror lived only thirty-two years, and reigned less than thirteen. He left an immense empire, which became the scene of many bloody wars. He was buried in the city of Alexandria. A golden coffin received his remains, and divine honors were paid to his memory in Egypt, as well as in other countries.

No character in history has offered more matter for discussion than that of Alexander the Great; but from the short account given here our young readers may form their own opinions, and perhaps feel encouraged to investigate for themselves.

EUMENES

EUMENES was born at Cardia, a small town in the Chersonesus, a peninsula in the southern part of Thrace. His father was a poor wagoner, but was able to give Eumenes a good education, because there were public schools in his day, where children of all ranks in life were taught. King Philip of Macedon chanced to be passing at one time through Cardia, and went to the exercise grounds to see the men and boys wrestling and boxing. On that occasion Eumenes was present, and showed so much energy and skill as a wrestler that Philip was charmed with him and took him into his service, where he remained for seven years.

When Philip died, Eumenes was raised to a high office under Alexander, on account of his talent for military affairs, and became one of that monarch's favorite officers, serving him for thirteen years. This was remarkable, because Eumenes was not a native of Macedon, and for that reason he refused to interfere in the disputes that arose after the death of Alexander, saying that it did not become him as a stranger to take part in the quarrels between the two Macedonian parties.

But when the troubles were all settled, the generals met to divide the various provinces and armies, and then Cappadocia and Paphlagonia fell to the share of Eumenes. Those

EUMENES

countries were not then subject to the Macedonians, so Leonatus and Antigonus were the two commanders selected to go with their armies and place Eumenes in power. However, they deserted him at the last moment for duties that gave promise of greater glory, and he went for aid with his army to Perdiccas, who was a most important person in Macedonia.

Perdiccas was very friendly to Eumenes, and not only took him into his confidence, but after a time conducted him in person to Cappadocia with a large force, and with one battle succeeded in establishing him in the government. Having placed guards and officers whom he could trust over the various cities, Eumenes accompanied Perdiccas as far as Cilicia, and would have gone back with him to his court, but there were provinces near Cappadocia still to be conquered, and it was thought best for Eumenes to be on the spot for that purpose.

When Perdiccas was engaged in a war with Ptolemy, Craterus and Antipater, two of Alexander's most distinguished generals, made war against him, and, as he could not then oppose them, he appointed Eumenes commander-in-chief of the forces in Armenia and Cappadocia. Neoptolemus, the captain of Alexander's life-guards, refused to submit to the rule of Eumenes, and gave him battle, but he was badly beaten, and fled to Craterus and Antipater with the few who managed to escape with him. He gave those generals an account of his defeat, and asked for assistance, particularly from Craterus, who was a favorite with the Macedonians. "They are so attached to you," said Neoptolemus, "that if they saw but your hat or heard the sound of your voice they would run to you with their swords in their hands."

This was true, and Eumenes knew it; therefore he did not tell his troops that they were going to contend against Craterus, which was a wise piece of generalship. He kept the secret entirely to himself, but took care so to arrange his army that a foreign force should fight against Craterus, because he dared not trust the Macedonians to do so. The battle was a desperate one, and although Craterus fought bravely, he was killed. Many passed over his body without recognizing it; but one of Eumenes's officers, who had known the dead general well, jumped from his horse and guarded the body until the battle was over.

Eumenes was raised to high honor on account of his victories, but the Macedonians were so indignant when they discovered that they had been led against one of their own countrymen whom they loved and admired as they did Craterus, that they passed sentence of death on Eumenes. Perdiccas, who had been a friend to Eumenes, would probably have turned against him too had he been alive, but he was slain in a mutiny in Egypt two days before the news arrived.

So Antigonus and Antipater took charge of the army against Eumenes, who again showed wonderful generalship; for he paid his soldiers so liberally, and divided spoils so justly, that when it was found that the enemy had distributed papers in the camp offering a large sum of money and high honors to him who should kill Eumenes, there was so much indignation that even the Macedonians went over to him again, and formed a body-guard of a thousand men for his protection.

Eumenes lost some battles and won others, and he was forced to move from place to place so constantly that he gave his soldiers permission to leave his command. This was partly for their own safety, and partly because it was inconvenient to fly before the enemy with so large an army. So when he retired to the castle of Nora, on the border of Cappadocia, he had only five hundred horse and two hundred foot-soldiers. This was well, because a larger number could scarcely have been accommodated in so confined a space. As it was, Eumenes found it difficult to give his men and horses proper exercise; but this is the way he managed it: for the men, the largest room in the fort was used for their walks, and they were urged to keep themselves in practice, to be prepared for flight. The horses were tied to the roof of the stable with strong halters, and then, by means of pulleys, they were so raised from the ground as to be obliged to stand on their hind legs. While in that position the grooms excited them with their voices and whips until they bounded furiously and tried to get their forefeet to the ground. Thus the whole body was exercised until the horses were out of breath and covered with sweat. That mode of treatment, with good food, kept them in excellent condition.

It was Antigonus who conducted that siege, and before he began it he invited Eumenes to a conference. "Oh, no," answered Eumenes; "Antigonus has many friends and generals to take his place in case of accident to himself, but the troops under my care have no one but me to command and protect them. Antigonus must therefore send hostages if he wants to treat with me in person."

"He must make the first application to me," returned Antigonus, "I being a greater man than he."

The reply Eumenes sent back was, "While I am master of my sword I shall never think any man greater than myself."

Then Antigonus despatched his nephew to the fort as hostage, whereupon Eumenes came out. The two generals had been friends and companions in earlier times, so when they beheld each other they embraced warmly. The conference lasted a long time, but as Eumenes insisted on retaining the government of his provinces, and demanded a large reward for his services besides, no treaty could be made.

During the interview a number of the enemy ran forward to have a look at the man who had caused the death of Craterus. Fearing that they might offer some violence, Antigonus called to them to keep at a distance, and even ordered them to be driven off with stones. They crowded up nevertheless; so encircling Eumenes with his arms, Antigonus commanded his guards to keep back the crowd, and with no little difficulty got him safe again into the castle.

The siege lasted until Antipater died, when Antigonus, whose mind was filled with schemes, turned his attention towards Macedonia. But he needed a competent general to assist him, so he raised the siege of the castle of Nora, after having obtained the oath of Eumenes to certain proposals of his, one of which was fealty to himself and to the royal family of Macedonia.

Then all the soldiers who had left Eumenes flocked to him from different parts of the country until he had a powerful army. This so displeased Antigonus that he ordered the siege to be begun again, but it was too late, for Olympias, the wife of Alexander, had invited Eumenes to go to her and protect her son, whose life she feared was in danger.

From that time Eumenes was a faithful ally of the royal family, with whom his influence became wonderfully great. But he was shrewd enough to be always on the lookout for

EUMENES

Antigonus, who was so jealous of him as to have turned his enemy. At last Antigonus really came; but Eumenes was prepared, and opposed him with such vigor when he attempted to cross the river, that four thousand of his men were captured, and the channel was choked up with his dead.

Not long after this bloody event, on hearing that Eumenes was ill, Antigonus, who had not abandoned hope of victory, advanced again. Eumenes was really too ill to command the army, but they would not move without him, so he had himself carried in a litter at some distance in the rear, so that his rest might not be disturbed by the noise. They had not gone far when the enemy appeared, marching down to the plain from the neighboring hills. Their armor glittered brilliantly in the sunlight, and the troops were so struck when they beheld the train of elephants with towers on their backs, and all the display of men and arms besides, that they grounded their arms and declared they would not stir another step without Eumenes.

On hearing this, Eumenes urged his slaves to hasten forward with his litter, and when he opened the curtains and waved his hand, the troops shouted for joy, challenged the enemy to come on, for they thought themselves invincible with him at their head. So did Antigonus, and when he spied the litter, carried about from one wing of the army to another, he laughed aloud, and said to his friends, "Yon litter is the thing that pitches the battle against us." And so he immediately retreated to his intrenchments.

There were two officers under Eumenes who had been jealous of him for a long time, so they formed a plot against his life, agreeing to make use of him in one more battle, and assassinate him immediately after. Antigonus managed during the next engagement to seize the baggage without being seen; but one of the jealous officers we have mentioned sent to ask after the battle that it might be returned.

Antigonus answered, "I will restore your baggage and treat you in all respects with great kindness if you will put Eumenes into my hands." The conspirators determined to deliver the brave man over to the enemy, so they took advantage of a favorable moment to fall upon him, snatch away his sword, and with his own girdle firmly bind his hands behind him.

When he was led through the midst of the men he had commanded, he asked to be allowed to speak to them. Mounting an eminence, he said, "What trophy, ye vilest of all the Macedonians! what trophy could Antigonus prefer to the one you are raising for him by delivering your general bound? Was it not base enough to acknowledge yourselves beaten merely for the sake of your baggage, as if victory dwelt among your goods and chattels, and not upon the points of your swords, but you must also send your general as a ransom for that baggage? For my part, though thus led, I am not conquered. I have beaten the enemy, and am ruined by my fellow-soldiers. But I conjure you by the god Jupiter, and by the awful deities who preside over oaths, to kill me here with your own hands. If my life be taken by another, the deed will still be yours. Nor will Antigonus complain if you take the work out of his hands; for he wants not Eumenes alive, but Eumenes dead. If you choose not to be the immediate instruments, loose but one of my hands, and that shall do the business. If you will not trust me with a sword, throw me bound as I am among wild beasts."

EUMENES

Some of the troops wept and would have granted his request, but others cried out, "Lead him on, and attend not to his trifling. He is only a Chersonesian who has worried us Macedonians with infinite wars; lead him on! lead him on!" And so they drove him forward.

But on account of their former friendship Antigonus could not bear to have Eumenes brought before him; therefore, when he was asked how the prisoner was to be kept, he said, "As you would keep an elephant or a lion." He soon ordered his heavy chains to be removed, however, and even permitted a slave to wait on him and friends to visit and bring him refreshments. Meanwhile, he was deliberating how to dispose of him.

At last the Macedonian officers insisted that he should be put to death,—they cared not how, so long as it was done; and Antigonus dared not postpone it. So the prisoner, after being deprived of food for three days, was executed.

The body was burned with honors, and the ashes were placed in a silver urn and sent to the friends of Eumenes in his native land. This was the end of one who raised himself to a high position entirely by his own efforts, but whose life will probably be of interest only to those who are fond of military adventure.

DEMETRIUS

DEMETRIUS was the only son of Antigonus, one of the generals who played an important part in public affairs after the death of Alexander of Macedon, in whose army he had served. Demetrius was singularly handsome, his expression being so beautiful that no painter or sculptor has ever been able to produce a good likeness of him. He had the faculty of being able to make himself both loved and feared; for socially he was an agreeable companion, and in time of war he was so persistent that nothing could deter him from obtaining what he sought. His two most prominent qualities were excessive love of pleasure and a passion for glory. The former prompted him to devote too much time to feasting, drinking, and other vices; but, on the other hand, he had many virtues. He was an exceedingly dutiful and affectionate son, a mild, generous conqueror, and a liberal patron of the arts. His passion for glory made him brave and encouraged him to study the military art so thoroughly that the warlike engines he either improved or invented showed peculiar skill. His surname was Poliorcetes, a Greek word meaning "besieger of cities," because in conducting sieges he proved himself a perfect genius. Here is a circumstance that shows how kind and affectionate was his natural disposition. When still a youth he had a companion named Mithridates, an excellent boy, who was always in attendance with him or his father,

Antigonus. Demetrius was very fond of Mithridates, and was, therefore, greatly distressed when his father sent for him one day and said, after having made him swear not to repeat what he was about to tell him, "My son, I have had a dream which makes me so suspicious of Mithridates that I have positively determined to destroy him." Demetrius could not warn his friend in words because of his oath, but the very day after his father had told him of his dream he drew Mithridates aside as though by accident, and with the point of his spear wrote in the sand, "Fly, Mithridates." The youth lost no time in acting upon this hint, but fled that night to Cappadocia. This is the Mithridates who founded a line of kings, he being the first of the name.

The first important military command was given to Demetrius when Ptolemy, king of Egypt, invaded Syria. Antigonus himself remained in Phrygia, but he sent his son, then just twenty-two years of age, as sole commander of his army. But inexperience made the young man rash, and he met with a great defeat near the town of Gaza. Eight thousand of his men were taken, five thousand were killed, and all his private property, including his tent and money, captured. Ptolemy afterwards returned everything except the prisoners, saying that he was fighting only for dominion.

Demetrius bore his defeat like a well-tried general, and immediately set to work to prepare for another battle, which soon took place with Cilles, Ptolemy's lieutenant. Cilles thought it a trifling matter to drive a young commander, already defeated, out of Syria, but he soon found that he had undervalued his antagonist, for Demetrius took him by surprise and captured him, seven thousand prisoners of war, and a large amount of treasure. He was not more delighted at the victory than he was at the opportunity it gave him of returning Ptolemy's generosity. So having obtained his father's permission, he sent back Cilles and his friends loaded with presents. This battle drove Ptolemy out of Syria.

Some time after, Antigonus and his son determined to free Greece from the slavery to which she had been reduced by Cassander and Ptolemy. This was a just and noble desire, and Demetrius set sail for Athens with a fleet of two hundred and fifty ships. He reached the Piræus, the harbor of Athens, before his approach had been made known, and as his ships were supposed to have been sent by Ptolemy, he got well into the harbor before the mistake was discovered; then the generals who had hastened to the shore were so frightened that they became helpless. Demetrius went upon the deck of his vessel, and, after motioning to the people on shore to keep silence, ordered a herald to make this proclamation: "Antigonus, my father, in a happy hour, I hope, for Athens, has sent me to give the citizens back their liberty, to turn out the garrison sent here by Cassander, and to restore to the country its ancient laws."

On hearing this the people threw down their shields and clapped their hands with delight, calling Demetrius their deliverer and benefactor. They invited him to land, but he would not do so until he had driven out Cassander's garrisons from other ports, as well as from Athens. This took considerable time, and then he made his entrance into the city, publicly announcing to the people that they were now free, and that they should receive from Antigonus, his father, a present of wheat, and a supply of timber sufficient to build a hundred galleys. So, after fifteen years, the Athenians had their laws and institutions again restored to them.

DEMETRIUS

But they were so servile in their gratitude that they showed themselves unfit for liberty. They bestowed such excessive honors on Demetrius as to be positively offensive, for they gave him and his father the title of king, though they had no claim to it, and called them besides their Tutelar Deities and Deliverers. But this was not all: by a common vote they decreed that each year was to be named by a priest of the two Tutelary Divinities, whose title should appear on all public documents. The figures of Antigonus and Demetrius, they decreed, should be wrought into the holy garments with those of the other gods; they built an altar on the spot where Demetrius first landed, calling it the "Altar of the Descent of Demetrius," and created two new tribes, called the Antigonid and the Demetriad. Their council consisted of five hundred persons, fifty being chosen out of each tribe. They added a hundred more to represent the new tribes, and further agreed that any ambassadors sent from Athens to Antigonus or Demetrius should have the same title as those sent to Delphi or Olympia to perform the national sacrifices, and that whenever Demetrius should visit their city he should be treated as though he were a god, the citizen who excelled the rest in his feast being promised money from the public purse for sacrifice. They also instituted a feast of Demetrius, and named a month in his honor.

Indeed, with all this disgusting flattery, Demetrius would have had his head completely turned if his father had not summoned him to undertake the reduction of Cyprus. He sailed for that island as soon as he received the order, fought a battle with Menelaus, the brother of Ptolemy, and defeated him. Then Ptolemy himself came with large forces and a numerous fleet, but Demetrius was prepared for him, and a great fight took place in the harbor of Salamis, the ancient capital of Cyprus, which ended in a complete rout of the Egyptian army. Ptolemy escaped with eight ships, the rest, with all their men, being taken or destroyed in the battle. Demetrius seized the arms, treasures, and military machines, and took them to his camp; but what added more to his glory than any victory could have done was his humane conduct. After he had given honorable funerals to the dead, he bestowed on the prisoners their liberty, and to prove to the Athenians that they were not forgotten he sent them full sets of arms for twelve hundred men.

Aristodemus was despatched with the news of victory to Antigonus, who waited in great anxiety to hear the result of the battle. This man was the boldest of all the court flatterers, and on this occasion he made it a study how to produce the best effect and to bring out the full importance of his welcome message. So when he crossed from Cyprus he bade the crew remain on board the ship, and, getting into a little boat, landed quite alone. When the anxious father heard that a messenger was coming from Cyprus he sent one person after another to get the news and hasten to him with it. But not a word could they draw from Aristodemus, who walked gravely and quietly towards the palace, determined to tell his story in his own way to Antigonus. He was so long about it, and looked so very grave, that it was generally believed by those who met him that his news was bad, and so thought the impatient Antigonus, who, no longer able to restrain his anxiety, ran out, followed by a crowd of people, and met the messenger at the gate. "Hail, King Antigonus!" exclaimed Aristodemus, holding out his hands and making a profound bow. "We have defeated Ptolemy by sea, and have taken Cyprus and sixteen thousand eight hundred prisoners."

DEMETRIUS

"Welcome, Aristodemus," replied Antigonus; "but, as you chose to torture us so long for your good news, you may wait awhile for the reward of it."

Then all the people saluted Antigonus as king, and for the first time gave him the title which the Athenians had bestowed on him. A crown was procured and placed upon his head, and shortly after he sent one to his son, with a letter addressed to "King Demetrius."

So elated was Antigonus with his success that he set out in person to invade Egypt, but he met with many difficulties; and as he was nearly eighty years old and very fat, he decided that it would be better to leave conquest to his son, and so returned home without having accomplished anything.

Now the Rhodians persisted in their friendship for Ptolemy; so Demetrius was ordered to fight them. He laid siege to Rhodes, and used on that occasion the most powerful of the engines he had invented. These "city-takers," as they were called, were the wonder and admiration of the world. The one used before Rhodes was the largest; it was a hundred and fifty feet high, supported on eight enormous wheels, and required three thousand four hundred men to move it. It was nine stories high, square at the base, and growing smaller as it rose. Each story was filled with soldiers, and there were windows from which all sorts of weapons were discharged against the enemy's walls. In spite of this formidable engine, the Rhodians made a brave defence, and held out for a whole year.

Demetrius had known for a long time that he was making little progress, so he rejoiced when a reasonable excuse for raising the siege presented itself. This came in the shape of an appeal for aid from the Athenians, whose city Cassander was besieging. Then a treaty was made with the Rhodians, who bound themselves to aid Antigonus and Demetrius against all enemies except Ptolemy.

Demetrius went to Athens with a fleet of three hundred ships and a large army, and not only drove Cassander out of Athens, but restored liberty by the terror of his arms to the whole of Greece. Then the Athenians thought no place good enough for him to occupy but the Parthenon itself, where he was supposed to be the guest of the goddess Minerva.

But he did not enjoy this new honor long, for several kings formed a league on purpose to attack Antigonus, and his son was called home. The old king headed the army himself; and although he said, "This flock of birds will soon be scattered by one stone and a single shout," he had his misgivings when he saw the tremendous army the kings had brought against him. The great battle was fought at Ipsus, and Antigonus fell pierced by a score of darts.

Demetrius managed, after several narrow escapes, to set sail for Athens, where he felt sure of a hearty welcome; he was therefore astonished when he received a message from the changeable and ungrateful inhabitants that they had resolved to receive no king within their walls. Demetrius was justly angry, but he was not in condition to avenge the insult; he merely sent a gentle remonstrance and a demand for his galleys, which were sent to him.

Not long after, fortune smiled on Demetrius again, for Seleucus, one of the most powerful of all Alexander's generals, became jealous of the vast territory owned by Lysimachus, and tried to strengthen himself by seeking a friendship with his former enemy, Demetrius; so he wrote to him, asking the hand of his daughter in marriage. This pleased Demetrius so much that he sailed for Syria at once, with his daughter and his whole fleet.

When Seleucus and Demetrius met, each gave the other a grand banquet, and after several unceremonious meetings they parted excellent friends. Seleucus took his wife with him, and they travelled in great state. He also brought about a reconciliation between Demetrius and the king of Egypt, whose daughter, Ptolemais, afterwards married Demetrius.

The ingratitude of the Athenians had been very galling to Demetrius, so when news came to him of disturbance in the city, he resolved to go and take possession of it by a sudden attack. But while passing along the coast of Attica he was overtaken by a violent storm, and lost most of his ships and men. It did not take him long to raise more troops, and with these he marched into the Peloponnesus and laid siege to the city of Messena. Thence he made an incursion into Attica and cut off supplies, so that the people were almost starved to death.

So great was the distress that any sort of food became acceptable. An instance is given of a father and son who actually came to blows over a dead mouse that fell from the ceiling, for they were so hungry as to have lost sight of every other consideration. Epicurus, the philosopher, saved his own life and the lives of his scholars by daily dividing a small quantity of beans.

Such being the condition of the Athenians, they were forced at last to open their gates to Demetrius, and sent ambassadors to know what sort of a treaty he would make with them. He entered the city, and issued a proclamation that all the inhabitants should assemble at the theatre. When they had done so, he ranged his soldiers in a line at the back of the stage, then coming forward like an actor, he gently upbraided the Athenians for their ill treatment of himself, but added that he forgave them, and would present them with a hundred thousand bushels of wheat, in token of reconciliation, to relieve their wants. He also appointed such magistrates as he knew would be most agreeable to them. Having thus settled matters in Athens, he next turned his attention to Macedonia, where, the king having died, his two sons quarrelled about the succession. Alexander, one of the sons, wrote to Demetrius asking his assistance, which was freely given. But after he had been in Macedonia a short time, Demetrius heard of a plot formed by Alexander to kill him, so in order to turn the tables on him he invited the young prince to sup with him. When the meal was nearly over, Demetrius rose and went out; the prince followed. "Kill him that follows me," said Demetrius to the guard. His order was forthwith executed. A friend who had accompanied Alexander said, "You have been just one day too quick for us, Demetrius."

The other prince had murdered his mother, and had thus made himself hateful to the people, who, as soon as they found no violence offered to themselves, proclaimed Demetrius king of Macedon.

Even then he could not rest, for his ambitious spirit demanded more power; so he marched with his troops against Pyrrhus, drove him out of Thessaly, and then besieged and took Thebes. But Pyrrhus was a brave man, and his conduct in battle won for him the greatest glory among the Macedonians, who kept constantly comparing his valor with that of their beloved Alexander the Great.

DEMETRIUS

Meanwhile, Demetrius was exciting their disgust because he was so theatrical in his manners, so haughty, and so fond of display. His robes were of the richest purple material, embroidered and edged with gold; his crown was the most gorgeous that had ever been worn by any Macedonian king, and even his shoes were gayly and elaborately ornamented. He lived in most luxurious style, and was so reserved that his subjects dared not approach him, or if they did he treated them with overbearing pride. He kept the Athenian ambassadors waiting two whole years before he would give them an audience, and when the Lacedæmonians sent one person to confer with him, he asked angrily whether they had really dared to send a single envoy. "Yes," they said, boldly, "one envoy to one king."

One day, when he was riding out and seemed to be in a more amiable mood than usual, several of his subjects approached him with petitions. They were so pleased to see him take the papers and gather them into his robe that they followed him; but when he reached the river he shook them all into the water, without having so much as opened them. Such acts were often repeated, until the Macedonians felt that Demetrius no longer governed them, but insulted them.

So, when he collected a great army to invade Asia, Pyrrhus and Lysimachus took that opportunity to attack Macedonia, and they were received with such favor that they divided the country between them. Then the soldiers of Demetrius deserted from his camp, and in order to save himself he put on a disguise and stole away.

For a while he was dejected, but his active spirit soon revived, and he collected an army, which he led into Asia Minor. There he had great success at first, but ill fortune overtook him, and after much suffering he was forced to seek the protection of Seleucus, his son-in-law. Seleucus knew it was dangerous to have within his territory a man who was so fond of bold enterprises; however, he granted him permission to stay two months. But the courtiers were displeased at this favor, and before the allotted period had expired they persuaded their king to send him to a strong fortress on the Syrian coast. There the prisoner was well attended and well fed, he had plenty of space for walking and riding, and a park with game for hunting, and those of his friends and companions in exile who desired to visit him had permission to do so.

At first restraint seemed irksome to Demetrius, but he sank into idle habits before very long, and passed most of his time in gambling and drinking. Such a life brought on a disease of which, in the course of three years, Demetrius died, at the age of fifty-four.

His remains were sent in a golden urn to Greece, where they were received by his son, Antigonus, who conveyed them to the city of Demetrius. As the galley passed along the coast, wherever it touched land the people sent chaplets to adorn the urn. When the vessel entered the harbor of Corinth, a famous musician played a solemn tune on the flute, to which the rowers kept time, and a troop of young men in arms stood in a line when the urn, covered with purple and surmounted by a royal diadem, was carried ashore. In tears and mourning Antigonus bore it to its final resting-place.

PYRRHUS

THERE was something in the bearing of Pyrrhus that excited terror rather than respect, and he had a peculiarity that no one could fail to notice. It was this: instead of teeth in his upper jaw he had one continued bone, marked with lines where the divisions of the teeth ought to have been. It was believed that he had power to cure the spleen by sacrificing a white cock, and by pressing with his right foot on the diseased spot while the patient lay flat upon the floor. All who were afflicted with the spleen, whether rich or poor, might at any moment apply to Pyrrhus, and he was willing to cure them, the only payment he ever demanded being a white cock for sacrifice. It was also said that the great toe of his right foot had a divine virtue in it, and when it was found in its natural state after his death, though the rest of his body had been reduced to ashes, no doubt remained that such was the case.

When Pyrrhus was a little child, his father, the king of Epirus, was driven from his throne by the Molossians, who made Neoptolemus king instead. Then Pyrrhus would certainly have been put to death had not some of his father's friends carried him off. They took him to King Glaucias of Illyria, who conceived such a fancy for the infant that he kept him, and had him educated with his own children until he reached the age of twelve; then the king went to Epirus with an army and placed his charge on the throne which was his by right of inheritance.

Pyrrhus ruled in peace for five years, but at the end of that period he went to attend the wedding of one of the daughters of King Glaucias, and during his absence Neoptolemus seized the throne again. Pyrrhus was then just seventeen years old, and did not possess the necessary means to assert his rights, so he went with his brother-in-law, Demetrius, to fight against Ptolemy. He distinguished himself at the great battle of Ipsus, and some time afterwards went to Egypt.

There he fell in love with Antigone, daughter of one of the wives of Ptolemy, and married her. She was a good wife, and loved Pyrrhus so much that she procured men and money to enable him to get back his kingdom. When he reached Epirus he was received with open arms, for Neoptolemus had been such a tyrant that all his subjects hated him. Still, Pyrrhus had too much consideration to dethrone him, so he proposed to share the government with him, and Neoptolemus was very glad to make that arrangement. It worked well for only a short time, for the two kings became jealous of each other, and this is what happened. It was the custom for the kings to offer sacrifices to the god Mars yearly in the Molossian country, and each time they made a vow to govern according to law, while the people swore to support the government. The kings were always attended on these occasions by a number of friends, and presents were exchanged among them all. The last time Pyrrhus and Neoptolemus sacrificed together, Gelon, one of the friends of the latter, presented Pyrrhus with two yoke of oxen. Myrtilus, cup-bearer to Pyrrhus, asked for the oxen, but his demand was refused. Gelon noticed that Myrtilus was not only disappointed but displeased, so he invited him to sup with him. After supper he urged his guest to become a friend to Neoptolemus and poison Pyrrhus. Myrtilus pretended to agree to the proposition of Gelon, but went straight home and told his master all about it. Pyrrhus then ordered him to take Alexicrates, his chief cup-bearer, to Gelon, and make believe that he could mix the poison better than any one else. Pyrrhus did this because he wanted to have sure proof of the plot. Gelon was thoroughly deceived, and so was Neoptolemus, who had urged on the conspirators. Everything seemed to be working so smoothly that Neoptolemus could not restrain his joy; and one evening when he had been drinking freely at an entertainment at his sister's house, he talked openly about the poison scheme and the probability that he would soon occupy the throne alone. Now there happened to be present a young woman engaged in the royal household, who was lying on a couch with her face to the wall. She was not observed, because she appeared to be sleeping; but she was wide awake, and not only heard all that Neoptolemus said, but ran early next morning to the apartment of Antigone, the wife of Pyrrhus, and repeated it to her. Of course Antigone warned her husband, but he did nothing until he had made sure that the majority of the Epirots were his friends and would stand by him; then he invited Neoptolemus to join him in a sacrifice, and killed him on the spot.

    He now had the government in his own hands, and at once undertook the Macedonian wars against his brother-in-law, Demetrius, with whom he had ceased to be friendly, and he fought with such skill and courage that even his enemies were filled with admiration. They could compare him to nobody but the great Alexander, and Hannibal called him the most skilful of all the renowned commanders. The Epirots exulted in the heroic deeds of their king, and when he got back home gave him the name of "Eagle." "If I am an eagle," he said, "you have made me one; for it is upon your arms and your wings that I have risen so high."

Not long after, on hearing that Demetrius was dangerously ill, Pyrrhus entered Macedonia and almost succeeded in conquering the country, but such tremendous efforts were made to repulse him that he was driven out. Then Demetrius raised an immense army, knowing that his dangerous neighbor would trouble him again. So he did, not only with his own army, but with the assistance of three other kings, and all their forces united.

The night before he entered Macedonia again, Pyrrhus dreamed that Alexander the Great called him, and that on going to him he found him sick in bed. Nevertheless, Alexander, after expressing great friendship for him, promised him his assistance. "How can you, who are ill, help me?" asked Pyrrhus. "I will do it with my name," returned the warrior, as, mounting a swift horse, he seemed to lead the way to victory.

Pyrrhus was so much encouraged by this vision that he hurried on to battle, and took one city after another until he met that part of the enemy's troops that were under the command of Demetrius. These had heard so much of Pyrrhus's feats, and of his uncommon gentleness towards those whom he had conquered, that they were for the most part ready to mutiny. Besides, a number of Epirots disguised themselves as Macedonians and went among their pretended countrymen, telling them to go over to Pyrrhus as they intended to do. This had the desired effect, and the Macedonian army declaring for Pyrrhus, Demetrius was only too glad to make his escape in disguise. So, without striking a single

PYRRHUS

blow, Pyrrhus became master of the camp and was proclaimed king of Macedonia.

He did not remain there long, however, for after a peace had been concluded with Demetrius, the Macedonians began to object to being ruled by a man whose ancestors had been their subjects, and he quietly went back to his own kingdom with his Epirot soldiers. Now was his chance to enjoy a life of repose and peace if he had so desired, but he could not rest quietly, and felt unhappy when not engaged in war. Therefore when the Tarentines, who were fighting the Romans, sent to ask him to command their forces, he eagerly accepted.

There was at the court of Pyrrhus a Thessalian named Cineas, who had studied oratory under Demosthenes, and whose words always had such weight that Pyrrhus said of him, "Cineas has gained me more cities by his speeches than I have won by the force of arms." Seeing Pyrrhus absorbed in preparations for the war in Italy, Cineas took occasion, when he was at leisure, to speak to him as follows: "The Romans have the reputation of being excellent soldiers, and have the command of many warlike nations; if it please heaven that we conquer them, what use, sir, shall we make of our victory?"

"Why, Cineas," replied the king, "when the Romans are beaten, there is no town, whether Greek or barbarian, that will dare to oppose us; we shall be masters of all Italy, whose greatness and power no man knows better than you."

"But," continued Cineas, after a short pause, "after we have conquered Italy, what shall we do next, sir?"

"There is Sicily very near," answered Pyrrhus; "a fruitful, populous island, easy to take."

"Is, then, the taking of Sicily to terminate our expeditions?" asked Cineas.

"Far from it," said the king, "for, if heaven grant us success in this, it will lead to greater things. Libya and Carthage will then be within reach, and after we have conquered them, will any of our enemies dare to resist us?"

"Certainly not," said Cineas, "for it is clear that so much power will enable you to recover Macedonia and to declare yourself sovereign of all Greece. But what are we to do then?"

"Why, then, my friend," said Pyrrhus, laughing, "we will take our ease, drink and be merry."

This was the answer Cineas had waited for, so he said, "And what hinders us from drinking and taking our ease now, when we have already in our hands that for which we propose to pass through seas of blood, through toil and danger, and through numberless calamities, which we must cause to others as well as to ourselves?"

Pyrrhus was troubled by what Cineas had said, but his ambition would not let him alter his purpose, so he sent the orator on to Tarentum with a great army, and afterwards set sail himself with more troops. But when he reached the Ionian Sea, he was overtaken by such a violent storm that his whole fleet came near being destroyed, and some of the ships were driven quite out of their course. Others were thrown on the rocky shore, and the one in which the king was seemed on the point of sinking; thereupon he threw himself overboard, and, after battling with the angry waves for some hours, reached the shore almost exhausted. The people near by did what they could for him and his men as the ships came in, and in a few hours Pyrrhus marched on to Tarentum with the remnant of his army that had survived the storm.

On hearing of the king's approach, Cineas went out to meet him, and, uniting their forces, the sovereigns proceeded to the field where Lævinus, the Roman consul, had encamped. But Pyrrhus sent forward a herald to propose to the Romans that they should take him as their mediator and settle all difficulties without fighting. Lævinus answered, "Tell Pyrrhus that the Romans neither accept him as a mediator nor fear him as an enemy."

Pyrrhus then moved forward; but when he beheld the Roman army drawn up in battle array he was amazed, and said to one of his friends near by, "Megacles, this order of the barbarians is not at all barbarian; we shall before long see what they can do." He was soon convinced that he had no mean opponents, but he exposed his person in the hottest of the fight and charged with the greatest desperation without once losing his presence of mind.

Presently, Leonatus of Macedon rode up to Pyrrhus to warn him of danger, and said, "Do you see, sir, that barbarian upon the black horse with white feet? he is constantly watching you, and seems to await an opportunity to attack you."

"It is impossible, Leonatus, to avoid our destiny," answered Pyrrhus; "but neither that Italian nor any other shall have much satisfaction in engaging with me."

While they were speaking, the man raised his spear and spurred his horse straight against the king, whom he missed. He killed the horse, however. Leonatus did the same to that of the Italian, and both animals fell dead together. Pyrrhus was caught and carried off by his friends, who brought down his assailant, though he fought fiercely to the last.

This incident made Pyrrhus more cautious, and, changing his robe and arms with Megacles, he charged on the enemy in this disguise. For a long time the battle was undecided, and, although his disguise saved the life of Pyrrhus, it very nearly cost him his victory. Many aimed at Megacles, and at last he was killed; his helmet and robes were carried to Lævinus, who, raising them on high, cried out that Pyrrhus was slain. The Roman army shouted for joy, and the Greeks were filled with grief and terror, until Pyrrhus uncovered his head and rode among them to assure them that he was still alive.

He then set his elephants against the enemy, and their horses were so frightened at the sight of the monsters that they turned and ran. Taking advantage of the disorder, Pyrrhus ordered his cavalry to charge, and the Romans were routed with great slaughter. He entered their camp, took possession of it, and gained over many cities that had sided with Rome, advancing to within thirty-seven miles of the great city itself. But his army was not then in a fit condition to take and hold Rome, so while he was waiting for more troops he sent Cineas to see whether he could not make terms of peace. Cineas carried all sorts of presents in his master's name to the women as well as the men; but they were refused. Cineas next put his eloquence to the test, and made a speech to the senate, offering such flattering terms that many seemed inclined to accept them. While the matter was being discussed, Appius Claudius, a noble old Roman, who on account of age and blindness had long since withdrawn from public affairs, ordered his servants to carry him to the senate-house. His chair was placed in the midst of the senators, and a respectful silence was observed by the whole body, who listened attentively when he began to speak. "Hitherto," he said, "I have thought my blindness a misfortune, but now, Romans, I wish I had been deaf as well as blind, for then I should not have heard of your shameful debate, so ruinous to the glory of Rome. Where now are your boasts echoed all through the world that if Alexander the Great had come into Italy when we were young he would not now be considered invincible, but either by his flight or his fall would have added to the glory of Rome? And yet you tremble at the very name of Pyrrhus, who all his life has been paying his court to one of the guards of that same Alexander. He is wandering about Italy not to help the Greeks here, but to avoid his enemies at home. Do not expect to get rid of him by entering into an alliance with him, for that would only open our doors to other invaders; for who is there that will not despise you and think you easy to conquer if Pyrrhus not only gets off without punishment for his insolence, but gains some of our colonies as a reward for his insult to Rome?"

When Appius ceased speaking, a unanimous vote was passed for war, and Cineas was sent back with this answer: "Tell Pyrrhus that when he quits Italy we will enter into a treaty of friendship with him if he desires it; but while he stays here we will fight him with all our force, even though he should defeat a thousand men like Lævinus."

Not long after, there was an engagement between the two armies near the city of Asculum, and the loss was so heavy on both sides that it was hard to decide which had gained the victory. Pyrrhus lost the fewer men, but when he was congratulated upon the result of the battle, he said, "One other such victory would utterly ruin me." For he had lost his best commanders and almost all of his particular friends, and he had no means of replacing them, while the Roman camp, on the contrary, was immediately filled up with fresh soldiers.

Now two offers were made to Pyrrhus, either of which he would have accepted had it been possible. The one came from the Sicilians, who asked him to free them from tyrants and drive out the Carthaginians; the other from the Macedonians, who wanted him to ascend their throne in place of Ptolemy Ceraunus, who had been slain. He was dreadfully perplexed, and grumbled at fortune for holding out to him two such glorious chances at once, but at last he decided in favor of Sicily, and sent Cineas on before, as usual, to treat with the various cities. The people of Tarentum were very angry when they found that he thought of leaving them in the lurch without having accomplished what he came for, but he haughtily ordered them to be quiet and await his pleasure, and so set sail.

He found everything in Sicily just as he had hoped; the people placed themselves at his command, and supplied him with such a large army and navy that he drove the Carthaginians before him and ruined their territory. At last he reached Eryx, the strongest of their cities, and, after making a vow to Hercules of games and sacrifices if in that day's action he should distinguish himself before the Greeks in Sicily as became his birth and fortune, he ordered the trumpets to sound the signal for battle. The enemy were soon driven from the walls, scaling-ladders were planted, and Pyrrhus was the first to climb one of them.

A crowd of warriors attacked him there, but some he drove back, some he pushed down from the walls on both sides, and others he slew with his sword until he had piled up a heap of dead bodies around him. Strange to say, he was not wounded in the least, and when the city was taken he remembered his vow, and offered splendid sacrifices to Hercules, and exhibited a variety of shows and plays besides.

PYRRHUS

But success did not improve Pyrrhus, and from a popular leader he changed into such a tyrant that the people of Sicily would no longer submit to him. Finding that he had made a mistake in trying to rule them harshly, he was glad when letters came from the Tarentines and Samnites complaining that they could not secure their towns from the Romans, and begging him to come to their aid. So, without appearing to run away from Sicily, he had a good excuse for returning to Italy. As he sailed away from the island, he looked back longingly and said, "Ah, my friends, how brave a field of war do we leave the Romans and the Carthaginians to fight in!"

Part of the enemy got to Italy before Pyrrhus did, and as he landed gave him battle. He lost a great many men and two of his elephants, and he was so badly wounded about the head that he was led from the field. This encouraged the enemy, and one of them, a tall, powerful man, advanced, calling for the king to come forth if he was still alive. This so excited Pyrrhus that, wounded and covered with blood as he was, he broke from his guard, seized his sword, rushed upon the challenger, and with one mighty blow cut him in two. This achievement amazed the barbarians, who, thinking that Pyrrhus must be a being of some superior sort, gave him no further trouble.

So he proceeded on his way until he met the Roman army, under the consul, Manlius Curius; a great battle was then fought, which after several hours ended in a splendid victory for the Romans. Others followed, until they gained the whole of Italy, and not long after Sicily fell into their hands also.

Thus, at the end of six years' hard fighting, Pyrrhus, though considered the bravest and best commander among the crowned heads of his time, found himself deprived of all hope of Italy or Sicily. So he returned with his army to Epirus, and, being joined by a body of Gauls, went to Macedonia, gained a victory there, and forced Antigonus, their king, to fly.

Next, at the request of Cleonymus, he marched against Sparta, but even the women of that city came out and helped to build barricades. Besides, they urged their husbands, fathers, and sons to fight with such desperation that Pyrrhus gained nothing, and so shifted his ground to Argos. On his arrival there the Argives requested him to retire, saying that they did not wish him to interfere with the affairs of their republic, because they could settle their troubles themselves. Pyrrhus pretended to comply, but Aristeas, who headed a strong party in Argos, and feared that his opponent was getting too powerful, opened the gates for Pyrrhus in the dead of night. Many of his troops entered and took possession of the market-place, but such a disturbance was created in getting the elephants through the gates that the citizens were alarmed, and many of them ran to the fortress and other places of defence to prepare to meet the enemy.

When day dawned, Pyrrhus was surprised to find the Argives ready for him, but his surprise was turned to horror when among the statues in the market-place he beheld one of brass representing a bull and a wolf in the act of fighting. The reason of this was that an old oracle had foretold that it was his destiny to die whenever he should see a wolf fighting a bull. He would have retreated, and sent orders to that effect to his son, who had remained outside the walls. But the messenger, for some reason or other, gave the contrary order,

PYRRHUS

and the prince entered the town with the rest of the troops and elephants, causing such a confusion that those within the walls who had been ordered to retreat fell in with the advancing forces, and the elephants became entirely unmanageable; they trampled down the soldiers, who rolled this way and that, wounding one another, while the enemy, taking advantage of the uproar, attacked them in front and in rear.

Throwing off his plume and helmet, so that he might not be recognized, Pyrrhus rode in among the enemy. It so happened that he was wounded through the breastplate with a javelin, though not dangerously; but he turned upon the man who struck the blow, and just at that moment the mother, an old woman, who watched the fight from a house-top, picked up a huge stone and threw it with all her might at the king. It struck him on the back of the neck; all grew black before his eyes; he dropped the reins and fell from his horse. The crowd did not know him, but one among them exclaimed, "It is Pyrrhus!" and, as the wounded king showed signs of returning consciousness, raised his sword and cut off his head.

This was the inglorious end of one of the bravest and most warlike monarchs of ancient times, whose mistake was the undertaking of enterprises more from love of action than from any well-directed plan. Another king, who lived when Pyrrhus did, compared him to a gambler, and said, "He makes many good throws, but never seems to know when he has the best of the game."

ARATUS

WHEN Aratus was a little boy only seven years old, his father, who was ruler of the city of Sicyon, in Greece, was put to death by a man named Abantidas, who thus made himself ruler instead. So great was the confusion in the royal household that Aratus was forgotten for the moment and made his escape.

He wandered about the city, too frightened to speak to any one or to know what to do, until he got to the house of Soso, his father's sister. He slipped in there and asked Soso to take care of him, for he knew that if his father's enemies got hold of him they would kill him too. Soso, being a kind-hearted woman, took the boy in, although she ran great risk in doing so, and, with the belief that the gods had directed him to her, hid him away until after dark, then sent him to Argos. His father had many friends and acquaintances there, who sympathized with Aratus, and received him with delight. He was sent to school, where he studied diligently and acquired a good education. Being a strong, healthy boy, Aratus took part in the public exercises, and became so expert in running, jumping, throwing the dart, boxing, and wrestling, that he won several prizes.

His father's death had made such an impression on his mind that he hated the very name of tyrant,—for the rulers had so much power that they were all called by that title,—and this feeling strengthened with age. Aratus constantly brooded over the injustice of his father's fate until he reached the age of twenty, when he resolved to free his native city.

Meanwhile, many changes and revolutions had taken place there. One tyrant had succeeded another, and now Nicocles was on the throne, having governed four months, and done considerable mischief in that time.

Aratus laid his scheme before two or three important personages, who tried to dissuade him from carrying it into effect, but when they saw that he was determined, and that his energy was tempered by remarkably sound judgment, they promised to lend him their aid. All the exiles from Sicyon came to him, anxious to be led back to their home; but it was necessary that everything should be done secretly. Among the exiles was one who had escaped from prison. He described to Aratus the point where he had got over the wall, also how it might be scaled there and the city taken by surprise. Aratus listened attentively, and sent to have the spot examined and the exact height of the wall measured. The report was favorable so far as the walls were concerned, but a gardener near by owned some uncommonly savage, noisy dogs, that made it almost impossible for any one to approach without being discovered.

Aratus thought he could manage the dogs, so went on with his preparations. It was easy to get a supply of arms without arousing suspicion, because robberies were so common, and the people from one territory so often made incursions into those of their neighbors, that everybody went armed. The scaling-ladders were made by one of the exiles, who, being a carpenter by trade, could work without attracting attention. Each of his friends in Argos supplied Aratus with ten men, he armed thirty of his own servants besides, and hired a few soldiers from Xenophilas, captain of a robber-band. These soldiers, after being told that they were going to Sicyon only to seize the king's horses, were ordered by different roads to a certain tower in the neighborhood to await their chief.

Caphesias, one of the exiles, was sent with five companions, disguised as travellers, to the gardener's house, where they were instructed to arrive after sunset and ask for a night's lodging. They were then to lock up the man and his dogs, and keep them out of the way. The ladders, being so made that they could be taken to pieces, were packed in corn-chests and sent forward in wagons hired for the purpose.

Now, Nicocles always had his spies in Argos to keep an eye on Aratus, of whom he was constantly in dread. Aratus knew this perfectly well, and so, to put the spies off their guard, he went to the market-place early in the morning, stood some time conversing with a number of people, and in various ways made himself observed. Then he anointed himself in the exercise ground, and gathering about him half a dozen young men with whom he was in the habit of feasting, he went home, chatting merrily with them as they walked along together. Shortly after several of his servants appeared in the market-place and made purchases, as if they were preparing for a feast.

The spies were thoroughly deceived, and said to each other, "It is certainly strange that so powerful a tyrant as Nicocles should feel the slightest fear of a young man who wastes all his money in drinking and feasting." So they went home, convinced that such a person needed no watching.

Immediately after his morning meal Aratus set out on his journey, and proceeded to the tower where the meeting with his men was to take place. In a few words he explained his intention, every man declared himself ready, and they marched forward, arranging their pace so as to reach the walls of Sicyon after the moon had set. Caphesias met them, and announced that he had locked up the gardener, but that the dogs had scattered before his arrival and made it impossible to secure them. Most of the company wanted to retreat when they heard that piece of news, but Aratus encouraged them with the assurance that if the dogs became troublesome he would not proceed.

When those who went first were fixing the ladders to the wall the dogs set up a furious barking, and to add to the din a large hound kept at the tower within the walls began to bark in return while Aratus and his men were climbing over so that they were in great danger of discovery. Just then the fortress bell rang for the change of guard, and Aratus heard them asking each other what could be the cause of the disturbance among the dogs. He and his companions kept well within the shadow of the wall, and were much relieved when the sentinel said it was the sound of the bell and the light of the torches used by the guard that had aroused the hound. Aratus knew then that he had a friend in the sentinel, and that many others in the city awaited his coming. Presently the cocks began to crow, and no time was to be lost. Having scaled the wall, Aratus hastened to the tyrant's house, followed by his men. The hired soldiers, who passed the night at the general's office hard by, were taken by surprise and captured without a single drop of blood being shed. By daybreak, the friends of Aratus had been summoned from various quarters, crowds of people, who had heard all sorts of true and false reports, had gathered in the public square to find out what had happened, and the whole city was in a state of excitement. Suddenly a crier appeared, and proclaimed aloud that Aratus, son of Clinias, had come back, and invited the citizens to help him to recover their liberty.

Shouts of joy rent the air; what they had hoped and prayed for had come at last. Crowds pressed forward to the tyrant's palace, and in a few moments the whole building was in a blaze. Nicocles made his escape from the city by a secret underground passage. The fire was extinguished in time to save the enormous riches of the tyrant, which were divided equally among the citizens and the soldiers Aratus had brought, and, strange to say, not a single life had been sacrificed. One of the first acts of Aratus was to recall fifty exiles that Nicocles had sent away, and no less than five hundred that had been expelled by other tyrants, some of whom had been away from their home for nearly fifty years.

The return of these exiles after so long an absence caused great trouble, for they wanted back their estates, many of which had been sold, and the purchasers refused to give them up. Then Aratus showed himself a high-minded, true statesman; for, feeling that he was unable to settle the difficulty, and knowing that the city was in danger of an attack from Antigonus, the Macedonian king, he determined to sacrifice himself for the good of his country. He therefore gave up his position as ruler and joined Sicyon to the Achæan League. This was a great council of the whole Greek nation that assembled twice a year and made laws for all the cities that chose to place themselves under its rule, each city sending representatives, who were elected by ballot.

ARATUS

Then Aratus served in the cavalry, and the generals thought very highly of him as a soldier, for he was as obedient and tractable as any man in the ranks.

Ptolemy, King of Egypt, had sent Aratus a sum of money when he returned to Sicyon, which had all been divided among the citizens, but they were so poor that it had not been enough, and the exiles would not be satisfied unless they got back the estates they had lost. So, finding that there was danger of serious trouble, Aratus determined to seek further aid from Ptolemy. Aratus had some claim on the friendship of this king, for he had always been in the habit of collecting for him the best works of the celebrated painters, some of whom were his personal friends. He had been asked to do this because he was an excellent judge of works of art, and because the Sicyon painters were considered the greatest of their time. So much was this the case that artists from other parts of Greece went there to study only to get the reputation of being of the Sicyon school.

So, as soon as Ptolemy heard of the arrival of Aratus in Egypt, he sent for him and made him a present of a hundred and fifty talents for the relief of Sicyon. On his return, Aratus sought the assistance and advice of fifteen of the citizens in the distribution of the money he had brought, and after a great deal of thought and management on his part, peace and contentment were at last established among the people; for each man felt that he had been fairly dealt with.

Aratus was now chosen general of the Achæan League, and immediately undertook a most daring and remarkable enterprise; it was the freeing of Corinth from Macedonian tyranny. This was of the greatest importance, because the possession of Corinth made a man master of all Greece on account of its position, and there were few kings who did not long to add Corinth to their territory.

This was such a bold and difficult undertaking that it has been called the last of the Grecian exploits, and its consequences prove it to have been one of the greatest ever recorded.

A complete victory attended the efforts of Aratus, who took the city with a body of four hundred picked men. After a night of anxiety and peril, during which he had seized the citadel, Aratus appeared in the theatre of Corinth. The people crowded to see him, eager to hear what he had to say to them. He came from behind the scenes in his armor and stood in the centre of the stage, his soldiers having previously arranged themselves to form an effective background. Aratus looked extremely careworn, and showed plainly how much he had endured. But this made him even more welcome to those whom he had come to liberate, and they greeted him with deafening cheers and cries of congratulation. He stood with his spear in his right hand until quiet was restored, then he began an oration in the name of the Achæans, persuading the Corinthians to join their league and to deliver over to them the keys of their city, which had not been in their power, as he reminded them, since the time of King Philip.

The Corinthians agreed to join the league, and Aratus, having seized the temple of Juno, placed a garrison of four hundred Achæans in the citadel, then went to the harbor of Lechæum, took twenty-five of the enemy's ships, four hundred Syrians, whom he sold, and five hundred horses.

The consequences of winning over the most important city of the Peloponnesus to the Achæan League show what a wise undertaking it was. Aratus saw that the cities of Greece divided were weak, but that if they could be united for defence and for the promotion of the common good, they would be strong. So, leading the Achæan forces from place to place, he never ceased in his labors until most of the prominent cities and states of Southern Greece had become members of the league.

In course of time the Ætolians grew jealous of the fast increasing power of the league; so, calling in the aid of the Lacedæmonians, who were enemies to the Achæans, they crossed over to the Peloponnesus and seized the city of Pellene. The soldiers rushed about from house to house, helping themselves to whatever treasure they could lay hands on, each claiming a wife or daughter of the citizens, whom he intended to marry. Every man marked his prize by putting his helmet on her head, and this it was that made them lose the city when Aratus marched in with his army. It happened in this way: one of the captives was a tall, handsome young girl, daughter of one of the wealthiest and most distinguished citizens of Pellene. She had been claimed by a captain, who, having put his helmet on her head, had placed her in the temple of Diana for safe-keeping. Hearing the noise caused by the arrival of the Achæans, she stepped out to see what was the matter, and stood in the gateway of the temple looking down upon the soldiers as they fought.

Now, so holy was the image of Diana in the eyes of the Ætolians, that whenever a priestess removed it from one place to another, people turned away their heads or covered their eyes, because they believed that to look at it would bring to them some dreadful misfortune.

The young Pellenian lady, being a priestess herself, and knowing of the superstition of the Ætolians, brought out the image of the goddess and held it up. As she stood with the helmet on her head and the image raised on high, she did not resemble an ordinary human being. The enemy, believing that they saw before them some divine apparition, turned away, covered their eyes, and ceased to defend themselves. Aratus immediately got the advantage, and, after killing seven hundred Ætolians, drove the rest out by main force. This action gained new honor for Aratus, and one of the greatest artists of the day painted a picture of the battle, which was considered a most wonderful exploit.

However, as many powerful states were preparing to oppose the Achæans, Aratus hastened not only to make peace with the Ætolians, but to form an alliance with them. He next turned his attention to Athens, which he wished to liberate, and made several attempts on her harbor, but failed each time. In one of these he broke his leg, and had to be carried into several actions in a litter. When this accident happened, it was reported that he was dead, and in order to flatter the Macedonians, under whose rule they then were, the Athenians made a public rejoicing.

Angry at such ingratitude, Aratus marched against them and entered their city, but they implored him to spare them, and he returned without doing them the least harm. Such humane treatment had its effect, and when Demetrius, their tyrant, died, the Athenians determined to strike a blow for liberty, and called the Achæans to help them. Aratus was not general then, because it was against the laws to re-elect him every year, so he held that office every other year, being chosen regularly twelve times.

When the Athenians sent for him he was in bed, too ill to rise, but he caused himself to be carried in a litter, so anxious was he to do what he could for them. For a hundred and fifty talents, twenty of which he furnished himself, he prevailed upon Diogenes, the Macedonian general, to give up the Piræus, Munychia, Salamis, and Sunium to the Athenians, and then the greater part of Arcadia joined the league.

Aratus was soon called to aid other cities, because Cleomenes, the Spartan king, attacked them; but he was so unfortunate as to meet with three defeats, one coming right upon the heels of another, and then it was decreed that he should have no more money provided for war. This made him so indignant that when the time came around again for him to be reappointed general of the army, he absolutely refused. As Achæan affairs were in a bad way, he was much blamed for giving up the helm to another pilot; but perhaps he did not feel capable of coping with so powerful a prince as Cleomenes.

Cleomenes had made himself absolute tyrant of Sparta, and now marched into Achaia to insist upon being made general of the league. He turned the Achæan garrison out of Pellene, and took not only that town, but so many besides, that the whole of Peloponnesus was in a tottering state, and dissatisfaction was felt on all sides. Even the Corinthians and Sicyonians were found to be in secret correspondence with Cleomenes, for they were tired of belonging to the Achæan League; they had lost confidence in Aratus, and wanted to get the power into their own hands.

Aratus was sent to punish the leaders, but he met with greater opposition in Corinth than he had expected, for the people would not suffer him to arrest anybody. They assembled at the temple of Apollo, and sent for him, intending either to kill or imprison him before openly revolting. He came leading his horse and pretending to feel no mistrust. When he reached the gate, a number of men arose and began to reproach him; but he mildly bade them to be less noisy, and not to crowd up the doorway to prevent others from entering. While he spoke, he drew back step by step, and pretended to be looking for somebody to take charge of his horse. Thus he got out of the crowd, and addressing each Corinthian as he came along, told him to hasten on to the temple. So without exciting suspicion he drew near enough to the citadel to order the governor to keep strict guard over it, then, mounting his horse, rode off towards Sicyon at full speed.

The Corinthians pursued him, but, failing to catch him, they sent for Cleomenes, and placed their city in his hands. Cleomenes would not touch the house nor any of the belongings of Aratus in Corinth, but sent for his friends and charged them to guard well all his effects.

Meanwhile, Aratus called a council of the Achæans, who decided to ask the aid of Antigonus, the Macedonian king. He approached with his army, and Aratus went by sea to meet him. Antigonus received him with honors, and soon learned to like and trust him, for Aratus was not only able to advise the king, but proved himself a most agreeable companion socially, and an intimate friendship grew up between them.

The arrival of Antigonus entirely changed the aspect of affairs. He lost no time in marching against Corinth, and made such a desperate attack that he got possession of the fortress, and Cleomenes retired to Mantinea. Then all the cities joined the Achæans again.

ARATUS

Antigonus entered Laconia shortly after this, and defeated Cleomenes near Sellasia, in a narrow pass between the two mountains Eva and Olympus. Cleomenes made his escape and sailed for Egypt, and Antigonus took Sparta. He then returned to Macedonia, where, being very ill, he sent his nephew Philip to Peloponnesus, but instructed him to be guided entirely by whatever advice Aratus should give him.

So he did as long as Antigonus lived, but when that king died and he succeeded to the throne he was less friendly towards Aratus; and when the Achæans became dissatisfied, and brought various charges, some real, some imaginary, against him, Philip willingly complied with their demand that he himself should look into the affairs of Greece. Even then he continued to be guided by the advice of Aratus, because it was of so much value to him that he could not act without it; but Philip was not a man who could bear prosperity. His character was bad, and he allowed himself to be governed too often by his passions. So the time came when he would no longer allow Aratus to thwart him in anything, and the more he saw that his actions were disapproved by the virtuous man the more he hated him. He had always feared the Grecian patriot, and that fear kept him within bounds, but when hatred got the better even of his cowardice his vices showed themselves clearly, and he became a cruel, unprincipled tyrant.

He was determined to rid himself of a man whom he could neither buy nor command, but dared not do so openly. He therefore had recourse to poison, ordering one of his generals to give it in small doses that would act slowly but surely. Aratus soon began to suspect it, but, knowing that he would gain nothing by making it public, he bore his sufferings silently. One day a friend who was visiting him expressed surprise at seeing him spit blood. He said, "Such, Cephalon, are the fruits of royal friendship."

The poison did its work, and before many months had elapsed the great statesman died, in the sixty-second year of his age. He was buried with honors, and a festival called Aratea was celebrated every year in his memory.

AGIS

WHEN the love of money made its way into Sparta it carried with it a train of evils, and the people who had been famous for their bravery, endurance, and simplicity became avaricious, effeminate, luxurious, and mean-spirited.

Such was their condition when Agis and Leonidas began to reign. Both kings were descended from royal houses, but they had been differently brought up, and did not resemble each other in their ideas. Leonidas had spent many years at the Persian court, and had formed a taste for pomp and display, while Agis was a true Lacedæmonian for simplicity. He had been reared in wealth and luxury, and indulged in every possible manner by his mother and grandmother, yet before he was twenty years of age he had adopted the plainest style of dress, and the old, simple Spartan customs. He was often heard to say that he only wanted to be king in order that he might restore the ancient laws and discipline of his country.

Not over seven hundred of the genuine Spartan families remained when Agis ascended the throne, and only a hundred of those possessed estates. The reason of this was that the law of Lycurgus, which made the father's estate pass to the eldest son, had been done away with, and so property had been all divided up, leaving only a few very rich people.

The rest were poor and miserable, and watched eagerly for any change that might bring relief.

Agis therefore determined to lay before the Spartan senate a plan for the new division of lands and for relieving the people from debt. The poor listened to him with pleasure when he went among them to find out how he could help them, and the young men showed themselves ready to make any change for the sake of freedom. But the old and the rich opposed him; they had been so long accustomed to their vicious way of living that they desired no other, and it displeased them to hear Agis constantly speaking of Sparta's ancient glory and wishing it might be restored.

However, he succeeded in gaining over three men of influence. These were Lysander, Mandroclidas, and Agesilaus. Lysander was a very prominent man, Mandroclidas was a shrewd, able one, and understood better than most others what was for the interest of Greece, and Agesilaus, though weak and avaricious, was uncle to Agis, and favored his plan not only because he was persuaded to it by his own son, but also because he had numerous debts which he hoped would be wiped out by a change in the government.

The sister of Agesilaus was Agis's mother. She had great influence in Sparta, and shared in the management of public affairs because her relations were numerous, she was very wealthy, and a large number of people owed her money. To her Agis next applied. He had a difficult task there, for she could not see any advantage to be derived from the changes her son proposed. But Agesilaus explained how the state would be benefited, and the young prince entreated his mother to sacrifice her wealth for his glory. "I cannot vie with other kings in display," said he, "for even the servants of the

AGIS

Asiatic monarchs are richer than all the Spartan kings put together, but if I can do something that will excel their pomp and luxury,—I mean the making of an equal division of property among all the citizens,—I shall really become a great king."

At last the mother was convinced, and as soon as that was the case she worked as hard as Agis did to carry out his views, going around among the other matrons and begging them to sacrifice something for the good of their country. These women all took part, more or less, in public affairs, consequently could influence their husbands; but many opposed Agis's scheme because the wealth was theirs, and they knew that if they consented to divide it they would lose the power and respect that property gave them. So they applied to Leonidas, the other king, and begged him, as the older man, to put a stop to the projects of Agis, whom they pronounced a very rash young man.

Leonidas was really inclined to serve the rich, but he dared not say so openly, because he feared those who were in favor of the change. However, he went about privately and spoke against Agis, telling the magistrates that his object in wishing to cancel debts and divide lands was not to serve Sparta, but to increase his own power.

Agis heard of how Leonidas was working against him, but all he did was to get Lysander elected Ephor, and through him propose to the senate his laws. After they were read, there was much discussion for and against them, and nothing was decided. Then Lysander called an assembly of the people, to whom he, Mandroclidas, and Agesilaus made addresses, urging them not to let the few insult the many and the majesty of Sparta be trodden under foot. They begged them to recollect the ancient oracles, which had bidden them beware of the love of money as a vice that would ruin Sparta, and then quoted a recent oracle, which had said they must by all means return to the state of equality regulated by Lycurgus. Then Agis stood up, and made a short speech, which he concluded in this way: "I will contribute as much as possible to the institution I recommend for your welfare. I will give up the whole of my estate, consisting of valuable lands, and six hundred talents (six hundred thousand dollars) in money, and my mother, grandmother, and all my friends and relations, who, you know, are the richest people in Sparta, will do likewise."

The people applauded the speech loudly, and rejoiced to think that at last, after three hundred years, they had a king worthy of Sparta. But Leonidas was more obstinate than ever, because he feared that he and his friends might be obliged to sacrifice their money and get little in return, while the honor would go to Agis. So the state was divided, the rich following Leonidas, while the populace clung to Agis. When the question was again brought before the senate and put to the ballot, the rich won it by only a single vote.

Lysander, who was still Ephor, was so angry that he determined to be revenged on Leonidas, so he brought two charges against him. One was that, as a descendant of Hercules, he had committed a crime in marrying a foreigner, and the other that, as a Spartan, he had been guilty of a capital offence in settling for many years in a strange country. Having set others to manage these charges, Lysander went with his colleagues to watch the heavens. This was a custom observed by the Ephori every ninth year. They would choose a starlight night, when there were neither clouds nor moon, and sit in silence, looking at the sky. If they chanced to see a shooting-star, they pronounced their king guilty of some offence against the gods, and he lost all his power until it was restored to him by one of the principal oracles.

Lysander assured the people that he had seen a star shoot, and Leonidas was accordingly summoned to answer the charges that had been made against him. But he was so frightened that he fled for refuge to the brass temple of Minerva, in Sparta. Thereupon Lysander persuaded Cleombrotus, the son-in-law of Leonidas and a prince of the blood, to lay claim to the throne. He did so, and was proclaimed king instead.

Soon after Lysander's term of office expired, and the new Ephori, being friendly to Leonidas, resolved to restore him to the throne. They also brought a charge against Lysander and Mandroclidas of cancelling debts and dividing property contrary to law. These two applied to the kings, saying, "These Ephori have no power except where a dispute arises between the two kings, and even then they have no choice, except to act for the public good; so it would be unlawful for us to notice them."

The kings saw the justice of this reasoning, and at once removed the Ephori and put others in their places. Agesilaus was one of the new ones, and when Agis heard that he had ordered a company of soldiers to waylay and kill Leonidas as he fled to Tegea, he sent others to defend him and bring him safe into the city.

Thus far all went well, and there was every appearance that Agis would succeed in what he had set out to accomplish; but the avarice of one man ruined everything. That was Agesilaus. He had fine, large estates; but at the same time he was deeply in debt. So he advised Agis not to carry out the whole of his plan at once, but just to cancel all debts, and then the rich would without doubt consent to the division of their lands, thus preventing any disturbance in Sparta. Agis was completely deceived by his uncle, and so was Lysander. An order was sent to the citizens to bring all their bills, notes, and bonds to the market-place at a stated time; these were piled up in a great heap and set on fire. While they were burning, Agesilaus exclaimed, "Never did I see so bright and glorious a flame."

The common people now pressed for an immediate division of the lands according to promise, and the kings ordered it to be done; but day after day Agesilaus found some excuse for postponing it. He was freed from debt, but he was by no means anxious to part with his lands, and this important point in the scheme of Agis remained unsettled until he was called to war in this way:

The Achæans expected an attack from the Ætolians, and so sent to ask the assistance of Agis. He had no difficulty in raising an army, for the young men who had just been released from debt were anxious to distinguish themselves, each hoping on his return to be rewarded with a piece of land. Agis preserved such excellent discipline that his army was admired everywhere, and marched from one end of the Peloponnesus to the other without the least disorder, but they had no opportunity to gain honors.

Meanwhile, affairs in Sparta were in a bad way, for Agesilaus had made the people so angry by constantly postponing the division of land, that the enemies of Agis openly brought back Leonidas and put him on the throne. Agesilaus would then certainly have been killed had it not been for his son, who was a great favorite in Sparta. He saved his father

AGIS

from the fury of the mob and helped him to escape from the city.

This happened just after Agis returned to Sparta, and during the commotion he fled for safety to one temple while Cleombrotus went to another. Leonidas advanced with a party of soldiers to seize Cleombrotus; he felt more angry with him for depriving him of his throne than he did with Agis, because Cleombrotus had married his daughter and ought to have shown more feeling for her father. Cleombrotus did not attempt to excuse himself, but his wife pleaded for him. Leonidas was touched by her appeal and desired her to stay with him, but commanded Cleombrotus to leave the country at once. The wife was too devoted to allow her husband to go into exile alone, so she put one of their children in his arms, took the other herself, and, after praying at the altar, departed with him.

As soon as Cleombrotus was gone, Leonidas turned out all the Ephori and put others in their places. Then he began to consider how he could get Agis out of the temple. First he tried persuasion, and told him that the people would willingly pardon a young man who out of ambition for glory had allowed himself to be deceived as he had been by Agesilaus. But Agis was suspicious, and treachery had to be resorted to.

Three young men who had always been his friends, but had now gone over to Leonidas, went constantly to see Agis, pretending friendship still. After a while they persuaded him to go to the baths, and each time accompanied him back to the temple, as if they were protecting him. One day, just as they came to the turn of a street which led to the prison, one of the pretended friends grasped his arm and said, "I take you into custody, Agis, in order that you may give an account to the Ephori of your government." Before he had recovered from his surprise, another threw a cloak over his head, twisted it tightly, and dragged him off to prison.

As this had been prearranged, Leonidas awaited them with the Ephori and such senators as were of their party, while a body of soldiers guarded the prison gates. Several questions were put to the prisoner, but he answered none until he was asked, "Do you repent of what you have done?" Then he replied, "I shall never repent of so glorious a design, though I see death before my eyes." Sentence of execution was immediately passed on him, and he was thrust into the decade, a dungeon where criminals were strangled. It was soon known throughout the city what had befallen Agis, and crowds flocked to the prison-grounds. Among the number were the mother and grandmother of the unfortunate man. They made an earnest appeal that he might be heard and judged by a full assembly of his countrymen, and called on one of the false friends to assist them, not knowing of his treachery. "No further violence shall be done to Agis," he said; "nor shall any harsh treatment be shown him; go in and see for yourselves if you please." So the two women entered the prison. The grandmother, an aged lady, highly esteemed in Sparta, was first shown into the decade. A few moments later the mother was ordered to follow. She obeyed, and a horrible sight met her gaze, for stretched upon the floor lay her beloved Agis, cold in death, while her mother's body hung lifeless from a rope attached to the ceiling. She was overcome with agony only for a short time; then recovering her composure, she embraced Agis, and exclaimed, "O my son, it was thy too great mercy and goodness which brought thee and us to ruin!"

AGIS

"Since you approve your son's actions, it is fit that you should share his reward," roughly said one of the treacherous friends, as he advanced and placed the noose around the poor, suffering mother's neck.

She made no resistance, for she was too miserable to do so. Her last words were, "I hope that all this may be for the good of Sparta."

Great indignation was expressed when the three dead bodies were exposed to view, for Agis was the first Spartan king who had ever been executed by the Ephori.

CLEOMENES

LEONIDAS continued to reign in Sparta until his death, and then he was succeeded by his son, Cleomenes. This young man had a great deal of spirit and determination, and as soon as he saw how the rich Spartans were living in ease and luxury, caring for nothing but their own selfish pleasures, while the poor were suffering, he resolved to put the laws of Lycurgus into effect once more.

He knew that Agis had lost his life in a similar attempt, but he was not to be turned from his purpose on that account. But he adopted a different method. He resorted to war, thinking thus to be furnished with an excuse for the changes he desired to make, and led his forces against the Achæans, who had given cause for offence. He met with splendid success, and covered his name with glory.

Then he returned to Sparta, and with part of his army fell upon the Ephori while they were at the public supper-table, and put them all to death. Next day eighty citizens, who he thought would be likely to oppose his plan, were banished, and all the seats of the Ephori, except one, were removed; that one Cleomenes himself occupied, and gave audience to the people. He explained to them how Lycurgus had established a council of Elders to act with the king in governing the country; but how in consequence of the wars the kings had been called from home and the Ephori, who had replaced the Elders, had become absolute rulers. He then recounted all the evils that had resulted, and said that if it had been possible for him to restore order without bloodshed he would gladly have done so, but in killing the Ephori he had acted for the good of Sparta, whose happiness and safety was his only aim. "The whole land is now your common property," he added; "debtors shall be cleared of their debts, and all those who are worthy of citizenship shall be made free Spartans, no matter what their former condition may have been."

Then the wealthy citizens, without exception, gave up their lands, and a new division was made. Even those that Cleomenes had banished got their share, for he promised that they should return as soon as quiet and order were restored. The old Spartan discipline and system of education were again introduced, the schools of exercise were reopened, and the public tables for dining re-established. Fearing that it might create jealousy were he to rule alone, Cleomenes took his brother Euclidas to share his throne, and that was the only time that Sparta ever had two kings of the same family.

It had been told to Cleomenes that the Achæans no longer feared him, because they did not believe that he would venture out of Sparta while affairs were undergoing a change. Therefore, to prove how ready his troops were to obey him, he made an incursion into the territories of Megalopolis, wasted the country far and wide, and collected rich booty. In one of his last marches he stopped a company of actors on the road, built a stage in the enemy's country, and offered a prize to the best performer. He devoted one day to this theatre, not that he cared much for such pleasures, but it was done out of bravado, to show the enemy that he felt too much contempt for them to give all his thoughts to the war. It was the custom among the Greeks to have players, jugglers, singers, and dancers attached to their armies, but no such people were ever seen in the camp of Cleomenes, for he and his men were too sober for that sort of diversion. They spent the greatest part of their leisure in exercising and conversation, and the young men were encouraged to make quick, bright answers, such as we have mentioned in the life of Lycurgus. The older ones took pleasure in teaching the younger, and the king himself was one of their best instructors, because of the example he set by his excellent conduct.

He was perfectly temperate, and as plain and simple in his habits as the commonest of the citizens. People who approached him were not awed by robes of state, rich carriages, pages, door-keepers, or display of any sort. They always found him in simple clothing, ready to meet them, offer his hand, and listen cheerfully and attentively to what they had to say, and it was more satisfactory to receive their answers from his own lips than to wait for it to come through secretaries. All these things won their hearts, and made them declare that Cleomenes was the only worthy descendant of Hercules.

At his supper-table couches, which were used instead of chairs, were placed for only three people, but when he entertained ambassadors or strangers more were added. No better food was provided on such occasions than usual, but the dishes were larger and there was more wine. After supper the table was removed, and a stand was brought in with a brass vessel full of wine, two silver bowls and cups, so that whoever chose to drink might help himself, though the wine was not offered to the guests. There was no music, nor was any required, for the king entertained the company himself by asking questions, relating anecdotes, and conversing, which he considered the best and most honorable method of gaining friends.

The Mantineans were the first people who asked the assistance of Cleomenes. He entered their city secretly by night, and helped them to turn out the Achæan soldiers commanded by Aratus. Then the Achæans assembled their forces, and Cleomenes challenged them to a battle, in which he defeated them. Aratus refused to be general of the Achæans when they got into such a bad condition, and then they invited Cleomenes to take that office, but, unfortunately, he was ill and had to go back home.

This ruined the affairs of Greece, for Aratus, who was jealous of the growing powers of Cleomenes, took advantage of his illness to call Antigonus into Greece. This was a shameful action, for it filled the Peloponnesus with Macedonians, who were hated by all the kings; besides, Aratus was the very person who had expelled them in previous years.

So when Cleomenes got well and announced his readiness to undertake the command the Achæans had offered him before, Aratus made proposals that he could not accept; he therefore declared war against him. Without giving the inhabitants time for preparation, Cleomenes entered Achaia and took several cities by surprise, then marched on to Corinth. The people hastened to pay their respects to him, and Aratus, seeing how they favored his rival, became frightened and fled.

Cleomenes won repeated victories, but at last, after making himself master of almost the whole of the Peloponnesus, he lost in one campaign all that he had gained, for fortune favored Antigonus, and many of the cities that had surrendered to Cleomenes went over to the Macedonians.

This misfortune was closely followed by another; for as he was marching back home, Cleomenes was informed of the death of his wife, a charming young woman, whom he loved very much. His sorrow was deep, but he did not neglect affairs of state on that account; he spent only one day at home with his mother and child, and then turned his attention to his public duties.

Now Ptolemy, King of Egypt, offered to help Cleomenes with troops, on condition that he would send his mother and his little son for hostages. It was a long time before the Spartan king dared to mention this proposition to his mother, but she saw that he had something unpleasant on his mind, and questioned both him and his friends so often as to the nature of it that at last he told her. She laughed heartily, and said, "Is this the thing that you have so often tried to tell me and were afraid? Make haste to put me on shipboard, and send this carcass where it may be of most service to Sparta before age renders it good for nothing and sinks it into the grave." This noble answer was acted upon, and the old lady with her little grandson embarked at once for Egypt.

Then, by freeing some of the Helots on condition that each paid a certain sum of money, Cleomenes collected an army of two thousand and made a sudden raid on Megalopolis, a city that was as great and powerful as Sparta. The inhabitants were taken completely by surprise, and nearly all of them fled to Messene. About a thousand men armed in defence of the city, but, finding it of no use, two of the most prominent of the Megalopolitans went to Cleomenes and begged him to restore it to its inhabitants. After a pause he consented, and sent the two men who had applied to him with a herald of his own to Messene, to tell the Megalopolitans that they might return in perfect safety if they would forsake the Achæans and declare themselves his friends and allies.

They refused, and Cleomenes was so angry because his gracious proposal met with no favor that he sent all the pictures and statues of Megalopolis to Sparta, and then destroyed the city. On his return home he immediately made preparations for a second expedition, and marched into Argos, laying the whole country waste. The enemy looked upon him as a wonderful genius; for with a very small army he had opposed the whole power of the Macedonians and Peloponnesians.

At last fortune favored the Macedonians at the battle of Sellasia, which Cleomenes was forced to fight, though he had only twenty thousand men with whom to oppose Antigonus, who had thirty thousand. Euclidas, one of the commanders, was slain, and out of six thousand Lacedæmonians whom he led to battle only two hundred were saved. Cleomenes escaped to Sparta, and, after advising the citizens to receive Antigonus, went with a few friends to the sea-shore, and embarked on some vessels that had been prepared for them.

Sparta surrendered as soon as Antigonus arrived, and the citizens had no cause to regret his presence, for he treated them very kindly, and, after sacrificing to the gods, left on the third day. His reason for going away so soon was that he had been summoned to Macedonia, where a dangerous war was going on. Although far gone in consumption, Antigonus would not desert his country in her need; he went home and won a splendid victory, but burst a blood-vessel when shouting with joy, "O glorious day!" A fever came on, and before long he was dead.

Cleomenes put out to sea after his escape from Sparta and sailed to Africa. He was welcomed by the king's officers and conducted to Alexandria, where, though he did not receive special honors, he was kindly treated. But after a time his dignified behavior and his charming and witty style of conversation won upon the king, who offered to send him back to Greece with vessels and money, to re-establish himself in his kingdom. Cleomenes was delighted with this offer, but before it could be carried into effect the king died, and all his hopes were blasted. The next ruler of Egypt did nothing but amuse himself, and Cleomenes knew it was useless to apply to him for assistance.

The king's prime minister was named Sosibius, and to him Cleomenes made a demand for a vessel to carry him and his friends to Greece, for he had heard of the death of Antigonus and of the war going on. Sosibius was afraid to keep so bold a man as the Spartan king against his will, yet he did not think it safe to let him go with the knowledge he had gained of Egyptian affairs.

While he was considering what to do, a Messenian named Nicagoras came to Alexandria. This man hated Cleomenes, who was unfortunate in owing him a sum of money, which he had not been able to pay when it came due. Cleomenes happened to be walking on the dock when Nicagoras landed.

"What business has brought you to Egypt?" he asked.

CLEOMENES

Nicagoras pretended to be friendly, and, after deceitfully paying Cleomenes a compliment, replied, "I am bringing some fine war-horses for the king."

"You had better have brought him some dancers and actors," returned Cleomenes, with a laugh, "for that is the sort of cattle he likes best."

Nicagoras smiled, but said nothing. A few days later he asked Cleomenes for the money he owed him, but did not get it. This made him angry, and he told Sosibius of the joke upon the king that Cleomenes had made when he arrived with the horses. He also wrote a letter, in which he accused Cleomenes of wanting to get supplies from Egypt in order that he might use them to seize some of her territory. This letter he gave Sosibius just before he sailed, and in due course of time it was laid before the king, who ordered Cleomenes to be invited into a large house, where he was to be retained and treated as formerly, but not suffered to go out.

It was unbearable to Cleomenes to be kept a prisoner; besides, he had reason to believe that he had not many days to live; so, when the king went on a journey, a stratagem which he had planned with his friends was carried into effect. It was customary for kings of Egypt to send a supper and some presents to prisoners whom they intended to set free. As soon as Ptolemy Philopator was well out of the way, the friends of Cleomenes announced that he had been released by royal command, and carried the necessary tokens to the prison gate. The keepers were entirely deceived, and, after Cleomenes had offered a sacrifice, accepted his invitation to the banquet that had been sent. Wine was served to them so plentifully that they became intoxicated, and while they were in that state the Spartan king put on his military tunic, and sword in hand rushed out of the house, followed by his friends, thirteen in number.

They went through the streets inviting the people to liberty. Their spirit and boldness won the greatest praise, but not a man ventured to follow or assist them. Two members of the royal family whom they met were killed on the spot. They then proceeded to the citadel, intending to force it open and join the prisoners to their party. But the keepers had got wind of their intention and had barricaded the gates. This was a grave disappointment, and after making another vain attempt about the city to arouse the people, Cleomenes stopped, and thus addressed his companions: "These people are so weak-minded that they fly from liberty; let us, therefore, die in a manner that will bring down no dishonor on our names." Each man then fell upon his own sword and killed himself. This happened after Cleomenes had been king of Sparta sixteen years.

The mother and son of Cleomenes, who had gone to Egypt as hostages, were overcome with grief when the news of his death reached them. The latter threw himself headlong from the top of a house, but was not killed, and when he was picked up he was very angry because he was not suffered to destroy himself.

When the king got home, he ordered the body of Cleomenes to be flayed and nailed to a cross, while the aged mother, her female companions, and her little grandson, were all put to death.

FABIUS

NOW we come to another able general, a Roman, and one who had quite as difficult a task to perform as Pericles had, though the circumstances were different, as we shall see. Fabius did not display the same foresight and skill that Pericles did, but he proved himself a man of great courage and strength of will. Like Pericles, he was an orator, and among his numerous speeches one of the most remarkable that has been preserved is his funeral oration on the death of his son.

Fabius was consul five times. During the first consulship he gained a great victory over the Ligurians, who were forced to run away and seek shelter in the Alps. But it was his policy to put off a battle as long as possible, so when Hannibal, the famous Carthaginian general, invaded Italy, he did not rush to oppose him, as the Romans wished him to do. The wildest terror and astonishment took hold of the people at Hannibal's approach, which certain unaccountable occurrences did not tend to allay. There were more than the usual number of thunder-storms, which was considered an unlucky omen; it was said, besides, that some targets sweated blood, and that certain reapers had found ears of corn filled with blood; also that it had rained red-hot stones, and that scrolls had fallen from heaven, on one of which was written, "Mars brandishes his arms."

Fabius shared the anxiety of his countrymen, and for this and other reasons would not meet the enemy; but Flaminius, who was consul also, insisted on doing so. Accordingly, he led the army into the field, and such a desperate fight ensued that, though a terrible earthquake took place while it was going on, none of the combatants knew anything about it. Fifteen thousand Romans were killed, and as many more were taken prisoners. It was in these words that Pomponius, the prætor, announced their defeat to his countrymen, who assembled to hear the result of the battle: "We are beaten, O Romans, in a great battle; the consul Flaminius is killed; think, therefore, what is to be done for your own safety."

This dreadful news created the greatest confusion, and it was decided to choose a dictator who should have entire control of public affairs. Fabius seemed best fitted for the office, and he was unanimously elected, Lucius Minucius being chosen for his General of the Horse, a very important office.

The first act of Fabius as dictator was a religious one. He assured the people that their late defeat was not owing to lack of courage on the part of their army, but to neglect of divine ceremonies by their general, and urged them not to fear the enemy so much, but to do something to gratify the gods. This he did not to encourage superstition, but to lessen the dread they felt of the enemy by encouraging the belief among his countrymen that Heaven was on their side. He then made a vow in presence of the people to sacrifice to the gods all the cows, goats, swine, and sheep that were produced in any part of Italy that year, and to expend a certain sum of money on the celebration of musical festivals.

FABIUS

In this way Fabius restored confidence, and then set out at the head of his army to oppose Hannibal again. He made no attack, but kept in sight of the enemy, always managing to secure the best positions, and thus keep them in a state of anxiety. But in course of time the Romans accused Fabius of cowardice in holding off so long; they became impatient, and called upon Minucius to lead them to battle. This tickled the vanity of the General of the Horse, who began to ridicule the conduct of the dictator. He said that the Romans were like spectators at a theatre placed on the mountains to witness the desolation of the country below, and asked the friends of Fabius whether he did not mean, by leading them from mountain to mountain, to carry them at last to heaven, or to hide them in the clouds from Hannibal's army.

These things were repeated to the commander, who was urged to risk a battle. "If I did so, I should depart from my resolution and prove myself a more dastardly spirit than they represent me. To fear for my country is no disgrace. The man who shrinks under slander and yields to the humors of those whom he ought to govern is unworthy of such a command as this."

Soon after, Hannibal, who was sorely in need of some good pasture-land for his horses, ordered the guides to lead him to the district of Casinum, but they misunderstood his foreign pronunciation, and conducted his forces to a valley bearing a similar name. This move suited Fabius precisely. He took possession forthwith of the surrounding mountains, and placed a guard of four thousand men at the only outlet from the valley. Thus hemmed in, Hannibal's army fell into the utmost disorder, and about eight hundred were killed. The guides were all crucified for punishment, but that did not relieve the army, and Hannibal was at his wits' end until he hit upon a stratagem. It was this: he caused two thousand oxen to have torches and dry fagots securely fastened to their horns, and when night came on they were lighted and the oxen were driven towards the mountains near the narrow pass guarded by the Romans, the army following in the dark not far behind.

At first the beasts moved along slowly, but when the fire burned down to their flesh they became mad with the pain, ran wildly in every direction, tossing their heads, and setting fire to the trees as they passed by. This was a mode of warfare the Roman soldiers had never experienced, and they became so bewildered that they fancied the enemy were approaching from every quarter to surround them. So they hurried from their posts to their camp on the mountains. Then Hannibal's men took possession of the deserted position, and the whole army, with all the baggage, marched safely through the pass.

Before morning Fabius discovered the trick, but, fearing an ambush, he kept his men under arms in the camp. At daylight he attacked the enemy in the rear, but Hannibal sent a body of Spaniards, who were accustomed to climbing mountains, to oppose the Roman troops, and they killed so many that Fabius had to retreat. This made him very unpopular, and he was regarded with open contempt by his army, who pronounced him a coward and an incompetent general.

He fell into disfavor with the senate too, because of the bargain he made for the exchange of prisoners. He agreed that after they had been exchanged man for man, those that were left over should be bought for a certain sum of money. When it turned out that there remained two hundred and

FABIUS

forty Romans unexchanged, the senate not only refused the money for the ransoms, but reproached Fabius with making a dishonorable contract and wishing to redeem men whose cowardice had placed them in the hands of the enemy. Fabius bore the injustice patiently, but resolved to keep his word with Hannibal. So he sent his son to Rome to sell lands, and so procured the sum required for the ransoms, which he paid himself. Many of the released captives offered to return him the money, but he refused it in every case.

About this time Fabius was called to Rome to assist at certain sacrifices, which were always performed by the dictator. Before leaving the army he gave Minucius strict charge not to engage the enemy during his absence; but he was not obeyed, and news followed him to Rome of a victory won by his forces. The populace flocked to the Forum, where they were addressed by the tribune, Metilius, a kinsman of Minucius. He praised the bravery of the victorious commander, and accused Fabius of cowardice and disloyalty, declaring that it was he and a few of his friends who had brought the Carthaginians to Italy, in order that he might be appointed dictator.

The only reply Fabius made was that he wished the priests to complete the sacrifices as soon as possible, that he might return to the army and punish Minucius for his disobedience. As the dictator had power of life and death, the people began to fear that he meant to execute Minucius. No one dared to say a word except the tribune, all other officers being deprived of authority during the existence of a dictator. He spoke boldly in behalf of his kinsman, and asked the people whether they would suffer him to become a sacrifice to the jealousy and ill will of Fabius. The effect of his harangue was very great, and it was decided that Fabius should retain his office, but that in the management of the war Minucius should have equal authority.

The enemies of Fabius thought he would be angry at such a humiliating plan, but they were mistaken, for he was too just and good a man to feel dishonored by it. He feared, though, that the country's cause would be injured by the rashness of Minucius, and therefore hastened back to his post. He found Minucius so arrogant and unreasonable that it was agreed to divide the army, he taking charge of the first and fourth legions, and delivering the second and third to his colleague.

Minucius was so exalted on account of his success that he made himself disagreeable by constantly boasting of how he had humiliated the dictator. Fabius said to him one day, "Do not forget that it is Hannibal, not I, whom you are to fight; but if you insist upon opposing me, let it be in striving for the preservation of Rome; for it would be a pity to have the people say that a man whom they have favored served them worse than he who was ill treated and disgraced by them." This speech had little effect on the younger general, who removed to a separate camp with the troops allotted to him.

Hannibal was informed of this division of the Roman army, and determined to take advantage of it. So, watching his opportunity, he placed a number of men in the ditches and hollows on all sides of Minucius during the night, and when day dawned gave the signal for battle. Fabius, who stood on a hill overlooking the scene of action, saw his countrymen gradually but surely losing ground, while one officer after another was cut down, and those warriors who fled were killed by the victorious Carthaginians. It did not gratify him to witness the defeat of his rival; on the contrary, he was deeply distressed, and with a heartfelt sigh said to those near him, "O Hercules! how much sooner than I expected, though later than his actions promised, has Minucius destroyed himself!" Then commanding his standard-bearers to advance, and his whole army to follow, he added, "Now, my brave soldiers, let us make haste to rescue Marcus Minucius; he is a brave man and a lover of his country. If in his haste to drive out the enemy he has erred, this is not the time to find fault with him."

Hannibal's men were frightened when they beheld Fabius coming up with his army, and retreated in great haste, lest they should be surrounded by the fresh troops. Seeing the change of fortune, as Fabius pushed on through the thickest of the fight to join Minucius, Hannibal called off his men and retired to his camp. He gave proof of the dread he had entertained of Fabius by this remark, which he made on entering his tent: "Did not I often say that this cloud which always hovered upon the mountains would one day burst upon us with the fury of a storm?"

After collecting the spoils from the field, Fabius retired to his own camp without making a single harsh or reproachful remark to his colleague. Minucius was so impressed by this forbearance on the part of a man whom he had sought to injure, that he gathered his troops about him and addressed them as follows: "Friends and fellow-soldiers, never to commit an error in the management of great affairs is beyond the power of men; but a good and prudent man learns by experience to correct his faults. Fortune has frowned upon me, without doubt, yet I have much to thank her for. In the compass of one day she has shown me that I know not how to command, but have need to be under the direction of another; from this moment I shall cease to contend for power over a man whom it is an honor to obey. Henceforth the dictator must be your commander in everything except expressions of gratitude to him. In that I will be your leader, by being the first to show an example of obedience and submission."

He then ordered the ensigns to advance with the eagles, and, himself following, led his army to the other Roman camp. On being admitted, he marched straight to the tent of the dictator, who came out as the sound of the approaching soldiers reached his ear. Then, fixing his standard before Fabius, Minucius saluted him in a loud tone by the name of Father, and his soldiers called the others their Patrons, a title that the freedmen of Rome bestowed on those who gave them their liberty. When silence was restored, Minucius thus addressed the dictator: "You have this day obtained two victories, Fabius,—one over the enemy by your valor, the other over your colleague by your wisdom and goodness. By the former you saved us, by the latter you instructed us; when we were suffering a shameful defeat from Hannibal, a welcome one from you restored us to honor and safety. I call you Father because I know no more honorable name; to my real father I owe my being, but to you I owe the preservation of my life and the lives of all these brave men." He ceased speaking, and threw himself into the arms of the dictator, while the soldiers embraced one another and wept tears of joy.

Shortly after this Fabius resigned the dictatorship, and consuls were again elected. It was the custom among the Romans for the consuls to command the army in turn when there was no dictator, and a difference of opinion arose among those who were now chosen as to the manner of

FABIUS

opposing Hannibal, some desiring to carry out Fabius's policy, while others were for giving battle and thus deciding the fate of the commonwealth. Among the latter was Terentius Varro, who was so popular that he managed to raise an army of eighty-eight thousand of the best fighting-men of Rome.

When his turn came to command, he posted his army at a village called Cannæ, not far from Hannibal, and at dawn of day had a red mantle raised above his tent as a signal for battle. As usual, Hannibal employed stratagems, but he proved himself in this fight, as in many others, a great general. In the first place, he stationed his men with their backs to the wind, which blew so hard that a perfect storm of sand and dust was driven into the faces of the Roman soldiers, who were thus prevented from taking proper aim. Next, all his best men were put in the wings, with this order,—that when the main body, which was weak, should give way as the enemy forced in upon them, the wings were to close around and give them battle in the rear. This was the chief cause of the Roman loss that day, which was very great.

Finding it impossible to recover ground, the consul, Varro, made good his escape with a few followers to Venusia, but Æmilius Paulus, another consul, who had been thrown from his horse, sat down upon a stone, covered with wounds, to await his death. He was so disfigured that even his friends did not know him and passed him by. Presently a young nobleman named Cornelius Lentulus recognized him, and, alighting from his horse, begged him to mount and save a life so valuable to his country. Æmilius refused, and insisted on the young man's resuming his seat on the horse; then, taking his hand, he said, "Go to Fabius Maximus and tell him that Æmilius Paulus followed his directions to the last, but it was hard fate to be overpowered first by Varro and then by Hannibal." As soon as Lentulus had ridden off, Æmilius rushed into the thickest of the battle and threw himself upon the swords of the enemy.

Hannibal had gained a splendid victory, and his friends urged him to pursue the flying Romans, assuring him that in five days' time he might sup in the Capitol. But he did not consider that a prudent step, and refused; whereupon Barcas, a Carthaginian, said, angrily, "You know how to gain a victory, Hannibal, but not how to use it."

The battle of Cannæ made a great change in the condition of Hannibal's army, for they now had regular supplies, which had not been the case before, and the greatest part of Italy submitted to the authority of the victorious general.

The Romans were in dire distress: what Fabius had predicted had really come to pass, and to him they now turned for relief. They had accused him of cowardice, but he was the only man in Rome who showed no fear. He walked about the streets addressing the men, checking the lamentations of the women, and doing his best to restore order. He caused the senate to meet, encouraged the magistrates, and became the moving spirit of every office.

It is much to the credit of the Romans that when Varro came home after his dreadful defeat, they received him with honors and even offered him the dictatorship, which, however, he refused. This conduct formed a striking contrast to that of the Carthaginians, whose generals were forced to endure a cruel death when vanquished, even though it could be proved that they were not to blame.

As soon as the Romans became convinced that Hannibal was not going to march into their city, they took heart and

FABIUS

renewed preparations to continue the war. Fabius Maximus and Claudius Marcellus were chosen to command, and they formed such a perfect combination, the one possessing the very qualities that the other lacked, that the Romans called Marcellus, who was a bold, active, high-spirited man, their sword, while Fabius, who was cautious, steady, and slow to give battle, they termed their shield.

During the course of this war each of these generals was consul five times, so that Hannibal constantly encountered them, and learned to dread the *sword* when in action quite as much as he did the *shield* when it was still. It was only by laying traps for them that he could hope for victory, and many failed before he at last succeeded in killing Marcellus. But Fabius was too prudent to be easily caught, though his friends attributed his escape to the favor of the gods.

Fabius made himself popular with the soldiers, because he treated them with uniform kindness and consideration. Once a young nobleman, who was noted for his courage, spoke of his intention to desert. Fabius heard of this, and sent for him. "I am sensible," he said to the young man, "of how your good service has been overlooked by the commanders, who are too apt to show favors in the wrong direction, but henceforth when you have complaints to make I trust you will apply to no one but me." He then gave the grateful soldier a horse and some other tokens of esteem, and from that moment there was not a more faithful or trustworthy man in the whole army.

At another time an officer reported that there was a young man from Lucania whose record was excellent in every particular except that he was frequently missing from his place at night. Upon making strict inquiries, Fabius ascertained that there was a certain pretty girl in the neighborhood with whom the soldier was in love, and it was in order to visit her that he so frequently went off. Fabius ordered the girl to be secretly brought to his tent, and when she arrived he summoned the Lucanian, to whom he said, "I know how often you have been missing from the camp at night; that was an offence against military discipline and the Roman laws; but I also know what a brave soldier you have been. In consideration of your services to your country I am willing to forgive you, but I have resolved to place over you a keeper who shall be responsible for your good behavior." He then led forth the young woman, who had been concealed behind a screen, and added, "This is the person who must answer for you; your future conduct will prove whether or no your secret rambles were on account of love."

It was by stratagem that Fabius took the city of Tarentum when the Carthaginians were only five miles away, and their general exclaimed, "Rome, then, has also got a Hannibal; as we won Tarentum, so have we lost it." He was surprised to find that others could set traps as well as himself, and acknowledged to his friends, privately, that he now thought it impossible to master Italy with the forces he had.

On his return to Rome, Fabius was received in triumph, and many marks of gratitude were showered upon him. Among others, his son was elected to the consulship, and an anecdote is related concerning this which shows how the consuls were honored. After his son entered upon the office, Fabius had occasion to speak with him one day while he was settling some point about the war. Either because he was unable to walk, or because he wanted to see how the young man would behave, he rode up to him on horseback. The consul observed his father at a distance, and sent word to him by one of the lictors to dismount and approach on foot if he had business with him. Many people were assembled at the time, and showed plainly how indignant they felt at having such an insult offered to so worthy and honorable a person as Fabius. But he instantly got down from his horse, ran towards his son, and embraced him tenderly, saying, "My son, I applaud your sentiments and your conduct. You know what a great people you command, and have a proper sense of the dignity of your office. This was the way that we and our forefathers took to advance Rome to her present glory; for we always considered the honor and interest of our country before that of our fathers or children."

And this was true, for the grandfather of Fabius, who was one of the greatest Romans of his day, actually served in a minor office under his own son, when he was consul, and when that son returned from the war in a triumphal chariot, rode on horseback as one of his attendants. It was his glory to show that, though as a father he had power over his son, he was proud to submit to the laws of his country and to her magistrates.

Now Cornelius Scipio, who had gained some victories over the Carthaginians in Spain, and had succeeded in driving them out of that country, returned home, and to show their gratitude the people elected him consul. Then he proposed a plan for ridding Italy of Hannibal and his army. It was this: to make Carthage the seat of war, and so compel the great general to go home for his own safety. Fabius did all he could to oppose such an undertaking, and won the senate over to his side. The fact is that he was jealous of the young conqueror, and did not want him to have the glory of driving Hannibal out of Italy: so when he found that in spite of his opposition the people esteemed Scipio more and more each day, he went to Crassus, the colleague of Scipio, and urged him to lead the army to Carthage if it was decided that it should go there.

This seems petty in so great a statesman as Fabius, but he had filled a prominent position so long that he could not bear to sink into the background and be replaced by a younger man. Crassus was a high-priest, and, as his religious duties would detain him in Italy, he refused to stir, whereupon Fabius made speeches to the people and the senate, in which he assured them that Scipio was not only running away from Hannibal, but he was draining Italy of her defenders, whom he was drawing into a foreign war that could be of no benefit. He succeeded in so far that the people became alarmed, and would let Scipio have only the troops that were in Sicily and three hundred of the soldiers who had served under him in Spain.

Meanwhile, the young conqueror was gaining victories, performing wonderful exploits in Africa, and sending home a great amount of spoils. At last news came that a Numidian king had been taken prisoner by the Roman general, that his men had been slaughtered, and that two camps of the enemy had been destroyed and a quantity of arms and horses captured. Then Hannibal was indeed compelled to hasten home, and the Romans rejoiced at the steps Scipio had taken. Never were they happier than when they beheld the Carthaginian army on shipboard leaving Italy.

Even then Fabius insisted that it was too soon to rejoice, for Hannibal was an enemy more to be dreaded under the walls of Carthage than ever he had been in Italy. But Scipio soon set at rest the fears thus raised, for he fought Hannibal and defeated him. Fabius did not live to see his prediction fulfilled, however, for he fell ill and died just after the Carthaginians left Italy. The expenses of his funeral were paid by the citizens, each one contributing a piece of money for the purpose, thus owning him as their father, and showing honor to him in death as they had done in life.

MARCELLUS

MARCELLUS was so brave and skilful a swordsman that he never refused a challenge or failed to kill his adversary. He was born of a prominent Roman family, and filled the offices of ædile and quæstor before he was made consul. He was raised to the latter position during the war between the Gauls and the Romans, which began not long after the first Carthaginian or Punic war had ended.

His first battle after he became consul was with the Gesatæ, a people of Gaul, who fought for pay. They marched with a tremendous army to Acerræ, a city on the banks of the river Po, to which the Romans had laid siege. The name of their king was Viridomarus. With ten thousand men he separated himself from the rest of his army, and destroyed the whole country round about.

As soon as Marcellus was informed of this, he left his colleague, Cneius Cornelius, to continue the siege, and, taking a number of cavalry and foot-soldiers, set out to put a stop to the destruction that the Gesatæans were dealing out. He marched rapidly until he met them at Clastidium, a little town that the Romans had won in battle from the Gauls. Marcellus had a small army compared with that of the enemy, and as soon as they saw him approaching and observed this fact, they felt so certain of being able to crush him with very little trouble that, without giving his men time for rest or refreshment, they immediately began an attack.

Marcellus spread out the line of his cavalry to prevent the enemy from surrounding him, until it nearly equalled theirs in length. Just as he was advancing to the charge, his horse took fright at the shouts of the Gauls, and turned back. Fearing that the superstition of his soldiers would cause them to regard this as an ill omen and so create disorder, Marcellus, with wonderful presence of mind, paid his adoration to the sun, and as it was the custom among the Romans always to turn around when they worshipped the gods, it appeared as though he had purposely made his horse jump back.

Just then Viridomarus recognized him by his attire as Roman consul. He therefore put spurs to his horse, and, brandishing his spear, challenged him to single combat. Marcellus knew him at once for the king of the Gesatæ, because his armor showed him to be royal, being composed of gold, silver, and gay colors. He therefore rushed upon the Gaul, and with one stroke of his spear pierced his breastplate and brought him to the ground. Two or three more blows ended the life of the king; then, jumping from his horse and taking possession of the dead man's arms, Marcellus raised them towards heaven and exclaimed, "O Jupiter, who observest the deeds of great warriors and generals in battle, I now call thee to witness that I am the third Roman consul and general who ever with his own hands slew a general and a king! To thee I consecrate the most excellent spoils. Do thou grant us equal success in this war."

When this prayer was ended, the Roman cavalry fought the enemy's horse and foot-soldiers at the same time, and gained a complete victory. Marcellus then gathered up the arms and baggage and returned to join his colleague, who was besieging Milan. But the Gauls made a desperate resistance, because Milan was the greatest and most populous of their cities, and it was not until Marcellus arrived that it was taken. The rest of the cities surrendered, and Italy became entirely Roman from the Alps to the Ionian Sea.

Marcellus was honored by the senate with the most splendid triumph that ever was seen in Rome. He appeared in the procession carrying the armor of King Viridomarus, which he had vowed to Jupiter. He had cut the trunk of an oak-tree, and dressed it up in the king's arms just as they had been worn, and with this trophy on his shoulder he was drawn in his chariot by four fine large horses through the town. The army followed, wearing their finest armor, and singing songs of triumph in honor of Jupiter and their general.

Some time later Hannibal entered Italy again, and Marcellus was sent with a fleet to Sicily to secure the aid of the Syracusans, who were then friendly to Rome. This was the beginning of the second Carthaginian or Punic war. After the battle of Cannæ, which was most unfortunate for the Romans, the few that were not slain fled to Canusium, and it was feared that Hannibal would march straight on Rome. So Marcellus sent fifteen hundred of his men to guard the city, and afterwards the senate ordered him to Canusium, to gather the troops that had fled there and place himself at their head for the protection of the country.

By this time the wars had carried off the chief of the Roman nobility and the best of their officers, but they still had Fabius Maximus and Marcellus. On these two distinguished commanders they chiefly depended, calling the former their *shield*, because he was slow and cautious, the latter their *sword*, because he was bold and active.

With the remnant of the Roman army that Marcellus could collect he marched to the relief of Nola, and, as everything was in confusion there, the citizens gladly placed themselves under his command. He drew up his forces within the gates, but ordered that nobody should appear on the walls. Seeing no signs of resistance, Hannibal supposed that no preparations for defence had been made, so he approached the city with very little precaution. The gate nearest to Marcellus was suddenly thrown open, and the best of the cavalry charged upon the enemy. The infantry rushed out, with loud shouts, from another gate, and while Hannibal was dividing his forces a third opened, from which the rest of the Romans emerged and attacked the enemy at still another point.

The Carthaginians were so taken by surprise that about five thousand of them fell, and the rest were driven back to camp. The Roman army was greatly encouraged by this victory, and the people elected Marcellus consul for the second time, in honor of the event. But when he returned to accept the office to which he had been unanimously chosen it happened to thunder, and the augurs thereupon pronounced the election disagreeable to the gods. Marcellus renounced the office without question, so great was the respect he entertained for the deities, but continued in command of the army, and returned to Nola. From that town he made excursions in the neighborhood to punish those who had taken sides with the Carthaginians. Hannibal met him, but his army was routed, four elephants were killed, and two were taken; but the worst blow he received was when three hundred of his cavalry deserted and joined Marcellus. Although the army of Hannibal was composed of men of all nations, some of whom were not friendly to one another, he had managed to keep them in harmony, and this was the first desertion he had ever experienced.

The Carthaginians next laid claim to the whole of Sicily, and Marcellus, who was elected consul the third time, sailed over to that island. Appius Claudius, as prætor, had been previously sent with a force to Syracuse, the chief city. To prove his friendship for the Carthaginians, Hippocrates, commander of the Syracusans, had killed a number of Romans at Leontini. This wrong to his countrymen made Marcellus very angry, so he besieged the city and took it by force, but did no harm to any of its inhabitants. Hippocrates sent a report to Syracuse that the Roman consul had killed every man and woman in Leontini, and so great was the tumult caused by this untruth that Hippocrates was enabled to make himself master of the place. Marcellus moved his whole army towards Syracuse, and sent ambassadors into the city to correct the false report they had heard about the massacre at Leontini. But Hippocrates was in power, and they were not received with favor; thereupon Marcellus began an attack by sea and by land, with Appius in command of the land-forces. Marcellus had sixty galleys, each with five rows of oars and furnished with every known sort of arms; also a huge bridge of planks laid upon eight ships chained together, bearing an engine for casting stones and darts. With these magnificent preparations he assaulted the walls, and might have won an early victory had it not been for Archimedes and his wonderful machines, that made all others appear trifling by comparison.

Archimedes was the most celebrated mathematician among the ancients, and, being a native of Syracuse, he contrived engines that greatly harassed the Roman army. He

MARCELLUS

had planned these engines for mere amusement while studying geometry, but his kinsman, King Hiero, of Syracuse, was constantly urging him to put them into practical use; so when the siege began he prepared to do so. He had already surprised people by showing how, by means of a pulley and cords, he could sit on the shore of a river and, with little effort, draw a boat loaded with passengers towards him. He boasted that he could move the world if he had a place for his apparatus. This seems to us of to-day a simple matter, but it was not so two hundred and fifty years before Christ, when Archimedes lived.

Well, the apparatus that this ancient scientist had planned for a siege was brought into play, and struck terror to the hearts of the Romans. It had power to rain down immense masses of stones and darts so rapidly and with such a noise that the soldiers were appalled. Their ranks and files were broken, and the men fell about in heaps. At the same time huge poles were thrust out beyond the walls, and from these great weights were dropped down on the ships, sinking them instantly. But what gave the Romans most trouble was a sort of iron hand with two claws fastened to a long chain and let down by a lever. This was driven with great violence into the planks of the galleys; then the other end of the lever was pulled down by a heavy weight, and the claws went up, raising one end of the boat far out of the water. Suddenly the weight was removed, the boat went down with tremendous force endwise into the sea, filled with water, and was sunk. Other vessels were whirled about by means of mechanical contrivances until they were dashed against steep rocks, and went to destruction with all on board.

Marcellus was soon compelled to draw off what ships he could save, and to sound a retreat to his land-forces. It was then decided to get close under the walls in the night, so that the darts which Archimedes threw to such a distance by means of his ropes and pulleys would fly over their heads. But a shower of darts aimed through openings in the walls soon convinced the Roman forces that there were engines adapted for short ranges as well as for long ones. Besides, immense rocks came tumbling down on their heads from the walls, and they were obliged to retire with such damage to their fleet, and such slaughter of their men, that they began to think they were fighting with superhuman beings. So terrified were they that the very sight of a piece of wood projecting from the walls, or a little rope thrown over, would send them flying, lest Archimedes might be about to try some new machine for their destruction.

Marcellus then put all his hopes in a long siege, since he was worsted in every assault he attempted, and while it lasted he took Megara, one of the earliest of the Greek cities in Sicily, overran a great part of the island, took many towns from the Carthaginians, and conquered all who ventured to meet him in battle. After a time a Lacedæmonian who went out to sea in a ship from Syracuse was captured by the Romans, and while Marcellus was treating with the Syracusans for his release, he noticed a tower into which it seemed that a body of soldiers might easily be introduced, because the walls near it were not hard to climb. So, at the celebration of the feast of Diana, when the Syracusans were drinking and enjoying themselves, Marcellus made his way into the tower with his men, and placed some of them as a guard on the outside. This was done during the night, and took the citizens completely by surprise. No sooner did the Roman general perceive the effect of his action than he ordered his trumpets to sound, and at the noise every Syracusan took to his heels,

MARCELLUS

supposing that the city had fallen, though its best fortified and most important quarter had not been touched.

Marcellus had no difficulty in stationing his men in the different quarters of the city after that, but he found it a harder matter to prevent them from setting fire to it and completely destroying every part. He is said to have wept when he looked down from his tower upon the beautiful city that was so soon to be plundered by his soldiers. He ordered, however, that no free person should be injured, and no slave killed or misused. The latter were all taken by the Romans, and so was the money in the public treasury, and the plunder was immense. Marcellus viewed the destruction with pain; but nothing afflicted him so much as the death of Archimedes, which occurred in this wise. So great was the interest that this scientist felt in his studies that when engaged in them he would often forget to eat, sleep, or bathe. When Syracuse was taken, he happened to be working out a problem that made him oblivious to all things besides; he therefore knew nothing of what the Romans had done. A soldier who entered his room and found him deep in thought ordered him to follow at once to Marcellus. He declined to obey until he had completed his diagram, whereupon the soldier drew his sword and slew him. Marcellus was very angry with the soldier who committed such a shameful deed, for he was always gentle, humane, and just even to his enemies, and in this respect set an example to his men which he could not excuse them for failing to observe.

On his recall to Rome, Marcellus took many beautiful ornaments from Syracuse to adorn the city, for up to that time it contained no fine specimens of art; weapons, spoils stained with blood, and trophies of war being the only decorations that pleased the fierce Romans. The Greek cities were, on the other hand, filled with fine statues, that nation being far advanced in the arts.

Marcellus did not have such a triumph as we have seen was given to other victorious generals, but he was honored with an ovation. That is, he did not pass through the city in a chariot, ushered by trumpets and crowned with laurels, but he walked, accompanied by musicians playing on flutes and pipes. His crown was composed of myrtle, which is a token of peace, and as he moved along he aroused feelings of love and admiration in his countrymen rather than of fear. This was the difference between a triumph and an ovation.

Marcellus was not without enemies, and when he was elected consul the fourth time they were so displeased that they sent for some Syracusans to come to Rome and make whatever accusations they could think of against him. These foreigners appeared when the senate met, and stood silently by while Marcellus took his seat in the consul-chair and proceeded to transact matters of business. When this was done, Marcellus left his place of honor and went to the one set aside for people who were accused, so as to give the Syracusans liberty to speak. But they were so impressed by the dignity of his presence in his robes of state that they were silenced until egged on by those who had summoned them. Then they made their charge, which was that although they had declared themselves friends to Rome, they had nevertheless been forced to suffer cruelties that other commanders had spared them. Marcellus answered, "Notwithstanding many instances of criminal behavior towards Rome, you have suffered nothing but what it is impossible to prevent when a city is taken by storm; that Syracuse was so taken was entirely your own fault, for when I asked you to surrender you would not listen to me, and you had not the excuse others have had of being forced on by their tyrants, for it was you, yourselves, who wished to fight."

When both sides had spoken, they withdrew, according to custom, while the votes were being taken. Although the Romans had not been altogether pleased with Marcellus for allowing his soldiers to plunder Syracuse, because King Hiero had always been friendly to their republic, yet they decided in his favor. Then the ambassadors fell at his feet, and, with tears in their eyes, asked him to pardon them and their countrymen. Marcellus was so moved by their entreaties that he not only pardoned them, but ever after showed favors to the Syracusans. Besides, he induced the senate to respect their liberty and their laws. Thereupon the Syracusans promised him that if at any time he or the members of his family should visit Sicily, they should be received by the citizens in festive attire, and public sacrifices should be offered to the gods on the occasion.

Since the defeat of the Romans at Cannæ not one of their consuls had dared to attempt a battle with Hannibal, but Marcellus resolved to march against him and drive him out of the country. The two armies met near the city of Numistro, and a bloody battle ensued. Night put a stop to it, but the next morning Marcellus drew up his army and challenged Hannibal again. But the Carthaginians retreated, and as soon as Marcellus had gathered the spoils which they left and buried his own dead, he marched in pursuit.

In all the skirmishes that followed he was so successful that the enemy regarded him with wonder and admiration. The next great battle between the Romans and the Carthaginians was fought near Canusium, and when Hannibal assembled his men just before it began, he said, "Exert yourselves, I entreat you, more than you ever have done; for you see that we can neither take breath after the victories the enemy have gained nor enjoy the least repose if we are victorious now unless this man be driven off."

Some mistaken movement on the part of Marcellus caused such disorder in his army that the day was decided in favor of the enemy. The general retreated to his camp, and, summoning his troops about him, reproached them thus: "I see the arms and bodies of Romans in great numbers, but not a single Roman do I behold." After they had begged his pardon, he added, "I will not forgive you while vanquished, but when you come to be victorious I will; to-morrow I will lead you into the field again, so that the news of our victory may reach Rome before that of our flight." This reproof made such an impression that, though many were dangerously wounded, there was not a man who did not feel more pain on account of it than he did from his injuries.

Next morning betimes the scarlet robe, the usual signal for battle, was hung out, and the companies that had disgraced themselves on the previous day were placed, as they had requested, in the foremost line. When this was reported to Hannibal he exclaimed, "Ye gods, what can be done with a man who is not affected either by good or bad fortune? he is the only one who will not suffer us to rest when he is victor, nor take rest himself when he is beaten. We shall have to fight with him forever, for his confidence when he is successful, and his shame when he is not, urge him alike to further exertions."

For a long time the battle was undecided; then Hannibal ordered his elephants to be brought forward and pushed against the Romans, thinking that it would be impossible for

MARCELLUS

them to resist such great beasts. They really did create confusion in the front line, but Flavius, a tribune, snatched an ensign staff from one of the companies, rushed forward with it, and wounded the foremost animal. He turned back, ran against the second elephant, the second against the next, and so on, until, the disorder increasing, Marcellus saw his opportunity, and ordered his cavalry to fall furiously upon the enemy. The rout was terrible, and the Carthaginians were driven to their intrenchments. Eight thousand of them fell, many being killed by the plunging and trampling of the elephants. Not more than three thousand of the Romans were slain, but almost all the rest were wounded. This gave Hannibal a chance to escape with the remnant of his army during the night, and move to a safe distance from Marcellus, who could not pursue him on account of the number of his wounded. The Roman army retired to Campania, where they passed the summer and recovered from their injuries.

During that season Hannibal employed his men in overrunning Italy and destroying right and left. This called down upon Marcellus the severe reproaches of his countrymen; they accused him of spending his time in enjoyment and leisure while the enemy were ruining the country. Such injustice Marcellus could not bear: so, appointing lieutenants to take charge of his army, he hurried to Rome, where he made so able a defence that he was appointed consul the fifth time.

Marcellus had built a temple out of the Sicilian spoils, which he now desired to dedicate to Honor and Virtue, but the priests would not consent to having two deities in one temple, because, they said, in case it should be struck by lightning they would not know to which to offer their sacrifices. So Marcellus began another temple. Now his dreams by night and his thoughts by day were all about Hannibal, whom he burned once more to meet in battle, but the omens were not favorable, and he feared to leave Rome. Some temples were struck by lightning; rats gnawed the gold in Jupiter's temple; it was reported that an ox had spoken, and that a boy had been born with an elephant's head. While such things were going on there was certainly something wrong with the gods, thought Marcellus.

A great many sacrifices had to be offered before the priests announced that the gods were appeased. Then Marcellus went forth to carry on the war. He fixed his camp between Bantia and Venusia, and then tried to draw Hannibal into a battle, but did not succeed. Meanwhile, some of the Roman troops that had been sent to lay siege to a certain town a little distance off were caught in an ambuscade, and twenty-five hundred of them were killed. This so enraged Marcellus that he determined to punish the enemy, and for that purpose drew nearer to them. Between the two armies was a hill, which seemed to possess so many advantages that Marcellus could not but wonder why Hannibal had not stationed his men there. He did not suspect that all the thickets and hollows were filled with Carthaginian soldiers, for Hannibal knew well enough that it was the very position the Romans would covet, and a most favorable one for an ambuscade. And indeed the Romans at once determined to seize it, and nothing else was talked of among the ambitious soldiers. So Marcellus made some offerings to the gods, and, as all the signs were favorable, set out with Crispinus, his colleague, Marcellus, his son, and two hundred and twenty Tuscan horsemen, to make a survey. On the top of the hill the enemy had stationed sentinels, who were so concealed among the trees and bushes that they could observe all that took place in the Roman camp without being seen themselves. The approach of Marcellus was therefore reported by them to the soldiers that lay in ambush, and when he was in their very midst, they rushed out suddenly from all sides, let fly a shower of arrows, and then charged with their spears and swords. The suddenness of the attack took the Romans so by surprise that they could not stand their ground. Marcellus and Crispinus were slain, besides forty of their men. Young Marcellus was wounded, but a party of the soldiers who were not injured picked him up and fled with him back to camp. To lose both their consuls in one action was the greatest misfortune that could have happened to the Romans.

When Hannibal heard that Marcellus was dead, he hastened to the hill, and stood for a long time gazing upon the form of the man who had been to him so fierce and troublesome an enemy; then, without any display of rejoicing or exultation, he ordered the body to be properly clad and honorably burned. The ashes were placed in a silver urn, on top of which was a gold crown, and this was sent to the son of Marcellus.

PHILOPOEMEN

Philopoemen lost his father when he was so young that some one had to adopt him. It was his good fortune to excite an interest in two philosophers of Megalopolis, the town in Arcadia where he was born, and they educated him so well that a certain Roman called him "the last of the Greeks," meaning that Greece did not produce one great man after Philopœmen.

When he was in command of the Achæan cavalry a funny incident occurred, which shows how simple his manners must have been and how plainly he must have dressed. A woman of Megara received a message that the general of the Achæans was coming to her house to supper on his way through the place. Her husband was not at home, and she was all flurry and excitement to get the meal ready in the short time she had. Presently a man arrived whom she took to be one of Philopœmen's servants, and she asked him to assist her in the kitchen. He threw off his cloak, and, at her request, began to chop wood. While he was thus engaged, the husband returned. "What is the meaning of this, Philopœmen?" he asked, in surprise. "I am paying the penalty of my plain looks," answered the general. He was not at all ugly, and he was large and strong, but he was unassuming, and had a contempt for any display of riches.

PHILOPOEMEN

From his childhood Philopœmen had a taste for a soldier's life, and learned to manage horses and handle weapons at a very early age. He would not engage in wrestling, because that sort of training was different from that of a soldier, which he greatly preferred. As soon as he had got through with masters and governors, he joined the citizens of Megalopolis in those private excursions to Laconia which were made for the sake of plunder, and he was always the first to march out and the last to return. His leisure he spent in hunting or in tilling the ground, for he owned a fine estate about a mile from the city, to which he went every evening. There he would throw himself on a common mattress, and sleep no more luxuriously than laborers did. Early in the morning he arose, and worked in the vineyard or at the plough until it was time to go to town and take part with his friends in public affairs. He believed that the surest way not to touch the property of others was to take care of one's own, and for that reason he gave so much attention to the improvement of his farm.

He spent many hours in the study of oratory and philosophy, but he was too apt to consider those who did not understand the tactics of war as drones useless to the commonwealth.

He was thirty years of age when Cleomenes, King of the Lacedæmonians, surprised Megalopolis by night, forced the gates, entered, and took possession of the market-place. When the alarm sounded, Philopœmen was one of the first to come out, but, although he fought with desperate courage, he could not drive the enemy off. But he kept Cleomenes engaged until all the citizens had escaped, and then, although he had lost his horse and received several wounds, he managed to make good his retreat.

The Megalopolitans went to Messene, and a short time after Cleomenes offered them their city back with all their property. They would gladly have accepted had it not been for Philopœmen, who said to them, "Cleomenes does not want to return your city to you; what he means to do is to get you back, and then, by becoming your ruler, keep the place more secure. He has no desire to watch empty houses and walls, and if you fail to return he will be forced to leave." The Megalopolitans saw the wisdom of this argument, and resolved not to return to their city. This gave Cleomenes an excuse for plundering and destroying the greater part of it.

King Antigonus then offered to assist the Achæans against Cleomenes, and joining his army to theirs, marched towards the enemy. In the battle which immediately took place, Philopœmen was wounded in both thighs, and a javelin that passed all the way through his body came out at his back, so that he could neither move nor get anybody to pull it out. Using all his strength, he broke it off, and then rode into the thickest of the fight, urging his men on with a desperation that ended in complete victory. It so happened that this glorious charge was made contrary to orders, and before Antigonus had given a signal which it had been agreed that the Achæans should obey. After the victory he asked why the cavalry had charged without orders and before he had given the signal. The answer was, "We were obliged, against our will, to go into action, because a young man of Megalopolis began the attack too soon."

"That young man has performed the office of an experienced general," replied Antigonus, with a smile.

Philopœmen's reputation was made, and Antigonus offered him an important command if he would join his army, but he declined. The young man then went to Crete, where he spent some years and gained much experience in war. By the time he returned home he had become so famous that the Achæans chose him for their commander. He found them a badly-organized company, riding miserable horses that they picked up anywhere, and so afraid to fight that they were apt to hire others to do it for them. Philopœmen went among the young men, rousing them to a sense of honor, and practising them in exercises, reviews, and mock battles, until he made such good soldiers of them that they became the wonder and admiration of every one. Philopœmen set them an example of courage by always going to battle at their head, and once when a general singled him out and rode with full speed at him, he stood perfectly still and awaited his chance, then with a violent blow of his spear laid his adversary dead at his feet. Thereupon the enemy fled. Philopœmen was then forty-four years old and his name was in everybody's mouth, for he was brave as the youngest, prudent as the oldest, and able to fight or command equally well.

He made great changes in the armor of the Achæans as well as in their mode of fighting. Not only was a taste for warlike things increased in the men, but the women shared it to such a degree that their daily expenses were diminished, so that the money thus saved might be spent for weapons, horses, and armor. The shops were filled with gold and silver breastplates and shields, the men spent their time on parade, and the women in ornamenting helmets and embroidering military vests. The very sight of these things tended to make the people courageous and ready to face danger.

At the battle of Mantinea, which the Achæans fought against Machanidas, the tyrant of Lacedæmon, Philopœmen had a chance to prove what his military improvements were worth, for it was his skill that won him the victory. With his own hand he slew the tyrant just as he had jumped a ditch in order to escape, and this was regarded as such a wonderful exploit that the Achæans set up his statue in brass at Delphi. It represents him in the act of killing Machanidas.

The Achæans had such confidence in Philopœmen that they were never satisfied to fight under another commander. They knew that no enemy felt able to stand up against him, and were willing to go into any action if only he led them on. The Bœotians feared him so much that, when they besieged Megara, they left their scaling-ladders planted against the walls and fled because they heard he was coming, although they were on the very point of success. Many other such instances are given to prove how Philopœmen ranked as a military commander.

Though a great man, Philopœmen could make mistakes, particularly where his vanity was flattered. He made a serious one when he left his own country in danger of attack and went to fight for the Cretans. He satisfied his ambition by so doing, and greatly distinguished himself, but it was not the act of a true patriot.

However, the Achæans could not get along without him, so as soon as he returned he was placed in command of their cavalry to fight Nabis, then tyrant of Lacedæmon. The first battle took place at sea, but Philopœmen was defeated, because his only experience had been on land; he soon redeemed his loss, however, for the enemy laid siege to Gythium, and he set sail for that place forthwith. He landed in the night, took them completely by surprise, burnt their camp, and killed a great number of them.

PHILOPOEMEN

A few days later, as he was marching through a difficult pass, Nabis met him suddenly. The Achæans were terrified, but Philopœmen reassured them by his coolness and presence of mind, and drew up his army in a manner just suited to the position. He then gave battle to the enemy, and put those that were not killed to flight. Peace was made with Nabis after that, but he was assassinated by the Ætolians some months later, and Sparta was thrown into great confusion. Philopœmen seized that opportunity to enter the city with his army and force it to join the Achæan League. Sparta was a city of such vast importance that the Achæans adored Philopœmen for taking possession of it.

The Spartans, on their side, were pleased, because they hoped to find in Philopœmen a man who would guard their liberty and preserve them from another tyrant. So they sold the house and goods of Nabis, and voted that the money realized thereon should be presented to Philopœmen. Timolaus was selected, being a personal friend to Philopœmen, to carry him the present. He went to Megalopolis for that purpose, and was entertained at Philopœmen's house, but when he observed the simple style of living and the dignified manners of the commander, he did not dare to offer the money, and returned to Sparta without having done so. He was sent again, but even then could not mention the present. The third time he summoned courage enough to tell Philopœmen that Sparta desired to show gratitude to him by means of a gift. The commander was pleased to hear what Timolaus had to say, but went straight to Sparta and advised the people not to tempt good men with money, but to use it to silence bad ones and make them less troublesome. He remained firm in his refusal of the present, and thus showed himself above bribery.

But later the Spartans had reason to rejoice that they had not shown honors to Philopœmen, for he punished them severely when they gave him cause to do so. Not only did he burn down their walls, put a great number of people to the sword, and banish others, but he actually abolished the laws of Lycurgus, and insisted that the Spartan children should be educated as Achæans. They submitted at the time, but took the earliest opportunity to secure the assistance of the Romans and re-establish, as far as possible, their ancient laws and customs.

Philopœmen was seventy years of age when he was elected general of the Achæans for the eighth time. He hoped to pass the rest of his life quietly, but such was not to be, for Dinocrates, a Messenian, who hated him, induced his countrymen to throw off the Achæan yoke. They therefore decided to seize Coronis, a town near Messene; but Philopœmen, on hearing of it, jumped out of his sick-bed, and travelled with all speed to Megalopolis, where he collected an army and moved towards Messene. Before reaching that place he met Dinocrates, by whom he was defeated. But a guard of five hundred came to the rescue of the flying troops; they rallied, and returned to the charge. Philopœmen, in fear of being surrounded, retreated upon rough ground, and tried to draw the enemy upon himself, but they would not risk a hand-to-hand encounter. They hurled their darts from a distance, however, until they drove him to such a steep place that he could not manage his horse. Even then he might have escaped, but illness had made him weak, and he was so fatigued that he could not make the attempt. With a sudden spring the horse threw him, and his head was wounded by the fall; he lay speechless so long that the enemy, thinking he was dead, turned him over and began to take off his armor. But he became conscious again, raised his head and opened his eyes, whereupon they bound his hands behind his back, and led him off in the most humiliating and insulting manner.

The Messenians were so delighted on hearing of the capture of Philopœmen that they thronged to the city gates to look at him, but even they shed tears when they beheld a man whose glorious deeds had astonished the world dragged along in such a shameful manner. He was shut up in a dark dungeon closed by an immense stone that was movable only by machinery, and a guard was placed to watch without.

Philopœmen's soldiers had fled; but when their general failed to appear they thought he must be dead, and reproached one another for having deserted him. On hearing that he was a prisoner they sent messengers to spread the sad news among the Achæans, who collected their army together in order to rescue him.

Meanwhile, Dinocrates sent a servant to the dungeon with a cup of poison, and orders not to leave Philopœmen until he had swallowed the dose. The prisoner was lying down, wrapped in his cloak. He was not asleep, for grief and trouble kept him awake. When the man approached with a light, he raised his head and asked, feebly, whether he had heard anything of his cavalry. The answer was that almost all had escaped. "Thou bringest good tidings, and we are not in all respects unhappy," returned Philopœmen. Then, without uttering another word, he drank off the poison and lay down. He was so feeble that his death followed soon, with little struggle.

Achaia was filled with grief when the death of Philopœmen was reported, and all the young men met at

Megalopolis, resolved to take speedy revenge. Choosing Lycortas for their general, they went to Messene, burnt, destroyed, and killed right and left, until the citizens made their submission. Dinocrates knew that he would receive no mercy at the hands of the enemy, and so killed himself; those who had voted for the death of the Achæan general did likewise.

The remains of Philopœmen were reduced to ashes and placed in an urn. With this his countrymen returned home in triumph, but at the same time with funeral solemnity. First marched the foot-soldiers, wearing crowns of victory, and followed by their captives in chains. The general's son, with the noblest of the Achæans, came next, carrying the urn, covered with ribbons and garlands. The cavalry, armed and mounted, brought up the rear, and as they passed along the people of the various towns and villages saluted the urn, then fell in with the procession, and followed to Megalopolis. After the interment the prisoners were stoned to death about the tomb. Many statues were set up and many honors shown to the memory of Philopœmen by different Grecian cities.

FLAMININUS

FROM his boyhood Flamininus was trained to the use of arms, because Rome was engaged in a number of wars, and as her young men grew up there was no lack of opportunity to make themselves famous. Therefore at a very early age they prepared themselves to become soldiers.

Titus Quintius Flamininus was only twenty years old when he was appointed tribune under the consul, Marcellus, in the war with Hannibal. Marcellus, as we have related in his life, was taken in an ambuscade and slain. Later, when Tarentum was recaptured by the Romans, Flamininus was appointed governor, and proved that he was quite as well able to fill such a post as he was to command an army. So great was the confidence he had in himself that he determined to run for the consulship without going through the stages of prætor and ædile as other men did.

It was an unheard-of thing for so young a person to aim at the highest office in the state, particularly as he had had no experience in public affairs; so some of the tribunes opposed him; but the senate left the matter to the voice of the people, and Flamininus was elected. He was not quite thirty years of age when this occurred.

Sextus Ælius was chosen for consul also. When the lots were cast to see what provinces each should go to fight, that of the Macedonians fell to Flamininus; and it was fortunate for the Romans that such was the case, because that department needed a general who was not violent, and Flamininus was remarkably gentle.

Up to that period the Greeks and the Romans knew little about each other, and it was important that the beginning of their intercourse should be agreeable if it was to be lasting. Philip was king of Macedon, and received his supplies from his own country for a war with the Romans; but should the contest last very long, he would have to depend on Greece for a great many things. Therefore the Romans felt the necessity of gaining the Greeks over to their side, so that they would not be friendly to Philip. In order to do this they had to have a general who was kind, gentle, courteous, pleasant in his bearing towards others, and, above all, perfectly just. Titus Flamininus combined all these qualities, and was, therefore, as a foreigner, more likely to gain authority over the Greeks than if he had been rash and ferocious.

No sooner was he elected consul than, feeling anxious to distinguish himself, Flamininus requested the senate to place his brother Lucius in command of the navy, and, selecting three thousand of the troops that had lately won glorious victories under Scipio, he crossed the sea and went to Epirus. His army encamped near the river Apsus, and, after examining the face of the country, he determined to make his way to the tops of the neighboring mountains. But the enemy held that position, and showered down their arrows from all quarters on the Romans; many were killed on both sides, but nothing was decided.

Meanwhile, some shepherds went to Titus and told him of a winding road by which they promised to lead him to the top of the mountain in three days if he would take them for guides. He believed them, and sent a tribune with four thousand foot and three hundred horse soldiers, that they were to lead. They marched only at night, and lay still in the hollows of the woods during the day, so that the enemy could not discover them, while Flamininus kept up some slight skirmishing to divert attention from them. Early on the day when he expected them to reach the top of the heights he drew out all his forces, and, dividing them into three parts, himself led the van along the narrowest path by the side of the river. The Macedonians had the best position, but although they harassed the Romans with their darts they did not subdue them.

When day dawned, there arose a smoke resembling the mist one sees about the tops of hills. As it was behind the enemy, they did not observe it, but it was the signal for which the Romans had been watching, and as it increased and mounted higher and higher they knew that it came from the fires their friends had lighted. Loud shouts rent the air as with renewed vigor they charged the Macedonians. The shouts were re-echoed from the tops of the mountains, and then the enemy fled. It was impossible to pursue them because of the steep ascent, but the Romans pillaged their camp, seized all the money and slaves, and became masters of the pass.

The Roman army was then led through Epirus, with so much order and discipline that nobody's property was injured. Though far from his ships and unable to procure the monthly allowance, Flamininus gave his men strict charge to buy all they required, and to plunder no part of the country. Now, this behavior formed such a contrast to that of the Macedonians, who on entering Thessaly had compelled the people to take shelter in the mountains, burnt their houses, and carried off all they could lay hands on, that several Greek tribes threw open their gates to the Romans, while others actually sent for Flamininus and put themselves under his protection.

They had been told by the Macedonians that the Roman invader led an army of barbarians ready to kill and destroy at every turn, and when they beheld a young man of mild, attractive manners, who spoke Greek well and desired to be just and humane towards them, they were greatly pleased with him, and began to believe that in him they might find the protector of their liberty. And they were right; for when Philip offered to make terms of peace, and Flamininus agreed on condition that the Macedonian troops were withdrawn and the Grecians left in freedom, it was plain that the Romans had come not to oppose the Greeks, but to fight for them against the Macedonians.

As Flamininus marched into Bœotia, the chief men of Thebes came out to meet him and show him honor. They were allied to the Macedonians, but the Roman general did not leave until he had talked them over to his side and made a formal league with them.

He next marched into Thessaly to continue the war with Philip. He had twenty-six thousand men in his army, of which the Ætolians furnished six thousand foot and three hundred horse; but Philip had quite as many, and each general was ambitious of the fame that he would secure to himself if he defeated the other. Both harangued their men just before going into battle, according to custom, and urged them to feats of courage, telling them that their foe was worthy of their steel, and the country in which they were fighting the most glorious spot in the world for victory.

FLAMININUS

The Macedonians, who always fought in a phalanx, which they formed by locking their shields together, made a charge with their projected spears that no army could withstand. The strength of such a phalanx was tremendous as long as it remained unbroken, but if the men got separated, and had to fight hand-to-hand with their heavy, unwieldy armor, they were at a great disadvantage. So at their first charge the Romans gave ground, but Flamininus attacked the enemy from the other side, broke the phalanx, and created so much confusion that they threw down their arms and fled. No less than eight thousand of their number were slain, and five thousand were taken prisoners. Philip himself would not have escaped had the Ætolians done their duty, but while the Romans went in pursuit of the enemy they stayed behind to plunder the camp. When the Romans got back and found nothing left for them they were very angry, and the ill feeling was greatly increased when the Ætolians claimed the victory, and declared that the Romans would have been put to flight if their cavalry had not protected them.

Flamininus, who particularly desired the praises of Greece, determined after that to manage everything by himself and pay no attention to the Ætolians. But they would not submit to being slighted, and out of revenge circulated a report that Flamininus was on the point of making peace with Philip at a time when he had it in his power to destroy his empire. Flamininus proved that this was not the case later, when he treated with Philip in person, for he granted him his kingdom only on condition that he would give up all claim to Greece and pay a large fine. Then all his ships, except ten, were taken from him, and his son, Demetrius, was sent to Rome as hostage.

Thus Flamininus put an end to the war. When the Isthmian games were celebrated, and an immense crowd had assembled to witness the exercises, a herald appeared in the arena and sounded a trumpet. All present were silent, and wondered what this could mean. They had not long to wait, for a crier proclaimed that the Roman senate and Titus Quintius Flamininus, the general and proconsul, having vanquished King Philip and the Macedonians, restored their lands, laws, and liberties to the Corinthians, Locrians, Phocians, Eubœans, Achæans, Magnesians, Thessalians, and Perrhæbians.

It was long since Greece had known peace, and the shouts of joy that went up as soon as the people had recovered from their astonishment were heard many miles away. If Flamininus had not hidden himself when he saw the crowd rushing towards him, he would certainly have been suffocated by their embraces, for they were beside themselves with delight, and declared again and again that none of their own statesmen had ever done so much for them as this foreigner, who had relieved Greece from her greatest distress and restored her liberty.

It may well be believed that great honors and gifts were heaped upon Flamininus wherever he went, but there was only one present upon which he set real value, and that was made by the Achæans in this manner. The Romans who, in the war with Hannibal, had the misfortune to be captured, had been sold here and there into slavery. There were twelve hundred of them in Greece, and when in the Roman army they now beheld their brothers, sons, and acquaintances free men and conquerors while they were slaves and captives, their position became unbearable. Flamininus grieved for them, but he was too honest to take them from their masters. The

Achæans bought them at five pounds a man, and, just as Flamininus was going to set sail, marched them in a body to the sea-shore and presented them to him. At that moment the Roman general felt fully repaid for his glorious services, and declared the return of his countrymen the most blessed part of his victory.

At his triumph the liberated slaves followed his chariot, each wearing a cap of liberty. To add to the splendor of this display, there were Grecian helmets, Macedonian targets, and long spears borne in procession through the city, besides thousands of pounds of massive gold and vast sums of coined money. Afterwards, Flamininus used his influence to have the hostage son of Philip returned to him.

There were more wars in Greece, beginning with an attack made by Antiochus, not long after peace had been made with the Macedonians. Flamininus went there again, added to the number of his achievements, and did not return to Rome until Greece was rid of her enemies and all her colonies were reconciled to one another.

Titus Flamininus was then raised to the very highest office in Rome, that of censor. His associate was the son of Marcellus, who had been consul five times. While Flamininus was censor, his brother Lucius, whom we have mentioned as being placed in command of the navy when Titus went to Epirus, was guilty of a shameful deed. He had a favorite boy, who went with him everywhere and loved him extremely. One day, when Lucius was drinking a little too freely, the boy said to him, "I love you, sir, so dearly that, wishing to please you, I came away from the show without seeing the gladiators, though I never saw a man killed in my life."

Lucius was delighted with the flattery, and replied, "Let not that trouble you, for you shall be gratified." He then ordered a convict to be brought from prison, and, having summoned an executioner, had him strike off the man's head in the very room where he was carousing.

When Marcus Cato became censor, he examined into the lives of the senators, which was part of his duty, and expelled Lucius for this shameful piece of cruelty.

Titus felt the disgrace so keenly that, appearing with his brother before an assembly of the people, he demanded that Cato should give his reason for casting a stain upon an honorable family. Thereupon Cato related all the details of the execution of the poor convict in the midst of a feast, and challenged Lucius to deny it if he could. Lucius was silent, and the censor was applauded for his justice.

Flamininus did not show his usual good sense on this occasion, for he was very indignant, and took sides with Cato's enemies in opposing all he said and did in the senate. Yet Cato had done no more nor less than his duty in disgracing a man too unworthy to be defended even by a brother.

Flamininus was much blamed for this, as well as for another action of his, prompted by desire for increase of fame. It was against Hannibal, the Carthaginian general.

Hannibal had been obliged to fly from his country and seek refuge here and there until, at last, worn out with old age and grief, he went to Bithynia, and put himself under the protection of Prusias, the king. The Romans knew perfectly well where he was, but saw no reason for interfering with the now harmless, unfortunate old man. But Flamininus was sent by the senate on an errand to Prusias, and, when he beheld Hannibal at court, declared that he could not stand seeing him alive. Prusias begged him not to trouble the old warrior, who was under the sanction of his hospitality, but Titus would not listen to him.

Hannibal had from the first felt little confidence in Prusias, and so he had ordered seven underground passages to be dug from his house, all running in different directions, and not visible above ground. When he heard that Flamininus was bent on taking his life he tried to escape through these passages, but found them guarded by the king's soldiers. He then knew that he had nothing to hope for, but was determined that Flamininus should not have the glory of killing him. So mixing a cup of poison, that he always kept in case of need, he took it in his hand and said, "Let us deliver the Romans from their cares and anxieties, since they think it too tedious and dangerous to wait for the death of a poor, hated, old man. Titus shall not have a conquest worth envying." He drank the dose, and died before Flamininus saw him again.

Some historians say that Flamininus was sent by the senate of Rome to kill Hannibal, because they felt that while a warrior who hated them as he did remained on earth they were in great danger. This is probable; for so generous and humane a man as Titus Flamininus would scarcely have been guilty of such a cruel deed; he was hasty and passionate, but he never nursed a feeling of hatred towards any one.

No further political or military acts of Flamininus are recorded, and he died in peace.

MARCUS CATO

THE Romans always called those who distinguished themselves, but received no honors through their ancestors, new men, and this was the name they gave to Cato, though he used to say that he was new only with regard to offices, but in so far as the services and virtues of his ancestors were concerned, he was very ancient.

Originally, his name was Marcus Priscus, but it was afterwards changed to Cato on account of his wisdom; for *catos* is a Latin word, meaning wise. Marcus Cato was a strong, healthy youth, with a florid complexion and gray eyes. He was brought up in camps and accustomed to a life of discipline and temperance, which fitted him for his later duties. Eloquence seemed to him such a necessary accomplishment that he studied hard to become a good orator, and the people of the neighboring villages would send for him to plead their causes because he did it so willingly and so well. Perhaps another reason for employing him was that he would never accept a fee. He was glad of the opportunity of exercising his talent, but he was all the while longing for military glory.

His first campaign was made when he was only seventeen years of age. Hannibal was then laying Italy in ruins, and not many years later it was Cato's pride to show the number of scars that marked his breast. He always marched on foot, followed only by one servant, who carried his provisions, even after he had risen to a high office, and he was so kind and considerate that when not on military duty he would wait on himself, and even prepare his own food. He never drank anything but water, except when his strength and spirits were exhausted, then he would take a little wine.

Cato had a farm, on which he lived when not engaged in war, and while there his habits were as frugal and economical as possible. The estate adjoining his farm belonged to a nobleman named Valerius Flaccus, a man of influence and great wealth. He often heard his servants speak of the laborious life his neighbor led; how he went early in the morning to the various towns in the vicinity to argue cases of law, and then returned to his own farm and worked hard with his domestics all day, afterwards sitting down with them and sharing their coarse food. They told, too, of many instances of kindness and consideration, as well as of the witty and sensible sayings of Cato. Valerius always wanted to know superior people, and liked to encourage those who were striving to do right, so he sent Cato an invitation to dine. The two men saw each other frequently after that, and Valerius discovered many excellent traits in Cato that only needed a chance for development; he therefore persuaded him to go to Rome and apply himself to affairs of state.

The young man soon gained friends and admirers, and Valerius helped him to rise to several high positions, until he became his colleague as consul and censor. All the young men of Rome tried to become public speakers because they had such an admiration for Cato, whom they called the Roman Demosthenes. From what is said of him by several historians, it is probable that he was quite as eloquent as the Greek orator. But few of Cato's admirers were willing to work as hard as he did in tilling his fields, or to live as plainly and dress as poorly. He always said that he did so in order that he might be the better prepared for hard service when his country needed him, and even when he was an old, gray-haired man he continued robust and healthy to the last. He inherited a beautiful piece of Babylonian tapestry, but sold it because, as the walls of his house were neither plastered nor whitewashed, he could not use it. In short, he thought that a man should own nothing that he could do without, and that it was better to have fields where food could be raised than a flower-garden that needed care. Only useful things had value in his eyes, but he carried this idea to an excess that made him cruel, for when a domestic grew old in his service he turned him off instead of taking care of him. When he was consul, he left his war-horse in Spain to save the public the expense of his freight, but it is a question whether it was a virtue to abandon an animal that had carried him safe through the war.

Perhaps a good idea of the character of Cato may be got from some of his sayings, which we will repeat. One day the Romans were very unreasonable in their demand for corn, and he attempted to argue with them. He began his address thus: "It is a difficult task, my fellow-citizens, to speak to the belly, because it has no ears." He was so displeased with the extravagant habits of the Romans that he said, "It is a hard matter to save a city from ruin where a fish is sold for more than an ox." On another occasion he declared that the Roman people were like sheep, that could not be made to stir alone, but would follow their leader in a body. The men to whom no one would listen could lead a crowd with the greatest ease. Wishing to encourage virtue, he said, in one of his speeches, "If it is by virtue and temperance that you are become great, do not change for the worse; but if intemperance and vice have made you great, change for the better; for you are already quite great enough." He found fault because the same persons were often chosen as consuls, and said, "Either you think the consulate worth little, or few worthy of the office." When the Romans sent three ambassadors to the king of Bithynia, one with the gout, one with a recently-healed fracture of the skull, and the third not much better than a fool, Cato said, "They have sent an embassy which has neither feet, head, nor heart."

One of his sayings was, "Wise men learn more from fools than fools from the wise; for the wise avoid the errors of fools, while fools do not profit by the example of the wise." He once made this jest about a fat man: "Of what service to his country can such a body be, which is nothing but belly?" He also said that in all his life he only repented of three things: the first was that he had trusted a woman with a secret; the second, that he had gone by sea when he might have gone by land; and the third, that he had passed one day without doing any important business.

To a wicked old man he said, "Old age has deformities enough of its own; do not add to it the deformity of vice." A tribune who had the reputation of a poisoner wanted to have a bad law passed, and worked very hard for it; whereupon Cato said to him, "Young man, I do not know which is more dangerous, to drink what you mix, or to confirm what you would make a law."

During his consulship with his friend Valerius Flaccus, he was sent in command of the army to fight the Spaniards, and while he was subduing their cities a great army took him by surprise, and he was in danger of being driven out of the country with dishonor. He sent to the Celtiberians for aid, and they demanded an enormous sum of money for their services. The Roman officers thought it shameful that they should be obliged to purchase assistance, but Cato said, "It makes no difference; for if we conquer, we shall pay them at the enemy's expense; and if we are conquered, there will be nobody either to pay or to make the demand." He gained the battle, and after that was successful everywhere. He often boasted that he conquered more cities in Spain than he had stayed there days. So much was he dreaded, that when he wrote letters to the commanders of several fortified towns ordering them to tear down their walls and towers, they immediately obeyed.

On his return home Cato was honored with a triumph, but he by no means felt that his work was done; on the contrary, he publicly offered his services to his friends and his country whenever they should be required, and continued to plead cases of law for those who sought him.

It was not long before he was called into action, for Antiochus the Great, King of Syria, marched into Greece with an army, creating no little commotion there, and the Roman forces were sent over to fight him. Antiochus blocked up the narrow pass of Thermopylæ, and added walls and intrenchments to those that already existed there. The Romans were at a loss how to approach, until Cato remembered that the Persians had made their way round the mountains and come upon Leonidas from behind when he defended the pass with three hundred Spartans. Under his direction, therefore, the troops began to ascend the mountain, but the guide, who was one of the prisoners, lost his way and wandered about among such dangerous precipices that the soldiers were in despair.

Cato saw the danger, and ordered his forces to halt, while he, with one Lucius Manlius, a dexterous climber, went forward in the middle of a dark night and scrambled among wild olive-trees and steep rocks until they found a path that seemed to lead down to the enemy's camp. There they set up marks to guide them on their return, and went to fetch the army. But when they had all reached the place and begun to march farther, the path suddenly failed, and they found themselves on the verge of a steep precipice. At last day dawned, and the Grecian camp with the advanced guard could be seen at the foot of the precipice. Cato halted and sent for the Firmians, saying that he wished to speak with them in private. The Firmians belonged to a Roman colony, and had proved themselves the bravest and truest of soldiers in time of danger. When they presented themselves, Cato said, "I want to take one of the enemy alive, so that we may learn who compose the advance-guard, what is their number, and what preparations have been made to fight us. But the business requires the speed and ferocity of lions rushing among a herd of beasts."

The Firmians required no second bidding, but promptly rushed down the mountain, surprised the guard and put them to flight, and brought back one of their number to Cato, as he had ordered. The prisoner, upon being questioned, said that the main body of the army was encamped in the pass with the king, but that six hundred selected Ætolians guarded the heights. Of such a small number, even though they were selected, Cato felt little fear, so he had the trumpets sounded, and started forward, sword in hand, shouting to his army to follow. When the Ætolians saw him advancing they fled to the main body, and created the wildest confusion among the forces.

At the same time Manius Glabrio, the Roman consul, attacked Antiochus from below, and entered the pass with his whole army. Antiochus was struck in the mouth with a stone, which knocked out several of his teeth, and caused such intense pain that he was forced to turn his horse and retire. His soldiers then lost heart, and pushed back through the narrow defiles, trampling each other down as the Romans crowded upon them, until all perished.

Cato gives an account of this exploit in his writings, and praises himself very much for it. He says, "All those who witnessed the action were ready to declare that Cato owed less to the people of Rome than the people of Rome owed to Cato; the consul, Manius, coming hot from the fight, took me in his arms and embraced me for a long time; he then cried out with joy that neither he nor all the people together could ever sufficiently reward Cato."

Immediately after the battle the consul sent Cato to carry the news of the glorious result to Rome. He arrived there in five days, and was the first to report the victory. Great rejoicings followed; the whole city was filled with sacrifices, and the Romans were made happy by the belief that they had power to conquer every sea and every land.

Cato was not prominent on the battlefield again after the victory he won over Antiochus, but he interested himself in politics, and made it his special duty to accuse criminals and have them arrested. One day he met a young man who had brought an enemy of his dead father to disgrace. Taking him by the hand, Cato congratulated him, and said, "You have done well; lambs and goats are not the proper sacrifices to offer to our dead parents: the tears and sufferings of their enemies are better."

MARCUS CATO

He was constantly accusing one person or another, and of course the tables were often turned on him, his enemies never losing the slightest chance of bringing him to justice. He was brought up before the court at least fifty times for various offences. The last trial took place when he was eighty-six years old, and on that occasion he was heard to say, "It is hard that I, who have lived with men of one generation, should be obliged to make my defence to those of another."

Ten years after his consulship, Cato stood for the office of censor, the very highest one in the republic. A censor had a great deal of power, and there were never more than two at a time. If one died during his term of office his place was not filled, because it was considered an evil omen for a censor to die; but the other one had to resign, and then two new ones were chosen. The office was held for eighteen months, and the duties were numerous. They consisted in taking the census, and this gave the name to the office originally, superintending the public morals, and inquiring into the life and manners of each citizen. The censors also had charge of the public money. They had the right to reprove or punish a person for not marrying, for breaking a promise of marriage, for any sort of dissipation or bad conduct, for extravagance in his household, or for failing to promptly educate his children; for the Romans did not think it proper for any one to follow his own free will without control. A censor could even punish a magistrate; he had power to expel a senator who led a vicious life, or to deprive a knight of his horse, and oblige him to go about on foot. In short, the Roman censors held themselves responsible for the public morals, and although they could not deprive a man of life or property as the courts of law could, they controlled his standing in society, and removed him either to a more honorable or less honorable tribe. They gave out contracts for all the public buildings besides, and saw that they were honestly filled.

So, when Cato stood as a candidate for this very high position, he met with much opposition, because some feared, others envied him. There were seven candidates besides, who promised to be very mild in their censorship, hoping thus to gain votes. Cato took a different course. He stood up in the rostrum and declared his determination, in case he should be elected, to punish every instance of vice, for he said that reform was greatly needed, and entreated the people not to choose the mildest, but the severest physician. "I am of that sort," he added, "and Valerius Flaccus is another; with him for my colleague, and him only, I could do good service to the country by putting an end to the growing luxury of the times."

The Romans showed themselves worthy of great leaders, for they chose the man who had promised to be a severe censor rather than those who would be likely to flatter them and overlook their faults. Cato and Flaccus were unanimously elected.

Cato's first action as censor was to expel many of the senators, and to place Valerius Flaccus at the head of that body. He next made an attack on luxuries, and ordered all things not absolutely necessary to comfort to be taxed so high that scarcely anybody could afford to indulge in them. This was all very well, but he made himself hateful to many by causing water-pipes to be cut, so that water might not be carried into private gardens and houses, and by having all buildings thrown down which jutted out into the public street. He lowered the price of public works so much that at last a party headed by Titus Flamininus complained of him to the senate, and had all the bargains and contracts he had made for the repairing and building of temples annulled, because the work at such prices could not be well done, and there was no advantage to the state in having bad jobs. They went further, and had him fined; but, in spite of some unpopular actions, the people must have been well pleased with their censor, for they erected a statue of him in the temple of the goddess of Health, and inscribed upon it, "In honor of Cato, the Censor, who by his wise discipline and good laws reclaimed the Roman commonwealth when it was sinking into vice."

In private life Cato was a good father and husband, and although he held so important a position in the state, the care of his family was never neglected. He chose his wife because she was well-born, for he said that women of good families were more ashamed of an unworthy action, and more likely to be obedient to their husbands, than those of mean birth. It was his opinion that a man who beat his wife or children laid sacrilegious hands on the most sacred objects in the world. A good husband he considered worthy of more praise than a great senator, and he admired Socrates, the renowned philosopher, for nothing so much as for having lived contentedly with a wife who was a scold, and children who were half-witted.

As soon as his son was old enough to study, Cato taught him himself. He had a slave named Chilo, who was an excellent teacher, but he did not choose that his son should undergo the humiliation of being punished by a slave if he happened to be backward in his studies. He taught the boy to wrestle, to throw a dart, to ride, to box, to endure heat and cold, and to swim the most rapid rivers. He also wrote histories of the ancient Romans for the boy's instruction, so that he was not obliged to stir from his father's house for knowledge. But he was not strong, and could not bear the severe discipline to which other young Romans were subjected; still he became an excellent soldier, and distinguished himself on the battlefield.

Cato had a peculiar method of managing his slaves, which he purchased among the captives taken in war. He always chose the youngest, because, like colts or puppies, they could be trained as he pleased. None of them were ever allowed to enter another man's house, unless sent on an errand by Cato or his wife. It was a rule with Cato that his slaves must either be busy or asleep, and he preferred those that slept much, because he thought they made better workmen if they had plenty of rest.

When he was a young soldier, he never found fault with the food that was placed upon his table, because he thought it undignified to quarrel with a servant on account of his stomach; but later in life, when he gave entertainments, he became exacting, and if any of the slaves waited carelessly or spoiled the food, he would beat them as soon as the meal was over. He managed to raise quarrels among his servants, because he feared some bad results if they were too united, probably an injury to himself or his family. If one of his slaves was guilty of a crime, he was accorded a formal trial, and then put to death in the presence of his fellow-servants.

Although Cato was very rich, he lost no opportunity to increase his wealth, even unjustly. He often said that the man who was truly godlike and fit to be registered in the lists of glory was he whose accounts at the end of his life should prove that he had more than doubled what he had received from his ancestors.

MARCUS CATO

Still, Cato was always an enemy to too much luxury, and constantly preached against it. Perhaps he was right in that, but he was certainly wrong when he thought it a disadvantage to become learned. The Greeks were far in advance of the Romans at that period in their studies, and when the two learned men, Carneades and Diogenes, arrived in Rome as ambassadors, and by their eloquence excited an interest in philosophy, Cato was alarmed lest the young men of his country should grow to prefer eloquence to fighting. He said very emphatically, "When the Romans come to study and understand Grecian literature, they will lose the empire of the world." But he was wrong, for Rome was never greater than when learning had reached a high pitch. She fell in consequence of irreligion and wickedness.

Cato's dislike of doctors was so great that he never employed one. Whenever any member of his family was ill, he prescribed herbs, with duck, pigeon, or hare. To be sure, he acknowledged that such diet made them dream, and that ought to have been proof enough that it was not proper, but Cato could not believe that anybody knew anything better than he did. Both his wife and son died under his medical treatment, but he himself happened to be strong, and so lived to a good old age in spite of his obstinacy.

His chief amusements were writing books and tilling the soil, and in a work on country affairs he gives, among other things, rules for making cake and preserving fruit; for it was his desire to appear acquainted even with such unimportant matters. To the very end of his life he kept himself busy with public affairs, and his last act in behalf of the state was the destruction of Carthage. It is true that he died before that end was reached, but it was he who urged on the war that led to the downfall of Hannibal, and on his death-bed he prophesied that Scipio was the person who would bring the third and last war against the Carthaginians to an end.

Scipio was at that time a very young man, and held only the office of tribune in the army, but Cato had witnessed extraordinary proofs of his conduct and courage, and his prophecy proved to be correct.

AEMILIUS PAULUS

THE Æmilian family was one of the oldest among the Roman nobility, and the subject of this chapter was descended from it. He lived at a time when Rome was full of celebrated men, and even among these Paulus was so conspicuous for bravery, honesty, and justice, that when he was nominated with thirteen others for the office of ædile he won it, though the remaining candidates were men of such merit that each, in course of time, became consul.

An ædile was an officer or magistrate who had care of the public buildings, games, and roads, and his position was one of great importance in Rome.

Later in life Æmilius Paulus was appointed augur, and then he showed how the worship of the gods might be called a science. The augurs were those priests who had so much power that they could encourage or put a stop to any public affair by interpreting the signs in nature or the flight of birds, favorably or otherwise, as they chose. While Paulus held this office he gave himself up to it entirely, studied all the ancient ceremonies, and never permitted even the most trifling of them to be altered or omitted. For he said that although the Deity might forgive neglect because He was merciful, yet it was dangerous for the state to do so, because those who were careless about trifles were sure to overlook important duties at one time or another.

He was likewise particular in observing the ancient Roman discipline in military affairs, even though by doing so he ran the risk of making himself unpopular with the soldiers; for he thought that it was impossible to beat an enemy unless the citizens were under strict control. It must be remembered that the Roman soldiers were at the same time citizens, who had votes in all the important civil and military affairs.

While the Romans were fighting Antiochus the Great, King of Syria, a war broke out in Spain, and Æmilius was sent there in command of the army. He went with all the dignity of a consul, though he was really only a prætor; but instead of having six axes carried before him as the other prætors did, he had twelve. He was very successful in Spain, and conquered two hundred and fifty cities there, but did not enrich himself at all by the war.

He had two wives. The first one was named Papiria, and became the mother of the renowned Scipio and of Fabius Maximus, who was consul five times. But the marriage was not a happy one, and resulted in divorce. Then Æmilius married again, and had two more sons.

When he was created consul, he was sent upon an expedition against the Ligurians, a warlike people, whose country was at the foot of the Alps. They had an army of forty thousand, and Æmilius had only eight thousand, but he routed them completely and shut them up within their walls. However, after destroying their fortifications, he returned their cities to them, set at liberty a number of prisoners, then carried off all their large ships and went back to Rome.

AEMILIUS PAULUS

He was anxious to be appointed consul a second time, but on being defeated at the election, gave it up and devoted himself to his duties as augur, and to the education of his children. He sent to Greece for professors, who instructed his boys in grammar, logic, rhetoric, modelling, and drawing, as well as in field sports and the management of dogs and horses. He was considered the most affectionate father in Rome, and was always present at the lessons and exercises of his children when not hindered by public affairs.

There came a time when the Romans were engaged in a war with the Macedonians. Perseus, who was then on the throne, was so well prepared that, although he was neither wise nor brave, he succeeded in defeating one consul after another, and the Romans began to wonder what could now be the matter with their army that had so long been the terror of more powerful commanders than the Macedonian king. At last, when they heard that he had engaged the Gauls and several other nations to join him, and was contemplating an invasion of Italy from the Adriatic shore, they thought it time to secure a general capable of managing so great an affair.

Paulus Æmilius was then sixty years of age, but he was in robust health, and the people turned to him in their need and called him to the consulship. At first he refused, for he no longer desired to hold office, but as he was daily urged to make his appearance at the Forum, he at last yielded, and placed himself among the candidates. He was unanimously elected, and put in command of the Macedonian war.

When he returned home he found his little daughter, Tertia, in tears, and asked her what was the matter. She put her arms around his neck, and, kissing him, said, "Oh, father, do you not know that Perseus is dead?" She meant a pet dog that had been brought up in the house with her. Æmilius replied, "That is a lucky incident, my child; I embrace the omen."

It was the custom among the Romans for those who were elected consuls to address the people from the rostrum and thank them for the honor. When Æmilius made his speech, he told them that he had applied for the first consulship because he wanted a command; but now they had applied to him because they wanted a commander; therefore he had nothing to thank them for. If they thought any other could manage the war better, he was willing to give up his charge; but if they confided in him, they were not to interfere with his orders, but were to supply him with the means of carrying on the war without question. For if they wanted to command their general, the expedition would be ridiculous. The Romans were much pleased with this address, and submitted, as they always did, to reason and virtue, in the hope that they might one day become masters of the world.

Paulus Æmilius set out at great speed, and soon reached the Roman camp. He did not fear Perseus, but he was struck with surprise and admiration when he beheld the strength of his army and the extent of his preparations. The Macedonian king had four thousand horse and nearly forty thousand foot soldiers, and he had chosen his position by the sea-side, at the base of Mount Olympus, with fences and barricades of wood on all sides. He felt very secure, and had no doubt that, with his immense wealth and great advantages, he could worry and tire out the consul.

Now, the habit Æmilius had formed of paying attention to details served him well, and led him to weigh every method of attack and to provide against surprises. When his soldiers showed impatience and presumed to give advice, he bade them not to meddle with what did not concern them, but to take care that they and their weapons were ready for use when their commander should see fit to employ them. He ordered the sentinels to stand guard unarmed, because he knew that if they had no means of defending themselves they would be watchful and not likely to fall asleep. He had wells dug along the foot of the mountain to provide plenty of fresh water for his men, and attended to many other such matters before he made his plans for battle.

Never were two great armies known to be so close together and yet to enjoy so much quiet. During the few days that Æmilius took for consideration he was informed that there was one passage that Perseus had left unguarded. It was a rough, difficult one, but a council was called to discuss whether or not to make an attempt through it. Among those present was Scipio, surnamed Nasica, son-in-law to Scipio Africanus. As soon as the expedition was decided on he was the first to propose himself for the command, and the second was Fabius Maximus, eldest son of Æmilius.

That very night they set out with about eight thousand soldiers, marched several hours, and encamped under the temple of Apollo, high up on Mount Olympus. During the march a deserter had made his way to Perseus and told him of the approach of Nasica. He was startled at the news, because, as Æmilius had remained quietly with his troops, there was no suspicion of any attack being made. Perseus immediately sent twelve thousand soldiers, under the command of Milo, to take possession of the unguarded pass. They met the Romans on the mountain, where a severe battle was fought. They were defeated, and those that were not killed threw away their armor, and, headed by Milo, fled shamefully back to camp.

This was a serious disappointment to Perseus, and he removed his troops in haste, but his friends encouraged him by telling him that his army was superior in numbers, and must be courageous, since they were fighting for the defence of their wives and children. Then Perseus pitched his camp again in a spot that offered every advantage for his army, and commanded that the Romans should be attacked as soon as they approached.

Meanwhile, Æmilius had rejoined Nasica, and advanced with his whole army. But when he beheld the enemy in all the magnificence of battle-array, his confidence was shaken, and he halted. The young commanders urged him on, particularly Nasica, who felt encouraged by his late victory. Æmilius turned to him with a smile, and said, "I would not hesitate were I of your age; but many victories have taught me the ways in which men are defeated, and forbid me to engage soldiers, weary with a long march, against an army drawn up and prepared for battle."

That night the moon, which was full, grew gradually dark, and became totally eclipsed. Æmilius had been prepared for this event by an astronomer in his army, and, as he had studied the cause of eclipses, he felt no superstitious terror with regard to them, and had informed his soldiers that there was to be one. But he was pious, and religiously observed sacrifices and the art of divination, so as soon as the moon shone out again, he offered up to her eleven heifers. When day dawned, he sacrificed twenty more to Hercules, without receiving a sign that his offering was accepted, but at the twenty-first there was a promise of victory for the Romans, and the captains were ordered to prepare for battle. The soldiers were so eager that Æmilius could scarcely restrain them, but he would not move until late in the afternoon, because he was too prudent to lead on his men with the sun shining full in their faces.

During the eclipse, the Macedonians were in a state of terror and amazement such as only the ignorant ever experience on account of the phenomena of nature. In their belief an eclipse portended some dire calamity, it was a sign of displeasure on the part of the gods, and by degrees a rumor spread to all parts of the camp that Perseus was on the brink of destruction, the eclipse having been sent as a warning.

Nevertheless, they presented a formidable appearance when the battle was about to begin. First marched the Thracians, men of enormous size, with bright, sparkling shields and great, heavy spears; then came the paid soldiers, differently armed. These were followed by a picked company of native Macedonians, brave, strong men in the prime of life, wearing scarlet coats and gilt armor. Last came the troops in phalanx called the Brazen Shields. The whole plain seemed alive with the flashing of weapons and armor, while the hills echoed the shouts of the soldiers as they cheered each other on. They marched boldly forward, and when the battle began, and Æmilius gazed upon the wall of Brazen Shields forming the phalanx, he was filled with dismay. He had never beheld such a sight before, and his heart misgave him. But he did not betray his real sensations as he rode through his army without breastplate or helmet.

It is not necessary to give the details of this conflict. It was fought within the space of one hour, and its fierceness was unparalleled. At one time Æmilus began to despair, and his men were on the point of running away, but, watching his chance, he divided up his forces and commanded them to make their way through the breaks in the enemy's ranks and fight them at many different points at once. In this way the phalanx was broken, and a hand-to-hand fight ensued. This resulted in a glorious victory for the Romans. The enemy were all cut to pieces; the plain and the lower part of the hills were covered with their corpses, and the river ran red with their blood. It is said that twenty-five thousand of their number fell.

On their return to camp that night the Romans were met by their servants with torches and led in triumph to their tents, which were brilliantly lighted and gayly decked with wreaths of ivy and laurel. When all were assembled, Scipio, the younger of the two sons who served under Æmilius, was missing. He was only seventeen years of age, but he had shown such wisdom for command and counsel, and such remarkable bravery in action, that he was universally admired. In spite of his victory, the general was overwhelmed with grief, and the soldiers were so afflicted at the sight that many of them left their suppers to seek the body of the youth among the slain. Soon the air was filled with the cries of men calling out for Scipio, for there was hope that he might not be dead. At last, late in the night, when everybody was beginning to despair of finding him dead or alive, he appeared with two or three of his companions, the fresh blood that covered them showing that they had pursued the enemy to the last.

For some unknown reason, Perseus had left the battle-field at the very beginning of the fight, and after it was over he fled with his cavalry, who had suffered no loss, to Pella. When the foot-soldiers joined them, they called them traitors and cowards, pulled them from their horses, and wounded

AEMILIUS PAULUS

several, so that the king, fearing for his own safety, turned into a by-road, took off his regal robes, and then led his horse, so that he might converse with his friends. But by degrees they all slunk away from him, one under pretence of tying his shoe, another of watering his horse, and a third of being thirsty himself. This was not so much because they feared the enemy as because they dreaded the cruelty of Perseus, who tried to lay the blame of his defeat on anybody but himself. On arriving at Pella he killed, with his own hand, two of his treasurers who presumed to give him advice, and after that everybody, excepting the Cretans, who hoped to get money from him, deserted him. These last were deceived, for he cheated them all, then sailed for Samothrace, and took refuge there in the temple of Castor and Pollux.

Then the Macedonians submitted to Æmilius, and in two days he was master of their whole country. He sent Cnæus Octavius with a fleet to Samothrace, not to seize Perseus, but to prevent his escape. Meanwhile, Perseus had made an arrangement with a Cretan, who owned a boat, to help him escape with his wife and children. An ancient proverb says, "The Cretans are always liars," and so it proved in this case, for the man who had promised to wait for the king and his family sailed away long before the appointed time. Then, in a fit of desperation, Perseus gave himself up to Octavius. When brought before Æmilius, the prisoner threw himself at his feet, embraced his knees, begged for mercy, and behaved in every way in a most abject, unmanly manner.

With an expression of mingled sorrow and indignation Æmilius looked at him, and said, "Wretched man, why do you take pains to prove that you deserve Fortune's frowns, and that you are now, and have long been, unworthy of the protection of that goddess? Why do you tarnish my laurels and make my conquests appear trifling by proving yourself a coward, unfit to be a Roman foe? Courage in the unfortunate is respected even by the enemy; but cowardice, though it meet with success, has ever been regarded with scorn by the Romans." He then gave Perseus his hand, raised him from the ground, and delivered him in charge of Tubero, his son-in-law.

Æmilius retired to his tent, where he remained for a long time in reflection; then, raising his head, he discoursed to the young men of his family and to others who were present on the uncertainty of human affairs, and drew a graphic picture of how, in one short hour, a great king had been humbled when at the very height of his power. He advised them not to be arrogant because of their victories, but to be humble and on the lookout for the misfortunes that the gods would surely send to counterbalance their present prosperity.

Having put his army into garrison for rest, Æmilius went on a visit of pleasure to Greece, and as he passed along he did much good by reforming governments and bestowing gifts. At Delphi he found a pillar of white marble, intended to support a gold statue of Perseus; he ordered his own to be placed there instead, saying that the conquered should make way for the conqueror.

He delivered up their country to the Macedonians, only demanding of them half the tribute they had been accustomed to pay their king. He would not even look at the piles of silver and gold in the palace of Perseus, but ordered them to be placed in the public treasury. The library he presented to his sons, who were men of letters, and to Tubero, his son-in-law, he gave a silver cup weighing five pounds, but that was all he took.

AEMILIUS PAULUS

Before leaving Greece, Æmilius told the Macedonians always to remember the liberty that the Romans had gained for them. But the Macedonians could not be grateful because their own laws were replaced by others, and their kingdom had been divided into four districts. They could see no advantage to themselves, particularly as in making these changes Æmilius had placed certain Roman senators to rule in Macedon. And they were not pleased with the law that forbade the people of different districts to marry or trade with one another. They were forced to submit, however, and, what was worse, all the nobility were commanded to remove immediately to Italy. Æmilius may have seen the wisdom of the laws he made for the Macedonians, but it is difficult to find how he could have excused himself for the horrible deed he committed at Epirus.

The senate had decreed that the soldiers who had fought under Æmilius against Perseus should have the spoils of the cities of Epirus. So Æmilius sent for ten of the principal residents of each city, and fixed a day for them to bring to him whatever silver or gold could be found in their temples and houses. With each of these he sent back a guard of soldiers to receive the valuables, as he said. But on the day appointed these soldiers rushed upon the people, seized and captured a hundred and fifty thousand of them, and destroyed seventy cities. In spite of all this ruin and destruction, the soldiers got so little for their share that they were very angry, and did not hesitate to let it be known when Æmilius sailed up the Tiber, in a galley taken from Perseus, all adorned with bright arms and gay colors.

They did not say in public that they were displeased because they had been cheated out of the riches they expected; they made another excuse for their complaints, and declared that they were because Æmilius had commanded in such a haughty, severe manner. Then Servius Galba, who had served under Æmilius as a tribune, and disliked him extremely, openly expressed his opinion that the general did not deserve a triumph, and that no honors ought to be shown him at all. He did more: he went around among the soldiers and told stories about Æmilius injurious as they were false. The tribunes then called an assembly and ordered Galba to repeat his charges against Æmilius, and when he had finished a vote was taken to decide whether the accused was worthy of a triumph or not. The first company of soldiers voted against it, but the commonalty and the senate showed their displeasure at such injustice, and the principal senators decided among themselves that something must be done to repress the boldness of soldiers who, if encouraged to deprive a worthy general of the honors of victory, would in time stop at no act of violence and wrong. Then they pushed through the crowd in a body, and ordered the tribunes to stop taking votes until they had spoken to the people.

It was Marcus Servilius, a prominent and highly-respected consul, who spoke as follows: "I am more than ever convinced of how great a general Paulus Æmilius must be, since he has performed such wonderful and honorable deeds with so mutinous and disorderly an army; but I am surprised at the Roman people, who, after rejoicing in triumphs over the Ligurians, will not allow themselves the pleasure of seeing the king of Macedon alive and led captive by the Roman arms. When a slight rumor of victory was brought to us a short time ago, you offered sacrifices and implored the gods to make it true; but now that the consul has returned with a real victory, you seem unwilling to behold the greatness of it. Perhaps you are afraid to rob the gods of their due honor, or wish to spare the feelings of Perseus; it would be much better to refuse the triumph out of mercy to the king than out of envy to your general. But you carry your malice so far that you permit a man who has never received a wound to discourse to you about the conduct of the war and the right to a triumph,—to you who, at the expense of so much blood, have learned to judge fairly of your commanders."

Baring his breast, he showed a mass of scars, and continued: "I glory in these marks before my fellow-citizens, for I got them in their service. Now go on, collect your votes, and I will mark those cowardly, ungrateful men who would rather have their fancies indulged than be properly commanded." This speech had such an effect that every soldier voted for Æmilius to have the triumph. We will give an account of how it was celebrated, because the word triumph gives no idea of the wonderful display.

Scaffolds were erected in the Forum and in all the public race-tracks, or circuses, as they were called, and these were occupied by spectators in white garments. The temples were open and filled with garlands and perfumes. Numerous officers kept the way clear for the procession, which on the first day consisted of the statues, pictures, and large images that had been taken from the enemy, drawn upon one hundred and fifty chariots. The triumph on this occasion lasted three days, because the spoils were so numerous.

On the second day a train of wagons brought the richest and most beautiful of the Macedonian arms, that shone and glittered in the sunlight. They looked as though they had been thrown together pell-mell, but they had really been placed with great judgment and care, to display the highly-polished shields, breast-plates, and targets to the best advantage. Arrows, horses' bits, points of naked swords, and long pikes stuck out on all sides, and made a terrible clatter as they moved along. Then came three thousand men carrying silver coins in seven hundred and fifty vessels, each containing three talents, or about three thousand dollars of our money. Others followed with valuable and beautifully-wrought bowls, horns, goblets, and cups.

On the third day the trumpets were sounded, just as they always were by the Romans at the beginning of a battle. A hundred and twenty fat oxen, with their horns gilded and adorned with garlands and bright ribbons, followed the trumpeters. Each ox was led by a young man, who wore a belt of curious workmanship, and behind them came boys with the gold and silver vessels for the sacrifice. Persons carrying the gold coin, in vessels that held three talents each, came next, and then followed the consecrated bowl, weighing ten talents, which Æmilius had caused to be made of gold and adorned with precious stones. This bowl was consecrated to Jupiter. It preceded the chariot of Perseus, in which were his armor and his crown. At a little distance his children were led captive, attended by a great number of governors and masters. The children, two sons and a daughter, were so young that they did not realize the misfortune that had overtaken them, but they were not the less to be pitied, and many Romans wept as they passed along. The captive king, clad in black, and wearing sandals according to the fashion of his country, walked alone. His appearance was that of a man whose reason was upset. He had sent to ask Æmilius to allow him to remain out of the triumph, and not make a public exhibition of him. His answer was, that it was in his own power to avoid the disgrace. Æmilius, who had a contempt

AEMILIUS PAULUS

for the cowardice of the king, meant that by putting an end to his life he could spare himself the pain of appearing as part of his own spoils. But he had not the courage to strike the blow.

Perseus was followed by a number of friends, all bowed down with sorrow, and after these were carried four hundred coronets of gold, which had been sent as a compliment to Æmilius by the cities he had rescued. Next came the victorious consul himself, riding in a magnificent chariot, wearing a purple robe woven with gold, and carrying in his right hand a branch of laurel. His army followed, chanting odes of victory and the glorious exploits of Æmilius, whom all admired but few envied. For, amidst all the honors that were showered on him, his heart was very heavy. Five days before the triumph, one of his younger sons, a bright lad of fourteen, had died, and three days after, the one aged twelve had followed his brother to the grave.

Æmilius bore the double blow with courage, and proved himself a hero in resisting the shocks of ill fortune as he had the spears of the enemy. He pitied the condition of Perseus, and had him made as comfortable in prison as possible, but the poor captive starved himself to death.

Æmilius, by his conquest of Macedonia, brought so much money to the treasury that it was many years before the Romans had any taxes to pay, and this of course they considered a great benefit. So popular was Æmilius, not only with the nobility but also with the people, that he was appointed censor, a position that gave him power to expel a senator, replace him by another when duly elected, and to disgrace such young men as led dissipated lives by depriving them of their horses. The censors valued estates also, and registered the number of the citizens; they had other duties, which are recorded in the life of Cato.

After a time the health of Æmilius failed, and his doctor sent him to Velia, in the southern part of Italy. He was very much missed by the Romans, who at last desired his presence for a solemn sacrifice. He returned, performed the ceremony, and then went home to dinner. It was soon found that his health had not improved as people hoped it had, for he became delirious shortly after he had eaten, and three days later he died. Not only his fellow-citizens, but also the Spaniards, Ligurians, and Macedonians who happened to be in Rome, assembled at the funeral to pay the last honors to this brave and generous hero, and there could have been no better proof of the justice which had marked his behavior towards all mankind without distinction.

TIBERIUS GRACCHUS

THE first Tiberius Gracchus was a very good man, who held, at different periods, the highest offices in Rome. After the death of Scipio, who conquered Hannibal, he married his daughter, Cornelia, and had twelve children. Then he died, and to Cornelia was left the bringing up and education of the family. She performed her task with such care and proved herself such an excellent mother in every respect, that her children were renowned for their ability and their virtues. But Cornelia lived to bury all except one daughter, who married Scipio the Younger, and two sons, named Tiberius and Caius, of whose lives we will now give an account.

These brothers loved each other dearly and resembled each other in some respects, but Tiberius, who was the older by nine years, was mild and gentle, while Caius was rough and passionate. Tiberius lived plainly and simply, while Caius was fond of rare dishes and fashionable attire. Both were public speakers, but Tiberius was quiet in his style and scarcely moved from one spot when speaking, while Caius had a habit of walking about and, when he became excited, of pulling his gown from his shoulders and making violent gestures. Besides, he would bawl so loudly that his voice sometimes lost its tone, and so spoiled his speech. To remedy this, he had a servant stand near him always with a sort of instrument called a pitch-pipe, used for regulating sound. Whenever his master's voice broke he would strike a soft note on this pipe, whereupon Caius would immediately check himself.

But to return to Tiberius. When he grew to manhood he was admitted into the college of augurs, and his first experience as a soldier was in Africa under the younger Scipio, who had married his sister. He shared the general's tent and imitated his brave actions, being the first at one of the sieges to mount the enemy's walls. He was much loved in the army, and his departure from it when he was called back to Rome caused considerable regret.

After that expedition he was appointed quæstor, or public treasurer, and went with the consul Caius Mancinus to the Numantian war. Mancinus did not lack courage and ability, but he was one of the most unfortunate generals Rome ever had, and, after losing several important battles, tried to decamp in the night. The Numantians found it out, seized the camp, killed many of the run-aways, and surrounded the whole Roman army so that they could not escape. Then Mancinus sued for peace, but the enemy declared that they would treat with nobody but Tiberius, who had a splendid character in the army, and whose father during the war in Spain had behaved honorably towards the Numantians. So Tiberius was sent, and by the peace he made saved the lives of twenty thousand Roman citizens, besides slaves and others of the army.

The Numantians then helped themselves to whatever was left in the Roman camp, even the quæstor's books and papers. This was unfortunate, for Tiberius could not return to Rome without his accounts, so he left the army, which was under march, and went back to Numantia with a few friends. He sent a messenger in to ask the magistrates for his books,

TIBERIUS GRACCHUS

whereupon he was cordially invited to enter the city. He was afraid to do so, but the magistrates went to him and, taking him by the hand, begged him no longer to look upon them as enemies. Then, not wishing to appear to distrust them, he went into Numantia, where a little feast was soon spread, of which he was requested to partake. Afterwards his books were brought to him, and he was asked to choose something from the spoils; but he accepted only some frankincense to be used in the public sacrifices, which he took to Rome.

There he found a great deal of dissatisfaction on account of the peace, which was not considered worthy of Romans, but the soldiers flocked to welcome him, for they loved him very much. Indeed, so great was his popularity with all classes that for his sake it was decreed that the consul only should be delivered up to the Numantians in chains, but that all the other officers should be spared.

Perhaps Scipio had something to do with this decree, for his influence was great, and he was fond of his brother-in-law. Now Tiberius had formed a plan for helping the poor of Rome, by which he hoped to cover his name with glory, but, unfortunately, it proved the ruin of his family. It was to divide all the land equally that Rome had gained by conquest. The rich people had managed, by fair and unfair means, to get possession of it, but Tiberius now proposed to divide it among the citizens without distinction.

Among the men whom he consulted before drawing up his law were Crassus, the high-priest, Scævola, an able lawyer, and Claudius Appius, whose daughter was his wife. These men, who were known for their virtues and intellect, approved of Tiberius's scheme, but the rich Romans did not relish the idea of sharing their estates with others, so they went among the people and told them that Tiberius was trying to overthrow the government and create a general confusion. They were wrong, for there never were milder laws proposed, there being no punishment of any sort decreed for those who had been guilty of unlawful deeds. And so the majority of the people thought, particularly when Tiberius mounted the rostrum and pleaded for the poor as follows: "The wild beasts of Italy have their caves to protect them, but the brave men who spill their blood in her cause have nothing left but air and light. They have no houses, no settled homes, but wander about with their wives and children from place to place, and their generals make fun of them when they urge them to fight for their sepulchres and domestic gods; for among a whole army there is not perhaps one Roman who has an altar that belonged to his ancestors, or a sepulchre in which their ashes rest. The private soldiers fight and die that the rich may become richer, and the Romans, who own not a foot of ground, are called masters of the world."

Speeches delivered by so prominent a man as Tiberius had such weight that nobody dared to oppose him in words; but still they did not give up. They knew that when the law came to be voted upon they could manage to defeat it if they could control only one tribune, for by the laws of Rome every tribune had to vote for a measure, one negative being enough to defeat it.

So they applied to Marcus Octavius. He was then tribune, and an intimate acquaintance of Tiberius. At first he refused to oppose him, but after much persuasion consented. Then there were daily discussions in public between Tiberius and Octavius, but they did not lead to a settlement. At last Tiberius forbade the magistrates to perform their various duties until the law was passed, and, besides, he put his seal upon the doors of the temple of Saturn, where the public money was kept, so that the quæstors could neither put anything into the treasury nor take anything out. He also threatened to fine the prætors if they disobeyed his orders; so government affairs were brought to a stand-still, and there was besides a conspiracy to assassinate Tiberius. Therefore whenever he went out he carried a sword-staff, called in Latin a dolo, and used by robbers in those times.

When election-day came, the rich men seized the voting-urns and carried them away by force. The confusion was very great, and Tiberius and his party resolved to fight for their cause. Manlius and Fulvius, two of the consuls, begged them not to do so, whereupon Tiberius, who felt great respect for them, asked what they advised him to do. "We cannot give advice in so important a matter," they replied, "but leave it to the senate." Tiberius consented; but when the senate met there was Octavius with his negative vote, and no result could be reached. Then Tiberius made this proposition: that Octavius should be deprived of his tribuneship; before all the people he took the young man by the hand and begged him to resign. Octavius refused. "Then we will leave it to the people," exclaimed Tiberius. "It is clear that there cannot be two tribunes so opposite in their ideas as Octavius and myself; one of us must resign: we will leave it to you to decide which it shall be." The assembly then adjourned until the next day.

When the votes were taken, a large majority decided in favor of Tiberius, who thereupon ordered his own servants to drag Octavius out of his chair. The whole proceeding was illegal, but the law was passed, and three commissioners were appointed to survey the land and see it equally divided. These were Tiberius himself, Claudius Appius, his father-in-law, and Caius Gracchus, his brother, who was at that time with the army before Numantia.

This was managed without disturbance; but the rich Romans feared that Tiberius was becoming too powerful, and took every opportunity to insult him. The populace of course defended him; and in order to keep their sympathies alive, Tiberius dressed himself in mourning and brought his wife and children into the crowd, asking that they might be provided for, because he did not feel that his life was safe.

About this time Attalus, King of Pergamus, died and left a will making the Roman people his heirs. Thereupon Tiberius proposed a law providing that all the ready money the king had left should be distributed among the citizens, to enable them to buy tools for the cultivation of their new lands. As to the cities in the territories of Attalus, they should be disposed of, not by the senate, but as the people should decide.

This brought matters to a worse state than before, and three or four of the senators made charges against Tiberius. The most important of these was that he had unlawfully deprived a tribune of his office. The others Tiberius could answer, but he was totally at a loss to find excuses for the last, so he dismissed the assembly.

He now began to see that not only the nobility but the people were offended at his having insulted the dignity of the tribunes, which until then had been sacred and honorable; so he tried to justify himself, after taking a day to prepare his speech, which was forcible and persuasive. Nevertheless it was clear that the popularity upon which he counted was gradually but surely diminishing. He therefore tried to have himself re-elected to the office of tribune, and sought in every way to increase the good will of the populace for himself. He proposed certain laws which favored them rather than the nobility, but when the day came for taking the vote, the opposite party were so much stronger than his—for all the people did not attend—that he spun out the time in discussions with the other tribunes, and then adjourned the assembly without arriving at a conclusion until the following day.

Meanwhile he appeared in the Forum, looking distressed, and with tears in his eyes told the citizens, "I fear that my enemies will destroy my house and take my life before morning." This had such an effect that several people pitched tents around his house and kept guard all night. At daybreak a soothsayer tried to drive the chickens out of their coop, and offered them food; but, as they would partake of none, it was pronounced a bad omen, and Tiberius was afraid to go to the Capitol. However, some of his friends called for him and assured him that everything seemed satisfactory; so he went, and was received with loud shouts of applause and welcome.

After he had seated himself he ordered the vote to be taken, but there was such a confusion caused by those of the two parties who were on the outside of the crowd trying to push their way in that nothing could be done. Flavius Flaccus, one of the senators, endeavored to make himself heard, but the noise was so great that he could not do so. However, he motioned to Tiberius that he had something to say to him in private, and an order was given that he should be allowed to pass through the crowd. He did so with difficulty, and told Tiberius that the rich men had formed a plan to have him assassinated.

Thereupon Tiberius, his friends, and servants tucked up their gowns, armed themselves with the staves which the officers used to keep off the crowd, and stood ready for defence. Those at a distance wondered what could be the matter, and, knowing that he could not make himself heard so far, Tiberius pointed to his head, meaning to show them that it was in danger; but they misunderstood him, and ran to the senate-house to say that Tiberius had asked them to put a crown on his head. Of course this was done by his enemies, but it created no little consternation, and the consul was called upon to punish the tyrant, as they now named him. The consul replied that he would not be the first to do violence, nor would he put to death any freeman who had not first had a fair trial; at the same time he added that if Tiberius should either force or persuade the people to any step that was not lawful, he would take care to stop it. One of the senators, at least, was not satisfied with the mildness of the consul; his name was Nasica. He started up and exclaimed, "Since the consul gives up his country, let all who choose to support the laws follow me." So saying, he threw the skirt of his gown over his head and hastened to the Capitol, followed by a great number of people. As they were for the most part well-known citizens, nobody ventured to stop them. They were armed only with staves, clubs, and pieces of broken furniture, but with these they fought their way through the crowd in the Capitol towards Tiberius. As some were knocked down and many were killed, others fled, and Tiberius followed their example. One of his enemies seized his gown, but he slipped out of it and ran with only his under garment. He might have escaped if he had been more sure-footed, but, unfortunately, he stumbled and fell flat upon the ground, whereupon a tribune, one of his colleagues, struck him a violent blow on the head with the foot of a stool. Other blows followed, and

TIBERIUS GRACCHUS

the fight continued until Tiberius and three hundred others lay dead.

The cruel and unnatural treatment of Tiberius's body proves that the trouble was all caused by the hatred of the nobility towards him personally. His brother begged to be allowed to bury him in the night, but, instead of that, his body was thrown into the river with hundreds of others.

The people of Rome were so angry at what had happened to their friend, as Tiberius had proved himself, that the senate dared no longer object to the division of the land. So Publius Crassus was chosen in place of Tiberius to see that this was properly done. Nasica, who had led on the attack against Tiberius, was so abused every time he appeared in public that he had to be sent out of the country for safety.

CAIUS GRACCHUS

CAIUS GRACCHUS was only twenty-one years old when his brother was so cruelly and unjustly slain. It was many years after that dreadful event before he took part in public affairs; it is true that he had been appointed one of the commissioners for the division of land, but he did not attend to it. Many thought it was because he disapproved of his brother's actions, but probably the true reason is that he feared his enemies, and knew his family to be less powerful than before. Be that as it may, Caius lived in retirement, and devoted much of his time to the study of public speaking, so that when he undertook to defend one of his friends against a certain charge, he did it so well that people pronounced him the very best orator in Rome.

He was elected quæstor, or public treasurer, to accompany Orestes, the consul, to Sardinia, and he was very glad to go, for he did not desire to become a politician, and would not have done so if he had not been forced into it. He was influenced, too, by a dream, for like most people of his time he was superstitious enough to believe in dreams. His was that Tiberius appeared to him, and said, "Why do you tarry, Caius? There is no escape; you are destined, as I was, to spend your life and meet your death in the service of the people."

CAIUS GRACCHUS

That winter in Sardinia was a very severe and sickly one, and Caius worked so hard for the comfort of the army, and was so successful in getting what they needed from neighboring places, that the senators in Rome began to feel jealous when they heard of his actions. "He will be even a more popular leader than his brother was," they said, and decided to prevent that if possible. So when some of the private soldiers were ordered home, Caius was requested to remain at his post. But he knew the reason for this, and became very angry. He caused much surprise by making his appearance in Rome when he was least expected, for people thought it strange for a quæstor to desert his general. He was therefore called before the senate to give an account of himself, and did it so satisfactorily that they regarded him as a much injured person.

"I have served in twelve campaigns," he said, "whereas I was not obliged to serve in more than ten; I have been with the general as quæstor three years, though the law required me to stay but one year; besides, I am the only man who went out with a full purse and returned with an empty one."

Afterwards other charges were brought against Caius; but he proved himself entirely innocent, and then asked for the tribuneship. All the noblemen opposed it, but people from all parts of Italy flocked to Rome in such numbers on purpose to vote for Caius that it was impossible to find lodgings for them. The nobility succeeded in having him elected fourth tribune instead of the first, but he soon proved by his wonderful eloquence that, in spite of them, nobody could be first but himself. He spoke with such force, and aroused the people to such a pitch of excitement by constantly referring to his brother and the dreadful fate he had met, that he always carried his audience with him.

His popularity was wonderfully increased, too, by the various laws he made, for all favored the people and increased their power in the government, while they lessened that of the senate. He further showed his respect for the populace by doing what no other public speaker had ever done: instead of turning his face towards the senate-house when making an address, which had always been the custom, he turned towards the people and spoke to them, which of course flattered and pleased them.

One of the laws Caius proposed was that three hundred Roman knights should be added to the senate, making six hundred in all; and as soon as it was passed he was appointed to choose the knights. The people liked this, because it gave them equal power with the senators, and that was what Caius always tried to do. His advice was asked whenever there was any public matter of interest to settle, and in every case he showed such honesty and good judgment that everybody was pleased, and foreigners felt themselves justly dealt with by the Romans. Not only did Caius plan new laws and make speeches, but he worked in other directions. It was he who proposed ways for colonizing cities, making roads, and building granaries, and after they were adopted he superintended the work, and people wondered at the number of things he undertook and accomplished. He was constantly to be seen with soldiers, scholars, builders, and mechanics of all sorts, and he showed himself master of the art of talking with them as well as when making a public address. He laid out beautiful, level roads, and was the first to place milestones to mark distances, and others to enable travellers to mount their horses without the aid of a groom. These things made him more and more of a favorite; for all classes of citizens felt the benefit of his undertakings.

CAIUS GRACCHUS

Once he closed an oration by announcing that he had a request to make which he hoped would not be refused. He did not tell what it was, but it was the general belief that he was going to ask for the consulship. However, when election-day came around he brought forward a friend named Fannius for that office. Fannius would not have been elected had it not been for the influence of Caius; but he asked it as a favor, and the people of Rome could refuse him nothing. He made no demand for himself, but with one voice he was chosen tribune the second time.

This displeased the senate, who were jealous of Caius's popularity, and in constant dread lest it might give him even more power than they had. So they resorted to a most undignified proceeding: first they took Livius Drusus, a fellow-tribune with Caius Gracchus, into their confidence, and with his aid resolved to outdo Caius in benefits to the public, even though they were dishonorable in so doing. If he proposed to form two colonies anywhere, they pretended to consider it a disadvantage to the citizens, but established a dozen in other places, and selected a large number of the most needy people for that purpose. If he proposed a law, they refused to pass it, but immediately made others that would appear to favor the poor citizens, whether they really did or not. In short, they showed plainly that their aim was to ruin Caius if possible, or, if not, at least to injure his reputation. Livius always took pains to make it known that whatever he did was by the advice and approval of the senate, whose chief desire it was to please the populace. Thus a better feeling arose towards the senate, who had formerly been looked upon by the plebeians as their enemy.

This would have been all right if their object had been good, but it was only to bring about the downfall of Caius that they sought. As this was not accomplished soon enough to satisfy the senate, they decided to send the obnoxious tribune out of the country, and an opportunity soon offered itself, when a proposition was made to repeople Carthage, which had been destroyed by Scipio; Caius was forthwith despatched to Africa to see to it. While he was gone, Livius Drusus lost no opportunity of seeking to make himself a favorite with the lower classes, flattering and gratifying them in a way that often seemed ridiculous even to them. He also brought charges of dishonesty in the division of the lands against Fulvius, who was a particular friend to Caius.

Caius completed his work at Carthage in seventy days, and then hurried back to Rome, where he had heard his presence was needed. He found that the people, after having been flattered by the senate and the tribunes, thought less of him than formerly, so he at once gave up his fine house on the Palatine Mount and went to live near the market-place, among the poorest and humblest of the citizens. Then he brought forward such popular laws that the neighbors flocked from all quarters to vote for them. But the senate persuaded Fannius, the consul, to command all who were not born Romans to leave the city at once. This was a most unusual proceeding, but Caius could not prevent it. However, he was very angry, and gave vent to his temper a short time after, which led to a quarrel between him and the other officers. There was to be a show of gladiators in the market-place, and the magistrates erected scaffolds, which they intended to let. Caius commanded them to remove the scaffolds so that the poor people might see the exhibition without being obliged to pay for it. Nobody obeyed his orders: so, the very night before the contest was to take place, he collected together a body of laborers, and worked with them to remove all the scaffolds. The common people were delighted when they saw the market-place cleared; but the officers were so angry that they resolved to be revenged.

Therefore, although at the next election Caius had votes enough to make him tribune the third time, his colleagues caused false returns to be brought in, and he was put out of office. This was a serious disappointment to him, which he took no pains to conceal. His adversaries were delighted at his defeat, and Opimius, who was chosen consul, immediately set to work to cancel several of his laws. This was annoying; but when the consul went a step further and began to question Caius's proceedings in Carthage, he put himself at the head of a party to oppose Opimius. It is said that Cornelia, his mother, helped him in this by sending several strangers disguised as harvesters into Rome to increase his party; but this is not certain.

A day was appointed when the laws of Caius were to be annulled, and for that purpose his party and the other met early in the morning at the Capitol. But, before business began, a private citizen, who was engaged with the consul in offering sacrifices, was murdered by the friends of Fulvius and Gracchus, who had taken offence at something he had said. Great excitement ensued, and the assembly broke up in alarm. Gracchus himself was terrified at the outrage, and tried to explain that he had no hand in it, but nobody would listen to him, and, finding that he could do nothing, he shut himself up in his own house, and so kept out of sight.

Early the next morning Opimius assembled the senate, and with the hope of still further exciting public feeling against the deed committed by the Gracchus party, had the body of the dead man exposed to view. But it did not have the desired effect, for the populace remembered how the senate themselves had murdered Tiberius and then thrown his body into the river, and they did not see why so much honor should be paid to a common citizen; besides, they still looked upon Caius as their defender and safeguard.

Opimius made a speech to the senate and explained the state of affairs, whereupon he was invested with power to protect the commonwealth and suppress all tyrants. He then ordered the senators and knights to arm themselves and to assemble the next day, each attended by two well-armed servants.

Fulvius and Caius made preparations on their side, collected the populace about them, and took possession of the Aventine Hill. But Caius had the good of his country so much at heart that he shed tears when he thought of the criminal action into which he had been drawn. He could not be persuaded to arm himself, but left his house in his usual dress, carrying only a short dagger at his side.

When the people were all gathered together on the Aventine Hill, Caius advised Fulvius to send his son to propose a settlement with the consul and the senate. He was a handsome youth, and made his modest speech with tears in his eyes. The senate were inclined to favor his proposition, but the consul said, "It does not become Fulvius and Gracchus to offer terms to the senate: they should, like loyal citizens, surrender at discretion to the laws and sue for pardon." The youth was sent a second time, but Opimius, who was determined to fight, had him locked up, and then with a company of soldiers started off to make the attack.

Before many minutes the fight was over, for the people could not hold out against experienced soldiers. Fulvius fled to a bathing-house near by, but he was discovered, dragged out, and put to death. Caius sought refuge in Diana's temple, where he would have killed himself had it not been for two faithful friends, who snatched away his sword and urged him to escape. He did so, and as he ran along, people shouted words of encouragement as they do to racers, but no one offered him assistance, nor would they furnish him with a horse, though he asked for one several times. He was accompanied by one servant named Philocrates, who loved him too much to desert him. Finding at last that his enemies were gaining upon him, Caius gave up the race and went into a little grove consecrated to the Furies. There, in obedience to his command, he was slain by his servant, who afterwards killed himself and fell upon his master's body.

A price of its weight in gold had been set upon Caius's head, so it was cut off and presented to Opimius on the end of a spear. It was found to weigh seventeen pounds, but this was owing to a cheat, for the person who secured it had filled it with lead. The bodies of Caius, Fulvius, and three thousand other rebels were thrown into the river, their goods were seized by the state, and their widows were forbidden to put on mourning. The son of Fulvius, who, it will be remembered, had gone to the senate with the articles of agreement, was brutally slain, although he had taken no part in the battle.

Caius and Tiberius Gracchus met with the same fate, yet there was less excuse for the conduct of the former than of the latter, for he was more of a popular leader and less of a patriot than Tiberius. His was the punishment of a rebel, while the death of Tiberius was a cruel, unjust murder. Tiberius headed his party out of principle, Caius because he wanted power.

So deeply did the commons regret the Gracchi that they erected statues to them in the most public parts of the city, consecrated the places where they were killed, and offered sacrifices to them at different seasons.

Cornelia bore her misfortunes with noble fortitude. Of the places which were consecrated to her dead sons she said, "They are monuments worthy of them." She went to live at Misenum, where she had many friends, to whom her house was always open for hospitality. Men of letters visited her constantly, and the various kings who were friendly to Rome showed their regard by sending her presents. She often spoke of her sons, and fondly recounted their actions and sufferings as though she were giving a narrative of some ancient heroes. She had always been proud of them, as this anecdote goes to prove: Once when they were little boys a noble lady called on Cornelia and showed her some costly jewels, asking to see hers in return. She left the room, and presently came back with Tiberius and Caius on either side of her, saying, "These are my ornaments."

After her death the Romans erected a statue to her, on which was this inscription—

"Cornelia, the Mother of the Gracchi."

CAIUS MARIUS

CAIUS MARIUS was born of poor but worthy parents, who earned their living by daily labor. They spent their days in an obscure country town, where their son was brought up in a quiet, humble manner.

Nevertheless his nature was warlike, and all through his early years nothing interested him so much as the exploits of warriors, whom he longed to imitate. He first served in the army when Scipio Africanus besieged Numantia, and fought so bravely that he was honored with an invitation to dine at the general's table.

In course of conversation one evening Scipio was asked, "Where shall we Romans find another brave general when you are gone?" "Here, perhaps," replied Scipio, placing his hand on the shoulder of Marius, who sat next to him. The young man was so flattered that he decided then and there upon a political life, and it was not very long before he obtained the office of tribune of the people.

His first act after his election was to propose a change in the system of voting, which lessened the authority of the Patricians. This made him popular with the Plebeians; but when, on the other hand, he opposed certain laws regarding the distribution of corn that favored the people, he lost their good will, but gained favor with the Patricians. So he was honored by both parties as a man who worked only for the public good, and not for the interest of any particular party.

When his tribuneship came to an end, Marius stood candidate for the office of chief ædile; that is, the one called curules, on account of the chair with crooked feet in which those officers sat while attending to business. The other was inferior, and was known as the plebeian ædile. Marius did not get the higher office, but he lost no time in applying for the lower one; failing to get that also, he waited a short time and stood for the prætorship. Then his perseverance was crowned with success, though it was said that he managed it by bribery. However, he was tried and acquitted, so probably the accusation was false.

While he was prætor he did nothing to distinguish himself, but when his term of office expired he was sent to Spain in command of an army, and did excellent service there in clearing the country of robbers. At that period the Spaniards were so uncivilized that robbery was not considered dishonorable, and so their country was filled with brigands, until Marius drove them out. On his return to Rome he was anxious to take part in the government, but he had neither wealth nor eloquence to recommend him. However, he increased his popularity among the common people by his industry, high spirit, and plain manner of living to such a degree that he gained offices which gave him power. Thus he was enabled to make a very lofty marriage with no less a person than Julia, a member of the illustrious Cæsar family. She was aunt to the celebrated Julius Cæsar, whose story is told in a later chapter.

Marius showed much fortitude in enduring pain when undergoing a surgical operation. Both his legs were covered with tumors, and he determined to have them cut out; so,

CAIUS MARIUS

refusing to be bound, he held out one limb and submitted to the painful operation without flinching; but when the surgeon was about to begin on the other he refused, saying, "I see the cure is not worth the pain."

When Metellus was made general in the war against Jugurtha, in Africa, he chose Marius for his lieutenant. That was a most difficult war, and gave Marius opportunities not only to distinguish himself by deeds of bravery, but to win the love of the soldiers by sharing their labors, their privations, and their dangers. Before long both Africa and Rome were sounding his praises, and many of the soldiers went so far as to write home that the war would never be brought to a close until Caius Marius was chosen consul. It is needless to say that Metellus became jealous of a man who was in such high favor, and when Marius announced that he was going home to stand for consul, the general said, "You ought to be content to wait for the consulship until this son of mine gets it too." But Marius thought otherwise, particularly as the son of Metellus was then but a boy, and went to Rome in time for the election.

He was received with open arms, and when he told the people that if he were made consul he would promise either to kill Jugurtha or to take him alive, they all voted for him. But he made himself disagreeable to the Patricians by enlisting in his army slaves and poor people, which Roman generals had never done, and by boasting of his own powers and speaking with contempt of the nobles. This pleased the populace, who considered him a very bold, high-spirited man, and encouraged him in his abuse of people who had won fame in the state, and excited their envy in consequence.

Now, when Marius went back to Africa it made Metellus angry to think that after he had almost brought the war to an end, and nothing remained but to take the person of Jugurtha, another should come to deprive him of that glory; so he retired, and left one of his officers to deliver up the Roman forces to Marius. It was not Marius, however, but Lucius Sylla who had the honor of receiving Jugurtha, an account of which is given in the life of Sylla. Marius could bear no rival in glory, and when his enemies declared that it was Metellus who began and carried on the war, and Sylla who gave it the finishing stroke, they sowed the first seeds of a violent quarrel which almost ruined the Roman empire.

The public attention was soon attracted towards another channel, however, for an army of more than three hundred thousand warriors, with their wives and children, came like a devouring flame from the shores of the North Sea, treading down, and driving before them like a drove of wild beasts, all that came in their way. Many generals and armies employed by the Romans to guard the northern part of Italy were shamefully routed, and this encouraged the advancing barbarians to push on towards Rome and possess themselves of the whole of Italy.

The reports that came to Rome from all sides were so alarming that Marius was ordered home to undertake the war. Though the law did not permit an absent man, or one that had not waited a given time after his first consulship, to be re-elected, the people would have no one but Marius; he was accordingly made consul a second time.

On his return, Marius was honored with a triumphal procession, in which Jugurtha in chains was led before the car of the conqueror. So great was the agony of the African captive that he lost his senses, and when, after the triumph, his ornaments and robes were dragged off of him and he was cast into a dark, damp dungeon, where he was starved to death, he exclaimed, with an idiotic smile, "O Hercules! how cold is this bath of yours!"

While marching, Marius trained his men to hardships by accustoming them to long, tiresome tramps, compelling every man to carry his own baggage and provide his victuals: so that afterwards "Marius's Mules" was a term applied to all hard workers who were patient and ready. Marius was fortunate in this: for some unknown reason the enemy changed their course and went first to Spain, which gave him ample time to exercise his soldiers, and to prove to them what he himself was. By his fierce manners when commanding, his stentorian voice and stern expression, they learned to obey, and their confidence in him increased to such an extent that they believed him to be the general of all others to inspire terror in the enemy. But what they put most faith in was his sense of justice, of which he gave several remarkable proofs. So well pleased were the Roman people with Marius that they elected him consul a third time, and as the year closed before the expected enemy came on, he was again re-elected, and Lutatius Catulus, a man highly esteemed both by nobles and commons, became his colleague.

Shortly after, the approach of the enemy was announced, and Marius passed the Alps and pitched his camp by the river Rhone. He took good care to station his army where they could be amply supplied with food and water, but remained perfectly quiet as long as possible. His reason was this: The enemy's soldiers were fierce-looking men, whose arms and mode of fighting were different from any the Romans had ever seen, and, like a prudent general, he wanted his men to become familiar with them, in order that they might not be awed merely because of their strangeness. When complaints of inaction reached his ears, Marius always replied that he was guided as to the time and place for fighting entirely by the oracles. And, in fact, he used to carry about in a litter a Syrian woman, named Martha, supposed to be a prophetess, who directed him with regard to sacrifices. This woman had given so many proofs of her skill that Marius's wife had sent her to be with the army, thinking that her prophecies would be of service. Whenever she went to sacrifice, Martha wore a purple robe, and carried in her hand a little spear trimmed with ribbons and garlands. Some people doubted whether Marius really believed Martha to be a prophetess, or only pretended to do so, in order to impress his soldiers, but she was certainly regarded with veneration by the entire army.

When the enemy ventured to attack Marius, they were received with a shower of darts and lost several of their men. Then they determined to march forward to the other side of the Alps, and so enormous was their number that they were six whole days in passing by the Roman fortifications. Whenever they were close enough to be heard, they would tauntingly ask whether Marius's men had any messages to send to Rome, because they expected to be there in a few days. As soon as they had passed, Marius began to follow, always encamping at some distance, and choosing safe, strong positions. The first serious battle took place at Sextilius's Waters, and after many hours of hard fighting the Romans gained a splendid victory. They killed or took prisoners a hundred thousand men, and got possession of their tents, wagons, and baggage. Many of these were voted a present to their general, who had shown extraordinary skill and courage.

CAIUS MARIUS

But Marius chose such arms and other spoils as would make the greatest show in his triumph; the rest he piled up for a splendid sacrifice. The army stood about in festive attire with garlands on their heads, and Marius, in a purple-bordered robe, had just taken a lighted torch and raised both arms towards heaven, when a party was seen approaching on horseback with great speed. Every one was silent and expectant. The men, who proved to be Romans, jumped from their horses, walked towards Marius, saluted him respectfully, and then announced that they brought news of his fifth consulship. The soldiers clashed their arms and shouted, the officers crowned Marius again with a laurel-wreath, and then he set fire to the pile and finished the sacrifice.

The rejoicings of the Romans were considerably dampened within a few days, however, when bad news came from Catulus. He was, as we know, consul at the same time with Marius, and though the latter had had no easy task in overcoming the barbarians, Catulus's had been a far more difficult one. He had crossed the Alps and posted his part of the army in Italy, placing the Adige River between him and the enemy, part of whose forces had continued on their way, though leaving quite enough in Gaul to oppose Marius. Catulus blocked up the river on both sides with strong fortifications, built a bridge, and put everything in readiness that he might not be taken by surprise.

But he soon found that all his efforts had been in vain, for the barbarians, who had come from a cold region, were so hardy and so strong that they felt a contempt for the Romans, and exposed themselves naked in a snow-storm just to make a display of their courage. It seemed easy for them to push their way through ice and snow to the very tops of the mountains, and then, using their broad shields for sleds, they slid down the slippery sides. They next set to work, like a body of giants, to fill up the channel of the river, pulling up trees by the roots and throwing them in, adding besides huge rocks and piles of earth. These with other bulky objects were forced by the current against the bridge that the Romans had built, and dashed upon the timbers with such violence as to shake their foundation. The Roman soldiers watched these proceedings with perfect astonishment, and when they saw their bridge going to pieces before their eyes, many of them were so discouraged that they left their camp and drew back. Catulus tried to persuade them to keep their post, but, finding it impossible to make them listen to him, he determined to do his utmost to save the honor of his country. It should never be said that a Roman army had fled if he could help it; so, ordering his standard to be pulled up, he ran to the front of the retreating soldiers and commanded them to follow him. He preferred to disgrace himself by deserting his camp rather than have his soldiers appear like cowards.

The enemy crossed the river, took all the spoils in the Roman camp, and spread themselves over the country, doing great damage wherever they went. Then Marius was recalled to Rome, and, instead of waiting for his triumph, he made all haste to get his army in order and join Catulus near the river Po, to prevent the enemy from advancing to the very centre of Italy.

Now, the part of the northern army that had so frightened the soldiers of Catulus were called the Cimbri, and the part that Marius had defeated were called the Teutones. The Cimbri either had not heard of the fate of the Teutones, or pretended ignorance, for they sent ambassadors to Marius to ask for lands and cities enough to accommodate them and their brethren, whom they were daily expecting to join them.

CAIUS MARIUS

"Who are your brethren?" asked Marius of the ambassadors.

"The Teutones," was the reply.

"Oh, do not trouble yourselves about your brethren," replied Marius, with a taunting laugh; "we have already given them land enough, which they may keep forever."

"The Cimbri will punish you immediately, and so will the Teutones when they join us," returned the ambassadors, angrily.

"But they are not far off," said Marius; "surely you would not be so unkind as to go away without saluting your brethren." As he spoke he gave a signal, and the Teutone commanders were led forth in chains.

No sooner did the Cimbri hear what had happened than they marched against Marius, and their king rode with a small party to the Roman camp, with a challenge to the general to decide by arms to whom Italy should belong. "The Romans never consult their enemies when to fight," said Marius; "however, the Cimbri shall be indulged on that point, and we will name the third day from this and the plain of Vercelli."

On the appointed day the forces were drawn up, and presented a magnificent array. Catulus had twenty thousand men, and Marius had thirty-two thousand. The Cimbrian infantry marched out of their trenches noiselessly, and spread themselves over a square mile, then the cavalry, to the number of fifteen thousand, came forth in great splendor. Their helmets represented the heads and open jaws of strange and frightful wild beasts, and these were surmounted by high plumes, making the men appear taller than they really were.

Their breastplates were of polished steel, and their shields were white and glittering. Each man carried two-edged darts, to be used at a distance, and a broad, heavy sword for hand-to-hand fighting.

Just before going into battle, Marius lifted his hands to heaven and vowed a hecatomb, which meant a hundred oxen, to the gods; Catulus vowed to consecrate a temple to the fortune of the day. Then the sacrifice was offered. As soon as Marius beheld the entrails of the animal he shouted, "The victory is mine!" and made the charge. It so happened that the chief part of the conflict fell to the legions of Catulus, which was a great disappointment to Marius. The battle took place in the summer, and the Cimbri, who had been bred in cold countries, could not stand the heat. The sun annoyed them dreadfully, they could scarcely breathe the hot air, and were forced to hold up their shields to shade their faces. The perspiration poured from them, and they were almost suffocated, while the Romans suffered scarcely any inconvenience. Then, too, the dust was so thick that the Romans could not distinguish the vast multitude of the enemy, and so were not appalled by it. In short, everything favored them that day, and at the very first charge the enemy's troops were cut to pieces.

Those that fled were followed by the Romans to their camp, where a shocking scene was enacted. The Cimbrian women met their husbands, fathers, and brothers, and murdered them as they ran in. That done, they strangled their little ones with their own hands, threw them under the horses' feet, and then killed themselves. A number of the men who were not killed by the women tied themselves by the neck to the horns or legs of the oxen, then goaded them on so that they were either strangled or torn to pieces. Nevertheless, about sixty thousand were taken prisoners.

CAIUS MARIUS

Although it was clearly proved that Catulus had left more of the enemy dead upon the field than Marius had, by the larger number of shafts having his name inscribed on them, yet the honor of the day was given to Marius, because of his former victory, and the applause he got at home was so great that he was called the third founder of Rome. He had indeed rescued his country from as great a danger as that which threatened her at the invasion of the Gauls, and the women and children drank to him and to the gods at the same time. The honor of the two triumphs would have been accorded to him, but either generosity or fear of opposition from Catulus's soldiers prompted him to share one with their general.

The war with the Cimbri brought Marius's fifth consulship to a close; then he was anxious to be elected again; but he was not an able statesman in time of peace: he was not popular with the nobility; besides, he preferred to be great rather than good, and showed plainly that, unless he held an office which gave him dignity, he would do nothing for his country's cause. He was not a true patriot, but he would make any sacrifice for position, and worked as hard for his sixth consulship as any man had ever done for his first one. He did not care how low he stooped if only he could gain favor with the people; that meant to him votes, for which he even resorted to bribery. And so he was elected, with Valerius Flaccus as his colleague.

But it would have been better if he had rested on his laurels, for by his conduct in his sixth consulship he excited the hatred of all parties. He had made an enemy of Metellus by his ungenerous behavior towards him in the African war against Jugurtha, and by means of bribery had kept him from being elected consul. Then he accepted a couple of lawless fellows named Glaucia and Saturninus for his friends, and with their aid committed many misdemeanors, the very worst of which was during the tribuneship of the latter. Saturninus proposed a law for the division of lands, and added a clause requiring the senate to swear to agree to any vote the people should carry, and never to oppose them. Marius had really been instrumental in the wording of this law, but pretended in the senate to oppose it, and said that no wise man could take such an oath. Metellus was the last senator to vote, and as he was a thoroughly honest man, and knew that such a law would lead to the ruin of the Roman constitution, he declared that he would not swear to support it. This was exactly what Marius wanted, because he knew it would make Metellus unpopular. A few days later, when Saturninus took the votes of the senators on his law, Marius stepped out and hypocritically declared that he was not so conceited as to believe that he could not make a mistake, so if the law met with favor he would willingly submit to it. This was the step he had intended to take from the start, but he wanted to produce a theatrical effect. The people clapped and applauded him, but the nobility were much displeased. However, fear of the populace led each senator to take the oath until it came to Metellus's turn. His friends begged him to do likewise; but, to a man who esteemed truth the first principle of heroic virtue, that was impossible. He left the Forum, saying to those who stood near him, "To do an ill action is base; to do a good one in which there is no danger is nothing more than common; but it is the duty of a good man to do great and good things, though he risk much by it." Metellus knew that he would be banished, and so he was; but he preferred banishment to dishonor.

CAIUS MARIUS

After a time Saturninus was guilty of such outrages that the principal men of Rome met at the house of Marius to see whether they could not find some means of punishing him. Then Marius was guilty of a mean, dishonest action, for he hid Saturninus and his friends behind a curtain, so that they might hear what was said, and, pretending to be ill, passed in and out from one party to the other, creating all the mischief he could between them. At last the senators became so violent that Saturninus and his set fled to the Capitol for protection. Soldiers were called out, and by order of the infuriated senators, who had discovered the trick, the friends of Marius, who were shut up in the Capitol, were besieged. The water pipes were cut, and, as no food had been provided, the prisoners could not hold out long. They called on Marius to save them, and he promised to do so if he could, whereupon the besieged men came down into the Forum, where, as they appeared, the people stoned and clubbed them to death. The consequence of all this was that Marius was thoroughly despised both by the nobles and commons, so much so that when the time came for the election of censors he dared not offer himself. So he built a house close to the Forum, and lived quietly for a long time, praying for war to break out, so that he might not remain entirely neglected and forgotten.

Sylla was now one of the consuls, and Marius hated him because he was popular with the nobles. The time came when the affairs of Rome were in such a state of disorder that Sulpicius, a bad man, who imitated Saturninus in his lawless deeds, formed a guard of six hundred, whom he called anti-senators, and set upon the consuls. This happened when the most warlike people of Italy had united to fight against Rome. Then Marius, who was sixty-five years old, wanted to command the army, but Sylla had been placed in his stead.

Sulpicius drove out the consuls and gave the command to Marius, who immediately began his preparations by sending two tribunes to relieve Sylla of his command.

Thereupon, with thirty-five thousand armed men, Sylla marched towards Rome, slew the tribunes Marius had sent, and made an assault, which forced Marius from the field. He made his escape from the city with a small party, and embarked on board a ship that happened to sail along just in the nick of time. A dreadful storm came up, and the party left the ship and wandered about on shore until they met a few poor shepherds, who relieved their hunger, but told Marius that a troop of horsemen were searching for him. That night was passed in the woods, and when day dawned Marius proceeded on foot, urging his companions not to desert him. Towards noon he approached a city on the sea-coast of Italy just as a cavalry company came in sight. He knew that they were searching for him, but fortunately there were two ships under sail in the harbor, so the whole party plunged into the sea and swam towards them. They were reached with little difficulty by all except poor Marius, who with age had become fat and unwieldy. However, two of his men kept his head above water until he got to one of the ships, the rest of the party having been taken on board the other.

By that time the soldiers arrived at the sea-shore, and called out to the seamen either to bring Marius back or throw him overboard; but he entreated them, with tears in his eyes, not to obey; and, after consulting among themselves, they decided that it would be cruel to place the old man in the hands of his enemies. So the soldiers rode off in a rage. A few hours later the seamen changed their minds; they did not intend to deliver Marius over to those that pursued him, neither did they feel safe in protecting him, so they solved the

CAIUS MARIUS

difficulty by steering for land and casting anchor at the mouth of the river Liris. They then advised him to go on shore and refresh himself, and rest until the wind was fairer, which, they said, would be the case at about sunset. Marius landed, and walked to a field near by, where he lay down and soon fell asleep. When he awoke, the ship was nowhere to be seen.

Alone, and deserted by all the world, the poor old general felt stupefied for some time. At last he collected himself, and on looking about discovered a hut in the distance. He raised himself with difficulty, for his limbs were stiff and sore, and waded through bog, ditch, and mud until he reached the hut, where an old man lived who worked in the fens. Falling on his knees, Marius implored him to protect one who, if he escaped his present danger, would reward him beyond anything he dreamed of. "If you want only to rest," said the man, who probably recognized his visitor, "my cottage will answer; but if you are flying from anybody's search, I can hide you in a more retired place." Marius desired him to do so by all means, so he led him to a little cave in the fen near the riverside, where he covered him with reeds.

Meanwhile, orders had been sent throughout Italy for a public search to be made for Marius, and whoever found him was to kill him. He had not been long in his hiding-place when he heard a tumult in the old man's hut, and, knowing that he must be the cause of it, he plunged into a puddle of thick, muddy water. But instead of escaping he only put himself in the way of his pursuers, who dragged him out all covered with dirt, and led him naked to the magistrates of Minturnæ, the nearest town. A Cimbrian horseman was selected to put the prisoner to death, and for that purpose he entered his chamber sword in hand. A dim light made the corner where Marius lay on the couch appear dark, but the

Cimbrian saw the prisoner's eyes flash as a terrible voice that had no human sound exclaimed, "Fellow, darest thou kill Caius Marius?" The barbarian dropped his sword and fled, crying, as he rushed into the street, "I cannot kill Caius Marius!"

Suddenly, as if by magic, everybody's anger was turned to pity and remorse. "How can we be so ungrateful towards the preserver of Italy? ought we not rather to assist and protect him?" they asked. "Let him go where he pleases to banishment, while we entreat the gods to pardon us for thrusting Marius, distressed and deserted, out of our city." So they went in a body to his room and conducted him to the sea-side, where lay a ship that had been provided for him. He set sail for Africa, where he hoped for a friendly reception; but he made a mistake, for the governor of Carthage was a Roman, who sent him this message: "Sextilius, the governor, forbids you, Marius, to set foot in Africa; if you do, you will be treated as a public enemy." On hearing this the exile was struck with grief and disappointment, but after a few days he sailed for the island of Cercina, there to await changes in public affairs at Rome.

When he was a child he lived in the country, and one day he caught in the skirt of his garment an eagle's nest as it was falling. It contained seven young eagles, and this was considered so remarkable that the augurs were consulted, and they said that not only should Marius become one of the greatest men in the world, but that he should be seven times in a place of high power. He never forgot this prophecy, and when his fate looked dark and gloomy he was buoyed up by the recollection that he had been consul only six times; so, with perfect faith in the augurs, he waited patiently at Cercina for his recall to Rome.

CAIUS MARIUS

News came to him at last that Cinna, the consul, had been driven out of the city by Octavius and his party because he had ruled too despotically, and that Cornelius Merula had been elected consul instead; also that Cinna had raised forces in other parts of Italy to oppose them. Nothing could have pleased Marius better. Not a moment was to be lost; he gathered about him a thousand Africans and Italian refugees, and with these set sail for his native land. He went ashore at Etruria, where so many of his countrymen flocked to greet him that, persuading the youngest and strongest to join him, he got together enough to fill forty ships, and then sent a messenger to Cinna to say that he was at his service.

Cinna was so delighted that he named Marius proconsul and sent him the fasces and insignia of office. "Grandeur does not become my present position," said Marius, whose role it was just then to appear humble. So, in the plainest of attire, and with an air of dejection that excited pity, he went to Cinna, saluted him and the soldiers, and prepared for action.

The first thing he did was to seize the provision-ships, take the seaport towns one after another, pillaging them, and slaying the inhabitants by thousands; then he blocked up the river so that no supplies could come by sea, marched with his army towards Rome, and posted himself on the hill called Janiculum.

Now, Octavius was one of the most upright Romans that ever lived, but he was so strict in his observance of the ancient laws and customs that the soldiers did not like him; so when Marius came on the scene they went to join him, and just before he entered the city Octavius was dragged from the rostrum and murdered.

Then the senate assembled and despatched a messenger to request Cinna and Marius to enter peacefully and spare the citizens. The former complied, but on arriving at the gate Marius stood still and declared that he would go no farther until his sentence of banishment was recalled. That was forthwith done, and he went into the city surrounded by a guard of Illyrian slaves, who had made their escape from the pens in Etruria and fled to him.

Without even the form of an election Cinna declared himself and Marius consuls, and then for five days there was nothing but massacre and bloodshed in the streets of Rome. At a word, or merely a nod of his head, the slaves of Marius would draw their swords and kill whoever failed to show him deference, so that even his friends approached him in fear and trembling. The most distinguished men of the state were butchered, and every town and road was filled with the soldiers, who hunted down those that fled or hid themselves. One betrayed another in order to shield himself; all friendship and confidence was destroyed; still Marius required fresh victims every day, and revelled in the scenes of blood.

The servants of a prominent citizen named Cornutus showed their affection for him at this trying time thus: hearing that he was to become a victim to the consul's fury, they concealed him in his own house, then took the body of a man about his size, cut off the head, put a ring that belonged to Cornutus on the finger, showed the body to Marius's guards, and then buried it with all the ceremonies they would have observed had it really been that of their master. The trick was successful, and Cornutus escaped in disguise to Gaul.

Mark Antony, the great orator, found a faithful friend in a plebeian, who would have protected him if he could have done so. The man was so pleased to have one of the most famous of Romans as his guest that he often sent to a neighboring tavern for some of the best wine kept there. One day the tavern-keeper asked the servant why he had suddenly become so particular about the wine he bought as to select the dearest. "Because we have Mark Antony at our house," answered the servant, innocently. No sooner was he gone than the tavern-keeper ran to Marius, who was then at supper, and told him where the orator was concealed. Marius clapped his hands with joy, and immediately sent an officer named Annius with some soldiers to bring him the head of the noble Roman without delay.

Arriving at the house, Annius stationed himself at the door while his soldiers went up a ladder and climbed into Mark Antony's chamber. He pleaded with them for his life, and exerted his powers of eloquence to such an extent that they were spell-bound and forgot their errand. Annius began to wonder at the delay after a few moments, and ascended the ladder himself. On looking in at the window he found his soldiers in tears, and the orator still addressing them. He jumped in, taunted them with their weakness, and, raising his sword, struck off the head of Mark Antony with one blow.

Catulus, who had fought with Marius against the Cimbri, tried very hard to stop the butchery that was going on in Rome, but, finding himself unable to gain any influence, he shut himself up in a small room and suffocated himself with the fumes of a charcoal fire. The horrible deeds committed by Marius's guard grew worse and more numerous, until Cinna's party, being struck with horror, killed every man of them in their camp.

Then news came that Sylla was advancing with a great army, and Marius was chosen consul the seventh time, in order that he might manage the war that must inevitably result. But he was getting old, and he feared Sylla so much, that the very idea of being obliged to fight him filled him with anxiety. He was wretched by day, and would start up from horrible dreams at night that would keep him awake for hours after. Like many a man before and since, he sought relief in drink, which only made his condition worse; for he was seized with a delirious fever, and died on the seventeenth day of his seventh consulship, despised by all. Rome was thus relieved of a cruel tyrant, who, though he was past seventy, was the first man who had been consul seven times, and had wealth enough to support the dignity of more than one king, complained of the ill fortune that caused him to die before he had got all that he had worked for.

SYLLA

NOW we come to a period when the purity and honesty of Rome had given place to riches and luxury, with all their accompanying evils; nevertheless, a man whose parents had been poor was still much blamed by the public if he happened to have become suddenly wealthy. So when Sylla boasted of certain exploits of his, a nobleman who was present said, "How can you be an honest man, who, since the death of a father who left you nothing, have become so rich?"

Lucius Cornelius Sylla was descended from a patrician or noble family, but his father did not distinguish himself in any way, and bestowed upon his son neither honors nor riches. He gave him a good education, however, for he was learned in the literature of his own country and of Greece. If Sylla had been as moral as he was intellectual, it would be a pleasanter task to write the story of his life; but he was intemperate, notorious for his low, vulgar tastes, and observed no law but that which his passions dictated. He was vicious in his youth and poverty, and no less so when he became old and rich. Indeed, he so squandered the public treasure when he got the chance that he was forced to let many cities that were allied to Rome buy their independence, in order that he might be enabled to replace the sums he had thrown away to gratify his own vile pleasures. On the other hand, he was a great general, won a number of important victories, and was of immense service to his country.

When Marius was consul the first time, Sylla was appointed quæstor, or public treasurer, and went with him to Africa to fight against Jugurtha. He gained high honors as a soldier, and won fame besides in this way: Some ambassadors of Bocchus, the king of Numidia, had suffered severely at the hands of robbers who stopped them on the road, and Sylla not only relieved their wants, but loaded them with presents and sent them back home with a strong guard. Thus he won the friendship of the king besides.

Jugurtha, who was son-in-law to Bocchus, had taken refuge at his court after his defeat, but Bocchus both hated and feared him, and was just turning over in his mind some means of getting rid of him when this affair with the robbers took place. He would not deliver up his son-in-law, but how could he better show his gratitude to Sylla, he asked himself, than by allowing him to seize his enemy? So Bocchus intimated to Sylla that if he would come to visit him Jugurtha should be his. This was such a tempting reward that, after communicating the matter to Marius, Sylla took a small party and set out upon the expedition, dangerous though it was. For when Bocchus had two such powerful men in his power he began to debate with himself which should be the victim. At last it seemed more to his advantage to give up Jugurtha, as he had promised, and so it was done.

Marius became very jealous when all the glory of his capture was given to Sylla, and he was still more so when the latter, who was anxious for fame, had a ring made with a seal, which he used on all his letters, representing Bocchus delivering Jugurtha to him. After a time, finding that the ill will of

SYLLA

Marius increased, Sylla left him and took command under his colleague, Catulus, instead. Then he was employed in the most difficult enterprises, and when it was his duty to supply the soldiers with provisions, he performed it so well that the army of Catulus had all they wanted, while the forces under Marius were suffering from hunger. This circumstance made Sylla still more hateful to Marius, and, added to others of like nature, led to civil wars and no end of tyranny and bloodshed.

When Sylla became prætor, or city magistrate, he was sent to Cappadocia to replace the king on the throne there, and succeeded without much trouble; it was his good fortune at the same time to be the first Roman to whom the Parthians had ever applied for friendship. These things, added to the fact that Bocchus dedicated several images of Victory in the Capitol, and close by them one of Jugurtha, in gold, representing his surrender to Sylla, caused the quarrel between Marius and Sylla to break out afresh. The former attempted to pull down the images, Sylla's friends opposed it, and the whole city was aroused to a degree that would have brought about ruin had it not been for the sudden breaking out of the Social War, which had been smouldering for a long time. This great event put a stop to the quarrel for the time being.

During the war, which was of the utmost importance to the commonwealth, Sylla distinguished himself much more than Marius did, and proved himself a commander of great ability. Towards its close he returned to Rome, and was rewarded with the consulship. At the same time he married Cæcilia, daughter of Metellus, the high-priest.

Sylla was glad to be consul, chiefly because his heart was set on getting command in the war now threatening with Mithridates, one of the most formidable enemies Rome ever

SYLLA ENTERING ROME

SYLLA

had. But he had a rival in Marius, who, though an old man, was just as full of ambition as ever, and, while Sylla was gone to the camp to arrange some matters, he got Sulpitius, one of the most wicked creatures that ever lived, to join him in creating a disturbance, and proclaiming, at the sword's point, whatever laws suited their purpose. Marius made himself commander of the army, put many of Sylla's friends to death, ordered their houses to be plundered, and, with the aid of Sulpitius, got the senate completely under his control.

Then he sent two prætors to Nola, where Sylla was quartered with his army, to announce the change. They delivered their orders so haughtily that the soldiers prepared to kill them on the spot, but at last contented themselves with breaking their fasces, tearing off their robes, and sending them away with many marks of disgrace. Then Sylla broke up his camp, and prepared to march on Rome at the head of his six legions. He was met by ambassadors, who entreated him not to advance with the intention of fighting, and assured him that the senate would certainly do him justice. He promised to encamp where he was, and even ordered his officers to mark out the ground for the camp; but as soon as the ambassadors were gone, he sent part of his army to take charge of the gate and the wall, and followed with the rest as quickly as possible.

The citizens got on the tops of the houses, and threw stones and tiles on the heads of the soldiers as soon as they appeared. When Sylla arrived, he ordered the houses to be set on fire, and, taking a flaming torch in his hand, gave the example. In doing this he had no thought for friends or relations, but was impelled by fury and the desire for vengeance to ruin his enemies, and cared not that the innocent and the guilty alike suffered. He got possession of the city, and, after driving Marius out, called the senate together and had him and others condemned to death. Sulpitius was betrayed by one of his slaves and killed. For this act Sylla gave the slave his freedom, and then had him thrown down the Tarpeian rock.

After re-establishing the power of the senate and proposing Octavius and Lucius Cinna for consuls, Sylla set forward against Mithridates. His first object was to relieve Greece from tyrants, and he accomplished this after taking Athens by storm and defeating the armies of Mithridates in two great battles. Then a treaty of peace was concluded, for Sylla was very anxious to return to Rome, where Cinna was committing such dreadful acts of violence that many prominent people had made their way to his camp for protection.

The two consuls had quarrelled, and Cinna had gone among the dissatisfied allies of Rome and raised a powerful army. Then Marius, who had fled to Africa, hearing of the trouble, returned to Italy, joined Cinna, and, with an immense horde of robbers and ruffians from all parts of the country, advanced on Rome. The senate were so alarmed that they offered to make way for Marius if he would shed no blood; but he paid no attention to them, and gave the signal for slaughter. His barbarians rushed on like wolves, sparing neither old nor young, men, women, nor children. The hideous massacre lasted for five days and five nights, during which Marius gazed on the horrid scene and seemed to delight in it. He had died, and Cinna had been killed in a mutiny of his own troops, when Sylla returned at the head of his victorious army, prepared for vengeance on the Marian party, whom he regarded as enemies to himself and to the republic.

SYLLA

After a short but severe fight he succeeded in making himself ruler, and then all who had taken sides with Marius, or who were even suspected of having favored him, were put to death without mercy. Fearing that any should escape, Sylla even produced a list of those he had doomed to death, and set a price upon their heads. Caius Metellus, one of the younger members of the senate, asked him how these evils were to end, and at what point he might be expected to stop. "We do not ask you," he added, "to pardon any whom you have resolved to destroy, but to remove doubt from those you are pleased to spare."

Sylla answered, "I know not as yet whom I shall spare."

"Why, then, tell us whom you mean to punish," said Metellus.

Sylla consented, and, without consulting any of the magistrates, at once condemned eighty persons. The people of Rome were very indignant at such an outrage; but without taking any notice of that, Sylla condemned two hundred and twenty the next day, and as many more on the day after. In an address to the public he had the impudence to say that he had posted up whatever names he could think of, but those that had escaped his memory should be published later. He went further in his cruelty, and made a law that any one who gave shelter to a proscribed person should be put to death, without exception, no matter how near the relationship might be. He who should kill a proscribed person was promised a reward of two talents, even though it were a slave who slew his master or a son his father. But the most unjust of all his laws was that which declared the sons and grandsons of condemned persons infamous, and confiscated their property.

It was not only in Rome that the lists of people who were to be killed were put up, but in all the cities of Italy. No temple of the gods, no hearth or home, was held sacred at this period; men were butchered before the very eyes of their wives and children, sons in the arms of their mothers. Many were sacrificed merely because the cruel Sylla had reason to hate them or wished to be revenged on them, but the majority simply because they were rich, so that it became a common saying among the murderers, "His fine house killed this man, a garden that one, a third his luxurious hot-baths." Quintus Aurelius, a quiet, peaceable citizen, who thought that there could be no charge brought against him unless it were the sympathy he felt for others, walked into the Forum one day to read the list of the unfortunates who were to die. Suddenly he came to his own name. "Oh, woe is me!" he cried, "my Alban farm is my offence." He had not gone many steps before a ruffian approached and killed him.

At Præneste, Sylla tried the inhabitants, or went through the farce of a trial, and had them executed singly, but, finding this tiresome, he collected them to the number of twelve thousand and ordered them to be cooped up and slaughtered. One person he would have spared, and that was the man at whose house he had been entertained; but the noble fellow said, "I will never owe my life to the destroyer of my country," and, mixing with the crowd, met his death with his fellow-citizens. The strangest proceeding was with Lucius Catiline, a wretch who had killed his own brother. He begged Sylla to place the dead man's name on the list of the proscribed, just as though he were still alive. This was done, and in return for the favor Catiline went and killed one Marcus Marius and brought his head to Sylla as he sat on his chair of state in the Forum, then washed his hands in the holy water at the door of Apollo's temple near by, no doubt thinking thus to cleanse himself from crime.

The next thing Sylla did was to declare himself dictator, though there had been no such office in Rome for a hundred and twenty years. It gave him power of life and death, of seizing property, of forming colonies, of building or destroying cities, of giving or taking away kingdoms. In short, it gave him power unlimited, and he exercised it in a most insolent, despotic manner. He presented bad women, actors, musicians, and the lowest of the freed slaves with territory and the revenue of whole provinces, and compelled women of rank, against their will, to marry some of the most depraved ruffians. We have recounted only a few of the horrible deeds of which Sylla was guilty, but they are enough to show that he was no less wicked than Marius.

Sylla held his dictatorship nearly three years; then, having made all the political reforms he thought necessary, he resigned, and left the people to choose consuls again. Strange to say, although the wicked man walked about in the Forum and elsewhere without a guard, nobody seemed to think of taking his life, though killing was such an everyday occurrence.

On the occasion of making sacrifices to Hercules he gave a magnificent entertainment, and the provisions were so abundant that a quantity was thrown into the river every day. The wine was of the finest kind, being at least forty years old. The feast lasted many days, and in the midst of it Sylla's wife died. But that event did not interfere with his pleasures; for the priests forbade him to approach her, or to have his house defiled by mourning, so he divorced her, and ordered her to be carried elsewhere before the breath was out of her body.

He was so superstitious that he obeyed strictly every law laid down by the priests, though he transgressed his own laws by sparing no expense either on his wife's funeral or on his sumptuous banquets.

The rest of his life was passed in the society of low people, with whom he sat drinking and feasting for whole days at a time, until he was seized with a loathsome disease that soon put an end to his existence. The very day before his death he had the quæstor, Granius, strangled by his bedside, because the latter wanted to keep the money due the state; hoping that when Sylla was dead he would not be obliged to give an account of it. Sylla was in the sixtieth year of his age, and had finished the twenty-second book of his autobiography just two days before his death. Some of his enemies tried to prevent his having the usual honors of burial, but the senate interfered, and his funeral was the most magnificent ever seen in Rome. His soldiers came from all parts of Italy to be present, and joined in the procession, which was headed by the senate, the magistrates, the priests, and the vestal virgins. Then followed the army, legion by legion, and all marched to the Campus Martius, where the pile was built.

Although such a cruel man, Sylla must have been a favorite with the Roman ladies, for they attended his funeral in great numbers, and sent two hundred and ten large baskets of spices; Besides these there was enough cinnamon and choice frankincense to make a full-length figure of the dead man and one of a lictor, both of which were carried in the procession. As soon as the corpse was laid upon the pile a strong wind arose, which blew up a flame sufficient to consume it in a few minutes. The ashes were deposited beside the tomb of the kings in the Campus Martius, where, according to Sylla's desire, a monument was erected bearing this inscription by himself,—"No friend ever did me so much good, or enemy so much harm, but that I repaid him with interest."

My young readers must not forget that the wars between Sylla and Marius were of the utmost importance, because they led to the destruction of Roman liberty; but neither of these heroes would have been so powerful had Rome retained her ancient virtues. She was on the brink of ruin because the nobles and the people had become corrupt, and after Sylla was gone new men arose to imitate his example, and new convulsions to disturb the public peace many times before a remedy could be found to cure the deep-seated malady.

CRASSUS

MARCUS CRASSUS lived at the same period with Pompey and Cæsar and Cicero, whose lives follow this, and he was one of the best public speakers in Rome. Often when others refused to undertake a case that seemed unimportant, he would give it so much of his time and attention that his fellow-citizens looked upon him as one who was ever ready to work for them. Besides, he had a pleasant way of greeting even the humblest of his countrymen, and of calling each by name, that added much to his popularity. This was unlike many rich men, and Crassus was enormously rich, for not only was he the owner of several silver-mines, but he had valuable lands and a host of slaves, whom he hired out. They were laborers on his estates, readers, writers, silversmiths, stewards, and household waiters. These he always overlooked himself, for he considered it the duty of a master to see that his servants were properly instructed in their various pursuits.

When Cinna and Marius got the power into their own hands, an account of which has been given in their respective lives, the father and brother of Crassus were killed, but he, being very young, was considered unimportant, and so escaped. But he knew that he was living in dangerous times, and therefore, taking with him three friends and ten servants, he fled to Spain, where he had once been with his father, and hid in a cave by the sea-shore. This cave belonged to a man

CRASSUS

named Vibius Pacianus, who was so pleased to know that young Crassus was safe that, after inquiring into the number of occupants of the cave, he ordered his steward to take a certain supply of food every day to a rock which he named and there leave it, promising him his liberty if he obeyed, but threatening death if he asked any questions or sought to find out for whom the food was intended.

Crassus lived in that by no means unpleasant dwelling for eight months, abundantly supplied with comforts and luxuries sent regularly by the friendly Pacianus, whose servants never saw him or knew whom they were serving. At last news came of Cinna's death, and then Crassus left his hiding-place and joined Sylla's army, where his services were very valuable. But Crassus had two grave faults: he was avaricious and covetous; so when Pompey was honored with a triumph, it made him very angry because he did not also get one. One day, when a citizen announced that "Pompey the Great was coming," Crassus asked, with a scornful laugh, "How big is he?"

Pompey's ability for war was so great that Crassus soon felt how useless it would be to compete with him: he therefore turned his attention to affairs of state, and became very influential. He was ambitious and covetous, as we have said, but not ill-natured or bad-hearted, and he was always ready to serve those who needed him. When Cæsar was going to Spain as prætor, his creditors wanted to stop him and take his things, but Crassus promised to see that they were all paid at a given time, and this was a noble act of friendship.

Crassus showed himself a good soldier in the war with Spartacus, the gladiator. There was at Capua a man who trained gladiators and kept them in confinement, not because they were criminals, but because they were his slaves, and he was cruel. They were for the most part Gauls and Thracians, and were made to fight merely to amuse their master and his guests. At last they determined to bear the imprisonment no longer, and two hundred of them formed a plot to escape. It was discovered, but not until seventy-eight had got off; these went to a cook's shop and armed themselves with all sorts of knives, hatchets, and spits, with which they marched noisily through Capua until they reached a place where they were able to defend themselves. On the way they came upon a wagon filled with gladiators' arms; they seized these, and then chose three captains, Spartacus being the chief and giving the name to the insurrection.

Spartacus was a brave, high-spirited man, superior to his condition both in intellect and disposition, for, unlike most Thracians, he was humane and gentle. When he first went to Rome to be sold, a snake coiled itself upon his face while he slept, and his wife, who was a kind of prophetess, declared it to be a sign that he would become powerful.

Well, the seventy-eight gladiators routed those Capuans who came out to fight them, and so got hold of all the weapons they required in place of the butcher-knives. Clodius, with a body of three thousand men, was sent from Rome, and he besieged the gladiators on a mountain that could be reached by only one narrow, difficult passage, which he kept guarded. The top of the mountain was covered with wild vines, of which the gladiators made strong ladders long enough to reach down a steep, slippery precipice on the opposite side to where Clodius had posted his army. By means of these ladders they all got down and made their way around to the Romans, who were taken completely by surprise and lost their camp. This gave the gladiators another

CRASSUS

supply of arms, with which they equipped a number of sturdy herdsmen and shepherds who had joined them.

Other prætors were sent from Rome, but Spartacus defeated them all, and his name began to be a terror in the land. But he was too sensible a man to suppose that his success would long continue against the forces that could easily be raised to oppose him; so he marched his army towards the Alps, intending to send every man to his own home, some to Thrace, others to Gaul. However, with their increase of numbers and repeated successes, they were not willing tamely to disband; they disobeyed their leader and went about ravaging Italy, until the senate, aroused to a sense of the danger that was likely to follow, sent out two consuls, each with a large army. In course of time both were defeated by Spartacus. Then Crassus was appointed general of the war, and a great many of the patrician young men volunteered under his command.

It was at Rhegium that he came upon the gladiators, and the first thing he did was to build a wall across the isthmus. This was a most difficult undertaking, but it kept the soldiers busy and the enemy from foraging; so when Spartacus, who had not considered the importance of this great undertaking, suddenly found his provisions failing and himself walled in, he spent the whole of one snowy, stormy night filling up a ditch with earth and boughs of trees, and so passed over a third of his army.

Crassus now began to fear that the gladiators would march straight to Rome; but his mind was soon relieved when they separated, for some reason or other, and part of them encamped on the Lucanian lake. He fell upon them without delay, drove them off, and would have put an end to them had not Spartacus come up just in time to rally them.

Meanwhile, Crassus had written to the senate to send Lucullus from Thrace and Pompey from Spain to his assistance. He now began to repent that he had done so, for he was always jealous of Pompey, who was a greater commander than he, and feared that he might arrive in time to carry off the honors. He therefore followed up Spartacus and his army with all speed, and gave them battle as soon as they made a stand.

When they brought Spartacus his horse, he drew his sword and killed him, saying, "If I am victorious, I shall get many better horses from the enemy; if I am defeated, I shall have no need of this one." Then, through showers of darts and heaps of slain, he made straight for Crassus, but did not reach him, though he killed two centurions that fell upon him together. He stood his ground, bravely defending himself, until he was surrounded by the enemy and cut to pieces.

Although Crassus had shown himself a good general and had gallantly exposed his person, he was only wreathing a laurel for the brow of Pompey, who met those that were escaping from the field, put them to the sword, and wrote to the senate, "Crassus has indeed beaten the gladiators in a pitched battle, but I have put an end to the war."

On his return to Rome, Pompey had a magnificent triumph for his conquest over Sertorius in Spain, but Crassus could not even accept an ovation, because it would have been undignified, seeing that he had defeated only fugitive slaves. The difference between a triumph and an ovation is explained in the life of Marcellus.

CRASSUS

Pompey and Crassus were both made consuls. They seemed pleased at first, but it was not long before they began to quarrel to such an extent that they could accomplish nothing of importance to the country. But Crassus, in order to increase his popularity, offered a great sacrifice to Hercules, entertained people at ten thousand tables, and gave them a supply of corn for three months. At the close of their consulship a Roman knight who was much respected mounted the rostrum and announced that he had had a vision, in which, he said, "Jupiter appeared to me and commanded me to tell you that you should not permit your consuls to go out of office until they are friends." The people cried out that they must become reconciled to each other. Pompey stood perfectly still and said nothing; but Crassus advanced towards him, and, holding out his hand, said, "I am not ashamed, fellow-citizens, nor do I think it beneath me, to make the first advances to Pompey, whom you called *Great* while he was but a beardless youth, and whom you honored with a triumph before he was even senator."

Somewhat later, Crassus was accused of being mixed up in the conspiracy of Catiline, but he was tried and acquitted by the whole senate. This was a plot to burn the city, and when the senate investigated it they naturally could not believe that a man who owned such an amount of property as Crassus did could desire to destroy it.

Now we come to the closing scene in the life of Crassus. He and Pompey were not really friends, although they had shaken hands to gratify an assembly of the people; so when Cæsar returned and desired to stand for the consulship he managed to reconcile the two, because he knew the importance of their influence. Having accomplished that, he formed the well-known league commonly called the First Triumvirate; and that was a sad day for the liberty of the Roman people.

Cæsar gained most by this league, for it helped him to the very top of the ladder of fame. Pompey agreed to it because he loved power, Crassus because he worshipped gold and saw a way to increase the millions he already had. So Cæsar was elected consul, and by means of persuasion and force the other two were associated with him. Pompey was appointed to the government of Spain, and Crassus to that of Syria, but he expected to extend it to India and the very shores of the Eastern Ocean,—not for fame, but for riches.

He first proposed to attack the Parthians, but they had been friendly to Rome; consequently the people opposed it, and would not let him depart until Pompey, whose influence was great, acted as escort. Even then Ateius, the tribune, met him at the gate, and tried to stop him by force, but, failing in that, he ran and got a pan of burning coals, on which he sprinkled incense, and called down the most horrible curses of certain strange and dreadful gods on the heads of the army. An imprecation of this kind was seldom used, because it was said that not only the person who used it, but his country, was sure to be unhappy. Therefore Ateius was much blamed for his rashness.

However, Crassus could not be stopped; so he put to sea, and after a stormy and dangerous voyage, and the loss of a number of vessels, reached Brundusium, whence he proceeded to Syria. The Romans met with little resistance, because they were not expected, and overran the greater part of Mesopotamia; but then Crassus committed a fatal error. Instead of following up his success and conquering the great city of Babylon, which he might have done with ease, he

CRASSUS

merely fortified the towns and returned into Syria to pass the winter. There he was joined by his son, Publius, who was sent from Gaul by Cæsar at the head of a thousand select horsemen.

Instead of devoting the winter to disciplining his army, as a great general ought to have done, Crassus spent his time inquiring into the revenues of the cities and weighing the treasures he found in the temple of Hierapolis, said to have been the richest in the world.

In the spring he took the field again with a splendid army; but part of it, headed by Cassius, the quæstor, tried to dissuade him from going farther, particularly as the soothsayers pronounced all the signs unfavorable. Crassus paid no attention to any of them, but marched straight on to the river Euphrates.

While he was crossing, there was a dreadful storm, accompanied by terrific peals of thunder and fearful flashes of lightning, and part of his bridge was destroyed. The spot he had marked out for his camp was struck twice by lightning; a richly-caparisoned war-horse ridden by one of the generals ran away, jumped into the river, and was drowned with the rider; and when the foremost eagle was moved in order for the march, it turned back of its own accord. These and other bad omens had a very depressing effect on the minds of the superstitious Romans, and it was increased when Crassus let fall the entrails of the animal he was sacrificing. However, his presence of mind did not desert him, and he said, with a smile, "See what it is to be old! but my sword shall not slip out of my hands in this manner, I promise you."

After crossing the river, Crassus was joined by an artful, wicked Arabian chief named Ariamnes, who led him to ruin. This man expressed so much friendship for the Romans, and flattered them to such a degree, that Crassus believed in him, and allowed him to become his guide because he knew the country so well. The traitor led the way along a smooth, easy road at first, but after a while he struck into a sandy desert, where not a drop of water nor a vestige of vegetation was to be seen for miles. No sooner was the imposture discovered than Ariamnes made his escape in the night.

The troops were worn out with their long, fatiguing march, and almost exhausted from thirst, when they were attacked by the Parthian forces under Surena, a man of high position, and one of the most remarkable commanders of his day. Crassus was so dismayed by the suddenness of the enemy's approach that he was scarcely able to draw up his army properly; however, after several changes one wing was at last placed under Cassius, the other under Publius Crassus, the centre being commanded by the general himself.

The Parthians came on, filling the air with a horrible din and loud bellowing, for they had instruments covered with leather and surrounded with brass bells, which they beat continually, because experience had taught them that nothing sooner disturbed the enemy than the dismal sounds they produced. Besides, they had a peculiar way of advancing and retreating as occasion required, firing their formidable arrows all the time, and drawing the enemy after them as they chose.

From the beginning the Romans fought at a disadvantage, and the battle was desperate and bloody. Young Crassus was sent with a detachment against the Parthian cavalry, and, although he showed himself a true hero, he and all his men were slain. The first knowledge the general received of his son's death was when the Parthians advanced again with loud shouts and songs of victory, holding the head of Publius on the point of a spear. "Does anybody know the family and parents of this young man?" they asked, in tones of contempt: "for it is not possible that so brave and gallant a youth can be the son of Crassus, the greatest coward and meanest wretch in the world."

This sight broke the spirit of the Romans more than all they had suffered. Crassus, though bowed down with grief, rode up and down the ranks and cried, "Romans, this loss is mine. The fortunes and glory of Rome stand safe in you. If you have any pity for me, who am bereft of the best of sons, show it in your revenge on the enemy. Put an end to their triumph; avenge their cruelty. Be not astonished at this loss; they who aspire to great things must expect to suffer. Lucullus did not defeat Tigranes, nor Scipio Antiochus, without some bloodshed. Rome has been blessed with great good fortune, but she has also known adversity, and it is through perseverance and fortitude that she has risen to her present height of power."

Thus he spoke, but his troops were not inspirited by his speech, and when he ordered them to shout for battle, although they obeyed, their shouts were feeble and unequal, while those of the enemy were bold and strong.

The fight lasted throughout the day, and the enemy's pikes did great execution; for they were so large and strong, and were pushed with such violence, that they often pierced through two men at once. When night came on, the enemy sent a message that they would give Crassus one night to bewail the loss of his son, if he did not in the mean time decide to go and surrender himself to King Arsaces.

The Romans were in a dreadful condition. Their wounded were lying on all sides, their dying groans and shrieks of agony filling the air, and preventing those who were able from paying proper attention to the burial of the dead. They could not remove the wounded without being observed by the enemy, and they dared not desert them. Flight was thus rendered impossible. They believed Crassus to be the cause of all their miseries, yet they called on him to speak to them; but he had given himself up to despair, and, having sought an obscure corner, had completely enveloped himself in a cloak, and lay stretched upon the ground.

Some of the officers tried to console him, but, finding it impossible to do so, they called a council of war and resolved to retire. This was therefore carried into effect as silently as possible, but as soon as the sick and wounded saw that they were to be deserted their doleful cries filled the whole army with confusion. Nevertheless they were left, and at break of day the Parthians fell upon them and killed four thousand. Their cavalry despatched a large number of stragglers on the plain, and then surrounded a hill where one of the Roman officers had stationed himself during the night with four cohorts, and put to death all except twenty, who cut their way through the enemy, sword in hand, and made their escape.

Crassus escaped to Caræ, and as soon as Surena heard where he was he determined to besiege the city; but, not wishing to do so unless he was absolutely certain that the Roman general was there, he sent an interpreter to the walls to summon Crassus or Cassius, and say that Surena desired an interview. When Crassus appeared, the man said that Surena was ready to conclude a peace with him on condition that he would give up Mesopotamia and be upon terms of friendship

CRASSUS

with the king, his master, for he thought that such a peace would be of advantage to both sides.

Cassius answered for the general, and desired that the time and place might be fixed as soon as possible for the interview. The interpreter, having obtained the information he sought, rode off.

Next day Surena led up his troops and began the siege, telling the Romans that if they wanted peace all they had to do was to deliver up Crassus and Cassius bound. The Romans were very indignant at having been so imposed upon, and at once made arrangements for their general to escape. This ought to have been kept secret, but Crassus told the whole plan to one of his guides, named Andromachus, a perfidious man, who repeated all he heard to the Parthians.

In the night Crassus marched out of Caræ with only four cohorts of foot-soldiers, a small number of cavalry, and five lictors, led by the false Andromachus. They got into some difficult places, and made little progress until day dawned, and then it was discovered that the Parthians were coming up. One of the Roman generals, who, with a small force, had reached a hill not far off, saw the danger Crassus was in, and immediately went to his aid. Then all the soldiers took Crassus in their midst, and, fencing him around with their shields, stoutly declared that no Parthian arrow should touch their general while any of them were left alive.

Fearing that Crassus might escape him after all, Surena resorted to stratagem. He instructed his soldiers to say in the presence of the prisoners that the king did not want to continue the war with the Romans, but meant to treat Crassus generously and to regain his friendship and alliance. These prisoners were soon after dismissed, and of course they reported to their general what the Parthians had said. After drawing back his troops, Surena, with a few of his principal officers, went over to the spot where the Romans were stationed, and, having unstrung his bow, offered his hand to Crassus, and said, "Our king has hitherto, though against his desire, given proofs of his power, but now it would be a pleasure to him to come to terms with the Romans and suffer them to depart in peace."

The troops were delighted, and urged their general to go with Surena to complete the peace, but he felt suspicious of the sudden friendship, and hesitated. Then they began to reproach him. "You are very willing to expose us to the weapons of the Parthians, but you dare not meet them yourself, even though they lay down their arms and ask for a friendly conference." This and other sneering remarks at last decided the fate of Crassus; and as he left he turned back and said, "All you Roman officers that are present will bear witness to the necessity I am under to take this step. When you are safe, pray tell the world that I was deceived by the enemy, and not that I was abandoned by my countrymen."

Octavius and Petronius, two officers, also a few soldiers, went forward with their general. The first persons they met were two of Surena's men, who addressed Crassus in Greek, and bade him send some of his soldiers to make sure that Surena and his company had no weapons concealed about their persons. "That is not necessary," he answered; "for if my life had been of any account I should not thus put myself in your hands."

Just then Surena himself, with half a dozen officers, advanced on horseback. "What is this I behold?" he asked,— "a Roman general on foot, when we are riding?" He then

CRASSUS

ordered a horse to be brought, and, as soon as Crassus had mounted, the equerries began to urge him forward. Octavius seized the bridle on one side and Petronius on the other, while the rest of the Romans tried to draw off those Parthians who pressed up to Crassus on each side. A scuffle ensued; Octavius drew his sword and killed one of the equerries; another came forward, and was killed also. Petronius received a blow on his breastplate, but was not wounded. Crassus was killed, and his head and right hand were cut off and sent to the Parthian king. The rest of his escort escaped.

Thus ended the tragic expedition that cost the lives of twenty thousand Romans and the imprisonment of ten thousand more. It had been undertaken by Crassus not for the glory of his country, but for the gratification of his ruling passion, love of gold, and he met the fate he deserved.

LUCULLUS

Lucullus was descended from a Roman family of distinction, and at a very early age was so impressed with the advantages of oratory that he made up his mind to devote himself to that branch. As he grew older he became remarkable for his eloquence, and made speeches, both in Greek and Latin, which showed considerable ability.

He had a brother named Marcus, whom he loved so devotedly that he could not be prevailed upon to accept a public office unless he also had one. This brotherly affection pleased the Romans so much that, although Marcus was the younger, he and Lucullus were elected ædiles at the same time. Ædiles were magistrates who had charge of public buildings, streets, roads, games, and processions.

Lucullus was only a youth at the time of the Marian or Social War, yet Sylla, the consul under whom he served, had such a high opinion of his honesty and talents that he employed him in enterprises of great importance. Sylla showed still further confidence in Lucullus when he made his will and appointed him guardian of his son, and neither this nor any other trust was ever betrayed.

Lucullus had nothing to do with the misery Sylla and Marius caused in Italy, for during that whole period he was in Asia on business. Shortly after the death of Sylla he was

LUCULLUS

chosen consul, with Marcus Cotta for his colleague. At that time it was proposed to begin the war against Mithridates again, and Lucullus was so anxious to command the Greek army that he left no stone unturned until he gained his point.

As soon as he got his appointment, therefore, he crossed over to Asia with his legion, and there met the rest of the troops that were to compose his army. Some of them had been badly disciplined, but Lucullus soon showed them what it was to have a real commander who would stand no trifling. While he was completing his arrangements, his colleague, Cotta, was so afraid of being outdone in the triumph of which he felt sure that he hurried on a battle; but he was defeated both by land and by sea, and nothing remained but for him to call on Lucullus for assistance. The soldiers did not wish their commander to go to Cotta, who, they said, had ruined himself by his own imprudence; but he told them that he would rather deliver one Roman out of the hands of the enemy than gain all the wealth the enemy had. He then marched against Mithridates with thirty thousand foot and twenty-five hundred horse soldiers.

Just as the challenge was accepted and the signal for battle given, there was a sudden explosion in the air, and an immense bright object, shaped like a barrel and of the color of melted silver, fell just between the two armies. Both were so affected by this wonderful occurrence that they parted without a single blow and retired to their camps. This took place in Phrygia.

Lucullus had been amazed at the size of the enemy's army, and, knowing that it would be impossible for them to get supplies enough for such myriads of men for any length of time, he caused his camp to be stocked with an abundance of provisions, and then resolved to wait.

Meanwhile, one dark, stormy night, Mithridates marched over to the country of the Cyzicenians, got there before daybreak, and posted himself upon Mount Adrastia. The Cyzicenians with Cotta's army had been beaten in the late battle, and had lost three thousand men and ten ships. As soon as Lucullus discovered that Mithridates had escaped, he followed, and posted his forces in the best places for cutting off the enemy's supplies. Then he called the soldiers together and said, "In a few days you shall gain a victory that shall not cost you one drop of blood." But the Cyzicenians, who were friendly to the Romans, were in a state of great alarm when they beheld Mithridates's troops in every direction, and wondered where Lucullus could be. They could see his camp plainly enough, but they had been told by the Persians that those were the Medes and Armenians, so they thought that there was no help for them with such an army on all sides. It was an immense relief, therefore, when a Roman made his way to the town and assured them that Lucullus was near. They could scarcely believe the good news at first, but when some soldiers arrived during the night they could no longer doubt.

Mithridates laid siege to Cyzicus, but Lucullus had so guarded the roads that the Persian could get no food for his soldiers, so he was obliged to lead them off. But Lucullus followed in a dreadful snow-storm, and the cold was so intense that many of his men perished. He overtook the enemy at last, however, slew a great number, and took fifteen thousand prisoners, besides six thousand horses and many camels. Mithridates then made his escape to the sea, leaving his generals to get off as best they could, but Lucullus fol-

LUCULLUS

lowed again, and again caused great havoc. It is said that in that campaign the Persians lost nearly three hundred thousand men in all.

There was great rejoicing in Cyzicus when Lucullus entered, but he had no time to make a long stay there, for he had resolved to go to the Hellespont to gather a fleet and pursue Mithridates into Bithynia, where he hoped to find him. But the Persian king heard of this, and made all haste to reach Pontus before Lucullus could stop him. A violent storm destroyed so many of his ships that for several days the shore was covered with the wreck which the waves threw up, and the king himself was only saved by pirates, who, when his ship was going to pieces, took him on their little boat, and, after passing through great suffering and danger, landed him safe at Heraclea, in Pontus.

Then Lucullus was advised by his officers to let the war rest awhile, but to that he would not consent. He pushed on into Pontus, where one city after another surrendered, much to the dissatisfaction of the soldiers, who preferred to take them by storm and so secure the plunder. But Lucullus was a mild, merciful man, and always rejoiced when he could gain what he desired with little bloodshed. This ought to have made him a favorite with his soldiers, but it was not so, for he was less popular than many a more brutal general had been.

He was resolute, however, and, once having started in pursuit of Mithridates, he stopped at nothing until he had chased that monarch into Armenia, where he placed himself under the protection of Tigranes, his son-in-law, who was king of Armenia.

Then Lucullus turned his attention to the reforms that were much needed in the Greek cities of Asia. The inhabitants had been for many years so oppressed by bad laws that any change could be only an improvement for them, and they soon had reason to bless that which Lucullus brought about. Their taxes had been so heavy that the poor creatures had been forced in many cases to sell their own sons and daughters, as well as the ornaments in their temples, in order to pay them, and, after that was done, had become slaves to their creditors, by whom they had been treated with horrible cruelty. When Lucullus came to their relief, after all the misery they had endured, he made himself universally beloved, and by the end of four years he had managed so well as to have freed the cities from debt and restored estates to their original owners.

Meanwhile, Appius Clodius was sent by Lucullus to Armenia as an ambassador, but when he got there he was ordered to wait for Tigranes, who was then engaged in a war in Phœnicia. He wasted no time, for while he waited he won over to the Roman interest many princes who had submitted to Armenia out of pure necessity, and a number of cities that Tigranes had conquered sent to let Clodius know that they were friendly to Rome. He promised them all the aid Lucullus could give, but desired them to remain quiet for the time being.

Tigranes was one of the haughtiest kings in the world, because he had been prosperous so long that he thought nothing was beyond his reach. He had conquered so many nations that several kings were servants at his court, and four in particular ran before him as footmen when he rode on horseback. When he gave audience, these captive kings were obliged to stand by with clasped hands, which was a token that they had forever resigned their liberty and were now the humblest of slaves.

LUCULLUS

When Tigranes returned, Clodius was admitted to his presence, and, without appearing in the least awed by his splendor, told him plainly that he had come to demand Mithridates, whom Lucullus claimed for his triumph, and that if he refused to give him up war would be declared. Such bold speech astonished Tigranes, who for more than twenty years had been used to the most servile conduct on the part of those to whom he deigned to grant an interview. However, he merely replied, "I will not deliver up Mithridates, and if the Romans begin war, I am able to defend myself." He was displeased not only at the way in which Clodius had spoken, but at Lucullus's having addressed him in his letter merely as king, and not as king of kings; therefore, in his answer, he gave Lucullus no title at all. But he sent Appius some magnificent presents. They were declined; then more were offered, out of which Appius selected a goblet, and returned the rest.

It must not be supposed that the haughty Tigranes had been kind or considerate to the fallen monarch for whom he now proposed to fight; on the contrary, he had treated him with contempt and kept him a prisoner in a sickly country some distance away. Now, for the first time, he was called to court and treated with respect.

When Appius Clodius returned to Lucullus, who was at Ephesus, he found that general enjoying the peace and good laws he had established in the Grecian cities of Asia by treating the inhabitants to all sorts of shows, processions, and trials of skill between wrestlers and gladiators. But without loss of time he went back to Pontus, put himself at the head of his troops, and prepared for war with Tigranes.

He had a long way to march, and subdued several cities on the route, but at last he reached the river Euphrates. It was so swollen by recent heavy rains that Lucullus stood wondering how he could collect boats to form a bridge for the passage of his army. In the evening the water began to subside, and by morning the river had returned to its natural size, which was so unusual that the people of the country declared Lucullus must be more than mortal. His importance was increased by a favorable omen that appeared just after the army had crossed. A number of heifers, sacred to the goddess Diana in Persia, and used only for sacrifice, appeared on the banks of the river while the army was going over, and one of them, leaving the flock, went and stood by a rock which was considered sacred to the goddess, and hung its head when Lucullus approached, as though offering itself for a victim. That animal, as well as a bull, was sacrificed to the Euphrates, and then the army rested before proceeding.

The next day Lucullus marched through Sophene, without doing the least injury to those who offered no resistance. When his men wanted to stop and take a fort which was supposed to be full of treasure, he pointed to Mount Taurus in the distance, and said, "Yonder is the fort you are to take; as for these things, they will of course belong to the conqueror." And so the Roman army moved on, crossed the Tigris, and entered Armenia.

The first man who told Tigranes of the approach of the enemy was executed on the spot, and after that no one had the courage to announce bad news until it could no longer be kept secret. Then Mithrobarzanes, one of the king's favorites, ventured to tell him how near Lucullus was, and the reward he got was a small army of cavalry and foot-soldiers, with which he was ordered to take the Roman general alive

LUCULLUS

and tread down his troops. He would have obeyed had he been able, for he fought bravely; but he was slain in the battle, his soldiers took to flight, and most of them were cut to pieces.

Then Tigranes retired to Mount Taurus, where he collected such a tremendous force that, as he viewed them, he turned proudly to those nearest him, and said, "My only fear is that I shall have Lucullus alone to fight, and not all the generals of Rome at once."

Lucullus, meanwhile, laid siege to Tigranocerta, the great city which the king had built, and when the grand Persian army came up he held a council of war. Some of his officers advised him to quit the siege and meet Tigranes with his whole army, while others thought it would be unsafe to leave so many enemies behind. Lucullus said both were right; so, dividing his forces, he left part to continue the siege under Muræna, while he led the other part to the battlefield.

He encamped on a large plain with a river in front of him, and his army looked so small as compared with that of the enemy that the Persian officers laughed at it, and cast lots for the spoils before the battle. Tigranes himself joined in the jeers of his officers. "If the Romans have come as ambassadors, they are too many; if as soldiers, they are too few," he said.

Next morning, at daybreak, Lucullus drew out his army, and as they marched in haste to a bend in the river, Tigranes thought they were retreating, and said to one of his generals, with a scornful smile, "Seest thou not, Taxiles, these invincible Romans taking to flight?" Taxiles answered, "Would indeed, O king, that some such piece of ill fortune might be yours; but the Romans do not, when going on a march, put on their best clothes or use bright shields and naked head-pieces, as now you see them; this is a preparation for war of men just ready to engage with their enemies."

While Taxiles was speaking, an eagle of the foremost legions moved to the right, by command of Lucullus, and the cohorts, according to their divisions and companies, formed in order and proceeded to pass over the river. Then Tigranes changed his tone, and, starting up as from a dream, exclaimed two or three times, "What! are these men coming upon us?" He then drew up his army in a hasty, disorderly manner, taking command of the main body himself, giving the left wing to the king of the Adiabenians, and the right to the king of the Medes.

As Lucullus was crossing the river, some of his officers bade him beware of that day, for it was an unlucky one to the Romans. "I will make it a happy day to the Romans," replied Lucullus. It was the sixth of October, and the anniversary of a defeat of the army.

Having thus spoken, Lucullus, armed with a breastplate of steel, formed of bright, shining scales, and wearing a fringed mantle, led on his men, sword in hand, to show them that the fight must be a close one. This was wise, because the Persians could only make use of their great, heavy weapons at a distance, and their armor was so unwieldy that unless they could use their pikes they had no means of defending themselves or attacking the enemy. Their legs and thighs alone were uncovered, and at those parts the Romans were ordered to deal their blows. But they had not much chance to do so, for with a cry of terror the Persians turned and fled, they and their horses, in heavy armor, falling upon the foot-soldiers and creating a panic. Their ranks were so thick and deep that they became entangled, wounded one another, and got trampled down, while multitudes were slain by the Romans, who followed them up and helped to increase the dreadful disorder.

Tigranes was among the first to fly, and when he met his son, who was sharing his misfortune, he took off his crown and bade him take it and save himself by another road if possible. Fearing to place it on his head, the young prince gave it in charge to one of his most faithful servants, who was afterwards taken prisoner by Lucullus. So that, besides killing nearly all the cavalry, and more than a hundred thousand foot-soldiers, the Romans secured a large number of captives and the crown of Tigranes. They lost only five men, and had one hundred wounded. Never was such a remarkable fight seen in the world, and one of the writers of the day said that the Romans were ashamed of themselves for having tried their arms against such a pitiful enemy.

Lucullus followed up his victory, took and burnt many of the royal palaces in Asia, and might have seized the kings themselves had they not fled like wild beasts and hidden themselves in the forests. Both Mithridates and Tigranes were so subdued that they never dared to make further resistance against the Roman army. Still, Lucullus could not derive all the advantage from his conquests that he ought to have done, for he was never a favorite with his troops, and after eight years of fighting they declared that they had had enough of hardship, and wanted to go home and enjoy their deserved repose.

Then the popular party in Rome, taking advantage of the complaints of the army, accused Lucullus of prolonging the war in order that he might lay up stores of wealth for himself, and at last succeeded in having him removed from command and Pompey made general in his stead. On account of this accusation many were opposed to allowing a triumph to Lucullus on his return to Rome, but some of the noblest statesmen used their influence to get this honor for him, because they thought he really deserved it. His procession was not as long as many others had been, but it made a splendid display of the arms and other warlike implements taken from the enemy. There were the cavalry captives, ten splendid chariots armed with sharp scythes and followed by sixty high officers of the Persian army. After these were drawn a hundred and ten war-vessels with brazen prows, preceding a massive gold statue of Mithridates six feet high, on which was his shield set with precious stones. Then came men carrying twenty large silver urns, gold cups, vases, arms, and a quantity of coin. These were followed by eight mules bearing golden couches, and fifty-six more laden with silver bullion. The procession closed with one hundred and seven other mules carrying two million seven hundred thousand drachmas in silver coin. A grand entertainment was provided for the whole city and all the neighboring villages besides.

Now the senate had hoped that Lucullus was going to support the Patrician party, which had suffered a good deal from the tyranny of Pompey, but they soon found their mistake, for he thought he had endured hardships enough, and had returned with the determination to pass the rest of his life in ease and luxury. He built for his own use superb villas near Naples and Tusculum, and had everything in such magnificent style that even the wealthiest men of the day were astonished. His gardens excelled those owned by any king of his time, and his houses were adorned with the most costly paintings and statuary that could be found. Lucullus was a man of learning and refinement, as was clearly shown by the splendid and costly library he collected. It was so complete that the learned men of the time never lost an opportunity to visit it, and they were always made welcome by the owner.

Like most people who become suddenly rich, Lucullus was fond of display. His beds were covered with costly quilts, his side-boards groaned under the weight of silver and gold drinking-vessels and dishes set with precious stones, and the variety and cooking of the provisions that were served to him daily were marvellous. When he entertained his friends, the most renowned musicians and comedians were engaged to perform for them, at an enormous expense.

Once, when some Grecian travellers were in Rome, they were invited to the house of Lucullus a number of times, but at last refused to go, because they feared he was incurring too great an expense for their entertainment. When Lucullus heard their excuse, he smiled, and said, "It is true, my friends, that some of the preparations are made for you, but the greatest part is for Lucullus."

He prided himself upon his extravagance, and nothing gave him more pleasure than to have it spoken of. Quite a moderate repast was set before him one evening when he chanced to dine alone; thereupon he summoned his chief cook and took him to task for it. "I thought that, as there were to be no guests, my master would not want an expensive supper," said the man, by way of apology. "What!" exclaimed Lucullus, "didst thou not know that this evening Lucullus sups with Lucullus?"

On entering the Forum, one day, he met Cicero, who stood conversing with Pompey. They were intimate friends of his, and, after saluting him familiarly, asked, "Are you at leisure to receive us at your house?" "Nothing could give me greater pleasure; come at once," answered Lucullus. "No, we will wait on you this evening," said Cicero, "on condition that you make no great preparations, but give us only what is provided for yourself." Lucullus objected at first, but, as they insisted, he turned to a servant who accompanied him and said, "I shall sup to-night in the Apollo." The friends did not suspect the stratagem, but this is what it meant: each dining-room had its own china and plate, as well as style of entertainment; the Apollo was the most magnificent of them all, and when the servants received an order to serve a meal there they knew that it was to cost no less than fifty thousand drachmas, and to consist of the very best of everything. Knowing only that Lucullus had merely named the dining-room, and not aware of the orders connected with it, Cicero and Pompey were amazed at the splendor of the repast that was laid before them a few hours later.

And so Lucullus lived on, taking no part whatever in public affairs, until, as he grew old, he lost his mind. Then the brother to whom he had always been devotedly attached took care of him and his estates. He died in the sixty-seventh year of his age, much regretted by the people, who attended his funeral procession in great numbers.

POMPEY

POMPEY was an exceedingly handsome man, and his manners were so pleasing and his conversation so agreeable that he early won the affection of his countrymen. He lived at the same time with Lucullus, whose life we have given, but, unlike that Roman, Pompey's tastes and habits were plain and simple.

Once, when he was dangerously ill and could eat scarcely anything, his physician ordered him a thrush, but, as thrushes were out of season, they were not to be found in the markets. Lucullus had them in his bird-houses all the year, and it was proposed to send to him for one. "Does Pompey's life depend upon the luxury of Lucullus?" asked the sick man. Then, without regard to the physician's order, he ate something that was easy to be had. That happened when he was middle-aged.

He was only nineteen years old when he served under his father in the war against Cinna. Lucius Terentius was his comrade, and slept in the same tent with him, but he had been bribed by Cinna to kill him while others set fire to the general's tent. Pompey found it out, and on the night set apart for the horrible deed he stole softly out of the tent after having gone to bed, and went with a guard to protect his father. As soon as Terentius supposed he was asleep, he crawled over to the bed and stabbed it in many places, thinking that Pompey was there. Then there was a mutiny among the soldiers, which it required all the eloquence young Pompey could command to quiet.

Cinna was killed not long after, and Carbo became ruler. This happened after the Romans had experienced so many calamities that any change was welcomed by them; but they soon found Carbo to be a most savage tyrant, and so rejoiced when Sylla returned to Italy.

Pompey was then at Picenum, where he raised an army of about seventeen thousand men. With this force he set out to join Sylla, and succeeded in doing so only after being attacked several times by the opposite party. He was just twenty-three years old when he elevated himself to the office of general, and Sylla was so struck by his appearance and the excellent condition of his army that he saluted him as Imperator when they met. This was an honorable title, and one that had never before been bestowed on a Roman who had not been in the senate; indeed, it was one for which such great generals as Scipio and Marius were fighting. But Sylla felt that Pompey deserved it, and his respect for that young man was so great that he would always rise and uncover his head when he approached. When he had made himself master of Italy and was declared dictator, he rewarded his principal officers handsomely; but to Pompey he gave most, knowing that he owed more to his services than to those of any other man.

Three years later Pompey was sent to Sicily, because the friends of Marius were fortifying themselves there. He retook the island, and was then ordered to Africa, where in forty days he drove out Domitius with his grand army. The Romans were astonished at his wonderful exploits, and on his

POMPEY

return prepared to receive him with every mark of honor and kindness. Sylla marched at their head to meet the hero, and, after embracing him affectionately, called him Pompey the Great, bidding all who were present to do the same.

Now, Pompey desired the honor of a triumph, and there can be no question that he deserved one; but Sylla was jealous of his fast-growing power, and said that no Roman who had not first been consul or prætor had ever had a triumph, and that such a proceeding would excite envy among other officers. But Pompey was determined, and said, "Do not forget that more people worship the rising than the setting sun." He meant that his power was increasing, while Sylla's was on the decline. Feeling the truth of this remark, and admiring Pompey's spirit, Sylla cried, "Let him triumph! let him triumph!" and so the young man had his way.

He might then have become a senator if he had chosen, but he preferred to seek extraordinary honors, and his triumph was certainly such. After it was over he took his place among the Roman knights, which pleased the populace immensely. But Sylla was anxious on account of the height of glory to which he had risen, though he dared not hinder him. He said nothing until Lepidus was raised to the consulship by Pompey's influence. Then, when Pompey passed through the Forum with a great train of followers, he cried out, "I see, young man, that you are proud of your victory; and indeed it was a great thing for you to obtain the consulship for Lepidus, the worst man in Rome, in preference to Catulus, the best and most deserving; but beware, for you have made your enemy stronger than yourself."

The truth of Sylla's words appeared shortly after his death, for Lepidus desired to become dictator, and armed himself for that purpose against Catulus, who had to call in the aid of Pompey. Lepidus was then driven out of Italy, and fled to Sardinia, where he died.

After a short season of peace and quiet, the senate ordered Pompey to Spain to support Metellus against the powerful Sertorius, whose activity and skill made him a most formidable opponent. When Sertorius heard of this addition to the Roman army, he said, "I shall want no other weapons than a rod and ferule to chastise the boy, but I fear the old woman." By the boy he meant Pompey, who was just thirty years old; Metellus was "the old woman." Though he spoke thus, he was really afraid of Pompey, and so made his plans with extreme caution. Metellus was less an object of dread, because he had given himself up to a life of luxury and pleasure quite unfit for a soldier.

The defeat of Lauron, narrated in the life of Sertorius, was a dreadful blow to Pompey, but he gained the next battle, which encouraged him so much that he hastened to attack Sertorius near the river Sucro. In that engagement he was wounded in the hand, and he would certainly have been captured had he not jumped from his horse and turned it loose towards the enemy. They were so dazzled by the rich trappings that they began to quarrel over them, as Pompey had expected, and so he made his escape. The war continued, with little success on either side, until Sertorius was murdered by his own officers, when it was brought to a close. Perpenna, who succeeded Sertorius, had taken charge of his private papers, and when Pompey took Perpenna prisoner he burnt them without reading them, because he feared they might cast disgrace on some of the most powerful men of Rome, and so be the cause of new wars. This was wise and prudent.

POMPEY

Pompey returned to Rome when the civil war was at its height, and Crassus was in command of the army. A great battle had just been fought, and five thousand slaves had fled; but Pompey met them and put them all to death, and then sent this message to the senate: "Crassus has beaten the gladiators in a pitched battle, but I have cut up the war by the roots."

The Romans were delighted to honor a man whom they had learned to love and admire, so they gave him a second triumph, and at the same time he was created consul, with Crassus for his colleague. One of the scenes that pleased them most was when Pompey appeared in the Forum with other Roman knights, each to give an account to the two censors of his actions in the war, and to demand his discharge. This custom was always observed, and each knight received, according to his behavior, marks of honor or of disgrace.

Pompey advanced, preceded by his lictors and leading his horse, amidst profound silence, everybody staring at him in admiration. The older censor spoke: "Pompey the Great, I demand of you whether you have served all the campaigns required by law?" He answered in a loud voice, "I have served them all; and all under myself as general." Loud cheers and applause greeted this reply, and the censors conducted the new consul to his home, followed by the multitude.

Though Pompey and Crassus were consuls together, they never could agree on any point, but kept up a continual quarrelling. When their term of office ended, a knight, who had never taken part in public affairs, mounted the rostrum one day before a large crowd of people, and said, "Jupiter has appeared to me in a dream, and commanded me to tell the consuls that they must not give up their office until they are friends." Pompey stood still and said nothing, but Crassus went to him, took his hand, and spoke as follows: "I do not think, fellow-citizens, that I do anything mean or dishonorable in making the first advance to Pompey, on whom you were pleased to bestow the title of Great when he was but a beardless youth, and for whom you voted two triumphs before he was a senator." Thus were they reconciled before they went out of office.

About this time the pirates had become so powerful in the Mediterranean that they attacked islands and seaport towns as well as ships, and persons of wealth, high birth, and intellect joined their band just as though their employment were an honorable one. They had watch-towers and arsenals, strongly fortified, and their fleets were gayly ornamented, as if they took a pride in their villany. They owned a thousand ships and four hundred cities, and were so powerful that they could insult Roman citizens without fear of punishment. Once they carried off two prætors in their purple robes, with all their servants and lictors, and at another time seized the daughter of Antony, a distinguished citizen, and would not release her until they had received a large ransom. When a captive declared himself to be a Roman, and told his name, the pirates would pretend surprise and fear, fall at his feet, and humbly beseech him to forgive them. Then they would dress him in a Roman gown, and place Roman shoes on his feet, so that they might know him another time, they said, and, putting out a ship's ladder when they were far out at sea, tell him he was free to go, and wish him a pleasant journey. If he hesitated, he was thrown overboard.

Of course trade and navigation came to a stand-still when every ship was in danger from pirates, and there was

POMPEY

reason to fear a famine in Rome: so, at last, Pompey was sent to clear the seas. This wonderful achievement was performed in four months: twenty thousand pirates were taken prisoners, and the rest were compelled to retire to Cilicia, which was too far from Rome for them to do further damage. The prisoners were not put to death; Pompey, was too humane for that; he gave them small tracts of land in various scantily-populated regions, thus offering them a chance to become honest citizens.

When the news was brought to Rome that the war with the pirates was finished, Pompey was considered such an able general that he was appointed over Lucullus to carry on the war against Mithridates and Tigranes, with more power than had ever been intrusted to any Roman general before. On his arrival in Asia he altered everything that Lucullus had done, merely to show that the latter no longer had authority, which was of course very galling to that general. For he had so disabled Mithridates and Tigranes that they could offer little opposition to Pompey, who got credit for the conquest that really belonged to Lucullus. Nevertheless, Pompey made some hard fights in different parts of Asia, and won some brilliant victories before the war ended; then, crowned with glory, he turned homeward, stopping in Greece by the way.

At Mitylene he witnessed the exercises of the poets, all of whom selected the actions of Pompey for their theme this year. He was so much pleased with their theatre that he took a plan of it, intending to build one similar, but larger, in Rome. Then he visited several other Greek cities, and lastly Athens, to which he presented fifty talents for improvements.

Rumors had reached Rome that Pompey was coming back with a powerful army for the purpose of establishing himself as sole ruler. But as soon as he landed in Italy he mustered his soldiers, bade each farewell, and sent him home, only requesting that none would fail to take part in his triumph. Then he went to Rome as a private citizen, and the whole city turned out to meet him with loud shouts of greeting.

His triumph lasted two days, and Rome had never witnessed one more splendid. Pompey's greatest glory was not in the fact that he had triumphed three times, for other Romans had done likewise, but that he seemed to have led the whole world captive; for his first triumph had been over Africa, his second over Europe, and his third over Asia.

At this time Cæsar was laying the foundation for future greatness. He had just returned from Spain, and wanted to be consul, and in order to accomplish this it was necessary that Crassus and Pompey should be friends, so that both would uphold him. He therefore set to work to reconcile them, which would have been all very well if the intention had been good, but it was only to serve himself that he wanted, and the union he formed, which is known in history as the *First Triumvirate*, proved a fatal blow to the constitution of Rome.

Then Pompey and Cæsar became fast friends and carried everything before them. Cicero and Cato were not on their side, so the former was banished and the latter was sent to Cyprus, it being necessary to get both out of the way. In effecting all this Pompey had taken into his service Clodius, one of the vilest wretches that ever lived, but in course of time he quarrelled with him, and Cicero was recalled.

For a while Pompey's popularity with the populace had not been so great as formerly, but he regained their good will when he was intrusted with the care of supplying the city with

POMPEY

corn in a time of scarcity. It was Cicero, the great orator, who induced the senate to appoint Pompey to that position, which was a most important one, because it gave him control over the merchant as well as the farmer. He sent agents to various places, and went himself to Sicily, Sardinia, and Africa, working with such success that he filled the markets with grain and covered the sea with his ships. So not only was there plenty in Rome, but she was even in condition to supply the wants of her neighbors.

Now Pompey married Julia, Cæsar's sister, and Cæsar married Calpurnia, the daughter of Piso, who was consul. These two men continued to be fast friends, but Cæsar was sent to Gaul with an army, and Pompey gave great offence by devoting himself to his wife and travelling about with her, instead of giving his whole attention to his country. But he gained public favor by opening his theatre and treating the people to all sorts of games, shows, gymnastics, and music, besides a battle of lions, and one of elephants, which was witnessed with wonder and delight.

A change had taken place in public affairs at Rome, and those who stood for offices now fought for them or got them by means of bribes. Some of the more honest citizens were so indignant that it was proposed to appoint a dictator, and Pompey was the man selected. But, fearing that as dictator he might become a tyrant, it was decided, after a great deal of debate, to appoint him sole consul. Before this happened his wife had died, so one bond between him and Cæsar was broken, and not many months after he became sole consul he married Cornelia, the daughter of Scipio, a young, beautiful, and highly-accomplished lady.

Meanwhile, Cæsar had made himself famous in Gaul, and his friends declared that his services to his country were so great that he deserved at least a second consulship. Pompey opposed this, saying that as there was no doubt that Cæsar wished to be released from command, he ought to return home to stand for office. The fact was that Pompey had no desire to share his government with any one; so, in order to weaken Cæsar, he demanded back the two legions he had lent him, under pretence that he was about to engage in a war with Parthia. Cæsar was not deceived, but returned the soldiers loaded with costly presents.

Not long after, Pompey was attacked by a dangerous illness. This was at Naples. He recovered, and the citizens offered sacrifices to celebrate the happy event. Others imitated the Neapolitans, until there was not a town or village in all Italy that did not rejoice publicly on account of Pompey's recovery. As he journeyed towards Rome he was greeted by crowds of people, who assembled from different quarters with garlands on their heads and lighted torches in their hands to see the hero, whose path they strewed with flowers. Such a display of affection was no doubt gratifying to Pompey, but it is said to have been one of the chief causes of the civil war, for it turned Pompey's head, and so increased his confidence in himself that he felt contempt for Cæsar's power, and believed that it would be very easy to subdue him.

When any one expressed anxiety about a war, and wondered where forces were to come from should Cæsar choose to advance on Rome, he said, "If in Italy I do but stamp upon the ground; an army will appear."

Cæsar was not idle. He slowly advanced towards Italy, and not only sent his soldiers to vote in the elections, but bribed such men as Paulus, Curio, and Mark Antony to take his side.

The time for which Cæsar had been appointed to command was drawing to a close, and, when the question of his removal arose, Curio made the demand that either Pompey's army should have a new commander or that Cæsar's should retain theirs. Marcellus then rose and pronounced Cæsar a robber, who should be looked upon as an enemy to Rome unless he would disband his army. Curio, with the assistance of Antony and Piso, demanded that it be put to the vote; the result favored Pompey, and the people clapped their hands for joy.

Pompey was not present, because it was not lawful for generals in command of an army to enter the city, so Marcellus, accompanied by the senate, went solemnly to meet him, and addressed him thus: "Pompey, I charge you to assist your country, for which purpose you shall make use of what troops you have, and levy what new ones you please."

Other senators spoke to the same purpose, but Antony, who was in favor of peace, read a letter of Cæsar's, in which he proposed that both he and Pompey should dismiss their armies and let the people judge which of them should rule. This proposition met with so much favor that Pompey found it more difficult to levy an army than he had supposed. Cicero then tried to bring about a reconciliation, and proposed that Cæsar should give up Gaul, disband all his army except two legions, and wait for another consulship. But Pompey and his friends would not agree to any such thing.

Just then news was brought that Cæsar was marching on Rome. That general was indeed on the road, but when he reached the banks of the Rubicon he hesitated whether to advance or recede. At last he exclaimed, "The die is cast!" and led his army over.

Such consternation had never filled Rome before, and the senate and magistrates ran to Pompey to find out what he meant to do. Tullus asked what forces he could command. After a moment's pause Pompey said, "I have the two legions that Cæsar sent back, and believe that I shall shortly be able to make up a body of thirty thousand men."

"O Pompey, you have deceived us!" cried Tullus; "let a messenger be at once sent to make terms with Cæsar."

"Now stamp upon the ground and call forth the forces you promised us," bade Favonius. Pompey made no answer to this raillery, and Cato said, "Let us choose Pompey for general with absolute authority, for the men who do great evils know best how to cure them." He echoed the opinion of all Rome in calling the war which Pompey had brought about an evil, but there was no help for it now, so he went in command of forces to Sicily, while the rest of the senators departed, each to his separate post.

Thus was the whole of Italy up in arms, though no one could say what it was best to do. People from the suburbs flocked to Rome, while those within the city were quitting it as fast as possible, and such was the confusion that everybody interfered with Pompey's plans, each giving advice according as he was affected by doubt, fear, or grief. Then, again, all sorts of rumors about the enemy filled the air, and those who reported them to Pompey were angry if he did not believe and immediately act upon them. At length, almost beside himself with the uproar, Pompey determined to leave the city, and, commanding the senate to follow, he did so as soon as it was dark. The consuls did not even wait to offer the customary sacrifices to the gods before going to war, so anxious were they to be with the general whom they loved even when they found fault with his management.

A few days later Cæsar entered Rome, but he behaved with so much kindness and consideration towards the inhabitants that their fears were soon at rest. He took all the money he wanted from the public treasury, and then went after Pompey, resolved to drive him out of Italy before he could be joined by his forces from Spain.

Pompey hastened to Brundusium, where he had a number of ships, and, having fortified the town, waited there until his whole army had embarked, then, after sending his father-in-law, Scipio, and his son Cnæus to Syria to provide war-vessels, he went on shipboard himself and sailed away.

Cæsar was surprised at the end of sixty days to find himself master of Italy, and without having caused the least bloodshed; but he could not follow Pompey, because he had no ships, so he marched to Spain, hoping to win over the forces there. In this he succeeded, and then passed the Alps again and proceeded through Italy to Brundusium. Thence he crossed the sea and landed at Oricum. One of his prisoners, who was a friend to Pompey, was then sent to propose that both armies should be disbanded within three days and all return to Italy.

But Pompey, who had got together a grand army of the very flower of Italy, suspected a snare, and so hastened to the sea and secured all the forts and shipping stations. Then Cæsar was forced to give battle or run the risk of starvation, because Pompey's men were so placed that he could get no supplies. So he daily attacked Pompey's entrenchments, and usually had the advantage, but one day he was in danger of losing his army, for Pompey put his entire detachment to flight and killed two thousand men.

Provisions began to be scarce with Cæsar, so he marched on to Thessaly, and Pompey's men were so rejoiced at this, as well as at their recent victory, that they urged him to follow. But some of the officers advised him instead to return to Italy, take possession, and proclaim himself victor. That he could not do, because Scipio and others of high dignity would then be left to the mercy of Cæsar, so he decided that the next best thing for Rome was to keep the war as far away from her as possible. He therefore followed Cæsar, with the intention of avoiding a general battle, but of wearing him out with sieges. However, after a time he yielded to the demand of his officers and began an engagement, though against his better judgment.

When Cæsar saw Pompey's army drawn up for battle, he exclaimed, "The long-wished-for day is come on which we shall fight with men, and not with want and famine." He then ordered the red mantle, the signal of battle among the Romans, to be hoisted before his tent, and his soldiers no sooner saw it than they ran to arms with loud shouts of joy.

It is unnecessary to give all the details of this memorable battle. Pompey had twice the number of men that Cæsar had, and the fight was a desperate one on both sides. There were the same arms, troops marshalled in the same manner, the same standards, the strength and flower of one and the same nation turned upon itself. The tenth legion, which Cæsar commanded, signalized itself, as it always did, and towards the close of the battle put the enemy to flight. Utterly disheartened and bowed down by grief, Pompey quitted the ranks and retired to his tent, where he sat down without

POMPEY

speaking a word until some of Cæsar's men entered. "What! into my camp too!" he exclaimed. Then, rising, he mounted his horse and rode away. He had very few people with him, and, finding that he was not pursued, he left his horse and walked slowly on. It must have been a sad moment for a man who for thirty-four years had been used to conquer when he found himself in his old age defeated and forced to fly from the battlefield. He passed on to Tempe, where, in a state of exhaustion, and burning with thirst, he threw himself upon his face and drank a deep draught from the river. He then went on to the sea-coast, and passed the night in the cabin of a poor fisherman. Next morning he went on board a boat, taking with him the freemen who had accompanied him, and bidding the slaves go to Cæsar and fear nothing.

A merchant-ship chanced to be lying off, just ready to set sail, and Pompey hailed it. The commander was a Roman citizen, named Peticius, who knew Pompey well, and no sooner did he recognize the fallen hero than he took him on board, and treated him with the utmost kindness and consideration. They sailed by Mitylene, where Cornelia awaited her husband. She was overwhelmed with grief when she beheld him with but one ship, and that not his own, but he consoled her as best he could, and assured her that he was ready to try his fortune again. For that purpose he sailed about and collected a navy, with which he determined to claim the hospitality of young King Ptolemy in Egypt. On arriving in Africa, he found that the king was posted with his army at the city of Pelusium. He sent a messenger to announce his arrival.

Ptolemy was very young, so, calling a council of his prime minister and ablest officers, he asked their advice. Some were for giving Pompey an honorable reception, while others advised the king to order him to depart, saying, "If you receive him, you will have Cæsar for your enemy and Pompey for your master. If you order him off, he may one day seek revenge, and Cæsar may resent your not having put him in his hands. The best method, therefore, is to send for him and put him to death. Thus you will do Cæsar a favor and have nothing to fear from Pompey. Dead men do not bite."

It was therefore decided that Pompey should be put to death, and Achillas was appointed to do the deed. He went in a small boat with Septimius, who had once been an officer under Pompey, and several others. They rowed up to the side of Pompey's ship, and Septimius greeted him in Latin, calling him Imperator, the highest title a Roman could have. Achillas saluted him in Greek, and invited him to step into his boat, saying that the water was too shallow near the shore for his vessel to go in. Pompey had his misgivings, but as by this time the coast was covered with troops, and several of Ptolemy's ships were ready to sail, there was nothing for him to do but obey. He therefore embraced Cornelia, who wept bitterly, and ordered one of his liberated slaves named Philip, and a servant named Scenes, to get into the boat before him. As he stepped in himself, he turned to his wife and repeated this verse of Sophocles:

> "He that once enters at a tyrant's door
> becomes a slave, though he were free before."

These were the last words he ever spoke to his friends.

As the boat was rowed to shore, Pompey noticed that not a man in it either spoke to him or showed him the slightest civility. That alarmed him, but he looked at Septimius and said, "Methinks I remember you to have been my fellow-

POMPEY

soldier." Septimius answered only with a nod, and Pompey did not venture another remark. When he was about to step ashore, he took hold of Philip's hand to steady himself, and, as he did so, Septimius ran him through the body.

Pompey seized his robe and covered his face, not allowing a single groan to escape his lips, while Achillas and others despatched him with many blows.

Cornelia, who had been watching her husband from the galley, gave a shriek that was heard on shore when she witnessed the murder. Her friends weighed anchor immediately, and a brisk gale carried them out to sea so fast that the Egyptians did not think it worth while to pursue them.

Having cut off Pompey's head, the murderers threw the body out of the boat naked, but Philip washed it and wrapped it in one of his own garments; then, after hunting about for a long time, he found some rotten planks, with which he set to work to build a funeral pile. While he was thus engaged, an old Roman citizen, who in his youth had served in the wars under Pompey, came up to him and asked, "Who are you that are preparing the funeral of Pompey the Great?" "I am his freedman," answered Philip. "Nay, then, you shall not have this honor alone," returned the other; "let me, too, I pray you, have my share in this pious office, so that I may not repent of having passed so many years in a foreign land. Let me have the honor of touching and wrapping up the body of Pompey, the greatest general Rome ever had."

Not long after, Cæsar arrived in Egypt, and when Pompey's head was presented to him he turned aside and shuddered; when Pompey's seal was laid before him he burst into tears. Achillas he put to death, and King Ptolemy, being defeated in a battle on the banks of the Nile, ran away, and was never heard of afterwards.

The ashes of Pompey were carried to his wife, Cornelia, who buried them at his country-seat near Alba.

CICERO

NOT much is positively known about the parents of Marcus Tullius Cicero, but he was born in the same year which gave birth to Pompey the Great. He became prominent at a very early age, for he was so quick and bright at school that the other boys wondered at him, and mentioned him so often at home that their fathers would visit the school on purpose to hear the clever pupil recite. He wanted to learn everything, but particularly poetry, for which he showed peculiar taste. His poem on the fable of Glaucus, which he wrote when a boy, still exists, and later in life he had the name of being not only the best poet but the best orator in Rome. Even at the present time his orations are considered perfect samples of rhetoric, but his verses have been cast into the shade by those of the many great poets that have followed him.

Scævola, a celebrated lawyer, taught Cicero all about the laws and politics of Rome; and his knowledge of military affairs, which was considered an important part of every Roman boy's education, he gained in actual service under the Consul Strabo, father of Pompey the Great. But he preferred to study philosophy and rhetoric, and returned to them just as soon as he could, devoting part of each day to declaiming in Greek and Latin.

His introduction into public life was made in defence of Roscius Amerinus, one of Sylla's emancipated slaves. Roscius was accused of having murdered his own father; Cicero defended him and won the suit. This happened when Sylla was at the height of his power; so, thinking it prudent to get out of the way after having defended a man whom Sylla had accused, Cicero determined to travel. He visited Greece, where he studied under the most learned men of the day; then he went to Asia and mingled with the great philosophers and rhetoricians. Like Demosthenes, Cicero began by having serious defects both in manner and delivery; but he took lessons of Roscius, the comedian, and Æsop, the tragedian, until he became so excellent in the art of oratory that when he was leaving Athens a learned scholar said to him, "You have my praise, Cicero, and Greece my pity, since those arts and that eloquence which are the only glories that remain to her will now be transferred by you to Rome."

He was thirty years of age when he returned to his native city, so much improved in public speaking that he excelled all the other orators, and soon became the most popular of them.

He was appointed quæstor, or public treasurer, at a time when there was great need of grain in Rome, and was sent to Sicily to procure it. At first the people complained of him, but he proved himself so just and reasonable that they afterwards declared they liked him better than any quæstor Rome had ever sent them. He gained further favor with the Sicilians by his prosecution of Verres, who had been their prætor and had filled the office very badly. Verres was convicted, and the Sicilians were so grateful to Cicero that later, when he became ædile, they sent him all sorts of presents from their island.

CICERO

Cicero owned a modest country-seat near Naples, and another at Pompeii, but he lived most of the time on the Palatine Hill, in Rome, so that people who desired to visit him needed not to make a journey. He had the good taste to live simply, though his wife had brought him a fortune, and he had besides plenty of money of his own. His companions were literary men, Greek and Roman, and he held a levee every day, as Pompey did.

Two years after he became ædile he was raised to the office of prætor, and presided at the courts of justice with great dignity and honor. But it had long been his aim to become consul, and he relied on Cæsar and Pompey to raise him to that office. They succeeded in doing so, and he won the blessings of his countrymen by crushing the conspiracy of Catiline. This he could only have done as consul, and he stood for that office in a complete suit of armor under his tunic, because he knew that Catiline and his party had determined to assassinate him. Their scheme was to put Cicero out of the way, make Catiline consul, and thus get complete control of the government into their own hands. It was bold and outrageous, but they might have succeeded had not the plot been revealed to Cicero, who exposed it in an oration, and thus saved Rome and drove Catiline from the city. When the people became aware of the danger they had escaped, they saluted Cicero as the father and deliverer of his country, and when he walked home from the market-place, after witnessing the execution of Catiline's principal assistants, all the houses were illuminated in honor of him, and he was followed by a train of the most distinguished of the citizens.

His authority at that time was very great, but he excited the envy of not a few because he was continually praising himself, and people grew tired of hearing him repeat again and again the benefit he had done his country in crushing Catiline. On the other hand, it must be admitted that, though he loved to sound his own praises, he did not envy others, and was always ready to give them whatever credit they deserved. This may be seen in his writings and in some of his sayings. For example, he called Aristotle "a river of flowing gold;" of Plato's Dialogues he said, "If Jupiter were to speak, it would be in language like theirs." When asked which of Demosthenes's orations he preferred, he answered, "The longest." When Cæsar was in power, Cicero obtained from him the Roman citizenship for a learned Greek, whose instruction he advised many youths to seek; and he gave several other instances of how highly he esteemed the merits of the virtuous and the wise. These are some samples of his bright repartee: When Crassus was going to Syria he wanted to leave Cicero his friend; therefore, on meeting him one day, he told him that he would sup with him. Cicero accepted the offer politely. A few days after Vatinius sent word that he wanted to make friends with him. "What!" said Cicero, "does Vatinius too want to sup with me?" This showed that he understood why Crassus wished to partake of his hospitality. A report was brought to Cicero of the death of Vatinius, and when he heard that it was false he said, "May the rascal that told the news perish because it is not true!" There was a man named Octavius, who was suspected of having African blood in his veins. He said, one day, when Cicero was pleading in court, that he could not hear him. "That is strange," returned the orator, "for you have holes in your ears." This was a mark of slavery among some nations; but the Africans wore earrings for ornament. There was a young man accused of having killed his father with poisoned cake. He was very insolent to Cicero, who cross-questioned him, and offered angry threats. "I had much rather have your threats than your cake," said Cicero. Publius Sestius had taken Cicero to defend him in an important case, but would not permit anybody to talk but himself; and when the judges were about to acquit him Cicero called out, "Make the best use of your time to-day, Sestius, for nobody will listen to you to-morrow." Marcus Appius said, in the introduction to one of his pleadings, that his client had desired him to try all that industry, eloquence, and fidelity in his cause could do. When he had finished, Cicero said, "What a hard-hearted man you are not to do any one thing that your client asked of you!" It need scarcely be said that Cicero excited a great deal of ill feeling by such cutting remarks, because they were often made merely for the sake of raising a laugh.

Lucius Cotta was censor when Cicero stood for the consulship. Cotta was known to be a great lover of wine, and often drank to excess. During the canvass, feeling thirsty, Cicero called for a cup of water; his friends stood close about him while he drank. "That is right," he said; "conceal me, for otherwise the censor may call me to account for drinking water."

Cicero had some enemies, but the most powerful of them all was Clodius, a bold, bad man, descended from an illustrious Roman family. Clodius hated Cicero so much that he determined to ruin him, and with that object in view caused the old law to be renewed which declared any one guilty of treason who had a citizen put to death without trial. This was a blow aimed at Cicero, who had executed those engaged in the Catiline conspiracy.

When Cicero was accused of this crime he put on mourning, and went around among the people humbly begging their grace. Nearly all the knights followed his example, and there were no fewer than twenty thousand young men of the best families walking about Rome in mourning attire, with hair untrimmed, supplicating the people for Cicero. But Clodius, with his lawless band of ruffians, met them at every turn, and pelted them with dirt and stones. At last matters came to such a pass that it was clear Cicero must either leave the country or fight. He applied to Pompey for assistance; but Pompey slipped out of the back door and avoided the interview. Cicero had often befriended him, therefore he dared not refuse, but as he was now Cæsar's son-in-law, and as Cæsar was no friend to Cicero just then, he preferred not to side with the orator.

Cicero next applied to the consuls; one advised him to wait until Clodius fell into disfavor, the other treated him roughly; but his friends, one and all, advised him to go into exile. So one night he started by land, escorted by a party of friends, and travelled until he reached Brundusium, whence he set sail for Greece.

No sooner did Clodius discover that he was gone than he pronounced a decree of exile against him, and then destroyed his farm, burned his villa and his city house, and on the site of the latter built a temple to Liberty. But in course of time Clodius made himself so obnoxious to the good citizens that Pompey went about among Cicero's friends urging them to get him recalled to Rome, and the senate declared that they would attend to no business whatever until that was done. Then Lentulus, the consul, used his efforts in Cicero's favor, and there was a bloody scene in the Forum in consequence. Milo, the tribune, summoned Clodius to trial for acts of violence, but the people collected in a body, drove Clodius out of the Forum, and gave a unanimous vote for the recall of the exiled Cicero.

So, at the end of about sixteen months from the time he had left, the orator returned to his native country, where he was received with every mark of honor. The senate met him at the city gates, and his entry resembled a triumph.

Not long after Milo killed Clodius, and Cicero was called upon to defend him against the charge of murder. But Cicero was a timid man; and when he beheld the crowd that had gathered to hear him, he was seized with a fit of trembling that seriously affected his delivery. That speech was said to be the worst he ever made, and was probably the reason why Milo was condemned.

Five years after his return from exile Cicero went to Cilicia as governor, and did such good service in driving the bandit tribes from the neighboring mountains that he was saluted by the soldiers with the title of Imperator.

When he went back to Rome he would have asked for a triumph, but the civil war was just on the eve of breaking out, and everything was in commotion. He tried very hard to reconcile the two leaders, Pompey and Cæsar, but, failing to do that, showed himself miserably changeable and undecided, first favoring the one, then the other. "Whither shall I turn?" he says in his epistles. "Pompey has the more honorable cause; but Cæsar manages his affairs with the greater address, and is more able to save himself and his friends. In short, I know whom to avoid, but not whom to seek."

He joined Pompey's camp in Greece after a time, but, on account of ill health, was not present at the battle of Pharsalia. At that battle Pompey was defeated and had to fly. Then Cato desired Cicero to command part of the army, but he declined, and announced that he would take no further share in the war. Thereupon some of the young warriors drew their swords, called him traitor, and would certainly have despatched him on the spot had it not been for Cato, who interposed and led him out of the camp.

Cicero then went to Brundusium, but when he heard that Cæsar was coming he began to tremble, for he did not know how the mighty conqueror would receive him. However, his fears were allayed when Cæsar appeared; for he saluted him as a friend, and then walked by his side and conversed with him.

Soon Rome became a monarchy, with Cæsar as ruler, and Cicero withdrew from public affairs and devoted himself entirely to philosophy and literature. He spent the greater part of his time at his country-house near Tusculum, where for recreation he would write poetry, sometimes producing as many as five hundred verses in one night. He rarely went to town, unless he wished to pay his respects to Cæsar or to vote him some new honors.

It was the assassination of Cæsar which called him to public life again and made him hope for political influence; but Mark Antony took Cæsar's place, and, as he was no friend to Cicero, the orator could do nothing for the moment. It was then that he composed some admirable orations known by the name of Philippic which are familiar to students of classical literature.

However, his ambition revived when he found young Octavio Cæsar disposed to be his friend, and with him he tried to bring about a war against Antony. But he was deceived, for as soon as Octavius had managed to obtain the consulship he formed an alliance with Antony and Lepidus, who had been Cæsar's friend, and Cicero's was one of the

CICERO

first names that appeared on the list of those they condemned to death.

While these things were taking place, Cicero was at Tusculum, and as soon as he heard of them he set out for a certain seaport, whence he hoped to set sail for Macedonia and join Brutus, who had formed an army there. He did embark, and sailed some distance along the coast; he then changed his mind and travelled by land. At times he thought of killing himself, but, after much uncertainty and various half-formed plans, he at last went to Capitæ, where he owned a pleasant house near the sea-side. As his vessel was rowed to shore, a flock of crows alighted on the sails, some cawing, others pecking at the ropes. This was considered a bad omen; but Cicero went to the house and lay down upon a lounge to rest. The crows followed, some settling on the window-sill, while one or two hopped on the lounge and tugged at the covers. Cicero's servants were so impressed by these ill omens that they asked one another, "Shall we stay to be spectators of our master's murder? Shall we not protect him, so innocent and so great a sufferer as he is, when the brute creatures give him marks of their care?" So, partly by persuasion, partly by force, they got him into a litter and carried him down towards the sea.

The assassins who had been sent from Rome, headed by Popillius, a tribune whom Cicero had once defended against a charge of murder, soon arrived. They went to the house and burst open the door; not finding the orator, they questioned a youth whom he had educated, and were told that he was in a litter then on its way to the sea. They ran in the direction pointed out, and when Cicero saw them approaching he ordered his litter to be set down. The poor old man, now in his sixty-fourth year, looked straight at the murderers, and some of them were so struck by his misery that they covered their faces while Herennius, the centurion, raised his sword and with one powerful stroke cut off his head.

The hands which had written the Philippics against Antony were also cut off and carried to Rome. Antony was holding an assembly for the election of magistrates, and when he beheld the head and hands of Cicero he said, "Now let there be an end of all executions." They were exposed together in a public place, and men wept when they beheld them and thought of the pure, amiable character that had met so cruel and unjust a death. About fifty-nine of this great man's orations have been preserved, though he wrote many more, which, with his other literary works, will give to those who care to study them a much better insight into the thoughts and feelings of Cicero than they can get in these pages.

CAESAR

IN the lives of Marius and Sylla mention has been made of Julius Cæsar, but, as he was one of the most renowned of the Romans there is much more to tell about him.

He was descended from the illustrious and noble Julian family, many of whose members distinguished themselves at different periods in Italy, but he was the most famous of them all. As a boy he was considered remarkably intelligent, and he was always so eager to learn that he gave promise at an early age of future greatness.

He was scarcely twenty years old when, after a season of disturbance in the government, Sylla became ruler of Rome, and he was forced to fly for his life. Sylla had reasons for disliking him, the principal of which was his relationship to Marius, who governed the opposite party; for Cæsar and Marius were first cousins. So many people were put to death merely for not siding with Sylla that Cæsar could not be ignorant of his own danger, so he left Rome and hid himself in a foreign country.

After a time Sylla's power grew weaker, and then Cæsar returned and soon became very popular with his countrymen. As a proof of this, he was elected to the office of high-priest when Metellus, who had held it, died, although two men of the highest reputation and great influence with the senate were candidates at the same time.

Not long after, Cæsar was appointed to the government of certain provinces in Spain, but he had spent so much money in entertainments and public shows that he was in debt, and his creditors refused to let him go until he had settled with them. He would not have known how to help himself had it not been for Crassus, one of the wealthiest men in Rome, who pledged himself to pay all his debts, whereupon he was allowed to depart. When crossing the Alps, he passed some villages whose inhabitants looked poor and miserable, and one of his companions said, "I wonder if those people want offices, or feel envious enough towards the great to quarrel with them?" To which Cæsar answered, "I assure you I had rather be the first man among these fellows than the second man in Rome." One day, when reading the history of Alexander, he burst into tears. His friends were surprised, and asked what ailed him. "Have I not just cause to weep," he asked, "when I consider that at my age Alexander had conquered many nations, while I have not a single exploit to boast of?"

But his ambition was soon gratified, for he conquered several tribes in Spain and made them subject to Rome. Besides, he settled many quarrels, and established such excellent laws that the provinces he had won were made happier by his presence. He became rich himself, and divided so much booty among his soldiers that they saluted him as *Imperator*, the highest title ever bestowed upon a Roman.

Then he returned home, and, having paid off all his debts, desired to stand for the consulship. Rome was divided into two great parties at that period, one led by Pompey, and the other by Crassus, but, knowing that his chances would be less if opposed by either, Cæsar brought about a reconciliation between the two leaders. The union thus formed between them and himself is known in history by the name of the *First Triumvirate*, and plunged the country into civil war.

Cæsar walked to the place of election between Pompey and Crassus, and was declared consul, with Bibulus for his colleague. The first thing he did after entering upon his new office was to make certain laws about the division of property and of grain, which so pleased the poorer classes that he became more popular than ever.

Bibulus was consul in name only, for he could do nothing against so powerful a person as Cæsar; therefore, finding that he was in danger of being murdered when he offered any opposition, he shut himself up in his house until his consulship expired. At that time Pompey filled the Forum with armed men, and thus got the laws passed which Cæsar had proposed merely to gain favor with the populace. In the same manner he secured for Cæsar the government of Gaul and Illyricum for five years with an army of four legions.

During his consulship Cæsar was guilty of one disgraceful deed, and that was getting such a depraved creature as Clodius elected tribune. His motive was to ruin Cicero, for it was through the influence of the bold, bad Clodius that the orator was banished; but this was before the wars of Gaul. We have now to follow Cæsar in a different course, and to show that after he went to Gaul he was equal as a warrior and general to the greatest the world had ever produced, and superior to many. In less than ten years he took by storm eight hundred cities, conquered three hundred nations, and fought with three millions of men, one million of whom he killed and another million he made prisoners.

So great was his influence over his soldiers that those who had been in no way remarkable before became heroes under his command, enduring the most dreadful sufferings and dangers that they might receive their reward from his hands; and he did reward them most liberally, storing up all the riches he got in the wars for that purpose alone, and never keeping more than his share for himself. Besides, he set them an example of courage and endurance by always exposing himself to danger and indulging in no comforts that they had not. This was the more remarkable, because he was a small man, his constitution was delicate, and he was subject to violent headaches and epileptic fits. He tried to strengthen himself by long marches and simple diet, and did in that way keep off many an attack. He usually slept, while on a march, in a chariot or litter, so that no time might be lost, and he travelled so fast as to excite surprise. He had been such a good rider from childhood that he usually sat with his hands joined together behind his back while his horse went at full speed. During his wars in Gaul he dictated letters to several people at once while riding, and it is said that he was the first person who sent letters to his friends who were in the same city with him when business was urgent. This was done to save the time that a personal interview would have required.

Cæsar won two victories in Spain, then left his army in their winter quarters and went to the river Po, anxious to find out what was going on in Rome. While he was there, numbers of Romans paid their respects to him, and to each he gave a handsome present or some promise for the future; thus the number of his friends constantly increased.

CAESAR

Suddenly he was summoned to join his army, and at their head won two such glorious victories over the Belgæ and the Nervii that the senate of Rome ordered sacrifices to be offered and all sorts of festivities to be kept up for fifteen days in honor of them. After settling the affairs of Gaul, Cæsar went back again to Lucca, near the river Po, for the winter, and did a great deal of mischief while there in this way: he had so much money that he could control the elections by bribery; so anybody whom he wanted in office he supplied with funds to buy votes, and of course in that way his power became greater and greater all the time.

Among the distinguished persons who went to visit him at Lucca were Pompey, Crassus, Appius, the governor of Sardinia, and Nepos, proconsul of Spain. At one time there were assembled a hundred and twenty lictors, with their masters, and more than two hundred senators. All these met in council, with Cæsar at their head, and fixed upon this plan: Pompey and Crassus were to be consuls again for another year, and Cæsar was to have a fresh supply of money and continue in command of the army for five years longer. It seems absurd for the senate to have voted Cæsar more money when he already had so much, and the honest men of Rome shook their heads and sighed; but what could they do? If Cato had been present, he would have spoken out boldly against such a decree, but he had been sent on an expedition to Cyprus on purpose to get him out of the way, and Favonius, who attempted to speak, was silenced because some of the people feared Pompey and Crassus, and others hoped so much from Cæsar that they were ready to grant him almost anything he might have demanded.

On his return to his army in Gaul, Cæsar found another furious war on his hands, for two of the most powerful

German tribes had crossed the Rhine to fight him. He killed four hundred thousand of them, and then pursued those that fled, because he wanted to have the honor of being the first Roman who ever crossed the Rhine with an army. So in the short space of ten days he built a bridge that was a wonder to all who beheld it, and, having crossed over with his army, drove two of the most warlike of the German nations to the woods, where they concealed themselves. Then he laid the country waste, sparing only those parts where the people declared themselves friendly to Rome, and at the end of eighteen days went back to Gaul.

His expedition to Britain was the most remarkable of all, and showed a great spirit of daring, for no other fleet had sailed into the Atlantic to make war, and it was not positively known that such an island as Britain really existed. Some writers had represented that there was in the north an immense territory, while others had stated that no such land existed at all. Therefore Cæsar may be said to have extended the Roman empire beyond the known world, for he went to Britain twice, and fought several battles, doing much damage to the inhabitants, but finding little to take, for they were too miserably poor and wretched. However, he received several hostages from the king, imposed a tribute on the island, and then went back to Gaul.

Sad news awaited him here; for his daughter Julia, who was Pompey's wife, had just died, and the great conqueror was much afflicted when he heard of it.

As winter came on, Cæsar went again to Italy, but he was soon recalled by a general uprising of the whole of Gaul; and although the season was a most severe one and the rivers were all frozen up, he performed some of the most wonderful feats that ever were known, appearing now here, now there, with such rapidity that the enemy never knew exactly where or when to expect him. At last the Gauls became convinced that Cæsar's troops could neither be conquered nor resisted, so they laid down their arms; and their principal general, approaching Cæsar as he sat on his throne, threw off his armor, and, placing himself at his feet, remained in silence until led away by the guard, who were ordered to keep him in safety to appear at the triumph.

By this time Crassus was dead, and the government of Rome had become so corrupt that tables were publicly spread out, where candidates for office sat to pay the people for their votes, and there was often much bloodshed in the Forum before an election could be decided. Many declared openly that they preferred a monarchy to such scenes, and hinted at Pompey as the person they preferred for their ruler; but Pompey pretended that he did not wish to become dictator, though he was all the while working for that position. Cato understood him, and, to prevent his taking any violent steps, persuaded the senate to declare him sole consul. This was done; and he continued at the same time to govern Spain and Africa, where he had stationed his armies.

This arrangement did not suit Cæsar or his friends, all of whom were jealous of the favor shown to Pompey; so Cæsar paid the debts of one tribune, sent money to another to build a public hall, and was so generous to many of the prominent men that his party increased wonderfully. This alarmed Pompey, who proposed that a successor be appointed to Cæsar in Gaul, and at the same time demanded the troops he had lent him. They were immediately returned, each man receiving a handsome sum of money from Cæsar as he bade him farewell.

The messengers who had been sent for these troops were so anxious to flatter Pompey that they told him he had nothing to fear from the army in Gaul; that they all preferred him to Cæsar, and would declare for him as soon as they entered Italy. This deceived Pompey, so that he did not deem it necessary to levy troops, and when Cæsar sent to demand a longer term as commander he was refused. He then made this proposition: that both he and Pompey should lay down their arms and become private citizens, thus leaving it to their country to decide what reward for his services each should receive. This seemed so fair that Curio, who made the demand in Cæsar's name, was loudly applauded, and wreaths of flowers were showered at him.

Scipio, Pompey's father-in-law, rose and proposed that if Cæsar did not lay down his arms within a certain time he should be declared an enemy to his country. Then a vote was taken to decide whether Pompey or Cæsar should disband his soldiers, and almost all the people were in favor of having the latter do so; but some of the senators became excited and talked angrily, while all were so grieved at the turn of affairs that they left the Forum and put on mourning.

Matters were not improved, and by no means settled, for when somewhat later Cæsar sent another proposition, such a violent uproar was the consequence that Antony and Curio, who spoke for him, were driven out of the senate-house with insults and forced to make their escape from Rome in a hired carriage, disguised as slaves. Cæsar wanted no better excuse for his future actions, for Antony and Curio were men of high standing, and it was easy to arouse the indignation of the soldiers by showing them how impossible it had become for any one who favored him to raise his voice in Rome with safety.

So he ordered an attack on Ariminum, a large city of Gaul, and sent troops under command of Hortensius, with orders to take it with as little disturbance and bloodshed as possible. He followed with the rest of his army, and marched straight to the river Rubicon, which divided Gaul from the rest of Italy. But there he hesitated, and began to weigh the difficulties and the daring of his enterprise. Many a man would have been daunted. Not so Cæsar: his courage rose with the occasion, and he cried out, "The die is cast!" as he proceeded to cross the river. He travelled so fast that Ariminum was taken that very day, and, as he advanced, not only individuals but the population of whole cities fled before him in terror and crowded into Rome.

Pompey was amazed when he heard that Cæsar was coming with his army, and as the news spread from house to house it struck terror to every heart, causing the wildest confusion throughout the city. Pompey had boasted in the senate that if he but stamped his foot all Italy would arm in defence of her territory. "Stamp your foot now," said Favonius, tauntingly. Although Pompey had as many soldiers then as Cæsar had, his friends were so alarmed at the reports constantly circulated that they forced him along with the general current. He issued a decree that from such a state of tumult nothing was to be expected but war, and, after ordering the senate and every man who preferred his country and liberty to the rod of a tyrant to follow him, left Rome. The consuls and most of the senators did likewise, but, when they heard how kindly Cæsar treated those he had conquered, many of them returned.

The account of how Cæsar pursued Pompey, who fled from place to place, and then went out to sea, is given in Pompey's life, so it need not be repeated here. Within sixty days from the time he entered Italy, Cæsar had made himself master of the country, and then he went to Rome, where, to his surprise, quiet had been restored.

He helped himself to what public money he wanted, though Metellus, the tribune, did his best to prevent it, and set out at once for Spain for the purpose of making himself master of Pompey's army there. Though often in great danger of defeat, he succeeded at last, and none of the soldiers escaped except the generals who fled to Pompey.

On his return to Rome he was created dictator, but within eleven days he resigned, declared himself consul, and was off to the wars again. He marched so fast that part of his army was left behind, while in the very depth of winter he put to sea and took two important towns of Greece, and then sent his ships back for the rest of the troops. But they were getting tired of so much fighting and marching, and many of the men were growing old and longed for peace and repose. So they exclaimed, "Whither will this man lead us again? Will he never let us be quiet? He carries us from place to place as if we had limbs of stone and bodies of iron; but even iron yields at last to repeated blows, and our very shields and breastplates cry out for rest. Our wounds, if nothing else, should make him see that we are but mortal men, subject to the same pains as other human beings. The gods themselves cannot force the seasons, or clear the winter seas of storms and yet he pushes forward as though he were flying from an enemy rather than pursuing one."

Thus they complained; but still they followed their general, for they would have considered themselves traitors had they done otherwise, and he led them against Pompey. A great battle was fought, and Cæsar lost so many men that when he retired from the field at night he said, "The victory to-day would have been of the enemy's side if they had had a general who knew how to conquer." Cæsar was almost as miserable as though he had been defeated, for he knew that he had not conducted the war properly and spent the whole night lamenting the mistakes he had made. He asked himself again and again why he had settled down to fight with Pompey in a barren country, where it was impossible to get food enough for his army, when he might have marched into a fertile one, and taken possession of some of the wealthiest cities in the world.

In the morning he raised his camp and marched towards Macedonia, where Scipio was stationed, and Pompey's men, thinking that he was running away because he was beaten, wanted to follow him. But Pompey was too prudent to risk so much; he preferred to tire out Cæsar's men by following at a safe distance, and laying a siege whenever a good and safe opportunity offered. He would have been wise had he stuck to this decision, but he allowed himself to be influenced by his officers, and so marched forward until he joined Scipio, and the two armies combined were so numerous that even Cæsar was dismayed when he beheld them drawn up in line of battle on the plain of Pharsalia.

It was Pompey then who made the attack, and the battle fought on that day was one of the most desperate ever seen. Cæsar, at the head of the tenth legion, broke into the enemy's ranks and drove all before him. When Pompey saw his cavalry flying he was beside himself, for he knew that all was lost. Retiring to his tent, he sat down without speaking a word, and buried his face in his hands. When the enemy engaged with his men just on the fortifications around the camp, he seemed to become suddenly alive to his position, and, starting up, exclaimed, "What! into my very camp?" He then disguised himself in old clothes and stole away. His journey to Egypt and his death there are related in his life.

Most of the infantry that were taken prisoners were joined to Cæsar's legions, and many distinguished persons were pardoned. Among these was Brutus, of whom more will be said hereafter. To the Thessalians Cæsar granted liberty for the sake of the victory he had won on their soil, before going in pursuit of Pompey.

Pompey had been assassinated before Cæsar reached Alexandria, and when his head was brought to him, he turned away in disgust. Ptolemy, the king of Egypt, handed over to Cæsar all the soldiers he found wandering about his country who had fought under Pompey, and they not only received favors, but were taken into the service of Cæsar, who wrote to his friends in Rome, "The greatest pleasure I have from my victory is the being able to save so many of my fellow-citizens, even though they have borne arms against me."

The king of Egypt had a sister named Cleopatra, with whom he was not at all friendly, and, indeed, had banished her from his country. When she heard that such a great warrior as Cæsar had come to Alexandria, she had herself carried to his palace rolled up like a bale of goods, and so interested him in her behalf that he induced her brother to let her share the government with him. Later, during the war which Cæsar fought in Egypt, the king was killed, and Cleopatra became queen.

The great general next went over to Asia, where Pharnaces, the son of Mithridates the Great, was engaged in a war. He totally defeated his army, and finished up the war so quickly that when he wrote an account of it to his friends in

Rome he put it in three well-known Latin words, *"Veni, vidi, vici,"* "I came, I saw, I conquered."

By the end of the year Cæsar was back in Rome, where he had been appointed dictator for another year, consul for five years, and tribune for life. So his authority was almost without limit.

After the battle in Thessaly the friends of the Roman republic had gathered in Africa under Cato and Scipio, so Cæsar could not rest until he had made a campaign in that country. After several battles he at last gained a complete victory, and returned to Rome, where he had one of the most magnificent triumphs that ever was seen. When it was over, he gave splendid presents to the soldiers, and feasts to the citizens, whom he entertained at twenty-two thousand tables.

The last of Cæsar's wars was fought in Spain, against the sons of Pompey. They were young, but they had collected such a numerous army, and fought with so much skill and courage, that Cæsar was in great danger. He was victorious at last, however, and when the battle was over he said to his friends, "I have often fought for victory, but this is the first time I ever fought for my life."

Then, although the Romans were displeased because Cæsar boasted of having destroyed the children and family of Pompey, one of the greatest of their statesmen, they were so tired of war that they made him dictator for life, hoping that the government of a single person would bring them peace. He was called the "Father of his country," and flattery poured in upon him from all sides, for even his enemies paid him compliments now, when his conduct was all that even they could desire. For he not only pardoned those that had fought against him in the field, but on some of them he bestowed honors. Among these were the two prætors Brutus and Cassius.

When his friends proposed that he should have a body-guard, he refused, saying that he would try to gain the affection of the people, which would be the best and surest guard he could possibly have. So he did everything to please them, and in order to gain favor with the army he sent colonies to people and rebuild Carthage, Corinth, and other places that he had destroyed.

But Cæsar was not a man who could sit still and enjoy the fruit of his great exploits: he was constantly making plans, which, if he had carried them out, would have brought almost the whole of Europe under Roman rule. All human designs, even though they may be excellent, as some of Cæsar's certainly were, are limited; but fortunately one of the best was carried into effect after Cæsar got through with his wars, and that was the correcting of the calendar. He called in the best philosophers and mathematicians of his time, and they formed such an exact calendar that it is in use to this day in Rome.

Now we come to the closing scene in Cæsar's life, for he enjoyed the lofty position for which he had fought so hard little more than a year. Various causes hurried on his end. He had offended the senate by receiving certain honors they conferred on him without rising from his seat, as he ought to have done. Then he had given offence by showing favor to people who were not worthy, merely for his own gratification. On one occasion Mark Antony offered him a crown. He refused it, and the next morning his statues were crowned. The tribunes imprisoned the people who had done this, but Cæsar turned them out of office for it. This proved that he was really anxious to be called king, though he had pretended that such was not the case.

So he became unpopular, and a conspiracy, in which Cassius and Brutus played the chief part, was formed against his life. His superstition was aroused because of several bad omens. Among these was the absence of his victim's heart when he was sacrificing, strange lights in the heavens, noises in the night, and wild birds that perched on the Forum. A soothsayer bade him prepare for great danger on the Ides of March. That day, when on his way to the senate, he met the soothsayer, and, with a light laugh, said, "The Ides of March are come." "Yes, they are come," was the answer, "but they are not gone."

Calpurnia, Cæsar's wife, who was by no means a weak-minded woman, had a horrible dream on the night before her husband was murdered, and begged him, with tears in her eyes, not to go to the senate-house. Finding that he was inclined to neglect her warning, she urged him to consult his fate by sacrifices. He did so, and, as the priests pronounced all the signs bad, he resolved to send Antony to dismiss the senate.

But one of the conspirators ridiculed him for listening to a woman's fears, and urged him to go to the senate, because the business to be transacted that day was of the utmost importance. So Cæsar felt ashamed of the weakness he had shown, and yielded.

When he entered, the senate rose to do him honor, and as he took his seat the conspirators gathered close about his chair. Cimber offered a petition, which Cæsar seemed unwilling to grant; and while he was speaking, Cimber seized his robe and pulled it from his shoulder. This was the signal for attack. Casca struck the first blow at the neck of Cæsar, and all the other conspirators rushed on him, so eager to share in his death that they actually wounded one another. He fought at first; but when he beheld Junius Brutus among his enemies, he was so grieved that he drew his cloak about him, and, having covered his face, fell without a struggle. He received twenty-three wounds, and his blood bathed Pompey's statue, at the foot of which he breathed his last.

Brutus turned to the senate and tried to explain the reason for the dreadful deed; but they were so dismayed that they fled, and the wildest confusion prevailed throughout the city when Cæsar's death was made known. Brutus, Cassius, and all who were suspected of having taken part in the murder were obliged to hide themselves or leave Rome, and their houses were burned to the ground. An account of the sufferings and death of Brutus will be found in his life.

Cæsar lived only four years after Pompey, and was fifty-six at the time of his death. It is said that for seven nights after that event a comet was visible in the skies, and was looked upon as a sign that the soul of Cæsar was received among the gods.

Cæsar was, besides a great general, one of the most intellectual men of ancient times, and his writings, which have many remarkable features, have been admired by students even up to the present day. His name became a title of honor for the Roman emperors, of whom there are twelve that bore it mentioned in history.

CATO THE YOUNGER

Cato belonged to a very distinguished family in Rome, the first member who made himself famous being his great-grandfather, Cato the Censor, whose life we have given.

Cato the Younger was left an orphan at a very early age, and his uncle, Livius Drusus, took care of him as well as of his brother, Cæpio, and his sister Porcia. He was not quick or particularly bright as a child, but he never forgot what he learned, probably because it gave him so much trouble to study his lessons. He was remarkable for excellent judgment and firmness, quite rare in so young a person, and he was fortunate in having Sarpedon for his instructor; for he was a well-bred, agreeable man, who preferred to govern by reason and kindness rather than harsh treatment.

Cato was so popular among the Roman boys that when Sylla gave the exhibition known as *Troy*, which was a tournament among the sons of noblemen, they accepted his son for captain of one side, but for the other captain they would have nobody but Cato, though several others were proposed.

Sylla, who had been a friend to the father of Cato, often sent for the two sons to visit him, and would talk familiarly to them, though he seldom did so to others. Sarpedon always accompanied the boys to Sylla's house, and liked to take them there, because he thought it would be to their advantage to gain favor with so prominent a person.

When Cato was about fourteen years of age, affairs at Rome were so disturbed that the house of Sylla, who was dictator, looked more like a place of execution than anything else, so many people being daily tortured and put to death there. Seeing the heads of several illustrious persons carried out, one time young Cato asked his teacher, "Why does not somebody kill this dictator?" "Because they fear him more than they hate him," was the answer. "Why, then, do you not give me a sword," asked the boy, "that I may kill him, and deliver my country from slavery?" Sarpedon was so struck by his pupil's stern, angry countenance as he uttered this speech that he watched him very closely after that, lest he should be guilty of some rash act.

He was asked one day whom he loved most. "My brother," he replied. "Whom do you love next?" was asked. "My brother," said Cato. "Whom do you love third?" Again Cato answered, "My brother," and so he would have repeated had he been questioned a hundred times more; for he loved nobody in the world as he did Cæpio, and the affection increased with years.

When Cato became a man he was made a priest of Apollo, and then he took his share of his father's estate and went to live in a house of his own. He had plenty of money, but he chose to live in the simplest possible manner and to devote himself to study. He took the most violent exercise to strengthen his body, and went bareheaded in all sorts of weather. His journeys were made on foot, even though his companions rode on horseback, because he preferred to accustom himself to hardships.

He first distinguished himself in the Servile war, which took its name from the slave Spartacus, who was the ringleader; and Gellius, who was prætor, wanted to reward him, but he refused, saying, "I have done nothing that deserves such notice."

He was then appointed military tribune to Macedonia, and when he reached the army the general gave him the command of only one legion. He at once set to work to discipline his soldiers, and succeeded so well that they became a terror to their enemies. They were devoted to Cato, who never commanded them to do anything without first doing it himself, and were never so happy as when he praised them.

While he was in Macedonia he received news that his brother was ill at Ænus, in Thrace. The sea was very rough, and no large vessel was at hand, but Cæpio needed him, and he was determined to go to him at all hazard. So, with two friends and three servants, he sailed in a little trading-boat. He narrowly escaped drowning, and arrived at Ænus to find that he had risked his life for nothing, for Cæpio was dead. This was a dreadful blow to Cato, who gave way to such passionate grief that those who had witnessed his fortitude on other occasions were astonished. He wept, he groaned, he embraced the dead body again and again, and refused to be comforted. Although so simple in his tastes, Cato spent vast sums of money on his brother's funeral, and erected a marble monument to his memory at Ænus that cost no less than eight talents.

He then returned to the army, and when his time of service ended the soldiers embraced him and parted from him with tears, spreading their garments at his feet and kissing his hands as he passed along, an honor that had seldom been paid to any Roman commander.

Before going home he made a visit to Asia to study the customs of the people. The following was his manner of travelling. Early in the morning his baker and cook would go forward to the place where he intended to pass the night. If they found no friend or acquaintance of their master, they would take lodgings and prepare his supper at an inn, without giving trouble to any one. If there happened to be no inn, they would ask the magistrates for lodgings; but they travelled with so little display that people often refused to believe they were Cato's men, and he would arrive to find no supper ready. Indeed, when he appeared it was no better, for he seemed an ordinary person to whom it was not necessary to pay attention. Sometimes he would take the magistrates to task and say, "Foolish people, why do you not learn to be more hospitable? All your visitors will not be Catos; so do not by your ill manners give them an excuse for taking from you by force what you give so unwillingly."

He met with a humorous adventure at Antioch. On his arrival there a crowd stood at the gates, the young men being ranged in a row on one side, and the boys in their best clothes on the other, while the priests and magistrates stood in white robes, with garlands on their heads. At first Cato was displeased, because he thought his servants had announced his coming; however, the people had evidently gathered to do him honor, so he desired his friends to alight, and walked with them towards the city gates. When they were near enough to be spoken to, an elderly man, with a staff and crown in his hand, advanced, saluted Cato, and asked, "How far behind is Demetrius, and when may we expect him?" Demetrius was Pompey's favorite, and just at that period

CATO THE YOUNGER

Pompey was at the height of his glory. Then Cato knew that the honors were not meant for him, and his friends laughed heartily at his mistake; but as he passed through the crowd he said, with a sigh, "Alas, poor city!"

Some time later the people of Antioch were ashamed of the way they had treated Cato; it was when Pompey insisted on showing that he regarded him as a more honorable person than himself, and praised him for the very simplicity that had made them neglect him. Pompey did not love Cato, and did not desire to share his power with him, but he could not help admiring and esteeming him. After Pompey showed such respect for Cato, every city through which he passed did the same, and he was feasted on all sides.

On his return to Rome he was made quæstor, or public treasurer, but he would not enter upon the office until he had studied its duties, and when he knew them he brought every one to account who had misused the public money, and turned out every servant who did not do his work faithfully and honestly. At first many complained, but they soon found that, although they were not so heavily taxed as before, the state had never been so rich, so they were satisfied, and as time went on there was no man in Rome whom the people trusted as they did Cato.

He had often refused to be tribune, because he did not desire that office, but when the time came that Rome was in danger, he worked hard to get it, in order that he might defend her liberty and her government; for the office of tribune gave great control, and a man holding it could, with his single vote, decide a point one way or another.

Cato was not remarkable as an orator, but at the time of Catiline's conspiracy he proved that he could speak with force when occasion called for it. Catiline had formed a plot to destroy Rome by open warfare; but Cicero exposed him, and he was forced to fly. The others who were connected with Catiline called him a coward, and resolved to set the town on fire, overthrow the empire, and cause other nations to make war on Rome. Cicero did not rest until he had found out every conspirator, and then laid the matter before the senate. Cæsar, who was an excellent speaker, and for reasons of his own not averse to political changes, made such an eloquent appeal in behalf of the conspirators, claiming for them a fair trial as citizens of Rome, that the senators were almost convinced of the justice of their cause.

It was on that occasion that Cato made the only speech that has been preserved to the present day. He asked Cæsar and others who were inclined to mildness how they dared advise a trial of traitors who were on the point of ruining the commonwealth. He charged Cæsar with being guilty himself, otherwise he would not attempt to rescue from justice the unnatural wretches who had sought to ruin their country. So earnest and eloquent was Cato that he carried his point, and all the prisoners were condemned to death on the spot.

Not long after this, Cato won the highest reputation by his opposition to the *First Triumvirate*, or the bond made by Cæsar between Pompey and Crassus by which they hoped to get complete control of the state. Cato fought hard at this period, and his life was in danger, when Metellus, the tribune, filled the Forum with armed men, in order that he might carry his law favoring Pompey. After the trouble subsided and Metellus had departed for Asia, the Romans saw the danger they had escaped, and blessed Cato as their preserver.

CATO THE YOUNGER

When Pompey returned, he tried to be friendly with Cato, because he thought that thereby his power would be increased; but Cato would not agree to any measures that did not seem of benefit to his country. Then Pompey turned to Cæsar, and these two powerful Romans worked together so successfully that Cato lost influence with the people. So when Cæsar proposed certain laws about the division of grain and lands, everybody took an oath to observe them except Cato, who did not think them wise or just. But it was ordained by the senate that any man who should attempt to alter the laws or refuse to take the oath should be severely punished. Cato's wife, children, and all his friends begged him to yield, but it was Cicero who forced him to do so, by using the argument that was sure to have effect, the safety of his country. "For," said he, "though Cato have no need of Rome, yet Rome has need of Cato, and so likewise have all his friends."

Then Cæsar was appointed to the government of Illyricum and all Gaul for five years, though Cato opposed it, saying, "You are placing a tyrant in your fortress." But for the time being he had lost his influence with the people, and Clodius, a very bad man, was declared tribune, while Piso, Cæsar's father-in-law, and Gabinius, one of Pompey's creatures, became consuls.

Still the men in power feared Cato, for they knew how much it had cost them to get the upper hand over him; besides, he was a friend to Cicero, whom Clodius hated. So it was decided to get him out of the way, and thus silence Cicero's eloquence. He was therefore appointed to the government of Cyprus.

He went there against his will, but fulfilled his office with so much ability and success that on his return to Rome he placed nearly seven thousand talents of silver in the treasury. That was an enormous sum of money, being equal to about eight millions of dollars.

The news of his success had reached Rome from time to time, and both banks of the Tiber were crowded with people who were anxious to do him honor when he went back home. The magistrates, the priests, and the whole senate were there too, but Cato rowed up the stream in a royal galley, never stopping until he reached the dock. When the money he had brought was carried through the streets, everybody gazed at it in astonishment, and when the senate assembled they praised him, and voted him the right of appearing at the public shows in a purple-bordered gown, and an extraordinary prætorship. This last was a great honor, because Cato was but thirty-eight years of age, and no man could be prætor until he was forty. All these honors were declined.

Not long after this, Pompey and Crassus, by agreement with Cæsar, who had crossed the Alps to confer with them, had themselves declared consuls. Cato felt sure that with such men at the head of the government Rome was in danger, so he resolved to stand for prætor, or public treasurer, knowing that he could do much in that office to diminish their power.

Pompey and Crassus were aware of that also, and assembled the senate unexpectedly, giving notice only to a few of the senators. They then declared that those who were chosen prætors should at once enter upon their office, without waiting, as was the custom, to see whether they should be accused by the people of having accepted bribes. In spite of this and other precautions, Cato was elected. Thereupon Pompey cried out, "It thunders!" Thunder was considered a bad omen among the Romans, so the assembly broke up at once, though nobody else had heard the sound. Afterwards, by means of bribery, Vatinius was elected prætor in place of Cato, but those who had been paid to vote for him ran away and hid themselves, while Cato, who had made a speech warning the people against Pompey and Crassus, was followed to his home by an immense crowd, who cheered him as he walked along.

Disturbances continued during the year, and corrupt practices in the elections grew to such an extent that when, at last, Cato became prætor again, he moved that a law be passed in the senate compelling every man who obtained an office to declare upon oath how he had managed it. This was unpopular, because no one would dare to offer bribes if he had to confess them, and if he did not get votes in that way there was little chance of gaining the election. So one morning when Cato was going to the tribunal a crowd of unruly people ran after him, calling names and throwing stones, so that it was with difficulty he made his escape unhurt. He succeeded in putting a stop to the bribery in this way: a certain sum of money was collected, and it was agreed that the candidates for office should use it in canvassing for votes, but if any man were found guilty of having offered a bribe, all the votes he brought in were to be destroyed. To see that it was fairly conducted, Cato was chosen to stand by the tribune who received the votes and examine into every proceeding connected with the election.

He did it honestly, but it made him unpopular with the chief men of Rome, who looked upon him as a sort of a spy upon their actions. Pompey was one of these and he did not hesitate to make some very harsh and insulting remarks about Cato; yet when affairs in Rome had gone from bad to worse, and the senate moved to create Pompey sole consul, hoping thus to re-establish a lawful government, Cato voted for him.

When Pompey heard of it, he sent for Cato, thanked and embraced him warmly, and begged his assistance in the management of his difficult office. Cato answered, "Nothing that I have ever said was spoken out of hate to you, Pompey, nor is what I do now out of love for you; all is for the good of the commonwealth. If you ask my advice in private, I will give it freely; but in public, whether you ask or not, I will speak my opinion openly." And so he did always.

Meanwhile, Cæsar, though in Gaul, was gradually, but steadily and surely, increasing his power in Rome. Cato warned Pompey more than once; but so great was the latter's confidence in the friendship of the conqueror that he paid no attention to the warnings.

As it was Cato's habit to speak his mind freely, he openly found fault with Cæsar's actions in Gaul, whereupon that general sent a letter to the senate full of charges against Cato. Cato laughed at them, and made each appear absurd as it was read aloud, and at last exclaimed, "It is not the sons of the Britons or the Gauls that we have to fear, but Cæsar himself, if we are wise." This made such an impression on the senate that it was at once decided to send some one to replace Cæsar. Then his friends demanded that if that were done Pompey should lay down his arms and give up his provinces too. "What I have foretold has come to pass!" exclaimed Cato; but he could not do much, for Cæsar was so exceedingly popular with the people that, though the senate saw the justice of Cato's remarks, they were afraid to oppose the general.

CATO THE YOUNGER

But when news came that the latter had seized Ariminum and was marching on Rome, then everybody turned to Cato in despair. "It is too late!" he exclaimed. "If you had believed me, or listened to my advice, you would not now be standing in fear of one man, or obliged to put all your hopes in one only." Pompey said, "It is indeed true that Cato has spoken like a prophet, while I have acted too much like a friend." Cato advised the senate to put everything in the hands of Pompey, saying, "Those who can raise up great evils know best how to cure them."

But Pompey did not feel that his forces were numerous or strong enough to oppose Cæsar, so he left the city. Cato followed Pompey into exile; but from that time to the end of his life he was so sad and dejected on account of the misfortunes that had befallen his country that he never cut his hair, shaved his beard, or wore a garland.

His advice to Pompey was of great value, and he got much honor for himself on account of his humanity; for not only did he postpone battles as long as possible, but he persuaded Pompey to ordain that no city subject to Rome should be destroyed, and that no Roman should be killed except in battle.

In Pompey's life will be found an account of his engagements with Cæsar, also of his death in Egypt. Afterwards his men declared that nobody should lead them but Cato, and he consented to do so; but it was necessary to increase his strength, and for that purpose Cato resolved to join his forces with those of Scipio, Pompey's father-in-law, who had made friends with Juba, the king of Mauritania.

So Cato set out across a desert country in the depth of winter, determined to lose no time. He had a great number of asses in his train to carry water and food, also many horses and carriages; still the troops suffered much during their seven days' march. Cato set them an example of endurance which they would have been ashamed not to follow. He was always foremost, and never made use of a horse or chariot during the entire journey. At last he reached Utica with his ten thousand men and joined Scipio.

Then Scipio, who held a higher office in Rome than Cato did, was on that account appointed commander-in-chief. He was inclined to kill all the people of Utica and burn the city, but Cato opposed it so strongly that he succeeded in preventing the cruel deed. Then the inhabitants requested him to take the command of the town and protect them against Cæsar, to which Scipio agreed. Utica was a very important city in Africa; so Cato set to work to fill it with supplies, repair its walls, and fortify it with ditches and ramparts. He also armed the young men and posted them in the trenches, while the rest of the inhabitants were kept close within the walls. Meanwhile, Scipio marched against Cæsar and gave him battle at Thapsus. A terrible defeat was the result, and opened the way for the great conqueror to march on into Africa.

When the news of this defeat reached Utica the people were almost distracted; so was Cato, but he appeared calm, and made a speech so full of hope and determination that confidence was restored, and the belief grew strong that it was not possible for even Cæsar to conquer such a man as Cato.

A large body of cavalry had escaped from Scipio's army and soon arrived at Utica. Cato desired to make use of them for the defence of the city, but they refused to act

CATO THE YOUNGER

unless he would drive out or destroy all the people, saying, "They have Carthaginian blood in their veins, and will certainly prove traitors." Cato would not listen to so cruel a proposal, and so the cavalry rode off; but he followed, and, with tears in his eyes, entreated them to return, if only for one day, so that those who desired to leave Utica might get off safely. They consented, and were placed at the gates and in the fortress.

Then the council of Utica sent for Cato, and, after thanking him for treating them in the upright manner he had done, told him that they had resolved to send messengers to Cæsar to ask him to have mercy on Cato and on them. "Should he refuse," they added, "we will fight for Cato as long as we have breath." After thanking them, Cato said, "I advise you to send without delay to intercede for yourselves, but for me intercede not. It is for the conquered to ask for mercy, and for those who have done an injury to beg pardon. For my part, I have never been conquered, and have had victory over Cæsar in all points of justice and honesty. It is Cæsar who ought to be looked upon as the defeated man, for he now shows himself guilty of the designs against his country, which he has constantly denied." As he walked away he was informed that Cæsar was coming. "Ah," he said, "he expects to find us brave men."

Scipio was all this time at anchor under a promontory near Utica, and Cato now provided ships for all those Romans who desired to join him, even persuading many who were loath to leave him to go. He saw them all embark, and then turned away without a word. That evening he supped with a large party of Uticans, and afterwards took his usual evening walk with his friends. When he went to his room he read Plato's book on the immortality of the soul, but he had not been thus occupied very long before he looked up and asked a servant who had taken away his sword. He received no reply, and went on reading; but presently he asked the same question again in a louder tone, and became so angry at getting a vague answer that he struck the servant, and demanded the weapon. Thereupon his son, who, having observed something strange in Cato's manner, had cautiously removed the sword, entered with some friends.

Cato looked at them fiercely, and said, "Am I deranged, that I must be disarmed and hindered from using my own reason? And you, young men, why do you not bind your father's hands behind him, that when Cæsar comes he may find him unable to defend himself? I need no sword to despatch myself, for if I but hold my breath for a while, or strike my head against the wall, it will do as well."

His son then left the room, weeping. To two of the friends who remained, Cato spoke thus: "Do you also think to keep a man of my age alive by force, and to sit here and watch me? or have you any arguments to prove that it is no dishonor for Cato to beg mercy of his enemy? If so, speak, and let me unlearn what I have been taught, and by Cæsar's help grow wiser. Not that I have determined upon anything regarding myself, but I would have it in my power to do that which I think fit to decide upon. Meanwhile, do not trouble yourselves about me, but go and tell my son that he cannot compel his father to what he fails to persuade him to." So they retired, and the sword was sent in by a little boy.

"Now I am master of myself," said Cato, as he received it, and carefully examined the blade. He then returned to his book, and after reading for a while fell asleep. Towards morning a noise was heard in his room; his son rushed in with some friends, and found Cato on the floor in a pool of blood. He had stabbed himself in the breast, and had fallen from the bed, throwing over a little table as he did so. He was not dead, and an attempt was made to bind up the wound, but he no sooner recovered consciousness than he tore it open, and instantly expired.

In less time than one might believe it possible the people of Utica had crowded about the dead man's door, calling him "their benefactor, their savior, the only free and unconquered man."

Cæsar was approaching, but neither fear of him nor their own party troubles could prevent their turning out in a body to do honor to Cato. They adorned his body, made him a magnificent funeral, and, after turning out in procession, buried him near the sea.

When Cæsar heard that Cato, with his son and a few others, had stayed at Utica, though the rest of the Romans had been sent away, he hurried forward with his army; for he had great regard for Cato. Upon being informed of his death, he exclaimed, "Cato, I envy thee thy death, since thou couldst envy me the glory of saving thy life." What Cæsar would have done had Cato been willing to owe his life to him cannot be known, but it is probable that he would have been merciful.

Cato was forty-eight years old when he died, and his name has come down to us of modern times as that of one of the purest statesmen and one of the most upright and persevering defenders of the liberties of Rome.

MARCUS BRUTUS

Marcus Brutus was remarkable for his honesty, his excellent disposition, and his fondness for study. He was a nephew of Cato, the philosopher, whom he loved and always tried to imitate. He was still a young man when he went with his uncle Cato to Cyprus to fight King Ptolemy. He conducted himself so well that he was highly praised on his return to Rome.

When the empire was divided into two parties under Pompey and Cæsar, it was generally believed that Brutus would join the latter, because in former times his father had been put to death by Pompey; but he took into consideration the public good rather than his own private feelings, and, believing Pompey to be on the right side, took part with him. He was sent to Cilicia as lieutenant, but, finding little opportunity for service there, he went to Macedonia, where Pompey and Cæsar were just preparing for a great battle. When he arrived, Pompey was so surprised and pleased at his joining him that he embraced and saluted him before all who were present as a person of great importance.

Brutus spent his whole time, except when in Pompey's company in study; and, although it was midsummer, exceedingly warm, and he had sometimes to wait a long while before

MARCUS BRUTUS

his tent was brought after him, he always managed to find a quiet spot where he could read and write.

Cæsar was so fond of Brutus that he ordered his commanders never to kill him on the field, but if possible to take him alive, charging them at the same time rather to suffer him to escape than to do him the least injury. So, after the famous battle of Pharsalia, when Pompey, being defeated, managed to escape to the sea, Brutus likewise fled, and made his way to Larissa, whence he at once wrote to Cæsar. He received a reply to his letter, in which Cæsar forgave him, expressed the greatest delight at his safety, and bade him come to him. He obeyed, and was welcomed by the great conqueror as one of his best friends. Nobody knew what direction Pompey had taken when he escaped from Pharsalia but Brutus, who suggested Egypt, and gave his reasons for so doing. He was right; but, as we know, poor Pompey had met his fate before Cæsar reached Ptolemy's kingdom.

Having secured Cæsar's forgiveness for himself, Brutus sought it for his friend Cassius and won it; for when he pleaded he did it with his whole heart and soul, and seldom failed. The first time Cæsar ever heard him speak in public, he said, "I know not what this young man intends, but whatever it be, he intends strongly."

Cæsar had so much confidence in Brutus that when he made his expedition into Africa against Cato and Scipio, he left him to govern Cisalpine Gaul. Brutus showed himself worthy of the trust, and when the conqueror returned, he was gratified to see how his glory had increased in the cities over which Brutus ruled; for while people in other provinces were miserable on account of the harshness and cruelty of their governors, those under Brutus were happy and contented.

Cæsar rewarded Brutus by appointing him prætor; but in so doing he offended Cassius, who thought that he ought to have been the first in that office, in consideration of the service he had done the state. Some ill feeling was aroused in this way against Brutus, and Cassius treated him with indifference for several months. It was his hatred of Cæsar which prompted him at last to seek Brutus's friendship again. Cassius, having determined to crush the dictator, knew that he could scarcely hope to succeed unless Brutus, who stood well with the people, would help him. So he went among his friends, and pointed out to them the danger of Cæsar's fast-increasing power, and sent them, one after another, to Brutus, to poison his mind against the man who loved him, and who hoped to make him his successor.

When this was done, he went himself to Brutus and made friends with him. He was plotting the assassination of Cæsar, and knew that if Brutus took part, the act would be justified in the eyes of the citizens. On taking leave of Brutus, he asked, "Do you expect to be present in the senate on the Calends of March? for Cæsar's friends intend to crown him king on that occasion." Brutus answered that he would not be there. "But what if they should send for us?" asked Cassius. "It will be my business, then," answered Brutus, "not to hold my peace, but to stand up boldly and die for the liberty of my country."

"But what Roman will suffer you to die?" asked Cassius, with emotion. "From you they expect tyranny to be crushed, for they are ready to suffer anything on your account, if only you will show yourself what they think you are, and do what they expect." They then embraced, and each went on his way to interview his friends. So the conspiracy grew.

MARCUS BRUTUS

On the Ides of March the senate met in a place that was particularly favorable for the purpose of the conspirators. It was a portico adjoining the theatre, and near the centre stood a statue of Pompey, opposite to which was a semicircle of benches. There they could assemble without exciting suspicion, and they hoped that the leading men of the city, who would be sure to be present, would stand forth and assert their liberty as soon as the deed was done.

Cæsar was so long in coming to the senate that it was feared the plot had been discovered. Such was not the case, however, but several bad omens and unfavorable sacrifices had made him suspicious and unhappy, so that when he did at last appear, it was with the determination to attend to no business of importance on that day.

When he took his seat, the senate being assembled, the conspirators gathered close about his chair, which stood just in front of Pompey's statue, as though they had an important petition to make, and, according to a previous arrangement, Tillius Cimber began to plead in behalf of his brother, who was in exile. The others joined their prayers to his, took Cæsar's hand, kissed it, also his head and breast, and became so violent that he stood up, whereupon Tillius caught his robe with both hands and pulled it from his shoulder. This was the signal, at which Casca, who stood behind the dictator, drew his dagger and struck at his neck. The wound was slight, and, snatching hold of the handle of the weapon, Cæsar cried aloud in Latin, "Villain Casca, what do you?" A great many blows followed, and Cæsar looked about to see if he could make his escape, but when he saw Brutus, the man he had loved and honored, with his dagger drawn against him, an expression of grief and reproach came into his face, and he ceased to resist. He merely covered his head with his robe, and so thick and fast fell the blows that the murderers in their eagerness actually wounded one another.

It had been suggested that Antony ought to be put out of the way too, in order to secure liberty for the commonwealth; but Brutus would not consent to so unjust an act, particularly as he believed that with Cæsar's death a change might be worked in so gifted and honorable a man as Antony that would go far towards the establishment of liberty.

Antony had been purposely detained at the door by Trebonius, who engaged him in conversation; but when the senators rushed out and he heard what had happened he thought his life was in danger, so disguised himself and fled.

Great excitement filled the city when the death of the dictator became known; but when it was found that there was to be no further bloodshed it soon subsided. Brutus went to the Forum and made an oration, which was loudly applauded by the crowd that gathered to hear him, and which restored confidence. Cicero and all the other orators spoke in favor of peace, and at last it was agreed that the conspirators should not be punished, but that their deed should rather be regarded as a blow for liberty, which ought to be rewarded.

So the provinces were divided among them, and then public attention was turned towards Cæsar's funeral. Antony spoke in favor of a public funeral, Cassius violently opposed it; but Brutus sided with Antony. This was a mistake; for when the Romans beheld the body of their beloved Cæsar, and Antony made a touching oration, holding up the bloody gown pierced with innumerable dagger-strokes, cries and lamentations filled the air, and many exclaimed, "Down with the murderers! Kill the assassins!" The whole city was aroused, and tables and benches were dragged from the shops round about and heaped together for a funeral pile. The body of Cæsar was placed on the pile, which was then set on fire, and the excited multitude seized the burning brands and rushed with them about the city, intending to fire the houses of Cæsar's murderers. Fortunately, they were warned in time to guard their houses and hide themselves.

Thinking discretion the better part of valor, Brutus stole out of the city, and made up his mind not to go back until the fury of the people had abated. Meanwhile, Octavius Cæsar, whom the great conqueror had adopted and made his heir, returned to Rome, and by distributing the money that the will had set aside for the citizens won so much favor that he soon got the better of Antony. He formed a powerful party among the soldiers that had served under Cæsar, a large part of the senate sided with him, and he was further strengthened by Cicero, who joined him because he hated Antony.

Then the city was again divided into two parties, many of the soldiers selling their services to the highest bidder, and violent quarrels between Octavius and Antony, the two leaders, took place.

Knowing that while affairs were in such a state he could do no good in Rome, Brutus went to Athens. He was kindly received, and became so absorbed in study among the learned men of the Academy that people thought he had retired from public life. But such was not the case, for he was all the time making preparations for war; and when he heard that several Roman ships were coming along the coast of Greece, laden with treasures and commanded by one of his friends, he went to a seaport to meet them. So great were his persuasive powers that he got possession of the ships, with a large sum of money they were carrying to Rome, and then set to work to raise an army. The Roman students at Athens had already been won over, and the soldiers that remained of Pompey's army and had wandered about Thessaly ever since his defeat joyfully flocked to join Brutus. The governor of Macedonia aided him, and in a very little while he found himself surrounded by a splendid army and an ample supply of horses and arms. He then went over to Asia, where Cassius had been equally successful. With such forces as these two leaders combined were prepared to bring into the field, success seemed sure.

Meanwhile, Octavius Cæsar had driven Antony out of Italy, but after making himself obnoxious to the senate, had made friends with him and Lepidus, and formed the second triumvirate, an account of which will be found in the life of Antony.

Brutus had heard of these alterations at Rome, and, being a man who never could be turned from a purpose when once he was convinced that it was right and honest, his eagerness to restore liberty to his country and save her from the power of the triumvirs was greatly increased. So he urged Cassius to move on with him to Europe without further delay. A strange story is told of a so-called apparition that appeared to Brutus one night just before he left Asia. He was so anxious about the preparations for the war he had undertaken that his sleep was disturbed, and he spent the greater part of the night making his plans, reading, and studying. Thus one night, after everybody in the camp had gone to rest, he sat quite alone in his tent, thinking about the great enterprise that lay before him. A dim light burned on a little table by his side. Suddenly he fancied some one came in; he looked up, and beheld a strange, horrible-looking being in the doorway. "What art thou?" asked Brutus, boldly. "Art thou god or man? And what is thy business with me?" In a deep, hollow, unnatural tone, the spectre answered, "I am thy evil genius, Brutus; thou shalt see me at Philippi." "I will meet thee there," replied Brutus.

When the apparition was gone, Brutus summoned his servants, but they declared one and all that they had seen no one enter his tent and had heard no sound. Early in the morning he went to Cassius and told him of his strange, unearthly visitor. Cassius belonged to the school of the celebrated philosopher Epicurus, whose disciples were taught to account for everything by a natural cause, so he argued in this way: "You know, Brutus, that in our sect we believe that not all we feel or see is real and true, and that the mind, like wax, readily receives impressions. These impressions are by the power of the imagination moulded into curious forms that do not exist in nature, as we constantly see in dreams. The mind is always in motion; but when the body, as in your case, is tired and distressed, the mind is in an excited and unnatural state. There is no reason for believing that there are such beings as demons or spirits, or that, if there were, they would assume a human shape or voice, or have power to affect us. At the same time I confess I wish there were such beings, and that they would help us in our sacred and glorious enterprise, so that we might not have to depend entirely on fleets and armies."

Brutus was comforted by this reasoning, and, taking courage again, he embarked for Italy. Cæsar and Antony, after having proclaimed themselves triumvirs for five years, raised a large force and marched to the plain of Philippi. There the two grand armies met, Cæsar encamping opposite to Brutus, and Antony opposite to Cassius. Brutus had fewer men than

Cæsar, but their arms and equipments were far more rich and splendid, for he had an idea that they would fight harder to preserve the gold and silver armor which he had given them than they would if it were less valuable.

Before the battle began there were many bad omens in the camp of Brutus and Cassius. The garland that the latter was to wear in the sacrifice was handed to him upside down; then the golden image of Victory that was carried in the solemn procession fell from the hands of the man who held it; birds of prey appeared about the camp, and swarms of bees flew into the trenches. The superstitious soldiers were so affected by these things that the soothsayers had trouble to calm them, and even the Epicurean philosophy of Cassius himself was shaken.

Brutus was all impatience for the fight, but Cassius desired to postpone it as long as possible. An officer in Brutus's army advised him by all means to tarry over the winter. "In what better condition do you hope to be by that time?" asked Brutus. "If I gain nothing else, I shall have lived that much longer," said the man. This answer so displeased both the generals that it was decided to fight the very next day.

As soon as it was morning, the signal of battle, the scarlet coat, was displayed, and Brutus and Cassius met midway between their two camps to make the final arrangements. Before they parted, Cassius said, "May the gods make this day successful! but, as the most important of human events are the most uncertain, and as we may never see each other any more, tell me what is your resolution concerning flight and death." Brutus answered, "When I was younger and less experienced, I was disposed to condemn Cato for killing himself; I thought it impious and unmanly to sink beneath the stroke of fortune or to run away from the divine course of nature. Now, in my own case, I am of another mind, and if our wishes are not realized in this undertaking I shall make no further attempt, but will die content with my fortune. I gave my life to my country on the Ides of March, and have lived since then a second life for her sake, with liberty and honor." Cassius smiled, and, embracing Brutus, said, "With these resolutions let us charge the enemy; for either we shall conquer, or we have no cause to fear those that do."

So the two commanders set about completing their arrangements, and then made the attack. Cassius was conquered, but Brutus was victorious. They would have carried the day had it not been for a mistake which caused their ruin. It was this: Brutus did not go to the relief of Cassius because he believed that, like himself, Cassius had gained a victory, and Cassius did not seek relief from Brutus because he thought that Brutus had been overcome. Brutus, on his return from plundering Cæsar's camp, began to wonder at not seeing Cassius's tent on the spot it had occupied high above the rest, and some of his men who had been reconnoitring assured him that something dreadful must have happened to Cassius. So he rallied his men and marched to the relief of his friend.

He found the camp deserted and Cassius dead; for, mistaking a party of his own men for the enemy, he had caused one of his slaves to put him to death when he saw them rapidly approaching his camp after his defeat. Brutus wept when he beheld the body of Cassius, and called him "the last of the Romans," for he said that Rome would never again produce a man of so great a spirit.

He then gathered together all that were left of Cassius's soldiers, promised each a liberal reward as recompense for what he had lost, and a great deal more if all would fight once again for him. Thus encouraged, the remnant of Cassius's army promised to do their utmost, and followed their new leader to his camp.

Meanwhile, Antony, having been informed of the death of Cassius, eagerly awaited the dawn of day, and returned with his entire force to the battlefield, showing the utmost anxiety to lose no time. This was his reason: during the land-fight of the previous day there had been a battle at sea, in which Brutus's fleet had so defeated Antony's that few of the vessels escaped, and, as they were bringing a fresh supply of soldiers, the loss was serious. Brutus had not yet heard of that engagement, and Antony's desire was to draw him into another battle before he should do so and become elated by his success. Besides, he knew that Brutus would scarcely consent to a second conflict just then if he heard of the success of his fleet, because he was thus enabled to get an ample supply of provisions, and had the best positions on land as well as at sea.

Nevertheless, it was three o'clock in the afternoon before Brutus led his men to battle. He showed himself an expert general and a brave soldier, determined to spare himself no peril if only he could gain the victory. Many brave men were slain in defending him, and one Lucilius, seeing a party of the enemy's horse galloping full speed towards Brutus, put himself in their way, and, when he was captured, told them he was Brutus. They believed him, and immediately sent forward a messenger to tell Antony that they had taken Brutus alive. Antony came out to meet them, because he was so pleased that he could not wait, and all the soldiers who heard that Brutus was coming gathered near to see him. Lucilius advanced boldly, and said, "Be assured, Antony, that no enemy either has taken or shall take Marcus Brutus alive. I am come here by a cheat put upon your soldiers, and am ready to suffer any punishment for it you may see fit to inflict."

All were amazed, but Antony, turning to those about him, said, "I see, fellow-soldiers, that you take it ill that you have been thus deceived, and feel yourselves injured on account of it; but let me tell you that you have taken a booty better than what you sought. For you were in search of an enemy, but you have brought me here a friend. Had you brought Brutus to me alive, I know not how I should have used him, but of this I am sure, that it is better to have such men as Lucilius our friends than our enemies." Having spoken thus, he embraced Lucilius, who forever after was his faithful friend.

The army of Brutus met with a total defeat, but with a few friends he made his escape and passed the night in a cave. Towards morning one of the friends said, "We must not stay here longer, for it is not safe; we must fly." "Yes, indeed," said Brutus, rising, "we must fly; not with our feet, but with our hands." He then shook hands with each of his companions, and thus addressed them: "It is a great satisfaction to me that all my friends have been faithful. If I am angry with fortune, it is for the sake of my country. As for myself, I am more happy than my conquerors, for I shall leave behind me that reputation for virtue which they, with all their wealth and power, will never acquire. It will always be said of them that they were an abandoned set of men, who destroyed the virtuous for the sake of the empire to which they had no right." He then entreated each of his friends to provide for his own safety, and drawing aside with Strato, who was one of the oldest and dearest, he fell upon the point of his sword and killed himself.

The body of Brutus was found by Antony, who commanded it to be wrapped in a rich purple mantle. After it was burned, the ashes were carefully placed in an urn and sent to the mother of Brutus.

ANTONY

MARK ANTONY lost his father when very young, and although his mother, who was of the family of the Cæsars, took great pains with his training and education, he formed a friendship with a bad man named Curio, who led him into all sorts of dissipation. After spending all the money his father left him and finding himself deeply in debt besides, he gladly accepted an invitation to accompany Gabinius, the consul, in his campaign in Syria. There he distinguished himself so that more important enterprises were intrusted to him, and he won a high reputation as a commander.

In ancient times it had always been said that the Antonys were descended from Hercules, and Mark was so proud of this that he dressed in imitation of that god as he appeared in paintings and statues. Besides, he had a noble bearing, his beard was full, his forehead large, and his nose aquiline, so when people looked at him they were really reminded of Hercules.

When Rome was divided into two parties, the one headed by Pompey and the other by Cæsar, Curio, Antony's bad friend, joined the latter and persuaded Antony to do the same. He went to Gaul, where he spent some time; then, being provided by Cæsar with money and credit, he returned to Rome, where he was first made quæstor, then tribune. In the latter office he was of the greatest service to Cæsar, and fled to him in disguise to report how the two questions had been put to the senate whether Pompey should dismiss his army or Cæsar his.

It was then that the conqueror marched into Italy, drove out Pompey, and placed Antony as tribune to govern Rome while he marched into Spain. Antony was exceedingly popular with the soldiers, but he was too lazy to pay attention to the wants of the people, and so committed many serious errors. But Cæsar would never listen to any charges against him, nor had he ever cause to complain of his lack of courage, skill, or energy in military affairs.

Indeed, he so signalized himself in the various battles that took place later that his reputation, next to Cæsar's, was the greatest in the army. After the celebrated battle of Pharsalia, in which he commanded the left wing, because Cæsar considered him his best officer, he was sent to Rome as Master of the Horse. That was an office next in power to the dictator, and Cæsar showed his high opinion of Antony in giving it to him.

But Antony was too fond of drinking and carousing, which gave great offence to the better class of Roman citizens; so when Cæsar came back from Spain, although he was very gentle with Antony and did much towards reforming him, he took Lepidus not Antony, to be consul with him. Antony's morals improved when he married, for Fulvia, his wife, had a good influence over him.

His friendship for Cæsar was so great, that when the murder of that conqueror was decided on, some of the conspirators made it their business to detain him in conversation outside the senate-house. He was much shocked when he

ANTONY

heard of the dreadful deed, but immediately took measures to prevent a civil war. He called the senate together the very next day, and secured the appointment to foreign countries of Brutus and Cassius, who had led the conspiracy. For himself, he aimed at becoming ruler-in-chief, and made the best of his opportunity when delivering the funeral oration in the market-place over the body of Cæsar. He expressed his horror at the murder, showed the bloody stains on the dead man's clothing, and called those that had committed the deed villains and assassins.

The populace grew so excited over his remarks that Brutus and his party were obliged to leave the city, and Cæsar's friends joined themselves to Antony, whose power became absolute. He got possession of Cæsar's papers, and carried into effect all that he had meant to do, appointed the magistrates named therein, recalled some from exile, and freed others from prison, as Cæsar's letters directed. His power was the greater because his brother Caius was prætor, and his brother Lucius tribune of the people.

But his schemes were thwarted by Octavius Cæsar, who came to Rome shortly after his uncle Julius was killed. Octavius made certain claims which Antony refused to grant, so he formed a strong party in the senate, and won over to his side Cicero and many others who hated Antony.

A report was carried to Antony that Octavius was plotting against his life, whereupon he went about and made offers to the old soldiers to take sides with him. Octavius did the same. Cicero was at that time a man of the greatest influence in Rome, and he did what he could to arouse the people against Antony. Finally he persuaded the senate to pronounce Antony a public enemy, and to order the two consuls, Hirtius and Pansa, to drive him out of Italy. A battle took place near Modena, in which the consuls were killed. But Antony was defeated and obliged to fly. It was then that he showed how great he was, for he bore all sorts of suffering and privation like a true hero, and set a wonderful example of patience and endurance to his soldiers.

Octavius was now satisfied, for he had desired only to humble Antony, not to destroy him. As soon as that was accomplished, he began to consult his friends as to the best manner of making his peace with the exile. It was brought about in this way:

After his defeat, Antony determined to make his way to the other side of the Alps, to join his army with that of Lepidus, whom he had befriended on several occasions. But when he came in sight of the camp he received no encouragement to approach nearer. However, feeling that he had little to lose, and possibly much to gain, he disguised himself in a large dark cloak, made his way into the trenches, and began to address the army of Lepidus. His speech had such an effect that Lepidus took alarm, and ordered the trumpets to be sounded, so that he could not be heard. But that night two of the soldiers, disguised in women's clothes, were sent by their comrades to confer with Antony. They advised him to make an attack on Lepidus, whom they offered to put to death. Antony would not listen to such a proposition, but the next morning he marched his men up to the river which divided the two camps, and was himself the first to plunge into the water and swim across. He was received by the soldiers, who not only held out their hands to help him ashore, but beat down the works to make way for his soldiers. So he entered the camp of Lepidus as absolute master. He did not take an unfair advantage of his position, though, for he

ANTONY

treated Lepidus with the greatest kindness, called him Father when he addressed him, and left him the honor of being general.

Octavius Cæsar, as we have said, was anxious to make a friend of Antony, because he knew that it would be a benefit to himself, so as soon as he heard how Antony had increased his forces by his alliance with Lepidus, he sent messengers to propose a conference. It was agreed upon, and the three leaders, Lepidus, Octavio Cæsar, and Antony, met on a small island. The conference lasted three days. It was decided that the three should divide the empire among them, and under the name of triumvirs they should have supreme authority for five years. This was called the second triumvirate. But before the three triumvirs separated a question arose which perplexed them. It was whom to destroy, each desiring to save his friends and get rid of his enemies. It ended by condemning friends and relatives with horrible, cold-blooded indifference. Cicero's head was offered to Antony in exchange for that of his uncle and the brother of Lepidus. Never was a more barbarous compact made, for these men consented to the death of their friends without even the excuse of hatred. Besides the three mentioned, hundreds of others were killed before the triumvirate was fairly established.

It was abominable to the Romans, who blamed Antony most of all, because he was older than Cæsar, and had more authority than Lepidus. He made himself still more obnoxious by going to live in the house of Pompey the Great, who had been the most temperate and decent of their citizens, and filling it with actors, jugglers, and all sorts of bad people, on whom he spent enormous sums of the public money, seizing it in many instances by violence and cruelty.

This lasted until the war with Brutus and Cassius broke out; then the army was divided between Antony and Octavius Cæsar, who marched into Macedonia, Lepidus being left in command of Rome. All the honor of this war belongs to Antony, for Cæsar was completely routed by Brutus in the first battle. However, Antony defeated both Cassius and Brutus at Philippi, Cæsar was sent home ill, and, after a short visit to different parts of Greece, Antony passed over to Asia.

There he returned to his former dissipations, and surrounded himself with wicked companions, to gratify whose coarse, low tastes he was often known to deprive some of the most virtuous citizens of all their wealth. His way was to pretend they were dead, and so seize their property. He presented his cook with a splendid estate as a reward for a well-served banquet, and did numerous other absurd things.

Later, he went to Egypt and spent some time at Alexandria, where he was entertained in a most sumptuous manner by the beautiful, gifted queen Cleopatra. He was suddenly recalled to Italy, because of a war which his brother and his own wife had declared against Octavius Cæsar; but before he reached there his wife died, and that event put an end to the trouble.

A reconciliation was effected between Octavius and Antony, which was strengthened by the marriage of the latter with Octavia, sister of Cæsar. After this took place a new division was made of the empire, the eastern provinces falling to Antony, the western to Cæsar, and Africa to Lepidus. Antony lived quietly for a couple of years, then went back to Asia, where he engaged in a long and difficult war with the Parthians. Never was a more splendid army gathered together

ANTONY

than the one he led; but he made many mistakes, and was at last badly defeated.

Cleopatra had joined Antony, and he was so much in love with her that he wanted to marry her. He therefore neglected Octavia, in consequence of which Cæsar brought serious charges against him in the senate, for it displeased the conqueror exceedingly to have so virtuous and noble a lady as his sister badly treated.

Antony, on the other hand, accused Cæsar of certain acts of injustice, and of taking upon himself too much power. Cæsar's answer was that he had put Lepidus out of the government because his conduct had been bad; that he would divide what he had got in war with Antony as soon as Antony gave him a share of Armenia, and that Antony's soldiers had no claims in Italy."

Upon this Antony prepared for war. He gathered together a splendid fleet of eight hundred vessels, of which Cleopatra provided two hundred, besides a large sum of money, and provisions for the whole army. If he had chosen to fight Cæsar by land without delay, he would have been successful, for Cæsar's preparations were by no means complete. But he was guided by the advice of Cleopatra, and waited until the Romans also had collected their fleet, and then the fight took place at Actium, on the sea. Even then he ought to have won the victory, for his fleet was twice the size of Cæsar's, and everything was in his favor; but the Romans set fire to all the Egyptian vessels except sixty, and long before the battle was decided those sixty hoisted sail, in obedience to Cleopatra's order, and put out to sea, a fair wind carrying them towards Peloponnesus.

That utterly ruined Antony's cause, for, like a weak, unprincipled general, he followed the Egyptian queen, and, after losing three hundred ships and five thousand men, his fleet gave up the contest. It was long before Antony's soldiers consented to believe that he had basely deserted them, but when at last the truth was no longer to be doubted, they submitted to the conqueror.

Antony went to Africa, utterly disgusted with life, and built himself a little house near Pharos, on a mound out in the sea, where he lived separated from all mankind. But he recovered from his fit of sulking when news was brought to him of the defeat of his army at Actium, that several powers had deserted him and gone over to Cæsar, and that nothing in Egypt remained to him. Having little to hope for, he determined to throw off care and enjoy himself. So he went to Alexandria, where he was again received by Cleopatra, whose palace was a scene of constant feasting and revelry.

There he remained until Cæsar marched against him with a large army, and then he had the mortification of seeing his fleet join that of Cæsar, while his cavalry deserted him and went over to the enemy also.

Cleopatra was so afraid that Antony might accuse her of having betrayed him that she sent him word she was dead. As soon as he heard the sad news he went to his room and requested Eros, a faithful servant, to kill him. Eros drew his sword as if he meant to obey, then turning away, slew himself, and fell at his master's feet.

"This, Eros, is well done," said Antony; "you show your master how to do what you had not the heart to do yourself." He then plunged the sword into his bowels, and threw himself on a couch near by to die.

ANTONY

Cæsar entered the city in triumph, and, mounting a platform in the exercise-ground, told the citizens that he freely forgave them for the sake of Alexander, who had built their city, and for the city's sake, which was too large and beautiful to be destroyed.

Many kings and great commanders asked for the honor of burying Antony, but Cleopatra performed that rite with royal splendor. Cæsar treated the queen with great respect, but when she was secretly informed that she was to be sent a prisoner to Rome, she had an asp brought to her in a basket of figs, and let it bite her arm. The poison did its work quickly, and Cæsar's messengers were surprised, when they went to capture the queen, to find that she had been dead several hours. Cleopatra was thirty-nine years old at the time of her death, and had been on the throne twenty-two years.

Antony was in his fifty-sixth year when he killed himself. He can scarcely be ranked among the great men of ancient times, for he had neither genius nor moral strength, and he was too much a slave to pleasure to be considered a good man, yet few possessed more devoted friends or warmer partisans. He lost his empire by his own fault, for he deserted those who were fighting for him, and his death is an example of unpardonable weakness.

SERTORIUS

QUINTUS SERTORIUS was born of a noble family in the country of the Sabines. His father died when he was very young, but his mother, whose name was Rhea, took excellent care of him and had him well educated. He was fond of oratory, and gained a reputation for his eloquence even in his youth; but his attention was early turned to war, and he met with success as a soldier.

He served first under Cæpio when the Cimbri and Teutones invaded Gaul. The Romans were put to flight, and Sertorius received several wounds, besides losing his horse; but he swam across the river Rhone in his armor and saved himself. The second time the Cimbri and Teutones came with their hundreds of thousands of men, threatening death and destruction on all sides, Sertorius volunteered to act as a spy in the enemy's camp, while Marius led the army. This required no little courage, for the enemy was a strange one to the Romans and a ferocious-looking race that might have terrified even the bravest.

Sertorius disguised himself as one of them so well that he was not discovered, and thus he was enabled to mingle with their troops and find out not only what they proposed doing, but their method of fighting and their habits. The report he carried to Marius was of the greatest importance, and in the war which followed he was so brave and able that he was advanced by his general to a position of honor and trust.

After the war with the Cimbri and Teutones was over, he was sent to Spain under Didius, the Roman general, in command of a thousand men, and took up his winter quarters at Castulo, a town of New Castile; but his soldiers behaved in such a disorderly manner and were so offensive on account of frequent drunkenness that the inhabitants lost all respect for them. They therefore called in the aid of the Gyriscenians, their neighbors, and attacked the Roman soldiers in their lodgings, slaying a great number of them.

Sertorius escaped with several hundred of his men and marched around Castulo to the gate by which the Gyriscenians had entered. It happened, fortunately for him, to be open; so, placing a guard there, he took possession of the city and killed all the inhabitants who were able to bear arms. Then he ordered his own men to put on the clothing and take the arms of those they had slain, and, thus disguised, to follow him to the city of the Gyriscenians.

The gates were thrown open at the approach of the supposed friends, but the Gyriscenians were soon undeceived, for many were killed; the rest surrendered and were sold as slaves. This manœuvre made Sertorius famous in Spain; and when he returned to Rome he was appointed quæstor to a part of Gaul. As the Marian war was on the point of breaking out, Sertorius's duties were to raise soldiers and provide arms, and a more active or diligent officer could scarcely have been found. Unlike most commanders, he continued to be a soldier at the same time, and exposed himself in the ranks so freely that in one of the engagements he lost an eye. But he gloried in this, for he always said that it was a badge of bravery of which he was more proud than a king of his coronet. Everybody treated him with the greatest respect, and when he entered the theatre he was always received with applause.

After Marius fled to Africa, at the time of the civil war in Rome, Sertorius joined Cinna's party, so when Octavius, the other consul, was victorious, Cinna and Sertorius left the city. They did not remain away long, however, but collected troops in other parts of Italy, and, being joined by Marius on his return, went back to Rome. The horrible scenes that ensued are recounted in the life of Marius, and need not be repeated. The conduct of his band of ruffians became so intolerable that Sertorius attacked them with his soldiers, as they lay encamped, and killed the whole body, consisting of four thousand. This was done for the relief of the city and for the good of his countrymen, after all argument and persuasion with Cinna and Marius had failed; for Sertorius never put any man to death to gratify personal revenge.

Not long after, Sertorius returned to Spain; but Sylla, who became consul at Rome after the defeat of the Marian party, sent a powerful force to oppose him, and he was obliged to fly to Africa for safety. He landed on the coast of Mauritania, but so many of his men were killed by the natives when they went ashore to get water that he was forced to make his way back to Spain.

On the journey he fell in with some Cilician pirates, whom he persuaded to join him, and together they forced themselves through a guard belonging to Sylla, and landed on the island of Ivica. Soon after, Annius, who was in command of Sylla's troops, appeared in the harbor with a numerous fleet and five thousand men. A battle ensued, and many of Sertorius's ships were driven on the rocks by a violent storm. Then Sertorius was in a dreadful plight. He could not go out to sea because of the storm, his vessel being a light one, and the enemy prevented his landing; so after being tossed about on the waves for ten days he escaped at last, and ran into a harbor on the Atlantic coast of Spain. There he met some seamen who had just arrived from the Canary Islands, and they gave such a glowing account of the wonderful climate, inhabitants, and productions of those "Islands of the Blest," as they were called, that, worn out with fatigue and disappointment, Sertorius longed to go there to rest, at a distance from the turmoil of war.

But the Cilician pirates wanted neither peace nor repose, so they refused to accompany him, and sailed back to the coast of Africa. Sertorius followed, and fought a battle with Paccianus, who had been sent by Sylla to assist a Moorish king to recover his throne. Sertorius defeated and killed him, and took nearly all his army prisoners; but he very wisely restored to the natives all their possessions and government, taking nothing for himself but what they offered him, and thus making himself exceedingly popular.

While he was considering where to turn next, the Lusitanians sent ambassadors to invite him to command their army against Sylla's troops, for they felt that Sertorius was to be trusted both for courage and judgment. He accepted the invitation, and left Africa for their country at once.

On his arrival he was appointed general of an immense army, many of the troops having volunteered because they wished to serve under so active and humane a leader. Sertorius carried on the war against four Roman generals, and fought with such skill and activity, appearing now here, now there, at most unexpected moments, that he won brilliant victories at every turn.

The Spaniards admired and loved him, but in order to gain their confidence before he began to fight their battles, he had made use of an interesting bit of artifice. He had been presented by a countryman with a milk-white fawn, of which he soon became very fond. It was so tame and gentle that it would follow him about wherever he went, and come to him when he called. Knowing that uncivilized people are apt to be superstitious, Sertorius decided to make use of this quality to gain favor with them, so he told them that the fawn had been presented to him by the goddess Diana, who was a huntress, and that it told him many secrets. If perchance he received private news that the enemy were giving trouble in any part of the country under his command, he gave out that the fawn had informed him of it in his sleep, and had charged him to keep the troops prepared. When he got notice of a victory gained by any commander under him, the messenger was kept out of sight, and the fawn was led forth crowned with flowers, while the people were told to rejoice at the good news which was to come. A few hours later the messenger was produced, and made to announce the victory which the fawn was supposed to have whispered to the general beforehand.

Sertorius did more for the Spaniards than merely fight their battles; for he taught them to keep their ranks and use their arms as the Romans did, instead of imitating savages in their mode of fighting. He founded schools, where the children of the nobility were instructed in Grecian and Roman literature, rewarded those who studied diligently, and he also introduced among the citizens the attire of his own countrymen. The soldiers were delighted with their gold and silver helmets, embroidered vests and coats, and the noble citizens were no less so when they saw their sons walking to school in fine gowns bordered with purple, particularly as Sertorius bore the whole expense of these, as well as of the instruction and rewards. Everybody loved Sertorius, and the boys who won the rewards, which consisted of golden balls worn suspended from the neck, were very proud of them. It was Sertorius himself who made the examinations and awarded the prizes.

Metellus was one of the Roman generals whom Sertorius had defeated in Spain, and after that happened Pompey was sent with fresh troops. When the soldiers that Sertorius had placed in a certain part of the country under Perpenna Vento heard that Pompey was coming, they took up their arms and demanded to be led against him at once, threatening otherwise to go to Sertorius, who, they declared, was able to defend himself and those that served him. So Perpenna, who feared to oppose Pompey, was obliged to yield, though he was jealous of Sertorius and objected to adding to his army.

Such a tremendous force was thus gathered together that it was almost impossible to control them, particularly as the larger part had been thieves and bandits, who knew nothing of discipline. They had several engagements of their own accord with the enemy, but were defeated each time and rescued, by Sertorius, until their confidence in him increased, and they became willing to listen to his advice. One day, in order to illustrate his plan, he caused two horses to be led into the field in the presence of his army. One was a poor, old, feeble animal, the other a strong, large one, with a remarkably thick, long tail. By the weak horse stood a robust, able-bodied man, by the strong one a weak little man. At a given signal, the strong man began to pull the weak horse by the tail, as though he would pull it out by the root, while the other man pulled out the hairs of the long, flowing tail one by one. The spectator, laughed heartily at the efforts of the strong man, who tugged and tugged without any result, and was forced at last to give up by the time the little man had stripped the large horse of every hair.

Then Sertorius said, "You see, my friends and fellow-soldiers how much more can be accomplished by perseverance than by force, and that things separated are not so strong as when united. Time is the friend of those who use their judgment and wait, and the enemy of those who rush forward on improper occasions." It was with such examples and speeches that Sertorius taught the barbarians to be less fierce, and to watch for favorable opportunities, rather than rush forward blindly, and so his influence grew.

Now the great Pompey was coming,—Pompey, the noble Roman general who had been honored with a triumph before he was old enough to have a beard. He passed over the mountains and pitched his camp near that of Sertorius. In every attack Sertorius had the advantage, and proved himself such a wonderful general that his fame reached even to Rome.

It was increased by the siege of Lauron. As soon as Pompey heard that Sertorius intended to besiege that place, he marched with his whole army to the foot of a hill a short distance off, and sent word to the citizens "to rest perfectly easy and watch him from their walls while he besieged Sertorius." When that general heard of it he laughed, and said, "I will teach that scholar of Sylla," so he called Pompey in ridicule, "that a general ought to look behind him rather than before;" he was then on the top of the hill, and pointed towards a body of six thousand soldiers in the camp, left there to seize Pompey in the rear as soon as he should begin the attack.

But Pompey dared not begin, so he had the mortification of seeing Lauron burned, while the inhabitants surrendered to his enemy, and said, tauntingly, "Pompey was at hand and could almost warm himself at the flames, but could offer no assistance."

At the end of a battle which took place between Pompey and Sertorius afterwards, the white fawn was missing, and its master was sorely grieved. However, during the night it was found wandering at some distance from the camp and brought back. Sertorius promised a large reward to the finder if he would tell no one of it, and immediately hid the fawn. A few days later he appeared in public with a cheerful countenance, and said that he had had a dream in which the gods had promised a piece of great good fortune. He then took his seat and began to speak to those who had brought petitions. Suddenly the fawn, that had been let loose by its keeper, came leaping towards Sertorius, laid its head upon his knee, and licked his right hand as it had been taught to do. Sertorius stroked the animal, and received it as though he had not seen it before, while tears filled his eyes, and the people gazed at him with wonder as a creature beloved of the gods.

Sertorius fought several more battles both with Pompey and Metellus, and won nearly all of them, so that it began to be generally believed in Rome that he would be back there before many months. Metellus was one of the greatest of Roman commanders, but he was getting old, and felt the superiority of Sertorius so keenly that he was anxious to get him out of the way; he therefore publicly offered a large reward to any Roman who should kill him.

Meanwhile, Sertorius gathered about him the senators who had fled from Rome to him, and established a government with Roman laws and institutions, giving all the offices to his own countrymen in order that he might prove that it was his purpose to restore liberty to them, not to make the Spaniards powerful against them. Thus he showed himself a true patriot, for he loved his country and wanted to return to it. When he was at the height of his power he sent word to Metellus and Pompey that he was ready to lay down his arms and go into private life if only he might be permitted to return home, declaring that he would rather live as the meanest of citizens in Rome than as commander of all other cities out of it. One reason for this was the deep affection he bore his mother, but he was not gratified by seeing her again, for she died while he was in exile. When he heard the sad news he was overwhelmed with grief, and would not leave his tent for seven days. He was prevailed upon to do so at last by his principal officers and other persons of note, who begged him to continue the management of public affairs.

Sertorius had created a powerful kingdom among strangers, which he had defended for more than ten years against the army of Rome under her ablest commanders. At last Perpenna, whose jealousy had grown year by year, and who was ambitious to command the army himself, began to conspire against his life, and went among the Romans trying to rouse their discontent. They dared not attack Sertorius openly, but did what they could to injure him in the eyes of the Spaniards until the conspiracy gained strength.

SERTORIUS

Letters were sent to the general announcing a great victory gained by one of his officers. The news was false, but Sertorius was deceived, and offered a sacrifice in honor of the joyful tidings. Afterwards, Perpenna invited all who were present to a supper, and while it was going on some of the conspirators pretended to be drunk and quarrelled among themselves. This displeased Sertorius so much, for he always insisted upon good behavior when he was present, that he threw himself back upon his couch, as though he wished not to see or hear what was going on. As he did so, Perpenna upset a glass of wine, which had been agreed upon as a signal. Thereupon the man who sat next to Sertorius struck him with his sword, and before he could recover from the blow threw himself upon his breast, and held both his arms while others killed him.

Perpenna then declared himself general of the army, but soon, proving himself unfit for the position, he was taken prisoner by Pompey, and executed as an enemy to his country. This ended the war in Spain; for all the men who had sided with the traitor were put to death also.

GALBA

Sulpicius Galba was a patrician by birth, and one of the richest men of his day. The wicked Nero was emperor of Rome when he became a man, and it was under his reign that Galba was proconsul both in Germany and Africa. Afterwards he was sent by the same emperor to govern Spain, and he filled his office so well that he became very popular. Indeed, he was so just and merciful that the cruel deeds committed by Nero horrified him. When Junius Vindex, general of the Roman forces in Gaul, rose against the tyrant and encouraged his soldiers to put him down, it was not difficult to gain Galba over to his side.

Galba mounted the tribunal to announce what he and Vindex hoped to do, and the crowd that had so long felt the tyranny of Nero gathered about the speaker, ready for any change that would offer relief. Galba was an old man, who inspired respect, and his actions while in Spain led to the belief that he could never be guilty of injustice; so the people saluted him as emperor. This was a surprise to him, for he was not prepared to take so decided and sudden a step as they supposed; he therefore refused the lofty title, saying that he offered himself to the service of his country merely as the lieutenant of the Roman senate and people.

GALBA

Nero had paid little attention to the movements of Vindex; but when he heard that Galba had joined him he started up, having just seated himself for his morning meal, and, in his excitement, overturned table, dishes, and breakfast. Without a moment's loss of time he assembled the senate and had Galba proclaimed a public enemy, and offered all his property for sale. Galba retaliated by selling everything of Nero's in Spain.

Many of the provinces declared for Galba, but two held out because their governors thought that they had as much right to succeed Nero as Galba had. These were Clodius Macer, of Africa, and Virginius Rufus, of Germany. Clodius had been guilty of so many wicked deeds that he feared to say what he wanted; for if he announced his intention to replace Nero, his enemies might assassinate him. Virginius, who commanded some of the best Roman legions, had often been urged by them to take the title of emperor, but he said, "I will neither take it myself nor will I suffer it to be given to any person but him whom the senate shall name."

So Virginius and Vindex fought a great battle, in which the latter lost twenty thousand of his men and then put an end to his own life. After this victory, Virginius was again urged to declare himself emperor by people who said that if he refused they would go over to Nero again. This so alarmed Galba that he wrote to Virginius, begging him to join with him in restoring the liberty of the Romans and preserving their empire. He then retired to a town in Spain called Colonia.

One evening during the following summer, just after Galba had gone to bed, a messenger arrived from Rome, who had made the journey in an incredibly short time, to inform him that Nero was dead and that the senate and people of Rome had declared him emperor. Two days later, Titus Vinius, with many others, came to confirm the news.

Now Galba began to wonder what Virginius Rufus would do for there was no man living who had a greater name than he had particularly since his victory in Gaul over Vindex. But he had said that the man named by the senate should be emperor, and, in spite of the entreaties of his army, he remained firm.

So Galba started for Rome. He was met near Narbo, a city in Gaul, by some members of the senate, who begged him to make haste to appear among the people, who were anxiously awaiting him. The litter, the decorations, and the attendants of Nero were sent to him also, but he preferred to use his own, which was regarded as a proof that he was above petty vanity.

Vinius, who had been one of the first to announce to Galba that he was emperor, persuaded him to assume a more regal appearance and manner, assuring him that he would make himself more agreeable to the Romans by so doing. Galba allowed himself to be led in this as well as in more important matters by this man, who was so unprincipled and so wicked that he soon ruined himself and made the emperor hateful to his subjects, as we shall see.

Galba determined to reform the extravagance that Nero had encouraged, but in doing so he went to the other extreme, and acted so stingily as to make himself ridiculous. He did this with the advice of Vinius, who was all the time helping himself most liberally from the public treasury.

Having got the old man completely under his control, this creature taxed the people just as heavily as Nero had done, and they blamed Galba for it, though he was really deceived himself, and made a dupe of by his ministers. Of course he was by no means blameless; but he was an aged man, and allowed himself to be led because he suspected no evil. This was weak, but he showed himself strong in keeping the soldiers to their duty,—for they had had great license in the previous reign,—in punishing those persons who, by bearing false witness, had caused the death of the innocent, and in various other ways.

What incensed the people against Galba more than anything else was that when Nero's ministers were ordered to execution, Tigellinus, the most infamous of them all, was spared. The reason for the mercy shown to him was that he had bribed Vinius with costly presents; but there was no man in all Rome whom the people were more anxious to be rid of. They now felt that there was nothing Vinius would refuse for money, and from that moment every act of Galba's was misrepresented. If he was merciful they attributed it to bribery, and if he was severe they thought it was because Vinius had not received his price.

The soldiers hated Galba because he refused to pay them for extra service, as Nero had done, and dissatisfaction in every part of the government grew worse day by day.

At last Galba took alarm, and with the belief that he was despised not only on account of his age, but also because he had no child to succeed him, he resolved to adopt a young man of distinction and name him his successor. Marcus Otho, a very bad person, who had been a friend to Nero in his pleasure-parties, was the person Vinius recommended; but while Galba hesitated a mutiny broke out among the soldiers in Germany, who proclaimed Vitellius, their commander, emperor.

As soon as Galba heard of this he knew that there was no time to lose, for he had unwisely made enemies of his soldiers, and could therefore expect no protection from them. Some of his advisers had named Otho for his heir, others had exerted themselves in favor of Dolabella, so Galba chose neither, but, without consulting any one, sent for Piso Lucinianus, a young nobleman of merit, and took him to the camp, where, in a speech to the soldiers, he introduced him as his successor to the empire.

Otho, who was present, was in a perfect fury, for he knew that he had been proposed for the succession, and the soothsayers had told him that he should be emperor after Nero. His friends, particularly those who had no positions to lose, and perhaps much to gain, advised him to seek his revenge. So he took great pains to win the good will of the soldiers, and thus to lay a plot for the destruction of those who stood in his way to the throne.

Early in the morning of January the fifteenth, Galba offered a sacrifice in the palace. When the diviner took the entrails of the animal in his hands, he said that there were signs of trouble, and that the life of the emperor was in danger. Otho trembled lest he should be discovered, but immediately hastened to the spot where he was to meet the soldiers. Not more than twenty-three awaited him, but when he appeared they saluted him as emperor, and carried him through the Forum towards the camp, flourishing their swords as they went.

As soon as Galba heard what had happened, he wanted to go out to the people, but Vinius prevented him from doing

GALBA

so until one of the guardsmen rushed in with a bloody sword in his hand, and announced that he had just killed Otho. "Who gave you the order?" asked Galba. "My allegiance and my oath," answered the soldier, amidst the applause of the people. Galba then expressed his intention to sacrifice to Jupiter, and was carried in a chair to the Forum for that purpose. No sooner had he arrived than the death of Otho was contradicted. Great excitement prevailed among the crowd gathered there, some urging Galba to advance, others to retreat, while his chair was pushed backwards and forwards, and almost knocked over. Suddenly a party of soldiers came up, and exclaimed, "Down with this private man!" while numbers ran about to get places on the porticos and other eminences, so that they might enjoy whatever spectacle was about to be presented. One of Galba's statues was overthrown as a signal for hostilities, whereupon a shower of javelins was aimed at the royal chair, and the soldiers advanced, sword in hand, to complete the work the javelins had failed in. Only one man in all the crowd of spectators did honor to the Roman empire that day in offering to defend Galba. That was Sempronius Densus, who called out to the soldiers to spare their emperor. But he was soon brought to the ground, and the royal chair was overthrown.

"Strike, if it be for the good of Rome!" cried poor old Galba, presenting his throat to the soldiers. He received several wounds in various parts of his body, and when he was expiring, one of the soldiers cut off his head. It could not be held up in the usual way because of its baldness, so it was stuck on the end of a spear, and twirled about for everybody to look at. When it was presented to Otho, he cried out, "Fellow soldiers, this is nothing unless you bring me Piso's too."

Not long after, Piso, who had taken refuge in the temple of Vesta, was slain, and his head, as well as that of Titus Vinius, was brought to Otho.

Forthwith the senate was assembled, and the very men who, seven short months before, had sworn allegiance to Galba, now swore to be faithful to Otho, and gave him the titles of Cæsar and Augustus.

Galba's body was carried away and secretly buried in the night. There were many in Rome who pitied his sad fate, but none who regretted him as an emperor; for though he was inferior to few of his countrymen in wealth, birth, and reputation, he had allowed himself to be governed by bad men to such an extent as to render himself obnoxious to his subjects.

OTHO

The new emperor began his reign by courting the friendship of the soldiers, which Galba had unwisely neglected. He made a speech to the senate which was remarkable for its mildness, gave his unexpired consulship to Virginius Rufus, and turned no consul out of office who had been appointed either by Nero or Galba. The oldest of them he promoted to the priesthood, and to all the senators who had been banished by Nero and recalled by Galba he restored what remained of their fortunes. So the Roman people began to flatter themselves that they were at last to have a government that would bring them peace and happiness.

Nothing gratified them more, or increased their affection for Otho so much as his punishing Tigellinus, the infamous wretch who had been the most brutal of Nero's ministers. Tigellinus was at his country-seat on the sea-shore when a messenger arrived to summon him to appear before the emperor. He always had a vessel in readiness, knowing that he might want to make his escape at any moment; but it did not avail him, for no amount of bribery could induce the messengers to let him off. However, he was determined not to give himself up to the fury of the people he had cruelly wronged, so, retiring to a private room under pretext of making some preparations, he cut his throat with a razor.

Otho had not been on the throne many days before he was called upon to oppose Vitellius, who, it will be remembered, had been proclaimed emperor by the legions in Germany before the death of Galba. Just at that time there were reports of wonderful miracles, though the author of them could not be found out. It was said that a number of people saw the reins fall from the hands of the statue of Victory mounted on a chariot in the Capitol, as though she no longer had power to hold them. A statue of Julius Cæsar that stood on an island in the river turned from west to east, they said, though there was no earthquake or hurricane to move it. Then the Tiber overflowed its banks. To be sure, it usually did so at that season, but never had it caused so much destruction. This was regarded as a very bad omen.

Vitellius had sent forward Cæcina, one of his best generals, to secure the passes of the Alps, while he remained in camp on the river Rhine. Otho collected a large army and marched against Cæcina. His men had been so long accustomed to a life of ease and luxury that the enemy undervalued their skill. Thus they won two victories; but then Cæcina made greater exertions, and brought men into the field who had had much experience in warfare. With these he completely defeated Otho's army in a hard-fought battle on the river Po, near Mantua.

One reason for this defeat was that Otho was not present at the battle; had he been there his soldiers would have felt encouraged to fight harder. For the safety of his person he had been persuaded to go to Brixellum, where he awaited the result. Vague rumors of the overthrow of his army reached him at first; but when the wounded joined him the bad news was confirmed. Otho's friends encouraged him to try again, and not to give up all for lost, while his soldiers

OTHO

crowded about him, kissed his hands, threw themselves on their knees and begged him with tears in their eyes not to abandon them to the enemy. One private soldier pressed forward with a drawn sword in his hand, and said, "By this, Cæsar, judge our fidelity; there is not a man among us but would strike thus to serve you." As he spoke he stabbed himself to the heart and fell dead.

For a few moments Otho stood perfectly still, looking at his men with little show of emotion of any sort. Then he spoke thus: "This day, my fellow-soldiers, which gives me such proofs of your affection, is preferable even to that on which you saluted me emperor; do not, then, deny me the greater satisfaction of laying down my life to save so many brave men. In this, at least, let me show myself worthy of the empire, and die for it. I am of the opinion that the enemy has not gained a decisive victory. Several nations declare for us, the senate is with us, and the wives and children of our opponents are in our power. But, alas! it is not in defence of Italy against Hannibal or Pyrrhus or the Cimbri that we fight; it is Romans against Romans, and, whether we conquer or fail, our country suffers and we commit a crime; for victory, to whichever it fall, is gained at her expense. I can die with more honor than I can reign, for by dying I shall establish peace in Italy, and save her from such another unhappy day."

No argument or persuasion could induce him to alter his resolution; so, taking leave of his friends and the senators who were present, he dismissed them; then wrote several letters and sent for Cocceius, his brother's son, then a little boy. To him he said, "You have no reason to fear Vitellius, for I have treated his family with the utmost tenderness and consideration. I had meant to adopt you as my son, but delayed it because I did not wish to involve you in my ruin if I failed. Remember, my boy, these my last words: do not entirely forget nor too well remember that you had an emperor for your uncle."

A moment after he heard a great noise outside. It was caused by the soldiers, who, seeing the senators departing, threatened to kill them for deserting Otho. Otho was obliged to assume a stern, angry air before he could quiet them and make them go also, and even then they obeyed very unwillingly.

In the evening, Otho had two swords brought to him, and, after carefully examining their points, sent away one and placed the other under his arm. Then he called his servants, spoke kindly to them, and made each a present of a small sum of money. Having dismissed them, he went to bed and slept soundly. Early in the morning he summoned one of his chamberlains and inquired if the senators were gone. On being assured that everything had been provided that they needed, and that they had all departed some hours previously, he said, "Go you, then, and show yourself to the soldiers, that they may not suppose you have helped me in killing myself and put you to a cruel death for it."

As soon as the man was gone, Otho fixed the hilt of his sword upon the ground and fell upon the point with so much force that he expired with one groan. The servants, who waited outside, burst into loud lamentation, which was echoed throughout the camp. The soldiers would not quit the spot, though the enemy were approaching. They dressed the body in magnificent attire and prepared a funeral pile. Many of them wept aloud and threw themselves on the ground in despair, while not a few slew themselves, after throwing their burning torches upon the pile.

OTHO

A plain monument was erected over the spot where Otho's remains were interred, on which was this simple inscription: "To the memory of Marcus Otho." He died at the age of thirty-eight, after having reigned only three months. The soldiers then took the oath of allegiance to Vitellius; but he was one of the most despicable, vicious, coarse wretches that ever lived, and was put to death after a reign of eight months, amidst the curses of the multitude.